Economics and History

Economics and History

Surveys in Cliometrics

Edited by David Greasley and Les Oxley

WILEY-BLACKWELL

A John Wiley & Sons, Ltd., Publication

This edition first published 2011

Originally published as a special issue of the *Journal of Economic Surveys* (Volume 24, Issue 5)

Blackwell Publishing was acquired by John Wiley & Sons in February 2007. Blackwell's publishing program has been merged with Wiley's global Scientific, Technical, and Medical business to form Wiley-Blackwell.

Registered Office
John Wiley & Sons Ltd, The Atrium, Southern Gate, Chichester, West Sussex, PO19 8SQ, United Kingdom

Editorial Offices
350 Main Street, Malden, MA 02148-5020, USA
9600 Garsington Road, Oxford, OX4 2DQ, UK
The Atrium, Southern Gate, Chichester, West Sussex, PO19 8SQ, UK

For details of our global editorial offices, for customer services, and for information about how to apply for permission to reuse the copyright material in this book please see our website at www.wiley.com/wiley-blackwell.

Library of Congress Cataloging-in-Publication Data

Economics and history : surveys in cliometrics / edited by David Greasley, Les Oxley.
p. cm. – (Surveys of recent research in economics ; 2)
Includes bibliographical references and index.
ISBN 978-1-4443-3780-8 (pbk.)
1. Economic history. 2. Econometrics. 3. History–Methodology. I. Greasley, David. II. Oxley, Les.
HC26.E266 2011
330.01'5195–dc22

2011013987

A catalogue record for this book is available from the British Library.

This book is published in the following electronic formats: ePDFs (9781444346695); Wiley Online Library (9781444346725); ePub (9781444346701); Kindle (9781444346718)

Set in 9/10.5 pt in Times by Aptara, Inc.

1 2011

CONTENTS

Notes on Contributors

Samuel Allen	Virginia Military Institute
Price Fishback	University of Arizona
Jonathan Fox	Max Planck Institute of Demographic Research
David Greasley	University of Edinburgh
Timothy J. Hatton	University of Essex and Australian National University
Kris Inwood	University of Guelph
Tim Leunig	London School of Economics
Brenda Livingston	University of Arizona
Les Oxley	University of Canterbury
Leandro Prados de la Escosura	University Carlos III, Madrid
Evan Roberts	University of Minnesota

1

CLIO AND THE ECONOMIST: MAKING HISTORIANS COUNT

David Greasley and Les Oxley

Cliometrics has been with us for half a century. At least it was in 1960 that the word itself was coined by Stanley Reiter to describe a style of quantitative history that linked clio, the muse of history with measurement or more succinctly metrics. Three years earlier a joint session of the Economic History Association and the National Bureau of Economic Research Conference on Income and Wealth was held in Williamstown, Massachusetts and many practitioners date the birth of cliometrics to those meetings. The task issue of the *Journal of Economic History* in 1957 was headed the integration of economic theory and economic history and contained some of the fruits of the pioneers' discussions and a summary of the proceeding by Simon Kuznets.

Regular workshops of cliometricians date from 1960 and the discipline laid strong foundations over the following decade, most especially in the USA. Fogel (1964) published *Railroads and Economic Growth: Essays in Econometric History*, which stimulated intensive methodological debate among historians worldwide. Very quickly the British Economic History Society commissioned a paper by Fogel 'The new economic history: its findings and methods' which was published in the *Economic History Review* in 1966. The 'new economic history' and 'econometric history' were at that time alternate labels for cliometrics.

The explicit connecting of economics with economic history was the hallmark of cliometrics as it developed in the USA. Reiter himself was a mathematical economist whose work included collaboration with economic historian Hughes to produce a paper, 'The First 1945 British Steamships' (Hughes and Reiter, 1958) published by the *Journal of the American Statistical Association* in 1958. That paper, along with a celebrated paper of two economists, Alfred Conrad and John Meyer, 'The economics of slavery in the Antebellum South', which also appeared in 1958 in the *Journal of Political Economy* are often associated with the birth of cliometrics (Conrad and Mayer, 1958). In a wider context the growth of cliometrics drew on the longer established traditions of quantitative economic history, and on concurrent developments in the social sciences and computing during the 1960s.

Economics and History, First Edition. David Greasley and Les Oxley

Cliometrics was sufficiently well established by the early 1970s for Penguin Modern Economics Reading to include *New Economic History*, edited by Temin (1973). His introduction to the *New Economic History* set out cliometrics' place within the wider discipline of economics by highlighting the distinctions between the classical and the historical economics schools which emerged in the 19th century. For Temin, the new economic history differed from the old by being a member of the classical economics family, not the historical economics clan; indeed his anthology introduced new economic history as a form of applied neo-classical economics. Early examples of Keynesian cliometric-style research can be found, including Brown's (1956) assessment of New Deal spending in the USA and the work of Matthews (1954) and Rostow (1948) on investment and British economic growth, but these were exceptions.

Chiefly the early cliometricians reinterpreted economic history through the lens of the neo-classical economist. Although in the USA the initial controversies surrounded the indispensability of railroads and the rationale for investing in slaves, in Britain the chief battleground between the old and new economic history centred on gauging the performance of Victorian entrepreneurs, and most especially on their choice of technology, see Lee (1977). A myriad of industry case studies appeared which carefully specified the circumstances of technical choice and these typically redeemed the reputations of Victorian entrepreneurs. At the macroeconomic level McCloskey (1970) emphatically denied Victorian Britain failed, by utilizing estimates of total factor productivity to show efficiency growth was on a par with that of the USA.

The heat of the early debates, the label of the new economic history, and the controversies surrounding counterfactuals and applying neo-classical economics to re-evaluate long-standing historical questions sometimes disguises the wider foundations of cliometrics. In that wider setting several intellectual traditions shaped the emergence and the subsequent evolution of cliometrics. The ones that now stand out include:

1. Quantitative history and most especially the construction of historical series of prices, wages and incomes, which have long traditions dating back to at least the 19th century.
2. Quantitative social science of the 1950s and 1960s which placed emphasis on empirical research, and the use of census and mass survey data. Sociologists for example, pioneered the use of sampling and significance testing to handle large volumes of social data, see Hudson (2000). The manipulation of large data sets was facilitated by concomitant developments in computing.
3. Econometric testing, including of macroeconomic business cycles models which developed strongly in the 1930s; see Morgan (1990). Tinbergen's (1939) *Statistical Testing of Business Cycles* published in 1939 drew on classical statistical methods but also set out the best practices for applied econometrics which eventually became embedded in cliometrics.
4. Cliometrics has been an evolving discipline, with its shifts in direction and emphasis in part reflecting new developments in economic theory. Most

importantly the return of growth theory to centre stage in mainstream economics and the development of endogenous growth models in the 1990s enabled cliometricians to reduce their reliance of neo-classical models and measures of residual productivity, see Greasley and Oxley (1997).

5. The evolution of cliometrics has also been strongly influenced by new developments in econometrics methods, most especially in the analysis of non-stationary time series following the work of Engle and Granger (1987).

In the following Section I, the five key forces which shaped the emergence and evolution of cliometrics are discussed within a survey of the historiography. Then in Section II the six chapters which form the substance of this volume are introduced and placed in the context of the wider discipline. Finally Section III concludes by considering what is next for cliometrics.

I

1. Quantitative History

The construction of long historical time series of key economic variables, most especially of wages, prices and human well-being has a long pedigree. In Britain the endeavours of Bowley (1900) and Wood (1910) stand out and their works on earnings and prices have been augmented by Beveridge (1939), Phelps Brown and Hopkins (1955), and more recently by Williamson (1995), Allen (2001) and Clark (2005). In France, the Annales School from the 1920s promoted the use of long run statistical series of population, prices and production to understand the past. The wider European historiography of prices and wages has been reviewed by van Zanden (1999). The early British studies of Bowley, Wood, and Phelps Brown and Hopkins had the objective of understanding shifts in living standards among particular groups of workers in a single country. In contrast Williamson and Allen incorporated purchasing power parities to compare wage levels across countries. Aside from allowing international comparisons of well-being over long time periods (dating back to the 13th century in the cases of England and Italy) these data have been used to consider issues of income and productivity convergence including during the first globalization 1870–1914. In recent years the international database on real wages has expanded to cover many parts of the world including Asia (Allen *et al.*, 2010) Latin America (Bertola and Porcile, 2006) and Australasia (Greasley and Oxley, 2004).

Estimates of production, national income and GDP have a historiography that long pre-date the contemporaneous data reported by governments after 1945. The history of national income accounting has been admirably surveyed by Maddison (2004) including the contributions of the 20th century pioneers, Colin Clarke and Simon Kuznets. In the case of British data Hoffman's (1955) estimates of industrial production deserve additional mention; they date from the 1930s and provide annual series for years from 1700. These data provided a platform for the subsequent estimates of Deane and Cole (1966), Feinstein (1972) and Crafts and

Harley (1992). Maddison's (2001) own GDP estimates incorporated purchasing power parity benchmarks to facilitate international comparison, and his wider discussion of alternative purchasing power parity approaches and the associated data sets illuminate the central issues surrounding the modern analysis of comparative economic growth.

Quantitative history built upon a great variety of scholarship. Political arithmetic, including Petty's constructions of national resources and capacity dates from the 17th century, and his work was followed by King's estimates of English national incomes in 1688, the Victorian Statistical Movement (see Cullen, 1975) and an explosion of governmental statistics in the 20th century. Historians, long before the birth of cliometrics, were avid measurers and their work, in addition to that on prices and wages, included the history of industries (Nef, 1932 and Wadsworth and Mann, 1931), agriculture (Rogers, 1866–1902), overseas trade (Schlote, 1932), overseas investment (Jenks, 1927), public finance (Hicks, 1938) and money and banking (Sayers, 1936). Quantitative approaches to economic history were flourishing before World War II, and subsequently gathered pace – see for example, Rostow (1948), Lewis (1949), Cairncross (1953), Matthews (1954), Thomas (1954) and Saul (1954). A decade later, around the time of cliometrics birth leading economists were also using long runs of historical data; notable examples include Phillips (1958) and Friedman and Schwartz (1963). Measuring was not novelty for historians when the pioneer cliometricians held their first workshop at Purdue University in 1960. The cliometricians were able to draw upon a long tradition of history by numbers as one ingredient in their new economic history.

2. Quantitative Social Science and Computing

Although economic history had long been a quantitative discipline, by the 1960s numbers gained greater prominence in history more generally. In part historians became more interested in the masses and in social as well as economic changes, as distinct from the history of elites, diplomacy and great men, see Hudson (2000). Summary statistics were a natural corollary to the history of the masses. Concurrent development in computing and the social sciences encouraged the growth of quantitative history. By the early 1970s introductions to quantitative methods for historians appeared and included practical guidance on computing. One well-known text, Floud (1973) noted that calculators which add and multiply could be bought for around £20, but those able to divide cost £35 (around £315 or £512 in 2009 prices, respectively, using the RPI and average earning to measure inflation, see www.eh.net, *Measuring Worth*). He also provided the details of a FORTRAN programme for calculating mean values.

The wider growth of the social sciences in the 1960s, most especially sociology and political science, paralleled the rise of positive economics. Often the textbooks spanned disciplines, for example, that of Blalock (1960), though written for sociology students and was widely used by economic historians. Sociologists pioneered the analysis of mass survey data using sampling theory and significance tests. Sociologists' work on families often overlapped with demographic history as well as social history more generally. Wrigley's (1966) article on family limitation in pre-industrial England shares common ground with the approaches of the sociologists and presaged influential work on English demographic history. Urban historians also made use of census data; Anderson (1971) utilized a sample of the 1851 UK Census to analyse family structure and migration patterns in Preston. Rather differently political scientists paid most attention to voting behaviour and historical analogues include Aydelotte (1963) and Reading (1973).

Cliometrics as it emerged in the 1960s was part of wider movement among the social sciences and history towards quantification. The cliometricians believed their new methods would bring clear answers to long standing historical debates. A similar mood of optimism was exuded by the social sciences, most especially in their ability to improve human well-being via public policy. Most obviously the new (Keynesian) economics held sway in the USA during the 1960s, reflecting a growing confidence among the practitioners, policy makers and politicians in the real-world utility of the social sciences, see Samuelson and Solow (1960) and their exposition of the Phillip's curve using US data. In essence cliometrics as it developed in the 1960s was a form of social science history which rested most especially on the methods and theories of economists.

3. Econometrics

Though sometimes labelled econometric history, very little use was made of regression methods by the pioneer cliometricians during the 1960s. Surveying the state of cliometrics at the end of first decade Wright (1971) concluded the new economic history had been distinguished by its use of economics not econometrics. Temin's (1973) anthology included only one paper that used regression methods, and a similar collection edited on behalf on the Economic History Society by Floud (1974) included only two. Even during the 1970s econometric estimation was not commonly employed by cliometricians. Reflecting on the achievements of the cliometrics school McCloskey (1978) highlighted that expertise with economic and most especially price theory was the defining skill of its practitioners. A decade later the same author's *Econometric History* (McCloskey, 1987) argued that that title originated as a verbal ploy – suggesting it was an attempt by cliometricians to appropriate the prestige of econometrics. Thus he reminds us that Fogel's seminal, and subsequently Nobel-prize winning work on railroads was subtitled *Essays in Econometric History*, although it contained only two elementary fitted straight lines to scatters of points.

Econometric history initially had very little to do with econometrics but made much use of economics and quantification. Gradually the use of regression methods assumed more prominence. The progression was mirrored in the papers latterly published in the *Journal of Economic History* including Gallaway and Vedder (1971) who utilized multivariate regression to show pull forces dominated the trans-Atlantic migration of 1860–1913, and Ford (1971) who used similar methods to explain how Argentine pull forces attracted British capital in 1880–1914. The shift to a style of econometric history that had clearer affinity with econometrics gathered pace during the 1980s as *Explorations in Economic History* became the house journal of cliometrics under the long and distinguished editorship of Larry Neal. Econometric estimation became the norm for *Explorations* papers, including in the areas of, for example, enterprise and technical choice where the early cliometricians had previously eschewed the use of econometrics, see Greasley (1982).

Thus by the 1980s the style of econometric history commonplace in *Explorations* had antecedents in the practices of applied econometrics pioneered by Tinbergen in the 1930s. In contrast cliometrics' other alternative label, the new economic history was beginning to look jaded 30 years on from the Williamsburg meeting. A later survey of the discipline by Crafts *et al.* (1991) associated the 1980s with a second phase of new economic history. In part these editors were reflecting on the richer range of theoretical perspectives deployed by cliometricians, ones that often did not always lead to the typical conclusion of first-generation work as reported by McCloskey (1978) 'The market, God bless it, works'. They also noted the heavier reliance on more sophisticated quantitative methods, with the authors in their anthology using autoregressive integrated moving average (ARIMA), vector autoregression (VAR), Logit and translog production functions. Cliometrics matured and became more eclectic in the 1980s. The virtues of precise specification and measurement demanded by the pioneers were sustained, but the theoretical and empirical models of cliometricians became both more econometric and more sensitive to the minutiae of history.

4. Economic Theory

The reinterpretation of economic history by the pioneer cliometricians rested primarily on applying the logic of economics to long standing historical issues. To a large extent the style of that economics was neo-classical. The impact was profound, most especially in the reinterpretation of US economic history. Even a cursory glance at standard US economic history textbooks, for example, Atack and Passell (1994) illustrate how explicit economic thinking transformed the understanding of national growth, westward expansion, trade, capital market integration, transport innovations, industrialization, slavery and economic fluctuations. The new economic history was also an export product and McCloskey (1987) once articulated the case for *Pax Cliometrica.* The British resisted, tempered in part by the greater use of insights from traditional historiography, but sometimes endorsed the product. Interestingly only 4 of the 10 papers in Crafts *et al.* (1991) were by British scholars. Yet progress had been made. All 14 papers in Temin's (1973) anthology were written by Americans.

Some critics argued that the pioneering cliometrician's revisionism amounted to an imperialism of elementary economic theory. Certainly the apparatus of neoclassical economics did not offer much insight into historical-institutional change. Yet the aspirations and agendas of cliometricians evolved, and they came to include tendencies towards greater eclecticism. Trust, uncertainty, creativity, credibility, institutions, agency and informational asymmetry are concepts that became incorporated in cliometricians' theoretical tool kits; for examples see O'Rourke

(2007), Greasley, Madsen and Oxley (2001) and Mitchener (2005). Cliometricians also re-invigorated long established theoretical perspectives, including those of Hechsher and Ohlin, and deployed them with new vigour and purpose, see Williamson (2002). Most dramatically, the return of growth theory to centre stage in main stream economics provided new opportunities for cliometricians to engage with and utilize the ideas of growth theorists.

Barro *et al.* (1995) argued that the disassociation in the neo-classical paradigm between theory and historical experience led to the virtual demise of research on economic growth by the 1970s, although economic historians, for example, Matthews *et al.* (1982) continued to highlight the importance of residual productivity. The new endogenous growth models, including those of Rebelo (1991) and Romer (1986) were able to explain continuing growth without recourse to exogenous technology, initially by showing that human capital formation might offset diminishing returns. A second generation of endogenous models paid more attention to the forces promoting technological progress by considering the private rewards for innovation and the possibility of public knowledge spillover, see Aghion and Howitt (1992). More recently unified theories which offer two and three stage interpretations of long run economic growth to integrate the Malthusian world of stagnant output per capita with the modern era of sustained output per capita growth have been constructed by Galor and Weil (2000) and Hansen and Prescott (2002). Concomitantly empirical analyses of economic growth surged from the 1990s.

Cliometricians have contributed much to the empirics of economic growth following the rise of endogenous theories, most especially in their extending of the analyses to periods before 1945 and by their supply of data. In the key area of human capital formation Goldin (2001), O'Rourke and Williamson (1999) and Baten and van Zanden (2008) have shown the value of historical data. The role of geography and natural resources in economic development, including issues of agglomeration, the resource curse and technology are further areas where the work of economists and cliometricians coincide. Lucas (2001), Krugman (1995) and Baldwin's (1999) analyses utilizing the new economic geography have clear cliometric analogues – for example, Keay (2007), Crafts and Venables (2001) and Greasley and Oxley (2010a). Sachs and Warner's (2001) analysis of the resource curse rested on post-1970 data, and scrutiny of their hypothesis with longer runs of data, for example, by Wright and Czelusta (2003), Greasley and Madsen (2010) and Huff (2002), have tempered their conclusions.

Among growth theories a schism exists between perspectives highlighting, respectively, the forces of geography and importance of institutions in economic growth. Cliometricians have a special place in the analysis of institutions, following the pioneering work of North (1990). Both theorists and empirical economists have built upon North's work, see Parente and Prescott (2000) and Acemoglu *et al.* (2002). The primacy of institutions in economic growth though has been challenged by cliometricians, notably by Sokoloff and Engerman (2000). The institutions versus geography in economic growth debates illustrate how the divisions between cliometricians and economists have blurred over the past decade. Cliometricians typically have constructed the data and the economists the theory, but the empirics of growth has become a common arena. A greater willingness on the part of economists to engage with historical data following the new developments in growth theory has been an important force in the evolution of cliometrics.

5. Time Series Methods

Cliometricians had by the 1980s became regular users of econometric methods. Some of the key debates in the second phase of new economic history, for example, those seeking to explain the rise in unemployment between the world wars made use of time series data and tests of statistical significance using regression methods, see Benjamin and Kochin (1979). Coincidental to the growing use of regression methods by cliometricians was a greater awareness among econometric theorists that classical regression analysis utilizing time series might lead to spurious results if the data series have trends. Engle and Granger (1987) pioneered the new methods of cointegration in an attempt to establish more robust long run relationship among time series variables. Their methods gained acceptance among cliometricians; for example, O'Grada (1993) provides an early new economic history example of the use of cointegration methods. Tests of Granger causality are a natural corollary to cointegration methods, and these were also utilized by cliometricians, see for example, Greasley and Oxley (1998).

Much of the initial work by cliometricians using the new time series methods was univariate analysis. Describing the trends and cycles of historical data long predated cliometrics. For US data the work of Kuznets (1930) and Burns (1934) stand out and Hoffmann (1955) provides an admirable survey of British research. The new time series methods provided opportunities for re-appraising long term production trends where the underlying data are difference stationary. The new methods were used to shed new light of key historical debates including the British Industrial Revolution and the Victorian climacteric, see Crafts *et al.* (1989) and Greasley and Oxley (1994). Following the work of Perron (1989) on structural breaks, the effects of major shocks on historical production trends were also investigated within a modern time series framework, for example, Greasley and Oxley (1996) analysed the First World War's effect on British industrial growth.

In a multivariate context the new time series methods by allowing the investigation of common trends among times series data contributed to the debates surrounding modern economic growth, most especially in relation to identifying income convergence among groups of countries. Times series tests of convergence typically find against multivariate convergence, see Bernard and Durlauf (1995) but Greasley and Oxley (1997) report time series evidence of convergence clubs. The method of common trends has also been used to identify developments blocks or groups of leading industries. Enflo *et al.* (2008) combined cointegration and causality analysis to gauge the role of electrification in Sweden's industrial growth, and Greasley and Oxley (2000) investigated the leading sectors of the British Industrial Revolution with similar methods.

II

Each of the chapters in this volume illustrates at least some of the foundations of cliometrics elucidated in the previous section. Cliometrics, as we have shown, has been an evolving discipline and the contributions reviewed here also help to show how the subject developed over the past half century. Most importantly each chapter surveys and builds upon a key area of cliometrics. Leunig (2010) takes us to the birth of cliometrics in his reflections on 'social savings', a concept introduced by Bob Fogel at the First Cliometrics Workshop at Purdue University in 1960 in a preliminary discussion of his later book, *Railroads and US Economic Growth*. Leunig takes issue with the view that the pioneer cliometricians simply applied economists' concepts to reinterpret history. In the case of social savings Fogel constructed a new concept to measure the consequences of technological change, and then applied the idea to overturn traditional historians' ideas on the importance of the railroads.

The concept of social savings built upon familiar ideas of marginal costs and the circumstances under which costs and prices would equate. Fogel formulated the concept to gauge the impact of new technology on economic growth, taking account of both the extent of a new technology's use and its additional value over previous technology. Social savings, measured as the gap between the supply price (of transport) made by the old and new technology, and the quantity of transport supplied (in 1890) was a simple yet enormously powerful device for gauging the importance of improved transport technology to US economic growth. In essence, because the US economy had good second best transport alternatives, the gains from railroads were shown to be less than traditional historians had believed, indeed Fogel's key conclusion was a denial that railroads were indispensable in US economic development.

Leunig performs valuable service in setting out the connections between social savings and alternative measures of gauging the welfare gains from a new technology. He highlights that the social savings from introducing improved technology equate identically to a shift in total factor productivity. Pioneer cliometricians, see McCloskey (1971), made much use of the price duals of production functions to measure total factor productivity. Fogel (1979) eventually set out precise definitions of social savings, but his wider work, including that with Engerman on industrial growth and slavery shows their understanding of production functions, the price dual and how these concepts can be used to measure efficiency and industrial growth, see Fogel and Engerman (1969, 1974). Leunig also explains why social savings do not usually equate to economists' standard measure of welfare, consumer surplus or with the results of growth accounting. Usually (and depending upon the shape of the demand curve) the rise in consumer welfare from improved technology will be lower than the social saving, and the gaps may be large when technological progress leads to large price falls and big output gains.

By setting out and clarifying the various measures for gauging the impact of new technology Leunig shows why cliometricians have reported diverse social savings results. He also surveys the wider use social saving, including those outside the railroad arena, and shows the potential for further use especially when the data needed to estimate consumer surplus are missing. Leunig is cautious about the likely growth of social savings studies, but while case studies of social savings are comparatively few, those estimating total factor productivity are legion. The distinctions and similarities between measures consumer surplus, social savings and total factor elucidated by Leunig provide a salutary reminder of the need for cliometricians and economists to specify carefully their purposes and methods.

The chapters of Inwood and Roberts (2010) and Prados (2010) illustrate and extend the long-standing traditions of quantitative history. Measuring human well-being has been an enduring concern among quantitative historians, and these chapters show how cliometricians are pushing forward the boundaries of the debates. Much of the early debates on living standards, for a summary see Taylor (1975) utilized real wage data, sometimes augmented by information on consumption per capita and life expectancy. The use of stature as a measure of well-being in history dates from the 1970s, see Engerman (1976) and Floud and Wachter (1982). The initial motivation of the stature studies was to provide for measurement of well-being for periods and populations (or sub-groups of populations including women and children) with no or at best dubious income data. Increasingly though anthropometrics has been seen as a credible and possibly superior measure of well-being, given its potential to reflect both an individual's material inputs and their usage of that sustenance, see Steckel (2008).

In their survey Inwood and Roberts (2010) highlight the value of explicit longitudinal studies which link early life conditions with later life health and longevity. They also review the myriad of studies which used estimates of stature from samples of populations at different points in time. The early stature studies typically utilized historical data from USA and Europe, but later studies had a wider geographical range, and Inwood and Roberts usefully draw attention to the conflicts with traditional income-based and the stature studies of living standards in history. Thus far explicit longitudinal historical studies, which chart early life and occasionally in utero (usually measured by birth weight) experiences with later life health and income outcomes have been limited, and Inwood and Roberts show clearly the potential value of cliometric work of this type.

In their survey they set out the key findings of modern (longitudinal) anthropometric studies, most especially Waaler (1984), and review the few parallel historical studies, highlighting the prospects for cliometric research. They consider both height and weight-body mass indexes and set out the key modern, essentially post-1945, research finding of the links to health, morbidity and mortality. Thus far parallel historical studies are small in number, and chiefly utilize data arising from research using US Civil War army records, see Costa (1993). However the potential for historical research does not simply arise from cliometricians utilizing the growing knowledge of the health sciences to construct better-informed history. Cliometricians, Inwood and Roberts argue, have the potential to make a particularly important contribution in documenting how the shape of the body mass–mortality relationship has changed across cohorts, periods and countries to provide a useful corrective to the perspective of some medical literature that appears to be searching for a stable or universal biological relationship.

Leandro Prados also draws and builds upon modern research, in his case on the United Nations Development Program's *Human Development Reports* (1990–2009) to construct new historical data on human development. Initially Prados reviews synthetic indicators of well-being, including the UN's Human Development Index (HDI) which has been published periodically since 1990. The HDI combines information on income, life expectancy and education in a composite index of development. Usefully Prados analyses the construction and criticisms of these data: he reviews the formulation of the individual series and discusses the merits of how income, longevity and education are combined. The value of synthetic indexes of development has been heavily criticized; see for example, Dowrick *et al.* (2003) and Pardos's discussion fully reflects the doubts surrounding the utility of the HDI. His main purpose however is to provide an improved HDI (IHDI).

The UN HDI provides a more optimistic indicator of developing countries well-being than measures of income per capita. Indeed Prados notes the tension between the pessimistic tone of the UN *Human Development Reports* and the more optimistic impression shown by the HDI. By including life expectancy, which grows relatively quickly in developing countries since 1945, HDI comparisons show developing countries performance in better light than do GDP per capita comparisons. Prados takes the view that the tension in part arises from defects in the construction of the HDI and he proposes a new measure which both adopts multiplicative weights for the three elements and, most importantly, new criteria for estimating the longevity and education components.

Prados utilizes the achievement function of Kakwani (1993), where an increase in the standard of living of a country at a higher level implies a greater achievement than a similar increase at a lower level. In particular for the social elements of the HDI, life expectancy and education, Prados derives the estimates with a convex achievement function, following Kakwani (1993), although the same procedure is not used for income. Thus, for example, in the case of life expectancy a gain at higher levels is weighted more heavily in the IHDI. Further by adopting a multiplicative aggregation of the three elements Prados is able to decompose the contributions of income, longevity and education in shaping the contours of the IHDI.

The results are striking, over the period 1870–2005 the IHDI rose by 1.4% p.a. compared to 0.9% p.a. for the HDI. The most important driver of the rise in the HDI has been the rise in life expectancy. However in comparison to the HDI the IHDI shows systematically lower levels of human development for developing countries. In the context of the conventional UN *Human Development Report* categories – 'low' is defined as <0.5 and high as >0.8, the IHDI mean level of development in 2005 at 0.455 falls in the low category, whereas the HDI shows a value of 0.711, close to the high category. Overall Prados argues that actual levels of development today are further below potential levels than the UN data show, and that greater investment in education and in improving life expectancy are, on the basis of the IHDI estimates, the route to improvement.

The contributions of Hatton (2010) and of Fishback *et al.* (2010) provide exemplary examples of the growing maturity of cliometrics. Fishback *et al.* provide a detailed survey of cliometric research into US income maintenance programmes, highlighting the patchwork, state and local level provision. They perform valuable service in gauging the overall level of US provision given the myriad and of diversity of the schemes, and they report it has been surprisingly high. Early cliometric research was sometimes criticized for a lack of sensitivity to the minutiae of historical experience, Fishback *et al.*'s survey show that the painstaking creation of historical data is now a hallmark of cliometrics.

Usefully Fishback *et al.* set the scene by articulating how the patchwork system developed and how expenditure grew. Five categories of welfare provision are considered; workers' compensation, mothers' pension, old age assistance, aid to the blind and unemployment insurance; and in each case the data of state and Federal provision is identified. These data provide a basis for analysing the geographic variation in spending and the extent to which state and city level differences persisted, including during the era of greater Federal spending from the 1930s. Fishback *et al.* also review why spending varied across states, and report new results on the political economy of unemployment compensation for the years 1940–2000, which shows higher spending persisted in some states irrespective of income and political shifts. Finally, these authors survey the cliometric literature which has gauged the impact of the various welfare programmes, highlighting that the effects spanned widely for example, to accident, crime, migration, wage and divorce rates and to the macro economy.

Cliometricians have always shown interest in gauging the effects of public policies. In his introduction to the *New Economic History*, Temin (1973) noted assessing government policies as one of the three key areas of the discipline (the other two he suggested were economic growth and economic institutions). The areas of policy Temin mentioned were, banking, land, transport subsidies and tariffs. Welfare policies were not mentioned. Fishback *et al.*'s survey illustrates how the boundaries of cliometrics have expanded over the past half century. The range of issues has grown, and approaches have become eclectic, with the impacts of public policies extended to consider a greater range of economic and social variables. Methods of analysis of have also changed substantially. Pioneer cliometricians made little use of econometrics. Coincidental with the rise of new time series methods from the 1990s was a growth in panel data estimation, which exploited both the cross-sectional and time elements of data. The dominant method of analysis revealed in the survey of Fishback *et al.* is panel data econometrics.

Tim Hatton's survey shows how a key area of cliometric research, the study of international migration, has evolved over the past 40 years. He highlights that the cliometrics of international migration has borrowed extensively from the parallel literature in economics, but that historical research utilizing pre-1914 data, when migration was essentially unfettered, has informed modern debates on the motives for and the effects of migration. Historical analyses of the Atlantic migrations were well established before the cliometrics revolution, and included the pioneering work of Jerome (1926), which argued migrants were pulled to the USA in numbers related to the business cycle. Ferenczi and Wilcox (1929) compilation of migration statistics provides an admirable early example of quantitative history. Pioneer cliometricians, including Gallaway and Vedder (1971) contributed the long standing debates surrounding pull and push forces in the Atlantic migrations and Pope (1968) considered British Empire migration more generally.

Interestingly it was the second-generation new economic historians including Hatton (1995) himself that placed migration decisions within coherent economic models which linked migration to expected future incomes from going or staying. Here cliometrics drew of the work of economists, but much extended their empirical boundaries. Parallel work constructing databases of international real wages; see especially Williamson (1995) with data series for years from the 1820s greatly enriched the understanding of international migration. These data were instrumental in advancing the debates of why European countries had varying out migration rates before 1914, and in gauging the impact of migration on incomes in the source and destination countries.

Computable general equilibrium (CGE) models have been an important feature of the cliometric analysis of the national wage and income effects of the mass Atlantic migrations before 1914. These models, as Hatton and Williamson (1998) show, allowed for the analysis of a richer array of migration effects, beyond those previously gauged, for example, by postulating counterfactual labour force changes and labour demand elasticities to estimate migration's effects on real wages. Thus CGE models have been used to gauge migration's effects on economic structure and trade, and to show how incorporating capital mobility influences the estimated migration–wage nexus. The cliometrics of migration provides excellent illustration of how the ideas of economists have been utilized but also augmented by economic historians using innovative methods and newly constructed data to provide sharper insights into key issues, including those of public policy and migration controls.

Greasley and Oxley (2010b) review recent development in time series methods and explore their use in cliometric research. Cliometricians, given their natural affinity with analysing long run data, have more to gain than most from time series analysis. Greasley and Oxley provide simple explanations of the potential and the pitfalls of using time series data and survey the tests now available to guide the best practice use of time series methods. Second-generation new economic historians made increasing use of classical regression methods with time series data in the 1980s, which made their findings vulnerable to the criticisms of Granger and Newbold (1974) that apparently significant relationships among times series variables might be spurious. Greasley and Oxley, in addition to illustrating the pitfalls, show how new methods of time series, including cointegration and causality testing, provide enormously powerful tools for understanding long run economic change.

The time series methods they illustrate are multi-faceted and range through uni-, bi- and multivariate and panel data techniques. These methods are now widely utilized and Greasley and Oxley gauge the extent of their use and the type of application by surveying the papers using time series methods published in *Explorations in Economic History* and *Cliometrica* since 2000. To illustrate and explain the methods they draw on their earlier research, including that used to identify structural changes and causes of the Industrial Revolution. Further, they explain how cointegration methods provide a basis for understanding the common features of times series, and show how issues of convergence and identifying the key drivers of economic change can be observed using these methods.

In addition to using their previous research to explain time series methods, Greasley and Oxley also report new research finding based upon recent developments in time series econometrics. In particular they show how test of multiple regime shifts proposed by Leybourne *et al.* (2007) can help identify the alternating stochastic properties of British industrial output and thus on the characteristics of the Industrial Revolution. They also explore how the structural time series model approach of Harvey (1989) can be used to help understand the trends and cycles in very long run data, illustrating the methods by analysing English real wage since 1264. Finally, Greasley and Oxley consider the potential of methods presently at the frontier of time series econometrics including the analysis of mildly explosive processes, see Phillips and Yu (2009) which may help the understanding of bubbles, and graphical modelling and its implications for causality testing.

III

The reconnecting of economics and economic history was at the heart of cliometrics as it emerged around 1960. In 1983 the Cliometric Society was formed and continued the tradition of annual cliometrics workshops. The US meetings are now augmented by World Congresses of Cliometrics. The Cliometric Society defines itself as an academic organization of individuals interested in the use of economic theory and statistical techniques to study economic history. Leunig's discussion of social savings provides a salutary reminder of the importance that the pioneer cliometricians gave to precise specification and to theory. The contributions in this volume also show how cliometrics has matured and evolved over the past half century. The range and the style of theories utilized are now broader. In some areas, for example, as Hatton shows in surveying the cliometrics of migration, coherent economic models became more firmly embedded in the historiography. The growing eclecticism of cliometrics in its use of economics is well illustrated by Fishback *et al.* (2010) in their analysis of the political economy of welfare in the USA.

In an important respect the Cliometric Society definition highlighting the use of economic theory and statistical techniques to study economic history does not fully capture the style of cliometrics discussed by Inwood and Roberts and by Prados. The construction of economic-historical data had a lead role in the growth of cliometrics, Often data construction has been informed by theory, most obviously in the estimation of GDP and real wages adjusted for purchasing power parity. Anthropometrics, though, and the measure of stature and body mass of past populations illustrates how the boundaries of cliometrics have expanded. That a grasp of price theory is no longer the defining skill of cliometricians appears palpable when, for example, an understanding of the medical sciences underpins some modern measures of economic well-being. The discussion of the HDI by Prados shows how crucial theoretical concepts remain to quantitative indicators of well-being. His IHDI utilized an achievement function proposed by Kakwani (1993), and its adoption would have important policy implications because the IHDI shows levels of well-being for developing countries well below those reported by the United Nations.

The pioneer cliometricians were tardy in their use of econometrics. Statistical methods are now central to cliometric research, and a diversity of approach has accompanied the growth. In part the fuller use of econometrics was stimulated by the growth of computers and most especially of software that facilitated estimation. As Greasley and Oxley show the development of new methods of analysis has been especially strong in relations to time series data. Economic historians have long had interests in measuring trends, cycles and the relationships among time series data. The new methods of cointegration and causality analysis have already delivered new interpretations, for example, of the causes of the Industrial Revolution, and promise much more. The statistical toolkit of cliometricians though now spans widely and includes panel data techniques and computable general equilibrium models, and much like for theory, no single approach now dominates.

Cliometrics put economics back into to economic history. There are now hopeful signs that cliometricians are helping to put economic history back into economics. Nowhere is this more apparent than in the once dormant but now vibrant field of economic growth. Theoretical models of growth now incorporate human capital, geography and institutions, and the empirical analogues sometimes are based on long spans of historical data. Cliometricians will always be interested in understanding the past for its own sake, but economic history also offers experimental data that are presently utilized only to a limited extent by economists. Maddison (2008) in a perceptive response to the stern review on climate change highlighted how its predictions of the future ignored the past. An optimistic view of the next 50 years would obviate the need for similar observations at cliometrics centenary celebrations.

References

Acemoglu, D., Johnson, S. and Robinson, R. (2002) Reversal of fortunes: geography and institutions n the making of the modern world. *Quarterly Journal of Economics* 107: 1231–1294.

Aghion, P. and Howitt, P. (1992) A model of economic growth through creative destruction. *Econometrica* 60: 323–351.

Allen, R.C. (2001) The great divergence in European wages and prices from the Middle Ages to the First World War. *Explorations in Economic History* 38: 411–447.

Allen, R.C., Ma, D., Bassino, J., and van Zanden, J.L. (2010) Wages, prices, and living standards in China, 1738–1925: in comparison with Europe, Japan, and India. *Economic History Review* 64: S1, 8–38.

Anderson, M. (1971) *Family Structure in Nineteenth Century Lancashire*. London: Cambridge University Press.

Atack, J. and Passell, P. (1994) *A New Economic View of American History*. New York: Norton.

Aydelotte, W.O. (1963) Voting patterns in the British House of Commons in the 1840s. *Comparative Studies in Society and History* 5: 134–163.

Baldwin, R.E. (1999) Agglomeration and endogenous capital. *European Economic Review* 43: 253–280.

Barro, R.J. and Martin, X. Sala I. (1995) *Economic Growth*. New York: McGraw Hill.

Baten, J. and van Zanden, J.L. (2008) Book production and the onset of modern economic growth. *Journal of Economic Growth* 13: 217–235.

Benjamin, D. and Kochin, L. (1979) Searching for an explanation for unemployment in interwar Britain. *Journal of Political Economy* 87: 441–478.

Bernard, A. and Durlauf, S. (1995) Convergence in international output. *Journal of Applied Econometrics* 10: 97–108.

Bértola, L. and Porcile, G. (2006) Convergence, trade and industrial policy: Argentina, Brazil and Uruguay in the international economy, 1900–1980. *Revista de Historia Económica* 37–67.

Beveridge, L. (1939) *Prices and Wages in England from the Twelfth to the Nineteenth Century*. London: Frank Cass & Co.

Blalock, H.M. (1960) *Social Statistics*. Tokyo: McGraw Hill.

Bowley, A.L. (1900) *Wages in the UK in the Nineteenth Century*. Cambridge: Cambridge University Press.

Brown, E.C. (1956) Fiscal policy in the thirties; a reappraisal. *American Economic Review* 46: 857–879.

Burns, A.F. (1934) *Production Trends in the United States since 1870*. New York: NBER.

Cairncross, A.K. (1953) *Home and Foreign Investment 1870–1913*. Cambridge: Cambridge University Press.

Clark, G. (2005) The condition of the working class in England. *Journal of Political Economy* 113: 1307–1340.

Conrad, A. and Mayer, J. (1958) The economics of slavery in the Antebellum South. *Journal of Political Economy* 66: 95–130.

Costa, D. (1993) Height, weight, wartime stress, and older age mortality: evidence from the Union Army records. *Explorations in Economic History* 30: 424–449.

Crafts, N.F.R. and Harley, C.K. (1992) Output growth and the British revolution: a restatement of the Crafts-Harley view. *Economic History Review* 45: 703–730.

Crafts, N.F.R. and Venables, A.J. (2001) Globalization in history: a geographical perspective. CEPR discussion paper 3079.

Crafts, N.F R., Leybourne, S.J. and Mills, T.C. (1989) The climacteric in Late-Victorian Britain and France: a reappraisal of the evidence. *Journal of Applied Econometrics* 4: 103–117.

Crafts, N.F.R., Dimsdale, N. and Engerman, S. (1991) *Quantitative Economic History*. Oxford: Clarendon Press.

Cullen, M.J. (1975) *The Victorian Statistical Movement*. Hassocks: Harvester Press New York.

Deane, P. and Cole, W.A. (1966) *British Economic Growth, 1688–1959*. Cambridge: Cambridge University Press.

Dowrick, S., Dunlop, Y. and Quiggin, J. (2003), Social indicators and comparisons of living standards. *Journal of Development Economics* 70: 501–529.

Enflo, K., Kander, A. and Schon, L. (2008) Identifying development blocks – a new methodology implemented on Swedish industry. *Journal of Evolutionary Economics* 18: 57–76.

Engerman, S.L. (1976) The height of slaves in the United States. *Local Population Studies* 16: 45–49.

Engle, R.F. and Granger, C.W. (1987) Cointegration and error correction: representation, estimation, testing. *Econometrica* 55: 1057–1072.

Feinstein, C.H. (1972) *National Income Output and Expenditure of the UK 1855–1965*. Cambridge: Cambridge University Press.

Ferenczi, I. and Wilcox, W.F. (1929) *International Migrations*. New York: NBER.

Fishback, P., Allen, S., Fox, J. and Livingston, B. (2010) A patchwork safety net: a survey of cliometric studies of income maintenance programs in the United States in the first half of the twentieth century. *Journal of Economic Surveys* 24: 895–940.

Floud, R.C. (1973) *An Introduction to Quantitative Methods for Historians*. London: Methuen.

Floud, R.C. (1974) *Essays in Quantitative Economic History*. Oxford: Clarendon Press.

Floud, R. and Wachter, K.W. (1982) Poverty and physical stature. *Social Science History* 6: 422–452.

Fogel, R.W. (1964) *Railroads and Economic Growth: Essays in Econometric History*. Baltimore: John Hopkins.

Fogel, R.W. (1966) The new economic history: its findings and methods. *Economic History Review* 19: 642–656.

Fogel, R.W. (1979) Notes on the social savings controversy. *Journal of Economic History* 39: 1–54.

Fogel, R.W. and Engerman, S.L. (1969) A model for the explanation of industrial expansion during the nineteenth century. *Journal of Political Economy* 77: 306–328.

Fogel, R.W. and Engerman, S.L. (1974) Time on the cross. *The Economics of American Negro Slavery*. Boston.

Ford, A. (1971) British investment in Argentina and Long Swings, 1880–1914. *Journal of Economic History* 31: 650–663.

Friedman, M. and Schwartz, A.J. (1963) *A Monetary History of the United States*. Princeton: Princeton University Press.

Gallaway, L. and Vedder, R.K. (1971) Emigration from the United Kingdom to the United States. *Journal of Economic History* 31: 885–897.

Galor, O. and Weil, D. (2000) Population, technology and growth: from Malthusian stagnation to demographic transition and beyond. *American Economic Review* 90: 806–828.

Goldin, C. (2001) The human capital century and American Leadership: virtues of the past. *Journal of Economic History* 61: 263–292.

Granger, C.W.J. and Newbold, P. (1974) Spurious regressions in econometrics. *Journal of Econometrics* 2: 111–120.

Greasley, D. (1982) The diffusion of machine-cutting in the British coal industry 1902–38. *Explorations in Economic History* 19: 246–268.

Greasley, D. and Madsen, J.B. (2010) Curse and boon: natural resources and long run growth in currently rich economies. *Economic Record* 86: 311–328.

Greasley, D. and Oxley, L. (1994) Rehabilitation sustained: the industrial revolution as a macroeconomic epoch. *Economic History Review* 47: 760–768.

Greasley, D. and Oxley, L. (1996) Discontinuities in competitiveness: the impact of the first world war on British industry. *Economic History Review* XLIX: 83–101.

Greasley, D. and Oxley, L. (1997) Time series based tests of the convergence hypothesis: some positive results. *Economics Letters* 56: 143–147.

Greasley, D. and Oxley, L. (1998) Causality and the first industrial revolution. *Industrial and Corporate Change* 7: 33–47.

Greasley, D. and Oxley, L. (2000) British industrialization 1815–1860: a disaggregate time series perspective. *Explorations in Economic History* 37: 98–119.

Greasley, D., and Oxley, L. (2004) Globalization and real wages in New Zealand 1873–1913. *Explorations in Economic History* 41: 26–47.

Greasley, D. and Oxley, L. (2010a) Knowledge, natural resource abundance and economic development: lessons from New Zealand 1861–1939. *Explorations in Economic History* 47: 443–459.
Greasley, D. and Oxley, L. (2010b) Cliometrics and time series econometrics: some theory and applications. *Journal of Economic Surveys* 24: 755–774.
Greasley, D., Madsen, J.B. and Oxley, L. (2001) Income uncertainty and consumer spending during the Great Depression. *Explorations in Economic History* 38: 225–251.
Hansen, G. and Prescott, E.C. (2002) Malthus to Solow. *American Economic Review* 92: 1205–1217.
Harvey, A.C. (1989) *Forecasting Structural Time Series Models and the Kalman Filter*. Cambridge: Cambridge University Press.
Hatton, T.J. (1995) A Model of U.K. Emigration, 1870–1913. *Review of Economics and Statistics* 77: 407–415.
Hatton, T.J. (2010) The cliometrics of international migration: a survey. *Journal of Economic Surveys* 25: 941–969.
Hatton and Williamson (1998) *Global Migration and the World Economy*. Cambridge, MA: The MIT Press.
Hicks, U.K. (1938) *The Finance of British Government 1920–1936*. Oxford: Clarendon.
Hoffman, W.G. (1955) *British Industry 1700–1950*. Oxford: Blackwell.
Hudson, P. (2000) *History by Numbers*. London: Arnold.
Huff, W.G. (2002) Boom or bust commodities and industrialization in pre-world war in Malaya. *Journal of Economic History* 62: 1074–1115.
Hughes, J.R.T. and Reiter, S. (1958) The first 1945 British steamships. *Journal of the American Statistical Association* 53: 360–381.
Inwood, K. and Roberts, E. (2010) Longitudinal studies of human growth and health: a review of recent historical research. *Journal of Economic Surveys* 24: 801–840.
Jenks, L.H. (1927) *The Migration of British Capital to 1875*. New York: A.A. Knopf.
Jerome, H. (1926) *Migration and Business Cycles*. New York: NBER.
Kakwani, N. (1993) Performance in living standards. An international comparison. *Journal of Development Economics* 41: 307–336.
Keay, I. (2007) The engine or the caboose: resource industries and twentieth century Canadian economic performance. *Journal of Economic History* 67: 1–32.
Krugman, P. and Venables, A.J. (1995) Globalization and the inequality of nations. *Quarterly Journal of Economics* 110: 857–880.
Kuznets, S. (1930) *Secular Trends in Prices and Production*. New York: NBER.
Lee, C.H. (1977) *The Quantitative Approach to Economic History*. London: Martin Robertson.
Leunig, T. (2010) Social Savings. *Journal of Economic Surveys* 24: 775–800.
Lewis, W.A. (1949) *Economic Survey, 1919–1939*. London: Unwin.
Leybourne, S., Kim, T.-H., and Taylor, A.M.R. (2007) Detecting multiple changes in persistence. *Studies in Nonlinear Dynamics & Econometrics* 11: 1–32.
Lucas, R.E. (2001) Externalities and cities. *Review of Economic Dynamics* 4: 245–274.
Maddison, A. (2001) *The World Economy: a millennial perspective*. Paris: OECD.
Maddison, A. (2004) Quantifying and interpreting world development: macro measurement before and after Colin Clark. *Australian Economic History Review* 44: 1–34.
Maddison, A. (2008) The west and the rest in the world economy. *World Economics* 9: 75–100.
Matthews, R.C.O. (1954) *A Study in Trade Cycle History*. Cambridge: Cambridge University Press.
Matthews, R.C.O., Feinstein, C.H. and Odling-Smee, J.C. (1982) *British Economic Growth 1856–1973*. Oxford.
McCloskey, D.N. (1970) Did Victorian Britain fail? *Economic History Review* 23: 446–459.

McCloskey, D.N. (1971) *Essays on a mature economy: Britain after 1840*. London: Methuen.
McCloskey, D.N. (1978) The achievements of the cliometric school. *Journal of Economic History* 38: 13–28.
McCloskey, D.N. (1987) *Econometric History*. London: Macmillan.
Mitchener, K.J. and James, K. (2005) Bank supervision, regulation, and instability during the Great Depression. *Journal of Economic History* 65: 152–185.
Morgan, M.S. (1990) *The History of Econometric Ideas*. Cambridge: Cambridge University Press.
Nef, J.U. (1932) *The Rise of the British Coal Industry*. London: Routledge.
North, D.C. (1990) *Institutions, Institutional Change and Economic Performance*. Cambridge: Cambridge University Press.
O'Grada, C. (1993), The Irish paper pound of 1797–1820: some cliometrics of the Bullionist debate. *Oxford Economic Papers* 45: 148–156.
O'Rourke, K.H. (2007) Culture, conflict and cooperation: Irish dairying before the Great War. *Economic Journal* 117: 1357–1379.
O'Rourke, K.H. and Williamson, J.G. (1999) *Globalization and History: The Evolution of the Nineteenth Century Atlantic Economy*. Cambridge, MA: MIT Press.
Parente, S.L. and Prescott, E.C. (2000) *Barriers to Riches*. Cambridge, MA: MIT Press.
Perron, P. (1989) The Great crash, the oil price shock, and the unit root hypothesis. *Econometrica* 57(6): 1361–1401.
Phelps Brown, E.H. and Hopkins, S.V. (1955) Seven centuries of building wages. *Economica* 22: 195–206.
Phillips, W.A. (1958) Relationship between employment and the rate of change of money wage rates in the United Kingdom. *Economica* 25: 283–299.
Phillips, P.C.B. and Yu, J. (2009) Singapore Management University Economics and Statistics Working Paper Series, No. 18-2009: 1–38.
Pope, D. (1968) Empire migration to Canada, Australia, and New Zealand. *Australian Economic Papers* 7: 167–188.
Prados, L. (2010) Improving human development: a long-run view. *Journal of Economic Surveys* 24: 841–894.
Reading, D. (1973) New deal activity and the states, 1933–39. *Journal of Economic History* 33: 792–810.
Rebelo, S. (1991) Long run policy analysis and long run growth. *Journal of Political Economy* 99: 500–521.
Rogers, J.E.T. (1866–1902) *A History of Agriculture and Prices in England*. Oxford: Clarendon.
Romer, P. (1986) Increasing returns and long-run growth. *Journal of Political Economy* 94: 1002–1037.
Rostow, W.W. (1948) *British Economy in the Nineteenth Century*. Oxford: Clarendon.
Sachs, J.D. and Warner, A.M. (2001) The curse of natural resources. *European Economic Review* 45: 827–838.
Samuelson, P.A. and Solow, R.M. (1960) Analytical aspects of anti-inflation policy. *American Economic Review* 50: 177–194.
Saul, S.B. (1954) Britain and world trade, 1870–1914. *Economic History Review* 7: 49–66.
Sayers, R.S. (1936) *Bank of England Operations 1890–1914*. London: P.S. King and Son.
Schlote, W. (1932) *British Overseas Trade from 1700–1930s*. Oxford: Blackwell.
Sokoloff, K.L. and Engerman, S.L. (2000) History lessons: institutions, factors endowments, and paths of development in the New World. *Journal of Economic Perspectives* 14: 217–232.
Steckel, R.H. (2008) Biological measures of the standard of living. *Journal of Economic Perspectives* 22: 129–152.

Taylor, A.J. (1975) *The Standard of Living in Britain in the Industrial Revolution*. London: Methuen.
Temin, P. (1973) *New Economic History*. London: Penguin.
Thomas, B.R. (1954) *Migration and Economic Growth: A Study of Great Britain and the Atlantic Economy*. Cambridge: Cambridge University Press.
Tinbergen, J. (1939) *Statistical Testing of Business-Cycle Theories*. Geneva: League of Nations.
Waaler H. (1984) Height, weight and mortality. The Norwegian experience. *Acta Medica Scandinavica* Supplement 679: 1–56.
Wadsworth, A.P. and Mann, J. de L. (1931) *The Cotton Trade and Industrial Lancashire, 1600–1780*. Manchester: Manchester University Press.
Williamson, J.G. (1995) The evolution of global labor markets since 1830: background evidence and hypotheses. *Explorations in Economic History* 32: 141–196.
Williamson, J. (2002) Land, labor, and globalization in the third world, 1870-1940. *Journal of Economic History* 62: 55–85.
Wood, G.H. (1910) *The History of Wages in the Cotton Trade during the past 100 years*. Manchester: Sherratt and Hughes.
Wright, G. (1971) Econometric studies of history, in M. D. Intrilligator. *Frontiers of Quantitative Economics*. Amsterdam: North Holland.
Wright, G. and Czelusta, J. (2003) Mineral resources and economic development. Paper presented at the conference on sector reform in Latin America. Stanford Center for Economic Development.
Wrigley, E.A. (1966) Family limitation in pre-industrial England. *Economic History Review* 19:82–109.
www.eh.net *Measuring Worth* (last accessed 19th September 2010).
Zanden van, J.L. (1999) Wages and the standard of living in Europe. *European Review of Economic History* 2: 175–197.

2

SOCIAL SAVINGS

Tim Leunig

1. Introduction

The cliometrics revolution that began in the 1960s is usually thought of as the application of formal economic modelling and econometrics to questions which had long interested economic historians, and which had previously been approached using primarily literary and archival techniques familiar to conventional historians. Although there is a considerable degree of truth in this understanding, it is incomplete, because the cliometric revolution also involved the development of new concepts, including 'social savings'.

This review of social savings will consist of six substantive sections. In Section 2, we will define social savings and compare it with other methods of assessing technological change, namely consumer surplus, total factor productivity and growth accounting. This will provide a theoretical underpinning and will be useful as a stand-alone section for those who are interested in the concept, but who have little interest in the particular ways in which it has been used by other economic historians. Section 3 will look in some detail at the early work of Robert Fogel, whose work on railroads represents the pioneering application of the concept of social savings to technological change in economic history. This section will not aim to adjudicate on the various criticisms made of his specific estimates, but rather to use the debates to explore the issues that are critical in actually constructing an estimate of social savings for an historical event. Section 4 will list and contrast the various other railway social savings estimates that have been compiled. Again, the aim is not to say whether railways were of more use in one country than in another, but rather to show the strengths and weaknesses of the social savings methodology, both in general and in the particular ways in which economic historians have actually applied them. Section 5 will go on to outline some applications of the social savings methodology to non-railway issues, and to explore other areas to which the approach could be used, perhaps profitably. Some very basic new social savings estimates will be presented, and these will again be used to explore the strengths and weaknesses of the concept. Section 6 will conclude, by summarizing what we have learned, and setting out some ways in which social savings estimates could

Economics and History, First Edition. David Greasley and Les Oxley

be improved in future, and setting out some areas to which social savings estimates could be applied by other researchers, whether economic historians interested in the past, or economists interested in present day issues.

2. The Definition of Social Savings, and a Comparison with Other Measures

The concept of social savings is defined as how much extra society would have to pay to do what it did after an innovation, without it. Algebraically, therefore, we can write that

$$Social\ savings = (c_{t-1} - c_t)Q_t \qquad (1)$$

where c represents marginal cost and Q total quantity, and where t means post-innovation and $t-1$ pre-innovation.

Assuming that the market is perfectly competitive, we can take prices as the measure of cost. In this situation, we can write that

$$Social\ savings = (P_{t-1} - P_t)Q_t \qquad (2)$$

where P represents price, and all other notation remains the same. Since data on costs as opposed to prices are usually very hard to come by, economic historians use this definition as a matter of routine, and as such *de facto* assume that markets are competitive, and thus that price is equal to cost.

Social savings are usually expressed as a percentage of national income, and can be thought of as equivalent to national income. Thus, if a million people get something for US$8 instead of US$10 as a result of an innovation, the social saving of that innovation is calculated as US$2 million, which can be taken to mean that society is US$2 million better off. Sometimes the benefits of an innovation are not monetized – for example time savings caused by faster transport. These time savings clearly have a value, but only those time savings that occur during hours for which people are paid form part of national income. Time savings for people who are commuting to work or engaged in leisure journeys are not captured in GDP but are clearly welfare enhancing. The value of this sort of time saving is captured as part of a social savings estimate. In this case a social saving estimate of a particular magnitude is still equivalent to a rise in national income of that magnitude, but does not imply that measured national income has risen by that magnitude. If railways save leisure travellers time that they value at US$1 billion, then they would be willing to pay US$1 billion for that time saving, and the railway has increased welfare by an amount equal to a rise in national income of US$1 billion, whether or not passengers have to pay the US$1 billion or whether it takes the form of greater consumer surplus, not captured by either the railway company or the national income statisticians.

2.1 *A comparison of Social Saving and Other Measures in Economics*

The social savings methodology is a way to calculate the value of technological change, but it is self-evidently not the only one. It is therefore useful to investigate how social savings compares with these other measures. We shall look at three alternative measures: consumer surplus, total factor productivity, and growth accounting, in turn.

2.1.1 *The Relationship to Consumer Surplus*

The standard measure of welfare, taught to generations of economists, is consumer surplus. Under competitive conditions, the area between the demand curve and the price represents the extent to which firms have transformed resources into items whose value to consumers outweighs their cost to society (where cost in turn is determined by competing uses for those resources). This remains the best definition of the welfare value of a new technology and therefore we shall look detail at this comparison.

Let us imagine that a technological change leads to a fall in the price of a product produced under perfectly competitive conditions. The rise in consumer surplus will be the previous quantity sold, multiplied by the fall in price, plus the area above the price and under the demand curve between the old and new quantities. The exact size of this area will depend on the shape of the demand curve. This can be written algebraically as

$$\Delta Consumer\ surplus = (P_{t-1} - P_t)Q_{t-1} + \alpha(P_{t-1} - P_t)(Q_t - Q_{t-1}) \quad (3)$$

The notation follows that of equation (2), and α represents a parameter determined by the shape of the demand curve.

Since we are interested in the relationship between the consumer surplus and social saving measures under different circumstances, it is helpful to express the change in consumer surplus as a proportion of the social saving estimate. When we do this, and setting $Q_t = 1$ without loss of generality, we find that

$$\Delta CS/SS = \alpha + (1 - \alpha)Q_{t-1} \quad (4)$$

Let us investigate three categories of value of α: $\alpha > 1$, $\alpha = 1$ and $\alpha < 1$.

α will take a value in excess of 1 only in the case of a Giffen good, characterized by an upwards sloping demand curve. By inspection of equation (3) we can see that if $\alpha > 1$, then $\Delta CS/SS > 1$, i.e. in the case of a Giffen good the social savings estimate of the value of technological change will understate the value as assessed by the consumer surplus method. The intuition is that the technological change that lowers the price of the product will also lower its consumption, since the income effect will outweigh the substitution effect. Since $Q_t < Q_{t-1}$, the social savings measure is multiplying the fall in cost by 'too small' a quantity. Giffen goods are, however, uncommon, and the possibility that the social savings estimate will be smaller than a consumer surplus estimate of the value of technological change is best thought of as a technical curiosity.

α takes the value of 1 when demand is perfectly inelastic. In that instance, equation (4) can clearly be seen to equal 1, i.e. the social savings and consumer surplus measures are identical. Note too that when $\alpha = 1$, equation (3) can be simplified to

$$\Delta Consumer\ surplus = (P_{t-1} - P_t)Q_t \tag{5}$$

Comparing equations (2) and (5) again shows that when the demand curve is perfectly inelastic, the consumer surplus and social saving measures of welfare are identical. Although demand is not generally perfectly inelastic, there exist circumstances in which this would be an accurate depiction. Let us take the case of a medical procedure, which is sufficiently cheap that everyone who needs it within a particular society is able to afford it, either because everyone is rich enough to purchase it, or because it is provided by an insurance- or state-provided healthcare system. Antibiotics or plaster casts for broken limbs would fall into this category in many countries, and in rich countries with collective healthcare systems of one form or another, the provision of kidney transplants is generally limited by the availability of kidney donors rather than inability to afford the procedure. A second category would be where demand is *de facto* determined by regulation. Few Californians have their car's smog emissions tested more often than is required by state law, and few British companies check their fire extinguishers more often than required by UK health and safety regulations. In both of these cases, therefore, demand is completely price inelastic. In these cases – unusual but not unheard of – the consumer surplus and social saving measures of welfare are identical.

Finally, α will take a value less than 1 in all other circumstances. Inspection of equation (3) shows that the ratio of consumer surplus to social savings is less than one, i.e. the social savings measure exceeds the consumer surplus measure of welfare. If the demand curve is linear α will take the value of $\frac{1}{2}$, and will take a value of less than one half if the demand schedule is convex. The classic example of a convex demand schedule is when demand exhibits constant elasticity.

A demand schedule characterized by constant elasticity of demand can be written algebraically as

$$Q = P^e \tag{6}$$

where e is the elasticity of demand, and other notation is consistent with earlier equations.

In this circumstance, the rise in consumer surplus is the integral of Q with respect to P (noting that in this case the equation has been written with Q as a function of P, rather than P as a function of Q, as is more common in graphical depictions of demand curves). Thus we find that, algebraically,

$$\Delta CS = \int_{P_t}^{P_{t-1}} P^e dp = \frac{1}{e+1}\left(P_{t-1}^{e+1} - P_t^{e+1}\right) \tag{7}$$

The relationship between the change in consumer surplus and the estimate of social savings in the case of constant elasticity of demand can be found by substituting equation (6) into equation (2) to find social savings as a function of

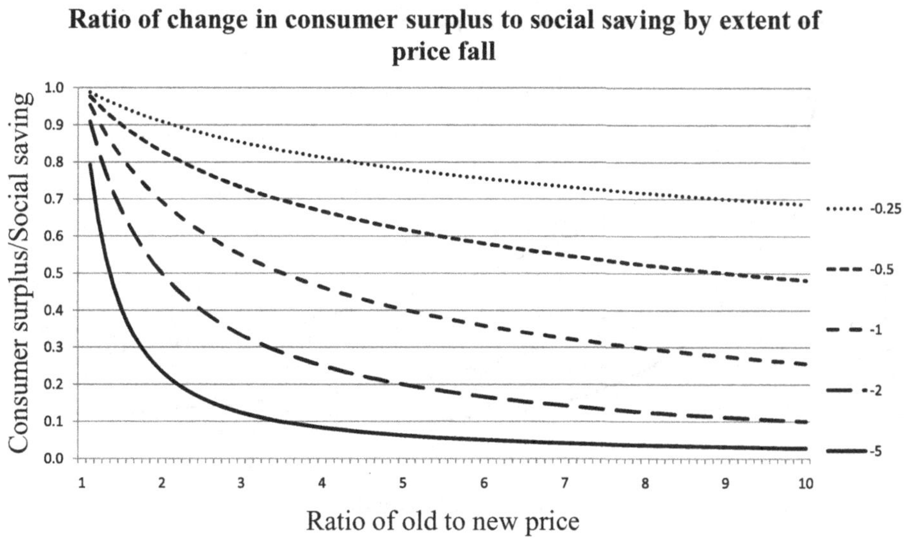

Figure 1. The Ratio of the Change in Consumer Surplus to Social Savings for Different Elasticities and for Different Price Falls.

price and elasticity of demand, and then dividing equation (7) by the amended equation (2). This gives the following expression:

$$\frac{\Delta CS}{SS} = \frac{P_r^{e+1} - 1}{(e+1)(P_r - 1)} \tag{8}$$

where P_r is the ratio of the pre-technology to post-technology price, i.e. $P_r = P_{t-1}/P_t$.

We can see immediately that the two measures of welfare diverge when P_r increases or when e becomes more negative, i.e. social savings overestimates consumer surplus by more when the price falls are larger, or when demand is more elastic.

Figure 1 shows us, for five different elasticities, the effect of an increase in the extent of the price fall on the divergence between consumer surplus and social savings estimates of the welfare gain from a new technology. Thus we see that at an elasticity of -1, the consumer surplus estimate of the benefit of a 10% fall in price is 95% of the social savings estimate. When the price fall is 2 to 1, however, the change in consumer surplus is 69% of the social savings estimate, 40% when the price fall is 5 to 1, and 26% when the price fall is 10 to 1. Figure 1 demonstrates the extent to which a large fall in price implies that the social savings estimate of the benefit of a new technology outweighs the 'true' measure of the welfare gain, as conventionally defined in economics.

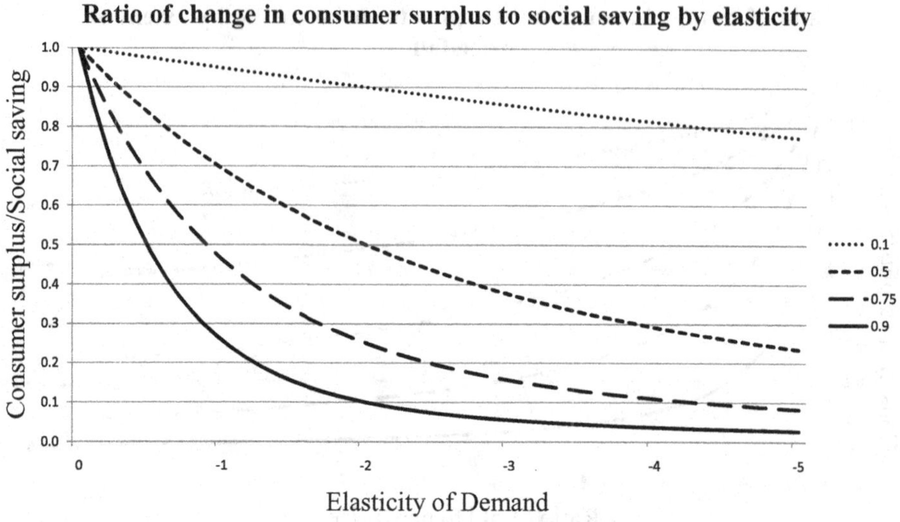

Figure 2. The Ratio of the Change in Consumer Surplus to Social Savings for Different Price Falls and for Different Elasticities.

We can also plot this information with the elasticities given on the *x*-axis, so that the different lines refer to different ratios of the old to new price. This is shown in Figure 2.

When we look at Figure 2 we can see clearly the extent to which more elastic demand implies a divergence between the consumer surplus and social savings measures of the value of the technology in question. If we take a 75% fall in the price of the product – not untypical for the sorts of products for which social savings studies have been carried out – we find that even at an elasticity of −1, the consumer surplus measure is only 46% of the social savings measure. At an elasticity of −2 the figure is 25%, falling further if demand is more elastic.

These calculations assume constant elasticity of demand, but the following two statements generalize to other functional forms that the demand curve can take. First, when the price fall is large, the extent to which the social savings estimate overstates the rise in consumer surplus is also large. Second, when the product in question is characterized by a highly elastic demand schedule, the extent to which social savings estimates overstates the rise in consumer surplus is again large. Clearly, when the product is price elastic, and when the price falls significantly, the divergence will be very great indeed.

We can see an example of this by looking briefly at Foreman-Peck's estimates of the consumer surplus value of passenger railways in 1865. He calculated that the fall in the price of transport – defined as being stage coaches prior to the railway – as being at least 8 to 1. In addition, he estimates that the elasticity of demand was constant at −1.3 (Foreman-Peck, 1991, pp. 75–76). Inserting these numbers into equation (8) tells us that a social savings estimate of the value of passenger rail transport in England and Wales in 1865 would be 4.5 times as high as the consumer surplus estimate. Foreman-Peck also presents altenative estimates, namely that the fall in price was 12 to 1, and that the elasticity was -1.5. Under those circumstances the social savings estimate would be 7.7 times as high as the consumer surplus estimate. Thus we can see that the difference between the two measures increases as the elasticity increases, and as the extent of the price fall increases, and that the extent of the divergence can be large.

A third factor is also critical in establishing the extent to which social savings and the change in consumer surplus diverge: the extent of previous demand. We have so far assumed that $Q = P^e$. If we assume an elasticity of -1, then if price is 1, quantity is also 1, whereas if price is 2, then quantity is 0.5. Imagine now that previous demand at a price of 1 was not 1 but 10, and that a rise in the price from 1 to 2 still leads to a fall in quantity of 0.5, i.e. to 9.5. In this case the demand schedule will take the form

$$Q = A + P^e \tag{9}$$

where in this particular case $A = 9$ and $e = 1$. When the demand curve takes this functional form, it is straightforward to see that, *ceteris paribus*, the change in consumer surplus and social savings estimates will converge as A increases. This is because both measures increase by $A(P_{t-1} - P_t)$, and therefore the ratio of the two measures converges as A increases. What this means in practice is that the greater the quantity sold in the pre-technological improvement world, the closer the two welfare measures will be.

This finding, along with the two stated earlier, tells us that the social savings and change in consumer surplus measures will be relatively similar for micro-inventions. If there exists a product with high levels of demand, whose price does not fall dramatically, and for which demand is relatively inelastic, then the two measures are likely to be relatively close in practice. If, however, the invention under consideration is a 'macro-invention', for which price falls are dramatic, for which previous levels of quantity sold are relatively small, and for which price elasticity of demand proves to be high, then it is likely that the social savings estimates will be hugely out of line with the conventional, and correctly defined, measure used by economists to value the welfare effects of improvements to technology, namely the rise in consumer surplus. As we will see later, this is an important finding that must be kept in mind when assessing the results of social savings studies.

2.1.2 *The Relationship between Social Savings and Total Factor Productivity*

Having looked in detail at the comparison of social savings and changes in consumer surplus, we will now look much more briefly at the comparison of social savings and changes in total factor productivity. Here, James Foreman-Peck has shown that there exists an identity between social savings and total factor productivity. This identity is best explained verbally. Social savings measures a resource saving, i.e. how much the technology has saved society when society produces the final quantity of goods. If society in fact produced the final quantity of goods both before and after the technological improvement, the saving measured by the social saving methodology would literally be a saving of resources needed to produce a given volume of output. Total factor productivity is defined as the ratio of outputs to inputs, and a rise in total factor productivity is defined as the rise in this ratio. Thus being able to produce a certain volume of output with fewer inputs represents a rise in total factor productivity, and total factor productivity can be thought of as identical to cost reduction – the very definition of social savings (Foreman-Peck, 1991; Harberger, 1998). We can see therefore, that the social saving and total factor productivity measures are in essence different methods of expressing the same thing, since both capture the fall in resources needed to generate a certain level of output. Strictly speaking, since social savings are habitually expressed as a share of national income, social savings equal the rise in total factor productivity multiplied by the industry in question's share of GDP (Crafts, 2004).

This in turn gives us a better understanding of the relationship between total factor productivity and rises in consumer surplus. It alerts us to the fact that total factor productivity numbers can be exposed to the same dangers that we saw for social saving numbers earlier. In essence, this is a classic index number problem. If we weight production by final quantities, we risk overstating the importance of the change that has occurred in previous years. There is in practice no perfect answer to this conundrum, even were the data to be as good as exists in the present day, let alone with the sort of data with which economic historians regularly have to deal.

2.1.3 *The Relationship with Growth Accounting Estimates*

Recent literature that seeks to place a numerical value on the impact of a new technology on society has commonly used a 'growth accounting approach'. This has been particularly common in papers that seek to assess the value of information and communication technology over the last 20 years. Thus, for example, Oliner and Sichel (2000) use this approach when assessing recent US growth performance, and van Ark *et al.* (2003) do likewise for Europe. In contrast Bayoumi and Haacker (2002) state that they use a social savings approach to make the same type of assessment, albeit for slightly different dates. (In fact, they calculate the change in consumer surplus not the social saving.)

The existence of these two sets of papers led Crafts (2004) to discuss the relationship between the two measures explicitly in this context. The fundamental intuition is as follows: 'The social saving concept was devised to answer the counterfactual question "how much faster was economic growth than it would have been in the absence of the new technology?" whereas growth accounting simply addresses the *ex post* accounting question "how much did the new technology contribute to growth?" and ignores issues of crowding out' (Crafts, p. 8). In essence then, growth accounting (implicitly) assumes that the resources used by a new technology would otherwise have remained idle, whereas the social savings estimate assumes that there was an opportunity cost to using them, which should not be included in any estimate of the value of the technology under consideration. As such, the growth accounting estimate will always exceed the social savings estimate. It will be important to remember this later, when considering whether social saving estimates are too high.

Thus we find clear and stable relationships between our four measures. Excluding cases in which price elasticity of demand is zero or positive, we find that a consumer surplus measure will always be lower than a social savings measure, which will in turn be equal to a total factor productivity estimate, and all of these will be smaller than a growth accounting estimate. Clearly, different estimates, prepared at different times and for different purposes can all have their own rationale. Nevertheless, the change in consumer surplus has the strongest underpinnings as a welfare measure, and in that sense the divergence should be seen as a potential – although as we will see, not necessarily an actual – issue with using social savings and other measures of welfare.

3. The Initial Application of Social Savings: Fogel's Work on American Railroads in 1890

The concept of social savings goes back to work by the then young Robert Fogel. Although now more famous for his work with Stanley Engerman on slavery, Fogel's initial career was built on his work as a graduate student on the history of the American railroads. As part of this body of work he developed and used a new concept, which he termed 'social savings'. He first introduced the concept of social savings in his 1962 *Journal of Economic History* article, 'A quantitative approach to the study of railroads in American economic growth: a report of some preliminary findings', following an oral exposition at the first annual Purdue Cliometrics meetings in December 1960. The subtitle of that article is appropriate: the paper is very preliminary in many ways. One way in which, looking back, it is clearly preliminary is that the explanation of the concept of social savings, its advantages and disadvantages, is not particularly clearly expressed, something Fogel himself admitted later (Fogel, 1979, p. 3).

Fogel's best definition of social savings came in his 1978 Economic History Association Presidential Address, published in the March 1979 issue of the *Journal of Economic History* as 'Notes on the social savings controversy'. In a section entitled 'The nature and limitations of the social saving model', Fogel wrote that 'I defined the social saving of railroads in any given year as the difference between the actual cost of shipping goods in that year and the alternative cost of shipping exactly the same bundle of goods between exactly the same points without the railroad' (Fogel, 1979, pp. 2–3).

Fogel initially applied the concept of social savings to American railroads in 1890. As we have mentioned, Fogel's first article appeared in 1962, and was followed by his 1964 book, *Railroads and American Economic Growth: Essays in Econometric History*. The first important aspect of Fogel's original article is the statement that an innovation's universal adoption does not demonstrate that it is of high value to society. That the railroad was pervasive is not in dispute. Its pervasiveness had led others, such as Christopher Savage, to state that the influence of the railroad in American development 'can hardly be over emphasized' (Savage, 1959, p. 184), while Rostow went further and saw it as 'decisive' in generating America's take-off into self-sustained growth (Rostow, 1960, p. 55). Fogel argued in contrast that were the railways to have been a tiny fraction cheaper than previously existing transport methods, and to have been perfect substitutes for them, then railways would have become pervasive while being of only limited value to society (Fogel, 1962, pp. 174–175). This argument was taken to its logical conclusion by Lebergott (1966, p. 439) who argued that if both modes of transport survived and competed, then neither could offer lower total costs to the consumer, and so the social saving must not only be small, but zero. This argument only holds if the two modes of transport are perfect substitutes, which is in reality an assumption too far. Even if the extreme case is rejected, Fogel's basic point that the pervasiveness of the railroad is not evidence of their importance to the economy remains strong.

The correct way to assess the importance of railroads needs to take into account the extent to which costs fall as a result of their invention, as well as the extent to which the railways were used. Hence the need for a measure such as social savings, which takes into account both the change in costs as well as the amount of traffic handled by the railroads.

The 1962 article set out the question about the role of the railroads that Fogel wanted to address, outlined the generally applicable social savings methodology that he would use to address it, and gave the results that he found when the method was applied to one element of that question. The general question was broad but simple: 'how much did railroads affect the nineteenth century American economy?', and the particular part that was answered in that original article was the extent to which interregional agricultural trade was facilitated by the railroad, as judged by the social savings methodology. Interregional trade was never perceived to be the most important aspect of railroads, but it served as a straightforward aspect to which the social savings methodology could be readily applied.

Fogel noted that the cost of railroad transport was dramatically lower than the cost of wagon transport. He presented basic data, which showed that were wagons to have been the only alternative to railroads, then the social saving of railroads would have exceeded one third of national income in 1890. In contrast, when the alternative to railroads was canals, then 'the social saving attributable to the railroad in the interregional transportation of agricultural products was about 1% of national income' (Fogel, 1962, pp. 195–196).

Fogel broadened the scope in his 1964 book. The 1962 article appeared essentially unchanged as chapter 2, supplemented by chapter 3, which constructed detailed estimates of the value of railroads to intraregional agricultural trade. Although the book contained other material, these are the two chapters that deal with social savings, and are the strongest sections of the book (Davis, 1966, p. 660). This brought the issue of adaption to the fore: to what extent should the counterfactual involve doing exactly what was done with the innovation, without it? Fogel noted this issue in his 1962 article but addressed it for the first time substantively in the subsequent book, and it remains critical to any proper understanding of the nature of social savings estimates.

In this case, the issue was that some land was used for agriculture because it was close to a railroad. Had the railroad not existed, the cost of shipping produce by wagon from that location would have outweighed its value, sometimes many times over. To say that the value of the railroad was the cost of shipping such produce by wagon is clearly not meaningful: the annual value of a railroad to a piece of agricultural land cannot exceed the value of the crops produced on that land.

For that reason Fogel developed two estimates, which he called (somewhat unintuitively) alpha and beta estimates. The alpha estimate preserves the pure assumption of the social savings methodology, namely that the value of the railroad is the additional cost of transporting everything that the railroad moved, without it. The alpha estimate is therefore best seen as an absolute upperbound, and in all probability something of an overestimate.

The beta estimate allowed some – inevitably *ad hoc* – adjustments, accepting that some activities only happened because of the existence of the railroad. In essence, this is a tacit acceptance that the implicit social savings assumption that demand is perfectly inelastic is not correct. As such, however, it risks moving social savings away from a clearly defined concept, and towards an estimate of consumer surplus. As we have noted, what matters in particular is that some land that was used for agriculture in the presence of the railroad would not have been used for agriculture in the absence of the railroad, because it was too far from a canal to be economically viable, given the cost of wagon transport. It is worth noting that although most of the counterfactual mileage is by canal, the dramatically higher cost of wagon transport means that 85% of the total 'alpha' social saving from the railroad comes from replacing wagon transport with railroad transport (Fogel, 1964, pp. 23–25, 46–47, 51, 73, 212–214). Thus the extent to which wagons would have been used without the railroad is critical in estimating social saving correctly. To try to eliminate farming that would no longer have been economic, Fogel assumes three things. First, he argues that 37 additional canals totalling 5000 miles would have been economically viable without the railroads (Fogel, 1964, pp. 92–93, and appendix A). Second, notwithstanding these additional canals, some land would no longer have been used for agriculture, and therefore the cost of shipments from that land should not be included. Third, a greater proportion of roads would have been improved, since these would have been the primary method of transport in a greater number of places. Depending on which adjustments are included, the estimate of the social saving for intraregional railroads falls as low as 0.8% of GNP (Fogel, 1964, pp. 214, 218; see also Davis, 1966, p. 661).

Finally, Fogel rather crudely extrapolates his results to cover non-agricultural products, but not passengers, finding that even on the alpha basis the total value of railroads in the USA did not exceed 4.7% of GNP in 1890, small enough for him to argue that railroads were not 'decisive' in generating self-sustaining growth (Fogel, 1964, p. 223).

3.1 *Criticisms of the Initial Social Savings Estimates*

The initial social savings estimates generated many criticisms, of many types. One group of criticisms were concerned with individual data issues, and thus relate to the application of social savings methodology to this specific example. These are important for assessing the social savings of American railroads at a specific date, but they are not important in understanding the strengths and weakness of social savings *per se*, save only to note that the quality of cliometric work will always be dependent to a huge extent on the availability, quality and suitability of the data. Although we will not go into individual data issues here, it is worth noting in passing that while equation (2) might imply that the data requirements for calculating social savings are relatively small, the reality is anything but: Fogel devotes an entire page of his 1979 article to simply listing the algebra, with definitions of over 50 different items (Fogel, 1979, p. 4).

In addition to criticisms of the data, economic historians also criticized the assumptions that underlie the concept and application of social savings.

The first such criticism concerned the (implicit) identity between price and marginal cost. In calculating social savings, Fogel had assumed that price was equal to marginal cost. Clearly the gain to society comes from a fall in costs, not from a fall in prices, since a fall in prices without a fall in costs represents a transfer from producers to consumers, not a net gain to society (McClelland, 1968, p. 114). This is a serious criticism not only at an intellectual level, but also at a practical one, as data on costs as opposed to prices are hard for economic historians to obtain. That said, those trying to calculate social savings are not the only cliometricians to assume away the difference between prices and costs.

Second, Fogel (implicitly) assumes that marginal costs for the previous technology do not change between the old and new output levels. (McClelland, 1968, p. 114). If the extra canals had been harder to build, or canal loading congestion had been an issue, then canal transport might have been more expensive in 1890 than Fogel assumes. Equally, if higher traffic volumes had allowed larger, more efficient canals or vessels to have been constructed, canal costs would have been lower than Fogel assumes. Again, this is a serious criticism, since assessing the cost structure for an obsolete technology facing significant rises in demand is not a straightforward counterfactual to develop, particularly if, like Fogel, you are trying to make an assessment in a period long after efforts to improve that previous technology have ended.

The third set of criticisms made of the social savings approach relate to what it excludes. Social saving clearly measures only the gain to direct beneficiaries of improved transport. Paul David pointed out that were transport-using industries to be characterized by declining long-run marginal costs, then an innovation such as railroads would, by lowering transport costs also lower the long-run costs of a host of other industries for which transport is an input by leading to an increase in output. He suggested that this could lead to benefits 10 times the estimates of social savings. This is a very strong claim, somewhat weakened by his failure to give any examples of such industries, let alone estimating the effect for such industries. Nevertheless, the point is clearly correct in principle, and it is not difficult to imagine examples (David, 1969, pp. 515–519). One such would be the Sears Corporation, which, by 1897, had a mail order catalogue, which ran to 786 pages, and included more than 7000 types of goods in the index, and perhaps 40,000 different products in all. Its scale was dependent on being able to ship very large numbers of goods to consumers quickly and reliably (Sears Catalogue, 1897). Canal transport was not a good substitute for railways for the Sears Corporation. Here, then, is an example of an important company who was able to reduce costs for consumers through economies of scale in purchasing, manufacturing, stock control, overhead management, and so on, and whose ability to do so was predicated on the availability of a transport network along the lines of that provided by the railways. More generally we could link David's criticism with the work of Alfred Chandler (1990), who argued that one of the reasons that the USA became the leading economic superpower was the scale and scope of its firms. Such scale demands ready access to transport, and the railways could be seen as part of preconditions for the success of the Chandlerian firm in many sectors. More generally, Atack and Passell set out that transition from workshop to factory that began in this period (Atack and Passell, 1994, chapter 17). Nevertheless, although benefits related to scale economies are not included in a social savings measure, benefits derived from scale of markets are included. That is, the benefits of (say) bringing more land into cultivation are fully captured within a social saving framework (Metzer, 1984, pp. 67–69).

A more recent critique of social savings comes from the work of Crafts and Mulatu (2006). This starts from two observations. First, that the spatial location of firms is endogenous to the generalized cost of transport, and second that the location of firms can affect the productivity of firms. This point is thus complementary to, but distinct from, the points made by David on scale economies. For David (and for Chandler) the point is that large firms can gain internal economies of scale, but that this is only economic if they can transport their products to dispersed consumers cheaply. For Crafts and Mulatu the point is that firms of any size can gain Marshall–Arrow–Romer agglomeration economies if they can locate near to each other, but again, this is only economic if they can transport their products to dispersed consumers cheaply. It is worth noting that Crafts and Mulatu find that the size of this effect, for Britain in 1911, is small, and do so for exactly the same reason as Fogel and Fishlow found that the social savings of American railroads were relatively small, namely that canals were already an effective transport technology. In addition, Crafts has also noted that if the transport using sector is characterized by imperfect competition, then a fall in the cost of transport will lead to an expansion of output in the transport using sector. Since marginal revenue exceeds marginal cost in the imperfectly competitive transport using sector, this expansion of output is welfare increasing in a way that is not captured by traditional social saving (or consumer surplus) studies. Crafts notes that this might increase estimates by 10% for the UK economy in the late 1990s (Crafts, 2004, p. 8).

The fifth set of criticisms relates to the failure of the social savings methodology to say anything about the changing structure of the economy. In many ways what was remarkable about the nineteenth century was not so much economic growth as structural change. It is not for nothing, for example, that the arrival of sustained economic growth is traditionally referred to as 'The Industrial Revolution', rather than 'The growth revolution'. Because social savings calculates only a value to a user whose demand is assumed not to change, it is unable to say anything about the role transport may have had in (for example), the movement from agriculture to industry either for a nation as a whole, or for one region of it. Williamson estimated social savings of transport improvements in the context of a general equilibrium model (Williamson, 1974, chapter 9), but this model had its criticisms (Kahn, 1988), and no other economic historian has produced social savings estimates within a general equilibrium framework. For that reason it is best to see social savings as failing to speak effectively to debates as to the changing structure of the economy.

Finally Boyd and Walton (1972) noted that multiplying the final quantity by the fall in price is equivalent to assuming that the price elasticity of demand is zero. Although as we have argued already there may be cases for which that is a good assumption, it is not a good assumption in general, and they show that it is not a good assumption for passenger transport. As such, it will lead to an overestimate of the welfare benefits of railways, perhaps by a huge margin. Boyd and Walton further argue that data generally exist to allow us to be more accurate as to the correct elasticity. In the case of passenger rail travel, the specific focus of their 1972 paper, they argued that there was sufficient evidence that a price elasticity of demand of around unity was strongly supported by the evidence. Thirty-five years later Leunig, following UK Department for Transport methodology, came to much the same conclusion. Fogel accepted this point in his 1979 paper, writing that 'it seems to me that Boyd and Walton were right in urging that we go beyond calculations based on the assumption that $E = 0$. It is time to move from guesses about the relevant elasticities to estimation of them' (Fogel, 1979, p. 11). What is important to note here is that moving from an elasticity of 0 to an elasticity of 1 does not alter the social savings estimate on a consistent basis across different social savings estimates. Fogel records, for example, that his agricultural social saving would be reduced by 28% were an elasticity of 1 to be used, whereas the equivalent figure for Fishlow's freight estimate is 48%, while Boyd and Walton found that the effect of using an assumption of unitary rather than zero elasticity was to reduce the estimated social saving by 45% for passenger transport (Fogel, 1979, p. 12; Boyd and Walton, 1972, pp. 249–250). At this point, however, what is being assessed is not social savings, but consumer surplus, and these figures are better seen as estimates of the extent to which different estimates of social savings overstate the welfare gain to society.

A modern evaluation of the quality of Fogel's early work on railroads would step back from some of the individual points about which contemporaries were much concerned. It would instead celebrate that the invention of the concept of social savings allowed economic historians, for the first time, to place a value on an innovation such as the railroads. In all of the criticisms that have been made, sight should not be lost of the fact that prior to the invention of the concept of social savings, no estimate had been made of the value of the railroads, one of the defining features of the nineteenth century economy. Until that date it was accepted as self-evident that railways, which had transformed the face of many nations, had also transformed the underlying economies of these nations. After the publication of Fogel and Fishlow's books, that assumption was no longer tenable. The numbers that they presented might not be correct, but the very act of presenting numbers that were reasonably well substantiated gave the profession a basis from which to begin more detailed work, and which gave a good sense of the broad order of magnitude of the results that were likely to be found.

Furthermore, the social savings methodology allowed Fogel and Fishlow to state which railways within the USA had the highest value to society. Surprisingly to those who had judged value from use, the most valuable lines were not the mainlines, for these tended to follow routes that already had good canal transport available. That they accounted for a large proportion of traffic did not mean that they accounted for a large proportion of the value of railroads to society. Fishlow, for example, finds that only 8% of the total social saving was attributable to the trunk lines (Fishlow, 1965, p. 93). The most valuable lines were those that replaced very poor (i.e. very expensive) wagon transport. Here there are shades of the later work by Ashauer (1989), who found that the most valuable transport infrastructure was that which completed a network, allowing efficient end to end journeys. It was the same for nineteenth century railways: what was valuable was getting rid of bottlenecks.

Second, preparing estimates of social savings methodologies forces economic historians to be explicit about the counterfactual. In many ways making a counterfactual explicit is the most appealing characteristic of all good cliometric work. When a non-cliometric historian says that something is critical, the reader is left wondering what would have been different had that thing not happened. With a properly defined counterfactual, the reader knows what the writer thinks would otherwise have happened, and can consider the evidence for that alternative.

One of the remarkable aspects of Fogel's book is his set of counterfactual canals. Noting that without the railroads, much land that was used for agriculture would not have been viable given the cost of wagon transport, Fogel asks the question 'would additional canals have been economic?' As we have noted, he argues that a network of 5000 miles would have been economic. But he does so not by considering a simple map, but by looking at detailed topological maps, in the manner of a would-be canal engineer. Fogel's counterfactual canals are supported by a wealth of evidence, including details on the route, and the gradients that would have been encountered along the way. Whether or not the reader finds the counterfactual convincing, there can be no doubt that this is a well-constructed counterfactual, allowing the reader to assess its merits or otherwise from a well-informed position.

From a modern perspective, and indeed since Fogel's 1978 Presidential address, we are much more aware of the extent to which social savings estimates, with their implicit zero elasticity assumption are in some sense untenable as measures of welfare. Looking back, there is no reason why Fogel, or any of his critics, could not have prepared consumer surplus estimates instead. After all, provided that one is prepared to assume constant elasticity of demand, or some other readily tractable demand schedule, and provided that one has some sense of the price elasticity of demand, it is not particularly hard to move from being able to make a social savings estimate to being able to make an estimate of the rise in consumer surplus. Of course, that is two more assumptions, but the pioneering cliometricians were rarely afraid to make assumptions, and any author who can devise 5000 miles of counterfactual canals could surely make a passable attempt to estimate price elasticity of demand.

That Fogel did not do so reflects the fact that although Fogel claimed to be trying to answer the question 'how much did railroads affect the nineteenth century American economy?', this was not really his question. To answer that question, a consumer surplus methodology would be appropriate. Instead, Fogel set out to show that railways were not indispensible. For this the social savings methodology was perfectly appropriate. After all, if a technology was not that important even when the price elasticity of demand was assumed to be zero, and the final quantity used to measure its value, then clearly it would not be important were a more realistic assumption of price elasticity to have been used. The creation of the concept of social savings needs to be seen in the context of wanting to create an upperbound estimate of the value of a technology. It is a strong intellectual creation in that context, but that does not mean that it can be used in all contexts without considering whether it is the appropriate criterion to use.

4. Comparing Different Social Saving Estimates

Table 1 sets out the findings of a broad range of social saving estimates for railways in different places and in different times. Before we go on to discuss the exact results it is worth noting that the quality of the individual results is extremely heterogeneous. Some are based on years of scholarly endeavour, while others appear to be little more than back of the envelope calculations. The lowest estimate is 0.5%, for China in 1933, while the highest overall estimate is in excess of 40%, for Brazil in 1913.

We need to be extremely careful when comparing the different social saving numbers. As we have noted already, the original definition of social savings included an implicit assumption that the price elasticity of demand was zero. Since the work of Boyd and Walton not all authors have followed this assumption, and therefore it is always necessary to check the different results have been compiled under identical elasticity of assumptions. In order to better facilitate comparison Table 1 uses zero price elasticity of demand throughout. For that reason some of the figures that appear in the table not identical to those in the original text, but instead use the data in the original text to construct a zero elasticity estimate.

Even once that change has been made in order to ensure comparability we still have to be extremely careful in using the numbers in Table 1 for comparative purposes for a very wide range of reasons.

Table 1. Various Estimates of the Social Savings from Railways.

Belgium		
1846	Freight and passenger	1%
1865	Freight and passenger	2.5%
1912	Freight and passenger	4.5%
Brazil		
1913	Freight	18%–38%
	Passengers	4.6%
China		
1933	Freight and passengers	0.5%
Colombia		
1924	Freight	4.8%
England and Wales		
1865	Freight	4.1%
1890	Freight	29.1%–31.6%
1843–1913	Passengers	1.5%–14%
France		
1872	Freight	5.8%
	Passengers	1.7%
Germany		
c1900	Freight	<5%
Mexico		
1910	Freight	24.9%–38.5%
Russia		
1907	Freight	4.6%
	Passengers	1.6%
Spain		
1878	Freight	7.5%
1912	Freight	11%
USA		
1859	Freight	3.7%
1859	Passengers	1.6%
1890	Freight	4.9%
1890	Passengers	4.8%

Notes: these estimates are based on zero price elasticity of demand wherever possible.
Sources: Belgium, Laffut (1983, p. 221). Brazil, Summerhill (2005, pp. 79, 85). China, Huenemann (1983, p. 228). Colombia, McGreevey (2008, p. 266). England and Wales, freight 1865, Hawke (1970, p. 196); freight 1890, Foreman-Peck (1991, p. 77); passengers, Leunig (2006, p. 665). France, Caron (1983, p. 45). Germany, Fremdling (1983, p. 135). Mexico, Coatsworth (1979, p. 952). Russia, Metzer (1976, pp. 75, 96). Spain, Herranz-Loncán (2006, p. 873). USA, 1859, Fishlow (1965, pp. 37, 52 n. 61); 1890 freight, Fogel (1964, p. 223); 1890 passengers, Boyd and Walton (1972, pp. 249–250).

First, these estimates have all been drawn up by different people: one of the most remarkable aspects of the social saving literature is that no author has constructed social saving estimates for more than one country. Different authors make different assumptions, which can have a very large effects on the final result. There can be no doubt that both Fishlow and Fogel are talented and conscientious researchers, and that both put forward strong reasons for the assumptions that they make. But their estimates of the extent of the social saving of railways in 1890 differ considerably. Fogel believes that the final answer is no greater than 5%, while Fishlow believes that it is double that amount, a difference of around US$0.6 billion. If two of the finest economic historians to study the problem cannot get closer than this, then we have to be aware that we cannot take any of the numbers in this table as being authoritative. The best estimates should be seen as legitimate, but we should recognize that other scholars of equal ability may well have chosen different but equally legitimate assumptions, and correspondingly come up with social saving estimates that differ by amounts that cannot be regarded as historically unimportant. The assumptions that matter here are largely in the treatment of data. In particular, estimating the cost using alternate modes of travel will never have an unambiguous answer. Counterfactual history is like that, particularly if we are considering a long period of time. Different scholars could make perfectly legitimate different estimates of the cost of non-rail freight in Brazil in 1913, for example. Indeed, Summerhill notes that there are different legitimate estimates of such costs, which is why he provides two different estimates himself. These two estimates are sufficiently different that his second social saving estimate is only half that of his first.

The second issue, which is equally important, relates to the fact that these numbers all come from separate research projects and were all designed to answer individual if related questions. Almost without exception the authors concerned have decided to answer the question ‘how valuable were railways in a particular country?’ None of them were trying to answer the question ‘were railways more valuable in country a than in country b?’ This means that none of the studies has been designed to facilitate international comparison. We can see this in any number of ways. As we have mentioned, different authors have made different assumptions about all sorts of different issues. In addition, the studies do not all relate to the same date. Thus we find a social savings estimate for Belgium 1846, and one from China for 1933. Nor is it the case that there is a convention that scholars estimate the social saving of railways at some particular point in a country’s railway history. For example, it would be possible to have devised a convention that said that the social saving of railways would be measured once three-quarters of the final railway mileage was built, or when a majority of interregional freight transport used the railway, or 50 years after the first railway line was opened. We could argue about the merits of any of these proposed conventions, but the fact is that without any form of convention our discipline has developed a set of estimates for different dates that are not readily comparable. Even were two studies to use exactly the same assumptions, if the results are that railways in one country were worth 5% of GDP in 1860, and they were worth 7% of GDP in another country in 1880, we cannot say in which country railways were more important, since we know that the effect of railways grew over the nineteenth century.

There are honourable exceptions. First, Summerhill estimated the social saving for railroads in Brazil for 1913, which is conveniently close to the date that Coatsworth had used earlier for his estimate of social savings for Mexico for

1910. Both are high-quality estimates of social savings, and it is reasonable to compare these two results at headline level. Second, Herranz-Loncán provides a high-quality estimate for social savings the Spanish railways for two separate dates, while Leunig provided estimates for the social savings of passenger railways for the UK for every single year between 1843 and 1912. Providing estimates for a long series of dates facilitates comparisons with estimates of passenger social savings in other countries, since it dramatically reduces the chance of having unaligned dates.

Were we to have two estimates, for two countries, for the same date and which use the same set of assumptions we could then compare the headline social savings estimates. Let us imagine for simplicity that we have such numbers, and that they relate simply to freight, and let us imagine that the results 5% are for one country and 10% for the other. We could conclude correctly that railroads had the larger effect in the second country, but we would still not know much about *why* railroads had a greater effect in the second country than in the first. There are many possibilities. It might be, for example, that the railways had the same effect per mile of track built, and that the only difference was that one country had built a much more extensive network than the other. Or it might be that both had the same networks, but that one was used less because of the existence of a better canal network, or perhaps because smaller differences in climate by region reduced the need for interregional transport of agricultural products. Or it might be that the country placed restrictions on internal trade, so that railways were little used (or not built). Social savings estimates, even at their finest, to some extent only define the historical question more accurately, rather than explain the historical reasons why railways were or were not important.

We can see this by looking at the numbers in Table 1. Broadly speaking, the estimates for more developed countries look similar to Fogel's original estimate. Recall that Fogel's estimate for the social saving of US freight railways was 4.7% in 1890. Hawke estimated 4.1% for British freight for 1865, and the estimates for other Northern European countries – which are generally of lower quality – did not diverge from this sort of level. Herranz-Loncán estimated 7.5% for Spain for 1878, rising to 11% by 1912, while Coatsworth's and Summerhill's estimates were around 20%–40% for Mexico and Brazil, depending on the exact assumptions used.

The obvious intuition is that later developing countries derived greater benefit from the railways because they had not constructed significant canal networks earlier on in the development process. Indeed, Fogel estimated that had there been no canals, so that railroads had replaced wagons in the USA, then railroads would have had a value of the order of 30% or more of US national income, in line with the later Coatsworth–Summerhill estimates for countries with limited canals. Presumably we would find that countries that did not invest in railroads gained more from the construction of the road network, and so on.

But in that context what do we make of the estimates for Russia (4.6%, 1907), Colombia (4.8%, 1924) and China (0.5%, 1933)? In the light of the Latin American results, we might expect high values for all three countries. Let us assume for a moment that these numbers are perfectly accurate, and that the methodology and assumptions are in line with those of Coatsworth and Summerhill. There are many alternative explanations. First, these countries may not have built a sufficient quantity of railroads. There may have been other routes that would have passed social (or even private) rate of return calculations but which were not built for a variety of reasons. Had those additional lines been built, then it is possible that the social savings result would have been in line with the Coatsworth–Summerhill figures. Second, it could be that these countries had particularly fine coastal shipping, river and canal networks, reducing the value of railways. Even if they did not, a flat country will enjoy lower wagon costs than a mountainous one. Third, the railway network may be run much more efficiently in one country than another, assessed either by cost or by speed and reliability. Fourth, one country may engage in much higher levels of internal or external trade than another country. Climatic variation, for example, increases potential gains from trade, in turn raising the potential level of social savings from improving transport links. Government regulations can reduce the incentives to trade, internally and externally. In this context as we have noted radically different social saving numbers can help us to define a question, as much as to answer it. It would be helpful were the convention to be that social savings results are expressed not only as a percentage of GDP but also in terms of their value (in absolute terms) per mile of track or per ton mile of freight carried. Were we to find not only that Russian railroads in total were worth less as a percentage of GDP than Mexican railroads, but that the difference was much less when we compare the value per track mile, we would then know that differences in the extent of railways explain at least part of the difference in the overall result. In short, there is much more work to be done, using existing studies as a starting point.

5. The Application of Social Savings to Non-railway Situations

The majority of social savings estimates relate to railways, and railways are the only technological improvement that have been extensively analysed using the social savings methodology. Nevertheless, there are examples of the application of the social savings methodology to other sectors.

One of the earliest and most important examples of the application of social savings to a technological improvement other than railways is von Tunzelmann's 1978 study of the effect of steam power on British industrialization before 1860. This contains a chapter that sets out to evaluate the importance of steam engines using the social savings methodology. In that chapter, von Tunzelmann assesses the value of steam engines in 1800. As such, what is being evaluated are stationary steam engines since neither the railway nor the steamship had been invented by this date. von Tunzelmann assesses both steam technology as a whole, and the improvements made by James Watt relative to earlier atmospheric engines. He finds that by 1800 steam engines, taken as a whole, were worth approximately 0.2% of GDP, with the improvements made by James Watt being valued at approximately half that total (von Tunzelmann, 1978, pp. 149, 157). What stands out from this study is the remarkably small figure that the social savings methodology places on the invention of steam engines. Against that, it is worth remarking that the date chosen for the study, 1800, is very early on. There are only 12,000 hp of Watt engines by that date (von Tunzelmann, 1978, p. 148). Clearly, assessing the social saving at a later date would give a much larger figure, both because there would be more engines installed by that date, and because the cost of operating steam engines will have fallen much faster than the cost of alternate technologies. This is particularly true once we get to the point at which there is sufficient steam power that it is no longer feasible to have replaced it all with water power. Wind power and animal power are considerably more expensive than water power in the British context.

Much more recently, Dan Bogart has used the social savings methodology to value the effects of turnpike trusts in eighteenth century England. He finds that turnpikes raised property income by around 20%. Given that a little over half of parishes had a turnpike by 1815, he therefore concludes that turnpikes increased total property income by 11%. This represents about 22% of the rise in real land rents between 1690 and 1815. On the basis that property income represents about 15% of national income, this implies that turnpike trusts 'generated a social saving of at least 1.65% of national income in 1815' (Bogart, 2009, pp. 149–150).

Both von Tunzelmann and Bogart are excellent scholars who produce work of a high quality. In this case both have applied the methodology correctly, and both have used data carefully. Of course, each has made assumptions, but neither set of assumptions appear at all unreasonable. And yet there is a sense in which the results are implausibly different to each other, since Bogart finds that turnpikes were worth eight times as much to Britain as the invention of the steam engine.

Again, we have the problem that we had with the railways: individual studies have been produced, for one thing, in one country, at one point in time. This makes it hard – and perhaps meaningless – to compare them. What would be more useful, once more, would be to have social savings estimates for a range of dates. Then we could see, for example, when – if ever – there was a sufficient mass of steam engines, or sufficient improvements in the steam engines, for the steam social saving number to exceed that of road improvements. The steam engine may not meet Rostow's definition of a breakthrough capable of changing the trajectory of the economy, but it seems unlikely that the social saving of stationary steam engines remained at just 0.2% as the nineteenth century progressed.

Social savings have been used for more novel goods as well. Bakker, for example, uses the social savings methodology to assess the value of cinema in the interwar era. Here the counterfactual is the previous technology, i.e., live entertainment. He finds that, in 1938, social savings were 2.3%, 0.32% and 1.37% of GDP in the USA, UK and France, respectively (Bakker, 2008, p. 381). These are radically different figures, but the advantage here – and the rationale for including it in this survey – is that all three estimates are constructed by the same author, for the same dates, using the same methodology, and the same assumptions. As such it is legitimate to compare them and to ask how it can be that social saving estimates are so radically different in the three countries. Although Bakker does not provide an explicit decomposition of the social saving figures, he notes earlier that live entertainment was much cheaper in Britain (Bakker, 2008, p. 142), which would lead to Britain having a lower social saving from cinema – $c_{t-1} - c_t$ is much lower in Britain than in either other country. Although the relative price of cinema to live entertainment was similar for the USA and France, live entertainment at a much higher market share in France. That French people's 'taste' for live entertainment at the same price ratio was greater than that of Americans should not surprise us: live entertainment in France would have been performed in French, but the vast majority of the world's films were in English. As such, cinema was a much worse substitute for live entertainment in France than it was in either Britain or the USA. Bakker argues that while 60% of the difference in cinema consumption between the USA and Britain can be explained by differences in relative prices, with only 40% to be explained by taste, the entire difference between cinema expenditure in France and the USA can be explained by differences in taste (Bakker, 2008, pp. 146–147). In this context, therefore, the lower rate of social savings in France relative to the USA should be seen as stemming primarily from differences in taste for cinema, which in turn stem from the relatively limited selection of films that were available in French. In contrast, as we have noted, a large part of the difference between the social savings estimates for the USA and Britain comes from the fact that live entertainment was dramatically cheaper in Britain than it was in the USA, although part of the difference is explained by a greater preference to live entertainment in Britain, taking into account differences in relative prices.

As well as social savings estimates that have been prepared, it is easy to think of social savings estimates that would be relatively straightforward to prepare. There are, for example, many other technological improvements, which could be analysed in this way. We know, for example, the costs of purchasing and operating civilian jet aircraft in both the 1960s and 1980s. In 1963 a Boeing 707 and Douglas DC-8 both cost around 1.2c per seat mile, including depreciation; by 1988 the costs of operating their successors, the Boeing 737 and McDonnell Douglas MD-80, were around 3c per passenger mile, which equates to around 2c per seat mile, in current terms (Sutton, 1998, pp. 463, 467). Even assuming implausibly that costs have not fallen since 1988, the current social saving from the Boeing 737 compared with predecessor aircraft is, as an order of magnitude, around US$30 billion per year, or around 0.2% of GDP (mileages from http://www.b737.org.uk/sales.htm). With more detailed data it would be perfectly feasible, and perhaps interesting, to document the rise in the social savings estimate for different types of aircraft over time.

We could also use the social savings methodology to assess the value of process as well as product innovations. Hounshell records that Ford was able to cut the price of the Model T Ford from US$960 to 360 between 1909 and 1916, a US$786 fall in 1916 real dollars (Hounshell, 1984, p. 224). Ford sold 577,036 Model Ts in 1916 (Hounshell, 1984, p. 224), giving a social saving estimate for that year of US$453 million, or about 1% of US GDP in that year, with steady growth in the intervening years. That the application of the concept of the production line by one car firm to the production of only one model of car can have a value of 1% of GDP in less than a decade is at one level quite remarkable. Yet the methodology is straightforward, and the data unambiguous. There are no issues connected with alternative technological trajectories, or of counterfactual canals or similar. We know what it cost to make a car in 1909 just prior to the implementation of the production line, and we know what it cost in 1916, just after the implementation. There is no reason to think that the 1909 figure would have changed in any meaningful way by 1916 had the production line not been invented, and the data on the number of cars sold in 1916 is clearly recorded. The social saving really is 1%, and that really is a large number. This sort of result reminds economic historians that interesting though railways and steam engines may be, the application of new production processes is also important, and should not be neglected. In particular, a new production process appears to have had rapid implications, whereas as the von Tunzelmann work shows, new products can take a long time to have a significant effect.

These two examples are given simply as illustrations that it is plausible to imagine that economic historians could create social saving estimates for a wide range of both product and process innovations, whose magnitudes might well generate at least further questions worth investigating.

6. Conclusion

Social savings represent a powerful addition to the economist and economic historians' arsenal of potential measures of the value of technological and other changes in the economy. The concept of social saving is of most use when data are too limited to allow a full assessment of consumer surplus. Since data on elasticity are not straightforward to calculate, and certainly never appear as data points in official or business records, the lower data requirements of social savings over consumer surplus offer considerable potential.

Social savings have been widely applied in the context of nineteenth century railways. Nevertheless, that set of research has in some senses been disappointing. This is because the studies have been undertaken by different scholars, for different dates, which apply to railways at different points in their development. Furthermore there is no standard set of assumptions for authors to use to ensure that their studies are readily comparable. As such the economic history profession has created a wide range of estimates, which cannot be readily compared with each other. As we have noted, the fact that scholars as eminent as Fogel and Fishlow, who agree on the validity of the methodology, do not agree on the size of the social saving available for the USA demonstrates the extent to which it is difficult to compare one study with another, or to take any one study as the authoritative judgement as to the social saving in any country at any given point.

We have noted that there are social saving studies of things other than the railways. von Tunzelmann studied steam, which in some ways is a natural complement to studies of the railway. Likewise Bogart's study of the value of turnpikes in the British Industrial Revolution is also similar to the studies of railways in that turnpikes are also a form of transport. Once more, we note that although both studies are of high quality it is hard to put them into context. As we noted the value of turnpikes in 1815 is roughly an order of magnitude greater than the value of steam by 1800. It must remain at least an open question as to whether turnpikes were really an order of magnitude more important for the British economy than steam at the start of the nineteenth century.

In this context Bakker's study of the cinema is of considerable interest. By comparing the value of the cinema for three different countries at the same date he opens up the potential of saying something comparative. As we have seen, Bakker's work suggests that both different prices and different tastes are important. Relative to the USA it is different relative prices that are most important in explaining the difference between the social savings valuation of the cinema in the USA and in the UK, whereas tastes are the biggest factor in explaining the difference in the social savings valuation of the cinema to France relative to the USA. Were these three studies to have been done by different people, using slightly different assumptions, and perhaps at slightly different dates we would not have the same confidence in our ability to compare the results, and thus to derive interesting conclusions.

This chapter has also argued that there are many other technological changes that could be assessed using a social savings framework. We calculated order of magnitude figures for the improvements in short-haul narrow-bodied aircraft. Given that these were relatively small improvements, in that we were not comparing the pre-jet age with the post-jet age, it should not be surprising that the value was of a relatively small size. We also noted that the methodology could perfectly well be applied to process innovations. We gave as an example the application of the production line by Henry Ford at the start of the twentieth century. Here we found that even over a small period of time the social savings results are quite large. This suggests that although new inventions may capture the imagination, economic historians should not underestimate the value of new methods of producing existing goods. The opportunity to increase welfare by making existing products more cheaply is potentially very large. In that context a social studies saving of the benefits of trade in existing low technology manufactured goods between more developed countries and, say, China in the last 20 years would be likely to yield a very high value indeed. It is not that the Chinese have, in the main, invented new goods of huge value, but they have demonstrated a consistent ability to produce a wide range of goods at much lower prices, freeing up money that consumers in developed countries are then able to spend on other welfare enhancing activities.

Given the limited interest and limited range of papers that use the social savings at methodology in recent years, it would be rash to predict a flurry of papers in the near future. If social saving studies are going to make a significant impact in economics and economic history in the future then it will be necessary for those who use the methodology to use it in a comparative setting wherever possible, or at least to facilitate comparison by producing studies that give figures for a wide range of dates, so that later scholars can more easily produce figures that are comparable. If that is done then it is certainly plausible that future social saving studies can hugely enrich our understanding of the past just as the original findings produced by Robert Fogel led to a dramatic reappraisal of the value of railroads to economic growth.

References

van Ark, B., Melka, J., Mulder, N., Timmer, M. and Ypma, G. (2003) ICT investments and growth accounts for the European Union. Groningen Research and Development Centre Research Memorandum No. GD-56.

Ashauer, D.A. (1989) Is public expenditure productive? *Journal of Monetary Economics* 23: 177–200.

Atack, J. and Passell, P. (1994) *A New Economic View of American History: From Colonial Times to 1940*. New York: Norton.

Bakker, G. (2008) *Entertainment Industrialised: The Emergence of the International Firm Industry, 1890–1940*. Cambridge: Cambridge University Press.

Bogart, D. (2009) Turnpike trusts and property income: new evidence on the effects of transport improvements and legislation in eighteenth century England. *Economic History Review* 62: 128–152.

Boyd, J. and Walton, G.M. (1972) The social savings from nineteenth century rail passenger services. *Explorations in Economic History* 9: 233–254.

Caron, F. (1983). In P. O'Brien (ed.), *Railways and the Economic Development of Western Europe, 1830–1914* (pp. 28–48). New York: St Martin's Press.

Chandler, A.D. Jr (1990) *Scale and Scope: The Dynamics of Industrial Capitalism*. Cambridge, MA: Harvard University Press.

Coatsworth, J.H. (1979) Indispensable railroads in a backward economy: the case of Mexico. *Journal of Economic History* 39(4), 939–960.

Crafts, N. (2004) Social savings as a measure of the contribution of the new technology to economic growth. LSE Department of Economic History Working Paper 06/04.

Crafts, N. and Mulatu, A. (2006) How did the location of industry respond to falling transport costs in Britain before World War I? *Journal of Economic History* 66: 575–607.

David, P.A. (1969) Transport innovation and economic growth: Professor Fogel on and off the rails. *Economic History Review* 22(3): 506–525.

Davis, L. (1966) The new economic history. II. Professor Fogel and the new economic history. *Economic History Review* 19(3): 657–663.

Fishlow, A. (1965) *American Railroads and the Transformation of the Ante-bellum Economy*. Cambridge, MA: Harvard University Press.

Fogel, R.W. (1962) A quantitative approach to the study of railroads in American economic growth: a report of some preliminary findings. *Journal of Economic History* 22(2): 163–197.

Fogel, R.W. (1964) *Railroads and American Economic Growth: Essays in Econometric History*. Baltimore, MD: Johns Hopkins University Press.

Fogel, R.W. (1979) Notes on the social saving controversy. *Journal of Economic History* 39(1): 1–54.

Foreman-Peck, J. (1991) Railways and late Victorian economic growth. In J. Foreman-Peck (ed.), *New Perspectives on the Late Victorian Economy: Essays in Quantitative Economic History, 1860–1914* (pp. 73–95). Cambridge: Cambridge University Press.

Fremdling, R. (1983). In P. O'Brien (ed.), *Railways and the Economic Development of Western Europe, 1830–1914* (pp. 121–147). New York: St Martin's Press.

Harberger, A.C. (1998) A vision of the growth process. *American Economic Review* 88: 1–32.

Hawke, G.R. (1970) *Railways and Econornic Growth in England and Wales, 1840–1870*. Oxford: Clarendon Press.

Herranz-Loncán, A. (2006). Railroad impact in backward economies: Spain, 1850–1913. *Journal of Economic History* 66: 853–881.

Hounshell, D.A. (1984) *From the American System to Mass Production 1800–1932: The Development of Manufacturing Technology in the United States*. Baltimore, MD: Johns Hopkins University Press.

Huenemann, R.W. (1983) *The Dragon and the Iron Horse: The Economics of Railroads in China, 1876–1937*. Harvard East Asian Monographs, Cambridge, MA: Harvard University Press.

Kahn, C. (1988) The use of complicated models as explanations: a re-examination of Williamson's late 19th century America. *Research in Economic History* 11: 185–216.

Laffut, M. (1983). In P. O'Brien (ed.), *Railways and the Economic Development of Western Europe, 1830–1914* (pp. 203–226). New York: St Martin's Press.

Lebergott, S. (1966) United States transportation advance and externalities. *Journal of Economic History* 26: 439–440.

Leunig, T. (2006) Time is money: a re-assessment of the passenger social savings from Victorian British railways. *Journal of Economic History* 66(3): 635–673.

McClelland, P.D. (1968) Railroads, American growth, and the new economic history: a critique. *Journal of Economic History* 28(1): 102–123.

McGreevey, W.P. (2008) *An Economic History of Colombia 1845–1930*. Cambridge: Cambridge University Press.

Metzer, J. (1976) Railroads in Tsarist Russia: direct gains and implications. *Explorations in Economic History* 13(1): 85–111.

Metzer, J. (1984) Railroads and the efficiency of internal markets: some conceptual and practical considerations. *Economic Development and Cultural Change*, 61–70.

Oliner, S.D. and Sichel, D.E. (2000) The resurgence of growth in the late 1990s: is information technology the story? *Journal of Economic Perspectives* 14(4): 3–22.

Rostow, W.W. (1960) *The Stages of Economic Growth: A Non-Communist Manifesto*. Cambridge: Cambridge University Press.

Savage, C.I. (1959) *An Economic History of Transport*. London: Hutchinson.

Sears Catalogue (1897).

Summerhill, W. (2005) Big social savings in a small laggard economy: railroad-led growth in Brazil. *Journal of Economic History* 65(1): 72–102.

von Tunzelmann, G.N. (1978) *Steam Power and British Industrialisation to 1860*. Oxford: Clarendon Press.

Sutton, J. (1998) *Technology and Market Structure: Theory and History*. Cambridge, MA: MIT Press.

Williamson, J.G. (1974) *Late Nineteenth-Century American Development: A General Equilibrium History*. Cambridge: Cambridge University Press.

3

LONGITUDINAL STUDIES OF HUMAN GROWTH AND HEALTH: A REVIEW OF RECENT HISTORICAL RESEARCH

Kris Inwood and Evan Roberts

1. Introduction

Understanding change in individual circumstances and behaviour across time is a key objective of research in many fields of economics, including economic history. Given a proper sampling method, inferences about changing circumstances can be made using independent samples of different individuals at different points in time, or cross-sectional data. Reliable inference about *changes* in behaviour and circumstance often requires repeated observations on the same individuals across time, or longitudinal data. Longitudinal data, although not a panacea for every inferential issue, allow researchers to disentangle individual- and period-specific effects in background and behaviour. In this chapter we review the literature in economic history and portions of closely related fields such as demographic and medical history that uses longitudinal data on human stature, weight and health to explain trends and determinants of living standards.

We discuss the following issues in the chapter. First, we review the rationale for using stature and weight as measures of human welfare. The questions in this literature are at least implicitly, and often explicitly, longitudinal. We then discuss empirical research into the relationship between conditions in early life, and later life health and mortality. Because height is a summary measure of nutritional conditions in the first two decades of life, studies of the relationship between height and health use the former to proxy for early life conditions. A related literature – largely but not entirely from epidemiology – seeks to understand the relationship between conditions in utero – often measured by birth weight – and health in later life (Barker, 1998). These areas of research revolve around the influence of environmental conditions on later health that are exogenous to the individual. Babies have no influence over their conditions in the womb, and children have very limited influence over factors that affect their net nutrition and attained height. Conversely, adult body weight may be appropriately thought of as a rational choice dependent on preferences, technology and relative prices (Philipson and Posner, 2003; Lakdawalla

Economics and History, First Edition. David Greasley and Les Oxley

and Philipson, 2009; Lumey *et al.*, 2010). Beyond a certain point increases in body mass are undesirable for humans, bringing an increased risk of morbidity, particularly cardiovascular conditions, and consequently increased risk of mortality (Gillman, 2004). The outstanding research question that we review in this chapter is if the relationship among body mass, morbidity and mortality has changed between historical and contemporary populations. Although as yet relatively few historical articles address this question, the first results suggest that the relationship between body mass and mortality has changed somewhat between nineteenth century and modern populations. To ground our discussion of longitudinal studies, we begin with an overview of anthropometric evidence of living standards and the new but fast-growing field of anthropometric history.

2. Anthropometric Measures of Living Standards

Anthropometric research infers living standards and health from measures of height and body mass. An interest in historical sources and in the long-term and historical experience of height and weight has grown substantially in the last 30 years, in part because anthropometric measures of welfare complement standard economic measures of welfare such as earnings or income. Anthropometric measures are helpful for historical and contemporary populations when reliable income data are not available, as in most countries before the early twentieth century, and in many developing countries today (Moradi and Baten, 2005; Heltberg, 2009). Reliable statistics on earnings or income are available only from the mid-nineteenth century for many countries, whereas anthropometric data can be found for some populations in the eighteenth century and earlier. The use of skeletal remains allows the measurement of heights and welfare for much earlier periods (Steckel and Rose, 2002; Steckel, 2005). Moreover, the use of alternative dimensions of living standards such as anthropometric measures or life expectancy is warranted by the expectation that monetary measures of income are not sufficient, and that human welfare is multi-dimensional (Fleurbaey, 2009). Even when reliable income data are available, the use of anthropometric measures may allow greater insight into inequality between sub-populations in the same country or region. Anthropometric research relies heavily on microdata that record individual characteristics such as height and weight. In the military and judicial records that are common sources for anthropometric history, socio-economic information such as occupation, literacy and ethnicity are also often available. This allows anthropometric analysts to calculate differences in mean stature or body mass by socio-economic groups or other subcomponents of a population giving insights into the long-term evolution of inequality between groups.

The anthropometric approach to measuring living standards takes a net nutrition perspective on human welfare. The two common measures used in anthropometric research are height and body mass, or body weight normalized for height. The common abbreviation for body mass, which we will use, is BMI. Adult height or terminal height is the product of both genetic and environmental influences (Silventoinen, 2003; McEvoy and Visscher, 2009). Genetic variation clearly accounts for much of the variation in stature within any population, and yet changes over several decades and differences between socio-economic groups in the average stature largely reflect environmental influences (Tanner, 1981; Faulkner and Tanner, 1986; Eveleth and Tanner, 1990; Bogin, 1999b). Between birth and the early twenties a human body has the capability to grow in stature. The most rapid periods of growth are from birth to 3 years, and in early adolescence. Males normally continue growing for longer than females, so that in well-nourished populations without significant gender inequality males are, on average, 11.5–12.5 cm taller than females. Three-quarters of the gender difference arises because boys grow for 2 more years at pre-adolescent rates (i.e. their growth spurt is delayed); boys also have a slightly larger growth spurt (higher amplitude and modestly greater length). But the body only puts energy taken in through food to the purpose of growth after fuelling immediate mental and physical activities, and fighting disease. Thus, the human potential for growth in stature can be compromised in three principal ways, which while conceptually separate, are not mutually exclusive. First, food intake may be restricted because food is in short supply, such as in a war or famine, or the relative price of food groups important to growth increases. Protein, especially milk protein, is particularly important for growth in human stature (Bogin, 1999b). Secondly, disease can retard growth by diverting energy to fighting disease, or causing inadequate absorption of the nutrients consumed. Finally, increases in the intensity or volume of physical activity without compensating increases in caloric intake also decrease the calories available for growth (Steckel, 2008). Conversely, the potential for stature growth will be enhanced if nutrient-rich food becomes more readily available or cheaper, disease incidence falls, or the physical intensity of daily activities decreases.

The net nutrition perspective that uses terminal stature as a measure of welfare is implicitly longitudinal because adult stature reflects the cumulative influence of environmental and economic patterns during the lengthy human growth period. Compared to other mammals, and even other primates, the human growth period is long in absolute length and compared to the potential lifespan (Leigh and Park, 1998; Bogin, 1999a; Leigh, 2001). Humans typically have two periods of rapid growth in stature; an infant growth spurt from birth to approximately 3 years, and an adolescent growth spurt that begins after 11 years of age. Although the conclusion of the infant growth phase is relatively uniform between individuals, the timing of the onset and length of the adolescent growth spurt differs considerably between individuals and is subject to both genetic and environmental influences. A constant genetic difference is that females normally begin their adolescent growth spurt 2 years earlier than males. In well-nourished populations, the adolescent growth spurt has begun earlier for both sexes, and concluded earlier, reflective of environmental influences. Human stature is most likely to be compromised from its genetic potential during the two growth spurts of infancy and adolescence. Correspondingly, changes in population stature for a birth cohort sharing a similar nutritional environment – such as being born and residing in the same region or country – will largely reflect net nutrition in infancy and adolescence. Decreases in average stature point to periods of decreased welfare from declining food consumption or increases in workload or disease, which are taken to be economic 'bads'.

Because height is a summary measure of net nutrition over 20 years, anthropometric studies of previous populations share a common inferential problem. Adult height and birth cohort alone identify a span of 20 years in which environmental influences might have changed growth relative to previous cohorts. Within that span of 20 years, there are two especially critical growth periods – infancy and adolescence – which researchers must examine for potential environmental changes that might have affected growth. To further complicate inference, the human growth cycle is flexible. Poor nutrition at an early age can be partially overcome with a compensating growth spurt later (Steckel, 1986). In severely malnourished populations, the attainment of terminal height can be delayed until the mid-20s (Bogin, 1999b). Thus, identifying changes in the average stature of a population does not identify the timing or cause of the change because the typical anthropometric study observes individual heights just once – in adulthood – but there are multiple years and multiple causes for a single change in height. These inferential issues do not invalidate the large and growing literature that uses height as a measure of human welfare, but do point to the desirability of longitudinal data that observes individuals at two or more points in time (Steckel, 2009b). While we concentrate in this review on what can be learned from longitudinal data, and emphasize their inferential advantages anthropometric historians have other options. Synthetic longitudinal data can be constructed from large cross-sectional studies of children (Steckel, 2009a). Aggregated data on correlates of net nutrition such as disease load, prices, and environmental conditions have been used to good effect by anthropometric historians to identify the timing of nutritional changes affecting particular cohorts.

3. Anthropometric History

Since the early uses of anthropometric evidence in economics during the 1970s, much effort has been devoted to establishing trends in population stature and body mass across different countries, explaining periods of change in average stature, and identifying periods of change still requiring full explanation due to the inferential problems just mentioned. We summarize some important findings in this literature and provide an illustrative example to set our discussion of the longitudinal research in anthropometric history in context. Readers desiring a more complete discussion of the evolution of this research area should consult the insightful review articles by Steckel (Steckel, 1995, 1998, 2009b). The use by economists and economic historians of anthropometric evidence – biological indicators that reflect the living standards of past populations – owes a considerable debt to human biologists (Tanner 1978, 1981). A seminal contribution in modern historical anthropometric research was the Steckel and Trussel use of growth velocities to demonstrate that the average age at menarche for American slaves was about 15. Because slave women did not bear their first child until an average age of 20.6 years, this finding implies that slaves were not bearing children as soon as they were physiologically capable (Trussel and Steckel, 1978). Steckel, Robert Fogel, Stanley Engerman and others initiated a stream of research that began to figure prominently in major journals and in the National Bureau of Economic Research's new Development of the American Economy (Engerman, 1976; Steckel, 1979; Fogel *et al.*, 1982; Engerman, 2004). Much of the early research in anthropometric history examined the United States and western-European experience, but since the mid-1990s the scope of this rapidly growing research has widened to include literally every settled continent. Because the American and European literature is of longer standing there is greater agreement about the trends in stature in these areas.

The most significant stylized fact to emerge from the anthropometric history literature is that North America and much of western Europe experienced a period of stagnating or diminishing stature during some portion of the nineteenth century. This finding provides an important qualification to the otherwise consistent evidence of improvements in the material standard of living during the nineteenth century (Komlos, 1998; Haines, 2004). The best-known experience of this phenomenon is the so-called antebellum puzzle in the United States (Komlos, 1987). The physical stature of successive cohorts of students entering the West Point military academy declined in spite of rapid economic growth before the Civil War. In a broad sense, the potential causes of the decline in stature – reduced calories relative to physical requirements for daily activities and fighting disease – are agreed upon, but in this case as in others it has proven challenging to identify with precision the relative importance of different influences (Gallman, 1996; Komlos, 1996; Coelho and McGuire, 2000; Steckel, 2000). The inferential problems discussed earlier mean that assessing the relative contribution of diet, disease and workload to changes in stature is demanding of both data and method (Haines *et al.*, 2003). Of course, the problem is complicated further because the relative contribution of these factors is likely to differ across cohorts and countries.

3.1 *Diet*

Before the advent of refrigerated transportation, proximity to nutrients was associated with being taller. People living in rural areas, and especially those living on farms themselves, were likely to be taller. Refrigerated transport and reduced transportation costs from the development of the railroad network reduced the rural height advantage around the turn of the twentieth century (Craig *et al.*, 2004). Milk because of its high protein:calorie ratio is important to human growth (Bogin, 1999b; Baten and Murray, 2000). The availability of fresh milk contributed to the rural height advantage. Economic historians have emphasized the role of relative price shifts in nutritional choices, and the variance of food prices for different population groups, such as urban and rural residents. Anthropometric research has shown that while urban and industrial growth did not lead to dramatic immiseration or starvation, it could contribute to reduced consumption at the margin. Even relatively small decreases in average food consumption could affect population stature if the changes were concentrated in lower income groups (Komlos, 1998).

3.2 *Disease*

Rural height advantages in the nineteenth century from diet were complemented by an advantage from lower rates of disease than urban areas (Haines, 2001, 2004). The urban penalty was not universal, with urban men in Belgium being taller than their rural peers (Alter *et al.*, 2004). Improved public health and food distribution saw the elimination of the urban height penalty in the United States by the mid-twentieth century although exactly when the urban penalty disappeared in different environments is not clearly known and probably varied (Steckel, 1995). The importance accorded to disease exposure in the anthropometric literature in populations before the modern health transition appears to be increasing.

3.4 *Work Intensity*

Industrial work and urban living contributed to declines in average stature, because industrial labour remained physically demanding. The calorie requirements of industrial workers were not greatly different from those of agricultural labourers (Komlos, 1996). However, it was recognized at the time that industrial workers were more likely to be malnourished relative to their work effort. Indeed, there was contemporary research into the food consumption and energy requirements of urban industrial workers (Oddy, 1970; Aronson, 1982). It was not until the turn of the twentieth century with the growing substitution of mechanical for human power in industrial work and the growth of white-collar work, that average daily calorie requirements in work decreased significantly (Komlos and Ritschl, 1995; Voth, 1996). The importance of work intensity for stature change in nineteenth century North America and Western Europe is not known to be large relative to the effects of diet and disease, although admittedly this may simply reflect the limited availability of evidence about individual-level variation in the demands of work.

3.5 *Inequality*

Anthropometric history has also shown inequality in societies for which few reliable surveys of money earnings or income survive. In the United States inequality in heights was most pronounced in the nineteenth century. Professionals and farmers were taller than clerical and skilled trades workers, with urban labourers being shortest on average (Steckel and Haurin, 1995). Similar degrees of inequality in height are evident in Canada, Australia and New Zealand, with the range between the tallest professionals or farmers and unskilled labourers being less than 5 cm (Whitwell and Nicholas, 2001; Cranfield and Inwood, 2007; Inwood *et al.*, 2010). Inequality in stature was greater in Europe. For example, in England the mean stature of 14-year-old boys at the elite Sandhurst school was 10–15 cm greater than orphans (Floud *et al.*, 1990).

3.6 *Gender*

An interest in inequality also motivates studies of the difference between male and female heights. Stature is an important and easily measurable aspect of sexual dimorphism or differences in body composition. The differences mainly emerge at puberty; at birth males are only 1% longer than females, but in adulthood men are, on average, 7% taller (Gaulin and Boster, 1985; Gustafsson and Lindenfors, 2004). The difference is primarily due to men having greater leg length in part because their pubertal period is longer than women's. Men also have a higher fat-free mass and a lower body fat percentage for a given weight. Sexual dimorphism in shape diminishes at advanced ages; both sexes tend to lose lean mass after age 40, so that even individuals with a stable weight have a higher body fat percentage as they age (Wells, 2007).

The magnitude of the sexual difference in stature and body mass varies between societies, and is susceptible to environmental, social and economic influences. Thus, differences in size dimorphism may reflect differences in net nutrition between the sexes from which, in turn, we may infer patterns of intra-household resource allocation that would otherwise remain hidden. Variation in the degree of dimorphism has been observed in pre-historic populations studied as well as modern groups (Frayer and Wolpoff, 1985). Because genetic variation occurs very slowly (Rogers and Mukherjee, 1992), changes in stature dimorphism are likely to reflect sex-specific changes in environment and living standards (Gustafsson *et al.*, 2007). The cause of variation in societal dimorphism continues to be debated by scholars in anthropology and biology (Eveleth, 1975; Gray and Wolfe, 1980; Holden and Mace, 1999; Nettle, 2002; Gustafsson and Lindenfors, 2004; Kanazawa and Novak, 2004; Gustafsson *et al.*, 2007).

Disagreement continues for several reasons. The magnitude of dimorphism is relatively small, and the samples used to measure it, particularly in prehistoric populations, are also quite small. Analyses seek to explain variation in the ratio of male:female stature within a range of roughly 1.04–1.12 (Gray and Wolfe, 1980). Explanatory influences are themselves difficult to measure in prehistoric populations. Although not widely discussed in the anthropological and biological literature, differing selection in samples even from the same time and place can influence measures of stature by sex and thus the apparent extent of dimorphism.

A critical question is whether or not the sexes respond similarly to nutritional conditions. The conventional conclusion is that "the growth of boys, from prenatal life to adulthood, appears to be more 'sensitive' to environmental factors than the growth of girls" (Bogin, 1999b). Although widely accepted in the anthropometric literature this hypothesis deserves further scrutiny, for two reasons. First, it follows from boys' growth being more sensitive to environmental conditions that sexual stature dimorphism should increase as stature itself grows. However, a recent study from Sweden using similar data sources for men and women found no increase in dimorphism over the twentieth century (Gustafsson *et al.*, 2007). Secondly, because stature in both sexes at a point in time is strongly influenced by socio-economic status, the degree of dimorphism will be influenced by selection into and composition of the sample. Average stature in both sexes can plausibly vary by 2–3 cm from the true population average if, for example, the sample is dominated by unusually tall (farmers) or short (urban workers) groups. Biases of this magnitude at plausible values of average stature will make the ratio of male:female stature different enough from the true value (1.05 vs. 1.07) that observed changes in the ratio could be the result of changing sample selection rather than true variation.

Historical research on women's stature and body mass is limited by the availability of systematic sources before the late twentieth century. Women appear in military and prison records less frequently and in a less representative way than men. Women in the military, for example, have tended to be nurses who represent a more highly selective group from all women than soldiers were from all men. Military nursing on a large-scale dates from World War I, and yet already by World War II the selection changed as the number of nurses increased and women began to serve in a broader range of auxiliary military roles. Similarly, the selection of women into prisons was different than for men. In Europe, North America and Australasia, women were (and are) imprisoned less often than men and for a narrower range of offences. Concerns about differential sample selection between the sexes are somewhat relaxed in the twentieth century because researchers have access to more systematic collection of data on children's heights in schools and, after World War II, population anthropometric surveys of adults. The shift from highly selective to representative sampling of women obscures the long-run trend in dimorphism.

Studies of female stature in Britain and Ireland, and among American slaves have been particularly important. After 1807 slaves in the United States were measured when shipped between ports; they comprise one of the few historical populations where a male and female sample was selected on the same principles. Steckel has used the slave manifests to show that both male and female slaves' growth was retarded in childhood, but caught up dramatically in adolescence. Nutrition was relatively poor for both sexes (Steckel, 1986).

Studies of the height of British and Irish prisoners from the nineteenth century illustrate the potential for using anthropometric measures to identify gender inequality. Oxley and Nicholas report a smaller gap between rural and urban stature in early nineteenth century Ireland than in England among female prisoners (Nicholas and Oxley, 1993). They argue that rural stature fell more rapidly for rural English women because their labour market opportunities deteriorated, reducing the returns from investing in growth and causing girls to receive less food than their brothers whose labour market prospects were better. Such interpretations of height decline are difficult to confirm from other sources although nonetheless it is agreed that adult women had poorer net nutrition than men because of labour market considerations (Floud, 1998; Harris, 2009). For example, in mid-nineteenth century Britain incarcerated women have been found to be 0.8 kg/m^2 lighter than men of the same age. On the same basic prison diet, 60% of women in prison gained weight whereas 70% of men lost weight (Horrell *et al.*, 2007, 2009).

There is also evidence of a long-run trend towards greater sexual dimorphism in heights from India (Brennan *et al.*, 1994; Deaton, 2008; Viswanathan and Sharma, 2009). The Indian research spanning more than a century has necessarily combined selective documentary evidence from the past, with more representative modern survey data. The latter have minimal selection issues between men and women. But the historical data, manifests of indentured labourers leaving India, are more complex because the selection of men and women into the pool of indentured labourers may have differed. Brennan *et al.* argue that the selection effect understates an estimated height decline and, strengthens the conclusion of growing dimorphism. Here, as in the other studies, the most important insight from research on men's and women's anthropometry is likely to be the connection between labour market returns and claims on nutritional resources in the household.

3.7 *An Example of Anthropometric Research from Cross-Sections of the Population*

The British prison data follow men and women through time but more commonly anthropometric researches rely on a cross-sectional source from which some longitudinal influence may be inferred. A useful example is provided by preliminary results from a project examining the evolution of physical stature in New Zealand (Inwood *et al.*, 2009, 2010). This analysis illustrates what can be learned as well as the limits of knowledge from conventional anthropometric research. A multivariate estimation on the first round of data from this project describing 4939 soldiers born in New Zealand and serving in the army during World War II is reported in Table 1.

Table 1. Maximum Likelihood Truncated (64 inches) Estimation of Stature, NZ-born Soldiers aged 21–49 years in World War II.

	Coefficient	$P>\|z\|$
Born 1890–1899	0.13	0.50
Born 1900–1904	−0.07	0.68
Born 1905–1909	−0.08	0.54
Born 1915–1919	0.14	0.20
Born 1920–1924	−0.15	0.41
Farmer	0.84	0.00
Labourer, farm	0.01	0.96
Professional–Clerical	0.47	0.00
Labourer, other	−0.19	0.13
Maori Name	−0.66	0.00
Constant	67.57	0.00
$N = 4939$		

Source: Inwood, K, Oxley, L. and Roberts, E. (2009) *Rather Above than Under the Common Size? Stature and Living Standards in New Zealand*, unpublished paper presented to the World Economic History Congress, Utrecht.

The truncated maximum likelihood regression model accommodates evidence that soldiers less than 64 inches tall may be underrepresented.

Inequality within the population is evidenced by the report in Table 1 that men from the professional and clerical class were six-tenths of an inch taller than labourers (the omitted occupational category in the regression are skilled tradespeople). These data, in themselves, cannot tell us if the working class disadvantage reflects poorer diet, more demanding working conditions or the disease burden of less healthy living and working conditions. The two-tenths of an inch height advantage of farm labourers over other labourers undoubtedly reflects the fact that the relative price of food was lower on the farm and that the lower population density of rural residents provided some protection from infectious disease. The estimation provides no way to disentangle the relative importance of the food price and disease exposure effects. Farmers were a full inch taller than non-farm labourers; presumably this reflects the combined influence of more limited disease exposure and greater wealth. Soldiers who enlisted with a name that was recognizably Māori (the indigenous population of New Zealand) were half an inch shorter than urban labourers. Mortality and morbidity among the Māori is known to have been disastrous in this period so it is not surprising to find that they were shorter as well (Pool, 1991). Again, however, we do not yet know the relative importance of nutrition, disease and work intensity to the loss of Māori stature relative to non-Māori New Zealanders.

The same regression framework allows us to say if New Zealanders were becoming shorter or taller over time. Somewhat surprisingly, in view of the experience of health improvement in many other countries at this time, successive birth cohorts of New Zealanders were *not* becoming taller after the turn of the century. There is no statistically significant difference in height between the reference group (men born 1910–1914) and any other birth group.

Anthropometric studies of this sort are not directly longitudinal in the sense of collecting evidence of well-being at different points in a life. Rather adult health is interpreted with reference to information about the person's early life experience (birthplace, birth year, etc). Thus, early-life environmental (broadly defined) influences can be seen to influence later-life health. Most anthropometric studies are implicitly longitudinal in this sense. In most cases, the evidence of earlier-life conditions such as birth location and date is collected at the time of measuring stature. The limitations of this process arise in part from the potentially confounding effects of survivor bias and also from the inaccuracy of human recall (Batty *et al.*, 2005; Kauhanen *et al.*, 2006; Haas, 2007; Murphy, 2009). Many people know their age and birthplace more or less precisely with some variation in precision by *inter alia* education, social class and migration status. More complex detail and information about other family members is likely to be correspondingly less precise.

An important and growing class of studies is able to obtain direct evidence of health at multiple points in a person's life. A number of studies attempt to correlate adult health experience with stresses received in utero. Research examining the children born in the aftermath of the Dutch winter famine of 1944 has been particularly influential (Lumey and Van Poppel, 1994; Lumey, 1998). The Dutch winter famine studies contribute to the extensive and varied, although still contested, evidence for the implications of foetal environment for adult health in the shape of risk for major chronic diseases, such as cardiovascular disease, stroke, hypertension, Type 2 diabetes and obesity; the best-known contributions are those of Barker (Barker, 1992, 1998, 2004). A large and growing literature investigates the 'natural experiment' consequences of severe famines for long-term health of survivors and even their descendents (Lumey *et al.*, 2010).

Another kind of anthropometric study that obtains direct evidence of health early and late in life is based on children who were examined medically in the early and middle decades of the twentieth century and then subsequently followed through to identify the adult and later life experience of health. For example, the Boyd Orr sample collected a great deal of diet and health information about 4999 children in 1937–1939 Scotland and England (Martin *et al.*, 2005). Fifty years later, another set of researchers retrieved the original records, located the children's National Health Records and thereby acquired long-term longitudinal data with rich detail about health and its determinants for children and again in later life. The Boyd Orr longitudinal data have supported a wide range of studies including, recently, analyses of the significant impact of early life conditions on adult stature and later-life health (Frijters *et al.*, 2010; Hatton and Martin, 2010). A number of other early twentieth century sources, many of them administrative in nature, have been matched to later life information to constitute new longitudinal data (Hart *et al.*, 2004; Starr *et al.*, 2004; Lawlor *et al.*, 2006; Batty *et al.*, 2009).

The inter-war Boyd Orr study was paralleled by the initiation of several longitudinal studies in the United States, some of which continued to the present day. Then, as now, the interest in longitudinal studies was interdisciplinary, with medicine, education and psychology to the fore. Particularly important were the Oakland Growth Study (1920–1921 birth cohort) that interviewed children and their families four times in the 1930s, and returned to them in the 1950s and 1972. The Berkeley Growth and Guidance studied a cohort born in 1929 from infancy. Similar longitudinal studies were started in Colorado, Iowa, Minnesota, Ohio and Massachusetts (Wall and Williams, 1970; Sontag, 1971; Mednick and Mednick, 1984; Young *et al.*, 1991). Somewhat atheoretical in their design and with relatively small sample sizes, these early longitudinal studies collected anthropometric information that makes them useful for subsequent research (Tanner, 1981; Himes, 2006).

In the post-war era, European governments launched a number studies designed from the outset to support life-course studies of human growth and health. A Medical Research Council Study begun in 1948, for example, collected information about British children born two years earlier. These children were later resampled at intervals to obtain true longitudinal data that have been used in a wide variety of studies (Wadsworth *et al.*, 2006). Additional longitudinal studies were launched in Britain and in western Europe during the 1950s and 1960s (Leon *et al.*, 2006; Power and Elliott, 2006; Stenberg and Vagero, 2006; Osler *et al.*, 2008). Some sources such as the 1946 cohort study begin following the subjects in early life, whereas others such as the Whitehall studies begin tracking people as adults and also reach backwards with the ex-post addition of early-life information (Batty *et al.*, 2009). In the United States, a large number of longitudinal projects were begun from the 1950s through 1970s. The US National Collaborative Perinatal Project study and Oakland Child Health and Development Study that contain birth cohorts from 1959 to 1967 have been followed up extensively for growth and health outcomes (van den Berg *et al.*, 1988; Hardy, 2003; Mei *et al.*, 2004; Klebanoff, 2009). The variety of sources and database design implies that historians of the second half of the twentieth century have at their disposal a diversity of sources supporting longitudinal anthropometric analysis although, admittedly, coverage varies by country and becomes more complete over time. Longitudinal sources offer the very considerable advantage over cross-sectional evidence that individual differences, for example, in onset of the growth spurt, which may be the focus of interest, do not disappear into cross-sectional averaging.

The limitation to this genre of analysis arises from the timing of the medical exam and the age at which people were examined. Very few if any research studies of health and physical well-being that follow individuals through time or provide personal identifiers allowing longitudinal reconstruction pre-date the Boyd Orr sample. Research on child health during the early 20th century was extensively reported and is invaluable for historical analysis, but it provides limited evidence about cohorts born in the nineteenth century (Harris, 1995). Hospital birth records allow the construction of longitudinal data but few records are available to document births before the mid-nineteenth century (Ward, 1993; McCalman *et al.*, 2008). The First World War military entrance exams such as those reported above support analysis of physical well-being and linkage to other sources for people born in the 1860s, but no earlier. Thus, the construction of longitudinal data from prison, hospital, military and other administrative sources usefully extends back into the nineteenth century the populations and cohorts for which the relationship between body composition and health can be examined over the life course.

Cohorts born before the 1920s can only be studied longitudinally by linking diverse original sources. In this respect, anthropometric research parallels the methods used to examine occupational and geographic mobility. Historical mobility studies in the 1960s and 1970s relied on hand searches and often were restricted to linking people who had not moved far from their original residence (Thernstrom, 1964). The development of complete machine-readable indices to population registers and censuses removed the restriction. Joseph Ferrie's 1996 book *Yankeys Now* pioneered the genre by tracing 2595 immigrants across the United States from 1850 to 1860 using census indices (Ferrie, 1999). More recently, systematic data mining techniques and inexpensive computing has permitted a generalization and expansion of Ferrie-type longitudinal data (Goeken, 2010). To construct these data, we need original sources describing the population at different times with similar identification variables such as name, race, birth date and location (and in some cases characteristics of parents). To connect together different original sources, the researcher matches individual characteristics that do not change over time (or change predictably, for example, age). It may be difficult to match individuals with widely shared characteristics (e.g. the surname of Smith) because there are so many potential matches in the different record sources. In practice the decision about matching individuals is inexact and probabilistic because of variations in the way names were recorded, age heaping, and errors in the original enumeration and transcribing the handwritten sources into a machine-readable format.

4. The Relationship Between Body Composition, Morbidity and Mortality

Determining if the relationship between body composition and health has changed is critical to using nutritional measures of living standards over time. Studies of living standards using anthropometric measures interpret increases in average height and body mass as indicative of higher real wages (due to lower food costs), lower disease incidence, or reduced physical intensity of work. In the absence of other changes to welfare these improvements to net nutrition can be interpreted as improvements to living standards. However, if the relationship between body composition and health changes, then changes in body composition over time cannot be interpreted as pure improvements in living standards.

To make the issue more concrete, consider the hypothesis that improvements in medical technology might lower the mortality risks of obesity. There are two separate, but not mutually exclusive, ways in which the obesity–mortality relationship might have changed. First, the obesity–mortality function could shift, giving a lower mortality risk at any given BMI. Secondly, the shape of the obesity–health function could change, lowering the mortality risk of an increase in BMI. We emphasize that these are hypotheses about possible changes, rather than established results, which we discuss later. If the obesity–health relationship has shifted, then the implicit price of obesity has changed. People are able to have their cake and eat it too. Conversely, an unchanging relationship between obesity and health across cohorts and countries is powerful evidence that the obesity–health relationship approximates a biological constant. If the obesity–health relationship is stable across time and place, we can compare changes in the population distribution of body composition among diverse populations, and forecast the implications of changing body composition. Conversely, if the obesity–health relationship has shifted substantially over just a century there is evidence that the obesity–health relationship is mediated by social and economic factors. Thus, a key question for historical longitudinal studies in anthropometric history is whether the height–health and body mass–health relationship has changed substantially over time.

In this section, we discuss historical and modern evidence on the relationship between height and weight, and morbidity and mortality. Weight and height direct our attention at different points in human life as critical in determining morbidity and mortality. While studies of height and health in later life address the relationship of early-life experience and later-life health, studies of weight and health seek to address the question of how behaviour in adulthood – closer to the end of the lifespan – affect morbidity and mortality. The two perspectives are not opposed. Morbidity and mortality risk can be affected by both growth period experiences, and adult experiences and behaviour. Yet the emphasis on early-life or adult experience as the primary cause of disease and mortality has shifted over the twentieth century (Kuh and Smith, 1993). Prior to World War II, researchers from a variety of disciplines emphasized the early-life antecedents of adult disease and mortality. However, in the 1950s and 1960s there was a much greater influence on adult behaviour – such as poor nutrition manifesting in overweight – as a primary cause of morbidity (Kuh and Ben-Shlomo, 2004). Interest in early life influences – often summarized by height in historical studies – resumed in the 1970s. The current epidemiological consensus is that morbidity and mortality risk are determined over the life span. Moreover, the relative contributions of early life and adult experiences and behaviour are likely to differ between individuals and between morbidities. The data requirements to answer this form of question are high. Conclusions are thus necessarily partial and inclusive – both early and later life experiences affect morbidity and mortality.

4.1 *Height and Health*

The ultimate question in studies of the relationship between height and health is the long-term relationship between the cumulative effect of childhood – or growth period – experiences and health in later life. Height in itself is not the variable of interest. Rather, height summarizes influences across the growth period. Particularly in retrospective or historical data, it may be one of the few reliable variables about early life experience available. In retrospective data collection, where respondents are asked about events occurring several decades earlier, recall of significant health events is likely to be biased or inaccurate (Coughlin, 1990; Friedenreich, 1994). Occupational and residential information is remembered quite accurately over 50 years, but childhood health is recalled less accurately (Berney and Blane, 1997; Batty *et al.*, 2005). Nevertheless, for living cohorts there are methods such as life-grid interviews that provide usable data on major life course events that may affect later health (Blane *et al.*, 1999; Holland *et al.*, 2000). Collecting new data is not an option for cohorts that are dead. Although there are surviving early twentieth century medical and social surveys that include health information and can be usefully re-examined by economic historians (Hatton and Martin, 2010), examining the relationship between early life (growth period) conditions and later life health requires height data for any studies of the nineteenth century and much of the early twentieth century. The medical literature on how life course influences shape morbidity and mortality particularly emphasize the importance for future research of obtaining information on the growth trajectory, and knowing more than attained adult height (Ben-Shlomo and Kuh, 2004). Economic historians might usefully try to uncover sources such as school health records that could provide more information on childhood growth trajectories.

4.1.1 *Height and Morbidity*

A significant amount of modern research on the association between height and morbidity has focused on the relationship between height and coronary heart disease. Across the population height has been shown to be inversely associated with the development of cardiovascular diseases. In other words, shorter people have a higher risk of developing cardiovascular diseases. Similarly, there is an inverse association between height and diabetes, with shorter men having a higher prevalence of diabetes, and greater levels of insulin resistance. Modern researchers who have been able to collect data on the components of height have found a stronger correlation between leg length and adult cardiovascular disease than total height. This correlation is significant because more of the environmental variation in height comes through variation in leg length than in torso length. That is, people who are shorter than their genetic potential due to deprivation in childhood tend to be shorter in the legs than they could have been (Elford and Ben-Shlomo, 2004; Lawlor *et al.*, 2004). The conclusion from modern research is that the inverse relationship between height and cardiovascular disease is most likely due to cardiovascular disease being a long-term consequence of conditions in childhood that are also reflected in height. Height has also been shown to be inversely related to stroke, respiratory disease and stomach cancers, and that the association is due to early life conditions manifesting in both reduced stature and disease (Davey Smith and Lynch, 2004). However, height is not associated with the development of hypertension (Whincup *et al.*, 2004). The emerging and important literature examining long-term consequences of famine for children will add further evidence (Lumey *et al.*, 2010). Already it seems clear that chronic malnutrition or repeated famine has much more serious impact than a single episode of food deprivation.

4.1.2 *Height and Mortality*

The relationship between height and mortality addresses indirectly the question of whether conditions in early life – reflected in height – also affect survival in the long run. The mechanisms for how early life conditions affect mortality and life expectancy are unclear in much of this research, opening up further questions rather than resolving issues.

Waaler's pioneering research with 1.7 million Norwegians demonstrated that height was associated with increased longevity in late-adult men, and that the effects were substantial (Waaler, 1984). Among men aged 55–59 at initial screening and followed for 17 years, the mortality of men standing 185–189 cm was half that of men 150–55 cm. However, while the relative risk for shorter men appeared dramatic, the population at risk was very small. Less than 8% of the population studied had an excess mortality risk of more than 50%. A subsequent follow-up of the same population for another 17 years to the year 2000, maintained Waaler's basic results. Men shorter than 165 cm had an elevated mortality risk, but above that height there was no increase in the risk of death over 25–34 years of follow-up (Engeland *et al.*, 2003). British researchers have found similar results in smaller samples. Height was inversely associated with all cause, coronary heart disease, stroke and respiratory disease mortality in a 20 year study of Scottish men (Davey Smith *et al.*, 2000). Similarly using data from the Whitehall study of British civil servants, an increase in height of 15 cm was associated with a 10% reduction in mortality risk (Batty *et al.*, 2006, 2009). A Finnish study showed even stronger support for the relationship with a 5 cm increase in height being associated with 10% declines in mortality risk (Jousilahti *et al.*, 2000). Recent papers using Asian and Australasian data from prospective medical studies found that a 6 cm (1 standard deviation) increase in height was associated with a 3% decline in mortality risk. This finding is significant because of the extension to non-European ethnic groups. No significant differences were found between the Asian and Australasian populations, suggesting this relationship is robust across different ethnic groups (Song *et al.*, 2003; Lee *et al.*, 2009). Moreover, studies of identical twins have demonstrated that the shorter twin had an increased chance of coronary heart disease mortality (Silventoinen *et al.*, 2006). In summary, the direction of the association between short stature and increased mortality risk is well established in modern research. The estimated size of the relationship varies across countries. This would be surprising if the association was a biological one with little variation, but the risk of short stature is likely to vary across countries and time depending on social and economic conditions. Estimating how the relationship has changed and why remains a challenge for economic historians.

The extensive modern research is complemented by just two historical studies addressing the same question directly. Engaging directly with Waaler's results Costa examined the mortality risk of stature in a sample of Union Army veterans (Costa, 1993). Her findings broadly paralleled the modern research. Mortality risk declined with increasing height after 160 cm and was lowest from 183 to 188 cm. Mortality risk began to rise again for very tall men. Subsequent research by Murray on the mortality risk of stature in a sample of elite Amherst college students complicates the historical picture (Murray, 1997). Murray found no relation between height and mortality risk. He concluded that the influence of height on mortality was mediated by social and behavioural factors. In economically homogeneous groups, such as elite college students in the nineteenth century United States, height may not be predictive of mortality. In an economically homogeneous sample, the variation in height is likely to be more genetic than reflective of environmental and economic conditions in childhood. Despite Murray's null finding, the similarity of the relationship in Costa's research with the extensive modern evidence suggests the height–mortality relationship is not unchanging, but certainly long-standing. Additional research on historical populations is necessary to show how the strength of the relationship has changed across time and space.

4.2 *Weight and Health*

Longitudinal studies involving weight are even more tightly constrained than studies of height by limitations on the availability and quality of evidence. Before the nineteenth century there was not adequate technology to accurately record human weights. While balance scales – such as the steelyard – have been used since ancient times they are of little value for measuring live weight (which moves). Fairbanks scales were perfected and mass produced in the United States by the middle of the 19th century, and were more stable and suitable for weighing people and animals. By the mid-1870s Fairbanks scales and similar designs manufactured elsewhere were used in anthropometric studies (Bowditch, 1877; Roberts, 1879). Ironically, the weight of platform scales, which were too bulky and expensive to have been used in the field and at muster stations, means we have little historical data on weight before the late nineteenth century.

Both historical and modern research show that individuals at the extremes of the weight distribution have a higher risk of mortality, with the risks mediated through specific diseases. Here we consider men only because anthropometric historical data on a longitudinal basis for women are scarce. Indeed, even modern medical studies have paid less attention to these issues for women (Kuh and Hardy, 2004). Although the mortality risk of being overweight dominates the academic and policy discussion today, being underweight was a more common health risk in industrialized countries before World War II.

The greater prevalence of underweight adults before World War II was related to the three contributors to net nutrition discussed above, namely caloric intake, disease burden, and physical intensity of daily living. Humans today, particularly in industrial and service work but also in agriculture, expend substantially less energy in work and transport activities than they did a century ago (Cutler *et al.*, 2003; Philipson and Posner, 2003). People in the past needed more calories just to carry out their daily activities. Moreover, nutritious food was expensive relative to income, both to acquire and prepare (Logan, 2006, 2009). Mass urbanization in the nineteenth century reduced the ability of western populations to produce their own food supplies that they could consume if they were unemployed or had reduced wages. Finally, common infectious gastrointestinal and respiratory diseases led to weight loss, and were associated with significant (but declining) mortality in the nineteenth century and first half of the twentieth century. Thus, despite the current policy and academic concern about overweight as a risk factor for morbidity and mortality, historical studies also show an important relationship between being underweight and later mortality.

4.2.1 *Weight and Morbidity*

Mortality – when not caused by accidents or suicide – is a consequence of specific illnesses. The relationship between BMI and specific morbidities mediates the relationship between BMI and mortality. Technological change in health care has changed the mortality risk of different morbidities over time, and the population prevalence of different morbidities has also changed. The changing mortality risk of BMI can be seen as the product of changes in these two terms. First there is the risk of contracting specific morbidities conditional on BMI, and second a risk of dying due to that morbidity in a given time period. As well as the risk of developing chronic diseases related to obesity, there is also evidence that the strain from obesity on the muscular–skeletal system may contribute to back and joint problems, and arthritis (Felson, 1996; Ferraro *et al.*, 2002; Symmons *et al.*, 2005). Modern health surveys in the United States, Europe and Australasia have also documented that self-rated health declines with increasing weight (Must *et al.*, 1999; Sturm and Wells, 2001; Jia and Lubetkin, 2005; Sach *et al.*, 2006).

Modern health research in developed countries on the relationship between weight and morbidity focuses nearly entirely on the relationship between excess weight and morbidity. Although there are substantial health consequences of malnutrition, and these remain a serious health concern in developing countries, in high-income industrialized nations a concern with the health consequences of being overweight has grown over the twentieth century (Czerniawski, 2007). Excess weight and obesity are associated primarily with a range of chronic conditions affecting the circulatory and metabolic systems. In particular, the link between being overweight and coronary heart disease has been a focus of medical research since immediately after World War II (Keys *et al.*, 1972; Kuh and Smith, 1993). More recently, the link between obesity throughout the life course, and the development of diabetes, has received significant attention (Forouhi *et al.*, 2004). Obesity in adulthood also contributes significantly to high blood pressure, a condition that can be a precursor to cerebrovascular conditions (stroke) and coronary heart disease (Whincup *et al.*, 2004). Overweight and obesity is also related to the development of site-specific cancers. Among men overweight and obesity is associated with a greater risk of kidney and stomach cancer (Davey Smith *et al.*, 2009).

Historical evidence on the relationship between weight and morbidity is limited to two recent papers using the Union Army data set that is central to research in this field (Costa, 1996; Johansen, 2000; Linares and Su, 2005). Unfortunately, the data required for understanding non-fatal sickness or morbidity estimates in historical populations is unlikely to exist for many populations. It is possible to study the relationship between body composition and mortality with observations at just two points in time. For example, soldiers who were weighed and measured upon enlistment can be linked to their single death certificate. Moreover, people die just once, and the event is well defined and thus well recorded in many societies. Conceptual and causal issues remain because the aetiology of how BMI at, say, age 18 influences mortality risk at age 50 is not entirely clear. Nevertheless, the data required to estimate a relationship can be generated from reasonably representative and available sources with well-understood selection criteria. Conversely, people fall sick frequently and the definition of being "sick" changes over time (Riley, 1990; Johansson, 2004). Moreover, people whose illnesses were recorded in, for example, friendly society or benefit fund records, may have been more likely to be sick – a common moral hazard problem in health insurance (Murray, 2007). Particularly in the past when medical care for many conditions was ineffective or counterproductive, and relatively expensive, most people did not present to a doctor for treatment. For the nineteenth century, the available sources to study morbidity at an individual level are limited. American Civil War veterans from the Union Army and members of sickness benefit societies are possible sources (Gorsky *et al.*, 2006).

Although primarily asking how health affected labour supply, Costa's 1996 study of 597 men from the Union Army data set also showed the effect of BMI on specific health conditions affecting labour force participation (Costa, 1996). Costa found that the relationship between BMI and non-participation in the labour market was 'remarkably similar' in 1900 and the late twentieth century. Non-participation was least likely at a BMI of 25, and increased at lower and higher BMI values. However, in the early twentieth century men were more responsive to changes in BMI. Costa also found that the relationship between BMI and specific diseases had changed. Whereas in modern populations heart disease risk increases with BMI, in the early twentieth century heart disease and BMI were negatively related. In a relatively small sample, however, Costa was not able to discriminate between specific morbidities.

Using an expanded version of the Union Army data set with 5600 men, Linares and Su (2005) were able to consider the relationship between BMI and four common chronic disease groups: cardiovascular, gastrointestinal, respiratory and rheumatism/musculoskeletal. Linares and Su's analysis examined the relationship of BMI with both the number of disease groups veterans contracted, and the occurrence of specific individual conditions. Although health guidelines define normal weight as a BMI between 20 and 25, Linares and Su found that the number of chronic diseases suffered by veterans was minimized at a BMI of 27, or slightly overweight by modern standards. Thus, the relationship between BMI and chronic conditions was U-shaped. Underweight and overweight were both associated with suffering more chronic disease. Moreover, the average BMI in the Union Army data set was 23.3, so most veterans had a greater than optimal number of chronic conditions.

When examining specific conditions, Linares and Su found a similar U-shaped relationship between BMI and the occurrence of cardiovascular, gastrointestinal and respiratory diseases. The curvilinear relationship was strongest for cardiovascular diseases. The risk of having a cardiovascular illness was nearly 50% greater for men with a BMI of 35 compared with men near the optimum BMI at 27. Similarly, extremely underweight men also had a much greater risk of cardiovascular disease. The pattern for gastrointestinal and respiratory diseases was slightly different: men with a BMI below 20 had a much greater risk of suffering these diseases than men at the optimum BMI of 27. The increased risk of gastrointestinal and respiratory disease was minimal for obese men, compared with men around the optimum weight. In contrast to the common U-shaped pattern, rheumatism and musculoskeletal diseases increased linearly with BMI. Although morbidity was related to BMI in the cross-section, Linares and Su found that weight change between medical examinations only affected the chance of gastrointestinal diseases. Men who had gained weight between examinations were significantly less likely to have contracted a gastrointestinal disease. It is critical to note the causality of this finding runs from the specific disease group to body mass. Gastrointestinal diseases are often associated with weight loss because of difficulty retaining food that has been consumed, rather than weight gain having a biologically protective effect against gastrointestinal disease. Conversely, although Linares and Su did not find strong evidence for it in their historical cohort, in modern studies there is *both* a statistical association and a causal physiological relationship between weight gain and cardiovascular disease (Rosengren *et al.*, 1999; Wannamethee *et al.*, 2005).

The small economic history literature on the relationship between BMI and specific morbidities comes exclusively from research using the Union Army data set. Thus, the results discussed earlier are not truly independent of each other. Unsurprisingly they point to similar results. However, the research using Union Army data is consistent with modern research. People at the extremes of the body mass distribution have a higher risk of contracting specific morbidities. The morbidity risks of being underweight were more common in historical populations. The issues of significant overweight and obesity were not unknown to historical populations, but less common than in contemporary cohorts. Limited data availability accounts for the dearth of historical research on the relationship between body mass and morbidity. Thus, opportunities for further research in this area are likely to be limited. Finding sources and assembling data from diverse historical records will remain the greatest challenge.

4.2.2 *Weight and Mortality*

The recognition that individuals at the extremes of the body mass distribution have a higher risk of mortality has been widely accepted in medical research and practice throughout the twentieth century. Moreover, it is established that the mortality risk of excess weight is specific to circulatory diseases, some cancers and diabetes. What is less clear is when in the life course excess weight is a particular risk. In the 1950s and 1960s when cardiovascular disease mortality in industrialized nations became an increasingly common cause of death, medical and epidemiological research emphasized excess weight in mid-adulthood as the most important risk factor. Since the 1970s, and particularly in the last two decades, medical and epidemiological research has paid increasing attention to other periods in the life course. Medical research has shown some mortality risk from excess weight in childhood (even if later BMI values are normal), and from fluctuations in adult weight that increase mortality risk even if an individual is in a normal BMI range much of the time (Kuh and Smith, 1993).

The inspiration for much of the economic history literature on the relationship between body composition and mortality was a large-scale Norwegian study (Waaler, 1984). Height and weight were measured between 1963 and 1975 as part of a tuberculosis-screening program, and deaths of the same individuals traced from 1963 to 1979. Waaler's research showed that the U-shaped relationship between body mass and mortality flattened as the age of initial measurement increased. All individuals measured at age 85 have a high risk of dying in the next 17 years, so the *relative* mortality risk for extremely slender or obese people is lower. Conversely, for individuals in their 20s and 30s the risk of mortality in the next 17 years is low, and people with extreme BMI values have a high relative risk of dying. With an extremely large sample, Waaler was able to show that the U-shaped relationship between mortality and body mass was also found after stratifying by height. Taller men with moderate BMI values had the lowest mortality risk. Again, taking advantage of the extremely large sample Waaler was able to show that the U-shaped relationship was strongest for particular diseases. Cerebrovascular (stroke) disease showed a strong U-shaped relationship with body mass, whereas cardiovascular diseases and diabetes had weaker U-shaped relationships. The excess mortality risk of being obese was greatest for stroke and diabetes.

Waaler's results have been supported by many subsequent studies. The most robust result is the substantial increase in mortality risk for obese (BMI $\geq$ 30) individuals in mid- and late adulthood (30–64). The relative risk of mortality for obese men has generally been found to be at least 50% greater than the mortality risk for men with a BMI between 20 and 25. For example, Calle *et al.* in a prospective study of more than a million United States residents over 14 years of follow-up found that 30–64 year old men with a BMI of 32–35 had an all-cause mortality risk 2.17 times higher than men whose BMI was between 23.5 and 25 (Calle *et al.*, 1999). Calle *et al.* found that smoking substantially modified the relationship between low BMI and mortality. Amongst non-smokers with no pre-existing major diseases, the relationship between BMI and mortality risk was J-shaped. Risk rose only slightly for very lean men (BMI below 20). A U-shaped relationship was found for smokers, both with and without a history of other diseases. Because of the significant smoking rates in industrialized countries from approximately World War I to the 1980s, the association between leanness and mortality is confounded by smoking behaviour (Pierce, 1989; Giskes *et al.*, 2005; Preston and Wang, 2006). In populations with very low smoking prevalence, such as Seventh Day Adventists who abstained from smoking for religious reasons, a positive linear relationship has been found between BMI and mortality risk (Lindsted *et al.*, 1991). Similar results have been found in other studies that controlled for smoking history in measuring the relationship between body mass and mortality (Lee *et al.*, 1993; Solomon and Manson, 1997; Singh *et al.*, 1999; Allison *et al.*, 2002). These studies typically showed that there was no adverse effect of a BMI as low as 19. The implications for historical anthropometric research are most profound in studying cohorts who were in adulthood during the twentieth century. The growing availability of anthropometric data from the two world wars in the twentieth century mean that increasing research will be done on these populations. It is unlikely that the available data sources for these historical populations will be able to control for smoking behaviour because what is typically available to researchers from military records are anthropometric measures in young adulthood, medical records from later in life and death records. For cohorts living mainly through the nineteenth century when smoking prevalence was much lower, the confounding effect of smoking on the BMI–mortality relationship is less of an issue.

A further issue raised by modern studies is when in the life course mortality risk is raised by excess weight. For example, a study by Hoffmans of Dutch men born in 1932, measured in 1950 for military service and followed for 32 years, found that the relative mortality risk of men overweight at 18 rose 'slightly' after 15 years, and 'steeply' after 20 years of follow-up (Hoffmans *et al.*, 1988, 1989). People can live with excess weight for several decades in childhood and early adulthood, but the risk rises over time. Because of the recent development of research interest in the links between childhood through early adult BMI and health in later life, many studies do not yet have enough deaths to test for a relationship between BMI and mortality. Thus, alternative endpoints such as the development of particular diseases are chosen. For example, there is no relationship between excess BMI in early childhood (3–6 years) and coronary heart disease in later life. However, BMI in later childhood (7–18 years) and early adulthood (18–30) was positively related to later development of coronary heart disease (Owen *et al.*, 2009).

A frequent finding in the epidemiological literature is that the relative mortality risk of being obese diminishes in the very elderly. In an older sample everyone has a high risk of dying, so the relative risk of being obese falls (Corrada, Kawas *et al.*, 2006). However, the difference in mortality rates between the obese and the lean may widen in older samples. For example, Stevens found that over 11 years of follow-up 1.5% of men aged 30–39 with a BMI between 18.5 and 25 died, compared to 3.6% of obese men. Among men aged 60–69, the mortality rates were 25.3% and 31.9%, respectively (Stevens, 2000). A related question to the mortality differences between groups is a comparison of the years of life lost in different BMI categories. Stevens found that on average the years of life lost for the obese was less than a year more than in the normal weight category. Although obesity carries health risks and raises relative mortality, the years of life lost due to obesity may be relatively modest. Recent work by Mehta and Chang advances this argument further (Mehta and Chang, 2009). Using data from the United States Health and Retirement Study, which studied individuals born between 1931 and 1941 from 1992 to 2004, they found the mortality risk of obesity only rose significantly for BMI levels above 35. People with a BMI between 30 and 34 – who have been found to have a significantly higher relative risk of mortality in many previous studies – had a mortality risk similar to people in the normal weight and overweight categories. Mehta and Chang attributed just 3% of observed male mortality to obesity, compared to 50% attributable to smoking. However, Mehta and Chang's conclusions are challenged by other recent research that forecast the life expectancy costs of obesity in the United States to rise (Stewart *et al.*, 2009).

The limited number of historical studies of the relationship between weight, or BMI, and mortality confirm the findings of modern research that extreme body mass values have a greater mortality risk. Historical research shows that mortality risk for men in their fifties and sixties is lowest at a BMI between 20 and 27. World Health Organisation guidelines for healthy weight currently define BMI values of 18.5–25 as a healthy weight (World Health Organization, 1999). However there is emerging evidence from large-scale epidemiological research that the increased mortality risk of having a BMI between 25 and 30 – categorized as overweight by WHO and other public health agencies – may be diminishing (McGee and Diverse Population Collaboration, 2005). The development of medical devices and pharmaceuticals to treat cardiovascular and related conditions may have reduced the cost of being slightly overweight. The mortality risks of obesity (BMI between 30 and 35) and severe obesity (BMI over 35) remain high. The proportion of the population classified as overweight or obese has been growing in most countries since the 1970s. The mortality risks of being obese do not appear to have changed substantially in the past century, but the population at risk has increased substantially. However, there is evidence that the risks of being moderately overweight have decreased through the twentieth century.

The only historical studies of the relationship between weight and mortality for cohorts born in the nineteenth century come from the United States. With the exception of John Murray's 1997 article on Amherst College students, the Union Army data provide the sole source of evidence on this topic (Fogel, 1993; Murray, 1997). Historical research on the relationship between weight and mortality has explicitly aimed to produce results comparable with modern studies. From the first article measuring the BMI-mortality relationship in an historical population, researchers have aimed to make comparisons with the contemporary literature (Costa, 1993). Comparisons with Waaler's pioneering 1984 study of Norwegian men have been particularly important in the historical literature (Waaler, 1984).

Costa and subsequent authors have drawn on data sets created of men who served in the Union Army during the American Civil War, and were born in the first half of the nineteenth century, when mean stature of American men was declining – a phenomenon known as the antebellum puzzle (Haines *et al.*, 2003). Using an early version of the Union Army data set Costa was able to study the relationship between BMI and mortality for 377 men who were weighed between the ages of 45 and 49 as part of pension exams (Costa, 1993). Compared to modern populations, the Union Army veterans were light, with an average BMI of 22.8 compared to a BMI of 25 among the Norwegian men measured in Waaler's research (Waaler, 1984). Over a 25-year follow-up period the risk of mortality was lowest for men with a BMI between 21 and 28. With a small sample Costa was not able to examine the risk of BMI for specific causes of death, but found that the relationship between weight and mortality was the same when men described as "very sick" were not included in the estimation. Costa concluded that the shape of the BMI–mortality relationship was the same in historical and modern populations, and that the location was similar with BMI risk lowest between 21 and 28. Using the same sample Costa also found that reduced stature was associated with higher mortality. With both stature and BMI rising in modern populations, the question is which effect dominates? Over the past century in the United States, at a population level the effects of increases in stature, reflecting better net-nutrition in childhood, have dominated the effects of increased BMI (Fogel and Costa, 1997).

Subsequent research with an expanded Union Army data set has modified, but not overturned Costa's conclusions. The U-shaped relationship between weight and mortality remains, but the slope of the curve has changed. Costa began with a sample of 1447 men, and the analysis of BMI and mortality risk included just 322 men. Recent research with the Union Army data has used samples of up to 10,000 men depending on sample restrictions, and compared the results to modern health surveys. For example, Henderson was able to use a sample of 9509 Union Army veterans examined after 1865 (Henderson, 2005). Henderson compared the Union Army cohorts born before 1845 with men in the first wave of the National Health and Nutrition Examination Surveys (NHANES I) carried out between 1971 and 1975. Henderson also found that the relationship between BMI and mortality was U-shaped and reached a minimum for men with a BMI between 20 and 30 in both cohorts. With greater sample size, Henderson was able to make finer conclusions on changes in the shape and location of the BMI-mortality curve. Henderson found that the relative mortality risk of extreme BMI values – both underweight and obese – was smaller in the nineteenth century. The overall BMI-mortality curve was flatter for the Union Army cohort. In the Union Army cohorts men with a BMI of 30–35 were approximately 26% more likely to die within 20 years of examination. In the NHANES I samples, men in the same BMI range were 49–60% more likely to die within 20 years of examination. Similarly, the mortality risk of having a BMI under 20 was greater in the twentieth century cohorts. Yet Henderson also found that moderately overweight men with a BMI of between 25 and 30 had reduced mortality risk in the twentieth century. Henderson concludes that twentieth century cohorts had higher fat-free mass for the same BMI – equivalent to a lower body fat percentage – increasing the chances of survival at BMI values in the normal and moderately overweight range (20–30).

Other authors have confirmed Henderson's conclusion that fat-free mass at a given BMI has increased since the nineteenth century (Costa, 2004; Su, 2005). Su compared a sample of 1238 men from the Union Army data set followed up over 18 years, with a sample of 861 from the NHANES follow-up sample. The incidence of obesity increased from 2.5% amongst the Union Army cohorts in 1890 to 28% in the NHANES sample measured in the early 1970s. Su found that in the Union Army cohorts underweight men had the greatest risk of death over 18 years, compared to men who were overweight. The difference was greatest in the first 9 years after follow-up – with a 20% difference in survival rates between underweight men and their heavier peers. But after 18 years the survival gap between BMI categories had narrowed significantly to just 12%. More of the underweight men died soon after their initial examination because some were already suffering from gastrointestinal diseases. While the same order of mortality risks was found in the NHANES cohorts, the mortality risks diverged over time. In the first 9 years the gap between the BMI categories was no more than 10%, but grew to 29% at 18 years. Just 40% of men who were underweight at initial examination in the NHANES survived 18 years, compared with 69% of overweight men. The optimal BMI for survival increased from a range of 20.6–23.6 in the Union Army cohorts to 22.7–27.3 in the NHANES cohorts. However, in both groups the optimal BMI for survival was in the middle of the distribution, the BMI–mortality relationship was again U-shaped. Using a larger sample with different age restriction, Linares and Su also examined survival rates over 20 years (Linares and Su, 2005). They also found a U-shaped relationship between body mass and mortality. Similarly to Henderson, they categorized body mass into the modern BMI categories of underweight (<20), normal weight (20–25), overweight (25–30) and obese (30+). Mortality was minimized with a normal BMI between 20 and 25, paralleling the results that Henderson obtained with the same data set. BMI was less strongly associated with deaths more than 9 years after measurement, emphasizing that current weight is most predictive of mortality.

The results obtained in the Union Army data sets are broadly paralleled by findings on Amherst College students (Murray, 1997). Men who were extremely thin or fat had a significantly elevated mortality risk, compared to men with a normal weight. Because the men were weighed at college in their early 20s, Murray's research examined the effect of early-adult body composition on survival to age 70. Even after controlling for height, men with a BMI below 18 were one-third more likely to die before age 70 than men of normal weight or moderate underweight (a BMI between 18 and 20). Men who were overweight (BMI > 25) were 45% more likely to die before age 70 than normal or moderately underweight men. Like the authors using the Union Army data set, Murray concluded that the BMI–mortality relationship was not significantly different in historical populations than contemporary ones.

A final piece of historical evidence on the weight–mortality relationship comes from a study of Scottish university students born in the 1920s, and followed until 2002 (Jeffreys *et al.*, 2003). The men, who were students at Glasgow University in 1948, were weighed in-person in 1948 and reported their weight in a postal questionnaire in the mid-1960s. Although the two weight measures were not collected in the same way, the independent timing of the two weight measures distinguishes this research from the Union Army research, where men who visited the doctor more frequently were weighed more frequently. Unlike the Union Army based research Jeffreys *et al.* found that weight in early adulthood was more strongly predictive of later-life mortality than mid-adult weight. Weight was most strongly predictive of cardiovascular disease mortality, and only moderately predictive of cancer mortality. Weight gain between early and mid-adulthood was not predictive of mortality. The failure to find an association between weight gain and mortality is inconsistent with the majority of the epidemiological evidence, and is likely to be due to mid-adult weight being self-reported.

4.3 *Weight and Height Together*

Following the literature we have, to this point, discussed separately the relationships among health, height and weight. Yet by definition any research that uses the BMI has information on stature. It follows that the relationship between height and mortality, and between body mass and mortality, are interdependent. Treating the relationships independently implies that the BMI–mortality relationship is stable across the height distribution, This assumption should be tested (Fogel, 2009). Put slightly differently, we need to investigate if each increment of height may require different increments of weight to maintain constant health.

Empirically, a key issue is whether people who are short but adequately nourished – as measured by BMI – are at a higher risk of death. People living through periods of rapid economic change – such as in contemporary developing countries, or now developed countries in the late nineteenth and early twentieth centuries – may be poorly nourished in childhood and thus short, but well nourished in adulthood and thus have a BMI in the healthy range. In a longitudinal perspective, the question is whether early life deprivation reflected in short stature could be compensated for by adequate nutrition later on (Fogel, 1994; Fogel and Costa, 1997).

Specifying mortality risk as a function of height, weight (and other control variables) is straightforward. Depicting the relationship for constant values of other controls requires an iso-mortality surface to be displayed graphically in two dimensions. Despite the straightforward nature of the iso-mortality curve, most research still depicts BMI–mortality curves (Henderson, 2005; Linares and Su, 2005; Su, 2005). A good example of the iso-mortality surface comes from Robert Fogel's 2004 book *The Escape from Hunger and Premature Death* (Fogel, 2004). The iso-mortality curves are formed in height–weight space (Figure 1), and are estimated from Waaler's 1984 data. The solid elliptical curves depict those combinations of height and weight (and thus BMI) that give a constant mortality risk. The dashed lines are lines of constant BMI (height/weight^2). Connecting the minima of each [solid] ellipse shows what weight minimizes risk at each height. Note that at the bottom, the line connecting the minima of each iso-mortality curves is to the right of the line depicting BMI $=$ 25, and then shifts across the line of BMI $=$ 25. Two important conclusions follow from this. First, even at the same healthy BMI short men are at a higher risk of death than tall men. Secondly, the BMI that minimizes mortality risk is not constant over height. For shorter men (175 cm), it is better to a little heavier, with a BMI of around 26. But for tall men it is better to be thin, with an ideal BMI of 22 for a man of 190 cm or taller.

This framework provides a way of recognizing that the relationship between body composition and health need not be an historical constant. Determining how the relationship has changed across time, and what the costs and benefits of that change have been is an appropriate task for economic historians. It is particularly important for future research to address more explicitly the question of how the relationship has changed across cohorts, similar to the research of Flegal and Gregg (Gregg *et al.*, 2005; Flegal *et al.*, 2007). Higher BMI values are strongly associated with increases in adiposity or fatness, placing greater strain on the circulatory system. Consequently, higher BMI values are most strongly associated with mortality from cardiovascular diseases. Although there is some modern evidence of an association between increased BMI and some forms of cancer, the historical evidence for this is very weak.

Historical research by economists has also demonstrated the mortality risks of being significantly underweight, a concern somewhat foreign to western populations in the past three decades. However, the aetiology of mortality risk for underweight and overweight individuals is somewhat different. A very low BMI is associated with higher mortality risk, but underweight itself is not really the cause of death. Morbidities such as gastrointestinal diseases or cancer cause the individual to have problems with eating or retaining nutrients, and the individual loses weight. Underweight is a symptom of the illness. Conversely being overweight is a cause of cardiovascular problems, and leads indirectly to mortality. Overweight is a cause of both the illness and mortality. Historical research has confirmed the findings of modern research that the extremes of the BMI distribution can have higher mortality risk. But in both the nineteenth century (gastrointestinal) and the twentieth century (smoking), the association of leanness with mortality is not likely to be causal.

Iso-Mortality Curves of Relative Risk of Dying for Height and Weight among Norwegian Males Aged 50–64, with Two Plots

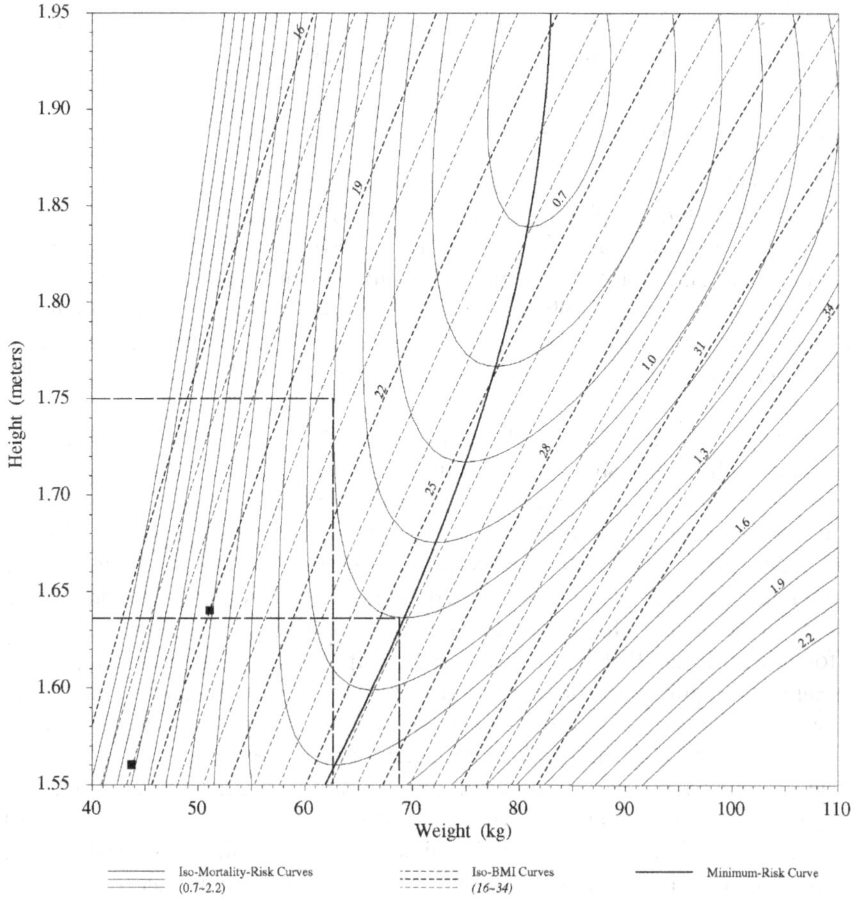

Note: The small dark squares show the effect of a 5 percent reduction in height and weight on the risk of dying. The large rectangles show the increase in weight required to offset the increased risk of dying due to long-term reductions in stature.

Figure 1. Reproduced with Permission from Fogel, R.W. (2004) *The Escape from Hunger and Premature Death, 1700–2100* (p. 64). Cambridge: Cambridge University Press.

Cliometric research has complemented the modern epidemiological literature by showing that the mortality and morbidity risk of overweight and obesity has changed over time. At least within the United States for which there is evidence across more than a century, the mortality risk of being moderately overweight appears to have dropped in the past 40 years. Precisely because the literature has shown these results to vary over time within one country with technological and behavioural change, we should not expect that the mortality risk and costs of being overweight would be the same elsewhere. Documenting changes over a century or more in the BMI–mortality and height–mortality relationship in other countries is an important area of research for economic historians.

5. Discussion and Conclusion

Historical anthropometric research continues to expand and, increasingly, to develop an explicit longitudinal dimension. Our survey of recent work in this area, most of which are longitudinal studies of human growth and health, spans the social and health sciences (principally history, economics and epidemiology). Research in this area, as Steckel (1998) observes, benefits greatly from communication across the disciplines. Health scientists increasingly exploit historical sources while social science historians are influenced by the advance of knowledge in the health sciences.

Economic historians are making a particularly important contribution of documenting how the shape of BMI–mortality relationship has changed across cohorts, periods and countries. This is a useful corrective to the presumption in some medical (not epidemiological) literature of a stable or universal biological relationship. The nineteenth century attracts particular interest in part because professional medical care was limited, infectious disease was common and patterns of economic change were very different than those before or after. The confounding of the BMI–mortality relationship by smoking was less prevalent although admittedly alcohol consumption was greater in the nineteenth than in the twentieth century. Of course, nineteenth century results will not be any more universal than those arising from more recent experience.

The economic historical approach also makes a significant contribution to the preservation and re-analysis of early medical and health studies and to the construction of longitudinal data by linking administrative sources of health information to population censuses and registers. The importance of the Union Army data sets is apparent at several points in the above survey. While this research will continue to be influential, the economic and social environment of the United States differed from that of other countries. If the relative price of food differed significantly in the United States from that elsewhere, for example, we would expect different patterns of food consumption to influence trends in BMI and health.

Historical sources are often complex in different ways than modern survey data because the former were not collected in a fully controlled way and for the most part were not collected in order to support scientific research. Of course both classes of data are sensitive to the challenges of attaining sample size for robust estimation and the need to consider selection into the sample and out of the sample through mortality, migration, etc. Many, but not all, modern surveys rely on a self-reporting of body measurements that may involve some misrepresentation of height, weight, and by derivation BMI (Gorber *et al.*, 2007). Until the age of 50 contemporary American men tend to overstate their height by about a centimetre, whereas women are relatively accurate. Individuals over 50 years old may misrepresent stature because they are beginning to shrink. Men slightly overstate their own weight, whereas women generally understate their weight until their late 70s (Thomas and Frankenberg, 2002).

The prison and military records used by economic historians generally rely on measurement by independent observers. Although the problem of self-reporting is less pressing in these historical sources, other challenges may present themselves. For example it is important to know if historical heights and weights were recorded with shoes and heavy clothing removed (men's shoes or boots can easily add 2–3 cm to measured heights, and a kilogram to weight). The precision of measurement unit may also be important. Heights recorded to the quarter-inch (0.6 cm) signal attentiveness to proper measurement. Heights recorded only to the whole inch are less desirable, as the historian has no way of knowing whether measurements were rounded up or down. Rounding increases imprecision; fortunately it need not bias the mean. A bigger concern might be inconsistency in methods of measurement across data sources, and across time within the same source (Shlomowitz, 2007). Age heaping is a common problem in historical sources although its significance for inference is likely to be limited to analysis of specific events in particular years; analysis of trends over 5- or 10-year birth cohorts is largely unaffected.

The precise dating of exposure to environmental or economic shocks is important for an emerging area of anthropometric research that examines the effects of conditions in utero (Lumey and Van Poppel, 1994; Lumey, 1998; Almond, 2006; Mazumder *et al.*, 2009; Song, 2009; Nelson, forthcoming). Epidemiological research shows that there are critical periods in human growth, from birth to 3 years of age and in adolescence (Bogin, 1999b; Gillman, 2004). An adverse shock during a critical period may have persisting consequences. Recent research in labour economics has shown that there are persistent effects for young adults who enter the labour market during a recession. A parallel question for anthropometric research is if the Great Depression, for example, had differential impacts on people who entered it during early or late childhood. Longitudinal studies in anthropometric history exploit these insights to measure *when* and how environmental and economic shocks matter.

Social surveys, censuses, the registration of demographic events and routine government data collection for social and health services since the 1850s have created a rich potential for further longitudinal anthropometric research on populations in many countries. The creation of longitudinal samples from diverse sources is a significant task, as Ferrie *et al*'s early life indicator project makes clear, but the payoff from well-designed studies is high (Ferrie *et al.*, 2009). It will be especially valuable to assess with evidence elsewhere the generalizability of the relationship between body composition and health already demonstrated for the United States from Union Army records.

The potential for construction of longitudinal samples even extends to intergenerational data. Data that span generations in turn raises the question of the interaction between genes and the environment (North and Martin, 2008; Conley, 2009). Many historical sources offer limited information with which to infer genetic background. Own and parental birthplace, and indicators of ethnicity are variables that were collected historically, and could proxy for genetic influences. The systematic compilation of family genealogies and samples that include siblings might be used to separate genetic and environmental influences. For example, research by John Parman uses a data set of brothers who served in World War II to examine the influence of height on educational attainment (Parman, 2009). Assembling this kind of data from historical records is possible in other countries and contexts. Data collection is likely to be even more involved than for other historical longitudinal research, as links must be made not only between one individual over time, but a sibling relationship must be identified. The use of sibling data sets may also permit some insights into questions of intra-household resource allocation.

Incorporating genetic influences into anthropometric studies, and using longitudinal-based anthropometric evidence in genetic studies, is likely to be more straightforward for studies of stature than weight. At an individual level, genetic inheritance influences stature more than than weight. Incorporating genetic influences will not solve all of the inferential challenges in anthropometric research. Without information on individual childhood conditions, stature will remain a reduced form for nutritional standards over the growth period. Inferential challenges remain for the study of weight or body mass and health, both morbidity and mortality. For example, evidence of a connection between body mass at time t and mortality by time $t + x$ may be powerless to explain what happens in the intervening x years. Two underlying relationships are possible. First, adult body mass at time t may be predictive of mortality by $t + x$ because strain is being placed on the circulatory system at time t. In this case body mass at time t has a causal relationship with mortality. Secondly, body mass at time t might have no independent effect on mortality, but be statistically predictive of body mass later in the interval $(t, t + x)$ that does have a physiological impact on mortality. Interpretation of historical results can be guided by cautious extrapolation from the current medical and epidemiological literature. Establishing a causal relationship between body composition and mortality in historical studies is a continuing challenge.

This chapter has surveyed the broad contribution of anthropometric history to understanding historical trends in living standards and the growing importance of historical longitudinal data to the interdisciplinary literature about human health. The extent and richness of both anthropometric and longitudinal research have expanded quickly during the past two decades, especially in economic history. Research opportunities continue to increase. We are in the early stages of a trajectory that will continue to contribute in unique and important ways to knowledge in history, economics and the social and health sciences.

Acknowledgements

We gratefully acknowledge helpful comments received from Richard Steckel, Bertie Lumey and the editor and referees of the original journal and financial support from the Royal Society of New Zealand, the Health Research Council of New Zealand, the Social Sciences and Humanities Research Council of Canada and our two universities.

References

Allison, D.B., Zhu, S.K., Plankey, M., Faith, M.S. and Heo, M. (2002) Differential associations of body mass index and adiposity with all-cause mortality among men in the first and second National Health and Nutrition Examination Surveys (NHANES I and NHANES II) follow-up studies. *International Journal of Obesity and Related Metabolic Disorders: Journal of the International Association for the Study of Obesity* 26: 410–416.

Almond, D. (2006) Is the 1918 influenza pandemic over? Long-term effects of in utero influenza exposure in the post-1940 U.S. population. *Journal of Political Economy* 114: 672–712.

Alter, G., Neven, M. and Oris, M. (2004) Stature in Transition: A Micro-Level Study from Nineteenth-Century Belgium. *Social Science History* 28: 231–248.

Aronson, N. (1982) Nutrition as a social problem: a case study of entrepreneurial strategy in science. *Social Problems* 29: 474–487.

Barker, D.J.P. (1992) *Fetal and Infant Origins of Adult Disease : Papers*. London: British Medical Journal.

Barker, D.J.P. (1998) *Mothers, Babies, and Health in Later Life*. London: Churchill Livingstone.

Barker, D.J.P. (2004) The developmental origins of adult disease. *Journal of the American College of Nutrition* 23: 588S–595S.

Baten, J. and Murray, J. (2000) Heights of men and women in nineteenth-century Bavaria: economic, nutritional, and disease influences. *Explorations in Economic History* 37: 351–361.

Batty, G.D., Lawlor, D.A., Macintyre, S., Clark, H. and Leon, D.A. (2005) Accuracy of adults' recall of childhood social class: findings from the Aberdeen children of the 1950s study. *Journal of Epidemiology and Community Health* 59: 898–903.

Batty, G.D., Shipley, M.J., Gunnell, D., Huxley, R., Kivimaki, M., Woodward, M., Lee, C.M.Y. and Smith, G.D. (2009) Height, wealth, and health: an overview with new data from three longitudinal studies. *Economics and Human Biology* 7: 137–152.

Batty, G.D., Shipley, M.J., Langenberg, C., Marmot, M.G. and Davey Smith, G. (2006) Adult height in relation to mortality from 14 cancer sites in men in London (UK): evidence from the original Whitehall study. *Annals of Oncology* 17: 157–166.

Ben-Shlomo, Y. and Kuh, D. (2004) Conclusions. In D. Kuh and Y. Ben-Shlomo (eds), *A Life Course Approach to Chronic Disease Epidemiology* (pp. 446–464). Oxford: Oxford University Press.

Berney, L.R. and Blane, D.B. (1997) Collecting retrospective data: accuracy of recall after 50 years judged against historical records. *Social Science and Medicine* 45: 1519–1525.

Blane, D., Berney, L., Smith, G.D., Gunnell, D.J. and Holland, P. (1999) Reconstructing the life course: health during early old age in a follow-up study based on the Boyd Orr cohort. *Public Health* 113: 117–124.

Bogin, B. (1999a) Evolutionary perspective on human growth. *Annual Review of Anthropology* 28: 109–153.

Bogin, B. (1999b) *Patterns of Human Growth*. Cambridge: Cambridge University Press.

Bowditch, H.P. (1877) *The Growth of Children*. Boston: Massachusetts State Board of Health.

Brennan, L., Macdonald, J. and Shlomowitz, R. (1994) A long run decline in final adult female height in India. *Man in India* 84: 9–13.

Calle, E.E., Thun, M.J., Petrelli, J.M., Rodriguez, C. and Heath, C.W. (1999) Body-mass index and mortality in a prospective cohort of U.S. adults. *New England Journal of Medicine* 341: 1097–1105.

Coelho, P. and McGuire, R. (2000) Diets versus diseases: the anthropometrics of slave children. *The Journal of Economic History* 60: 232–246.

Conley, D. (2009) The promise and challenges of incorporating genetic data into longitudinal social science surveys and research. *Biodemography and Social Biology* 55: 238–251.

Corrada, M., Kawas, C., Mozaffar, F. and Paganini-Hill, A. (2006) Association of body mass index and weight change with all-cause mortality in the elderly. *American Journal of Epidemiology* 163: 938–949.

Costa, D. (1993) Height, weight, wartime stress, and older age mortality: evidence from the Union Army records. *Explorations in Economic History* 30: 424–449.

Costa, D. (2004) The measure of man and older age mortality: evidence from the Gould Sample. *The Journal of Economic History* 64: 1–23.

Costa, D.L. (1996) Health and labor force participation of older men, 1900–1991. *Journal of Economic History* 56: 62–89.

Coughlin, S.S. (1990) Recall bias in epidemiologic studies. *Journal of Clinical Epidemiology* 43: 87–91.

Craig, L., Goodwin, B. and Grennes, T. (2004) The effect of mechanical refrigeration on nutrition in the United States. *Social Science History* 28: 325–336.

Cranfield, J. and Inwood, K. (2007) The great transformation: a long-run perspective on physical well-being in Canada. *Economics and Human Biology* 5: 204–228.

Cutler, D.M., Glaeser, E.L. and Shapiro, J.M. (2003) Why have Americans become more obese? *Journal of Economic Perspectives* 17: 93–118.

Czerniawski, A.M. (2007) From average to ideal: the evolution of the height and weight table in the United States, 1836–1943. *Social Science History* 31: 273–296.

Davey Smith, G., Hart, C., Upton, M., Hole, D., Gillis, C., Watt, G. and Hawthorne, V.. (2000) Height and risk of death among men and women: aetiological implications of associations with cardiorespiratory disease and cancer mortality. *Journal of Epidemiology & Community Health* 54: 97–103.

Davey Smith, G. and Lynch, J.W. (2004) Life course approaches to socioeconomic differentials in health. In D. Kuh and Y. Ben-Shlomo (eds), *A Life Course Approach to Chronic Disease Epidemiology* (pp. 77–96). Oxford: Oxford University Press.

Davey Smith, G., Sterne, J.A.C., Fraser, A., Tynelius, P., Lawlor, D.A. and Rasmussen, F. (2009) The association between BMI and mortality using offspring BMI as an indicator of own BMI: large intergenerational mortality study. *BMJ* 339: b5043.

Deaton, A. (2008) Height, health, and inequality: the distribution of adult heights in India. *American Economic Review* 98: 468–474.

Elford, J. and Ben-Shlomo, Y. (2004) Geography and migration with special reference to cardiovascular disease. In D. Kuh and Y. Ben-Shlomo (eds), *A Life Course Approach to Chronic Disease Epidemiology* (pp. 144–164). Oxford: Oxford University Press.

Engeland, A., Bjorge, T., Selmer, R.M., Tverdal, A., Engeland, A., Bjorge, T., Selmer, R.M. and Tverdal, A. (2003) Height and body mass index in relation to total mortality. *Epidemiology* 14: 293–299.

Engerman, S. (1976) The height of slaves in the United States. *Local Population Studies* 16: 45–49.

Engerman, S. (2004) Personal reflections on the 1982 special anthropometric issue of social science history. *Social Science History* 28: 345–349.

Eveleth, P.B. (1975) Differences between ethnic groups in the degree of dimorphism. *Annals of Human Biology* 2: 35–39.

Eveleth, P.B. and Tanner, J.M. (1990) *Worldwide Variation in Human Growth*. Cambridge: Cambridge University Press.

Faulkner, F.T. and Tanner, J.M. (1986) *Human Growth: A Comprehensive Treatise*. New York: Plexum Press.

Felson, D.T. (1996) Weight and osteoarthritis. *American Journal of Clinical Nutrition* 63: 430S–432S.

Ferraro, K.F., Su, Y., Gretebeck, R.J., Black, D.R. and Badylak, S.F. (2002) Body mass index and disability in adulthood: a 20-year panel study. *American Journal of Public Health* 92: 834–840.

Ferrie, J., Rolf, K. and Troesken, W. (2009) '. . . Healthy, Wealthy, and Wise? Physical, Economic and Cognitive Effects of Early Life Conditions on Later Life Outcomes in the U.S., 1915–2005.' Long-run Impact of Early Life Events II Workshop, National Poverty Center, University of Michigan, March 2009.

Ferrie, J.P. (1999) *Yankeys Now: Immigrants in the Antebellum United States*. New York: Oxford University Press.

Flegal, K.M., Graubard, B.I., Williamson, D.F. and Gail, M.H. (2007) Cause-specific excess deaths associated with underweight, overweight, and obesity. *JAMA* 298: 2028–2037.

Fleurbaey, M. (2009) Beyond GDP: the quest for a measure of social welfare. *Journal of Economic Literature* 47: 1029–1075.

Floud, R. (1998) Height, Weight, and Body Mass of the British Population Since 1820. NBER Historical Working Paper 108. Cambridge: National Bureau of Economic Research.

Floud, R., Wachter, K. and Gregory, A. (1990) *Height, Health and History: Nutritional Status in the United Kingdom, 1750–1980*. Cambridge: Cambridge University Press.

Fogel, R. (1994) Economic growth, population theory, and physiology: The bearing of long-term processes on the making of economic policy. *The American Economic Review* 84: 369–395.

Fogel, R.W. (1993) New sources and new techniques for the study of secular trends in nutritional status, health, mortality and the process of aging. *Historical Methods* 26: 5–43.

Fogel, R.W. (2004) *The Escape from Hunger and Premature Death, 1700–2100*. Cambridge: Cambridge University Press.

Fogel, R.W. (2009) *Some Common Analytical Errors in Explanations for the Secular Improvement in Health and Longevity*. Chicago: Center for Population Economics, University of Chicago.

Fogel, R.W. and Costa, D.L. (1997) A theory of technophysio evolution, with some implications for forecasting population, health care costs, and pension costs. *Demography* 34: 49–66.

Fogel, R.W., Engerman, S.L. and Trussell, J. (1982) Exploring the uses of data on height: the analysis of long-term trends in nutrition, labor welfare, and labor productivity. *Social Science History* 6: 401–421.

Forouhi, N., Hall, E. and McKeigue, P. (2004) Life course approaches to diabetes. In D. Kuh and Y. Ben-Shlomo (eds), *A Life Course Approach to Chronic Disease Epidemiology* (pp. 165–187). Oxford: Oxford University Press.

Frayer, D.W. and Wolpoff, M.H. (1985) Sexual dimorphism. *Annual Review of Anthropology* 14: 429–473.

Friedenreich, C.M. (1994) Improving long-term recall in epidemiologic studies. *Epidemiology* 5: 1–4.

Frijters, P., Hatton, T.J., Martin, R.M. and Shields, M.A. (2010) Childhood economic conditions and length of life:, evidence from the UK Boyd Orr Cohort, 1937–2005. *Journal of Health Economics* 29: 39–47.

Gallman, R. (1996) Dietary change in antebellum America. *The Journal of Economic History* 56: 193–201.

Gaulin, S. and Boster, J. (1985) Cross-cultural differences in sexual dimorphism: is there any variance to be explained? *Ethology and Sociobiology* 6: 219–225.

Gillman, M.W. (2004) A life course approach to obesity. In D. Kuh and Y. Ben-Shlomo (eds), *A Life Course Approach to Chronic Disease Epidemiology* (pp. 189–217). Oxford: Oxford University Press.

Giskes, K., Kunst, A., Benach, J., Borrell, C., Costa, G., Dahl, E., Dalstra, J., Federico, B., Helmert, U. and Judge, K. (2005) Trends in smoking behaviour between 1985 and 2000 in nine European countries by education. *Journal of Epidemiology and Community Health* 59: 395–401.

Goeken, R. (2011) New methods of census record linking. *Historical Methods* 44, forthcoming.

Gorber, S.C., Tremblay, M., Moher, D. and Gorber, B. (2007) A comparison of direct vs. self-report measures for assessing height, weight and body mass index: a systematic review. *Obesity Reviews* 8: 307–326.

Gorsky, M., Harris, B. and Hinde, A. (2006) Age, sickness, and longevity in the Late Nineteenth and the early twentieth centuries: evidence from the Hampshire friendly society. *Social Science History* 30: 571–600.

Gray, J.P. and Wolfe, L.D. (1980) Height and sexual dimorphism of stature among human societies. *American Journal of Physical Anthropology* 53: 441–456.

Gregg, E.W., Cheng, Y.J., Cadwell, B.L., Imperatore, G., Williams, D.E., Flegal, K.M., Narayan, K.M.V. and Williamson, D.F. (2005) Secular trends in cardiovascular disease risk factors according to body mass index in US adults. *JAMA* 293: 1868–1874.

Gustafsson, A. and Lindenfors, P. (2004) Human size evolution: no evolutionary allometric relationship between male and female stature. *Journal of Human Evolution* 47: 253–266.

Gustafsson, A., Werdelin, L., Tullberg, B. and Lindenfors, P. (2007) Stature and sexual stature dimorphism in Sweden, from the 10th to the end of the 20th century. *American Journal of Human Biology* 19: 861–870.

Haas, S.A. (2007) The long-term effects of poor childhood health: an assessment and application of retrospective reports. *Demography* 44: 113–135.

Haines, M.R. (2001) The urban mortality transition in the United States, 1800–1940. *Annales de démographie historique*: 33–64.

Haines, M.R. (2004) Growing incomes, shrinking people – can economic development be hazardous to your health? Historical evidence for the United States, England, and the Netherlands in the nineteenth century. *Social Science History* 28: 249–270.

Haines, M.R., Craig, L.A. and Weiss, T. (2003) The short and the dead: nutrition, mortality, and the "Antebellum Puzzle" in the United States. *Journal of Economic History* 63: 382–413.

Hardy, J.B. (2003) The collaborative perinatal project: lessons and legacy. *Annals of Epidemiology* 13: 503–511.

Harris, B. (1995). "The health of the schoolchild: a history of the school medical service in England and Wales."

Harris, B. (2009) Gender, health and welfare in England since industrialization. *Research in Economic History* 26: 157–204.

Hart, C.L., Taylor, M.D., Smith, G.D., Whalley, L.J., Starr, J.M., Hole, D.J., Wilson, V. and Deary, I.J. (2004) Childhood IQ and cardiovascular disease in adulthood: prospective observational study linking the Scottish Mental Survey 1932 and the Midspan studies. *Social Science and Medicine* 59: 2131–2138.

Hatton, T.J. and Martin, R.M. (2010) The effects on stature of poverty, family size, and birth order: British children in the 1930s. *Oxford Economic Papers* 62: 157–184.

Heltberg, R. (2009) Malnutrition, poverty, and economic growth. *Health Economics* 18: S77–S88.

Henderson, R.M. (2005) The bigger the healthier: are the limits of BMI risk changing over time? *Economics and Human Biology* 3: 339–366.

Himes, J.H. (2006) Long-term longitudinal studies and implications for the development of an international growth reference for children and adolescents. *Food and Nutrition Bulletin* 27: S199–S211.

Hoffmans, M.D.A.F., Kromhout, D. and De Lezenne Coulander, C. (1988) The impact of body mass index of 78,612 18-year-old men on 32-year mortality from all causes. *Journal of Clinical Epidemiology* 41: 749–756.

Hoffmans, M., Kromhout, D. and Coulander, C. (1989) Body Mass Index at the age of 18 and its effects on 32-year-mortality from coronary heart disease and cancer. A nested case-control study among the entire 1932 Dutch male birth cohort. *Journal of Clinical Epidemiology* 42: 513–520.

Holden, C. and Mace, R. (1999) Sexual dimorphism in stature and women's work: a phylogenetic cross-cultural analysis. *American Journal of Physical Anthropology* 110: 27–45.

Holland, P., Berney, L., Blane, D., Davey Smith, G., Gunnell, D.J. and Montgomery, S.M. (2000) Life course accumulation of disadvantage: childhood health and hazard exposure during adulthood. *Social Science and Medicine* 50: 1285–1295.

Horrell, S., Meredith, D. and Oxley, D. (2007) Anthropometric measures of living standards and gender inequality in nineteenth century Britain. *Local Population Studies* 79: 66–74.

Horrell, S., Meredith, D. and Oxley, D. (2009) Measuring misery: body mass, ageing and gender inequality in Victorian London. *Explorations in Economic History* 46: 93–119.

Inwood, K., Oxley, L. and Roberts, E. (2009). Rather above than under the common size? Stature and living standards in New Zealand. *World Economic History Congress*. Utrecht.

Inwood, K., Oxley, L. and Roberts, E. (2010) Physical stature in nineteenth century New Zealand—a preliminary interpretation. *Australian Economic History Review* 50, 262–283.

Jeffreys, M., McCarron, P., Gunnell, D., McEwen, J. and Davey Smith, G. (2003) Body mass index in early and mid-adulthood, and subsequent mortality: a historical cohort study. *International Journal of Obesity* 27: 1391–1397.

Jia, H. and Lubetkin, E. (2005) The impact of obesity on health-related quality-of-life in the general adult US population. *Journal of public health* 27: 156–164.

Johansen, S. (2000) *Family Men: Middle-Class Fatherhood in Industrializing America*. New York: Routledge.

Johansson, S. (2004) The health transition: the cultural inflation of morbidity during the decline of mortality. *Health Transition Review* 1: 39–65.

Jousilahti, P., Tuomilehto, J., Vartiainen, E., Eriksson, J. and Puska, P. (2000) Relation of adult height to cause-specific and total mortality: a prospective follow-up study of 31, 199 middle-aged men and women in Finland. *Am. J. Epidemiol.* 151: 1112–1120.

Kanazawa, S. and Novak, D. (2004) Human sexual dimorphism in size may be triggered by environmental cues. *Journal of Biosocial Science* 37: 657–665.

Kauhanen, L., Lakka, H.-M., Lynch, J.W. and Kauhanen, J. (2006) Social disadvantages in childhood and risk of all-cause death and cardiovascular disease in later life: a comparison of historical and retrospective childhood information. *Int. J. Epidemiol.* 35: 962–968.

Keys, A., Aravanis, C., Blackburn, H., Van Buchem, F., Buzina, R., Djordjevic, B., Fidanza, F., Karvonen, M., Menotti, A. and Puddu, V. (1972) Coronary heart disease: overweight and obesity as risk factors. *Annals of Internal Medicine* 77: 15–26.

Klebanoff, M.A. (2009) The Collaborative Perinatal Project: a 50-year retrospective. *Paediatric and perinatal epidemiology* 23: 2–8.

Komlos, J. (1987) The height and weight of West Point cadets: dietary change in antebellum America. *Journal of Economic History* 47: 897–927.

Komlos, J. (1996) Anomalies in economic history: toward a resolution of the "Antebellum Puzzle". *The Journal of Economic History* 56: 202–214.

Komlos, J. (1998) Shrinking in a growing economy? The mystery of physical stature during the industrial revolution. *Journal of Economic History* 58: 779–802.
Komlos, J. and Ritschl, A. (1995) Holy days, work days, and the standard of living in the Habsburg Monarchy. *Journal of Interdisciplinary History* 26: 57–66.
Kuh, D. and Ben-Shlomo, Y. (2004) The life course and adult chronic disease: an historical perspective with particular reference to coronary heart disease. In D. Kuh and Y. Ben-Shlomo (eds), *A Life Course Approach to Chronic Disease Epidemiology* (pp. 15–40). Oxford: Oxford University Press.
Kuh, D. and Hardy, R. (2004) A life course approach to women's health: does the past predict the present? In D. Kuh and R. Hardy (eds), *A Life Course Approach to Women's Health* (pp. 3–22). Oxford: Oxford University Press.
Kuh, D. and Smith, G.D. (1993) When is mortality risk determined? Historical insights into a current debate. *Social History of Medicine* 6: 101–123.
Lakdawalla, D. and Philipson, T. (2009) The growth of obesity and technological change. *Economics & Human Biology* 7: 283–293.
Lawlor, D.A., Ben-Shlomo, Y. and Leon, D.A. (2004) Pre-adult influences on cardiovascular disease. In D. Kuh and Y. Ben-Shlomo (eds), *A Life Course Approach to Chronic Disease Epidemiology* (pp. 41–76). Oxford: Oxford University Press.
Lawlor, D.A., Martin, R.M., Gunnell, D., Galobardes, B., Ebrahim, S., Sandhu, J., Ben-Shlomo, Y., McCarron, P. and Davey Smith, G. (2006) Association of body mass index measured in childhood, adolescence, and young adulthood with risk of ischemic heart disease and stroke: findings from 3 historical cohort studies. *American Journal of Clinical Nutrition* 83: 767–773.
Lee, C., Barzi, F., Woodward, M., Batty, G., Giles, G., Wong, J., Jamrozik, K., Lam, T., Ueshima, H. and Kim, H. (2009) Adult height and the risks of cardiovascular disease and major causes of death in the Asia-Pacific region: 21 000 deaths in 510 000 men and women. *International Journal of Epidemiology* 38: 1060–1071.
Lee, I.-M., Manson, J.E., Hennekens, C.H. and Paffenbarger, R.S., Jr (1993) Body weight and mortality: a 27-year follow-up of middle-aged men. *JAMA* 270: 2823–2828.
Leigh, S.R. (2001) Evolution of human growth. *Evolutionary Anthropology* 10: 221– 236.
Leigh, S.R. and Park, P.B. (1998) Evolution of human growth prolongation. *American Journal of Physical Anthropology* 107: 331–350.
Leon, D., Lawlor, D., Clark, H. and Macintyre, S. (2006) Cohort profile: the Aberdeen children of the 1950s study. *International Journal of Epidemiology* 35: 549–552.
Linares, C. and Su, D. (2005) Body mass index and health among Union Army veterans: 1891–1905. *Economics and Human Biology* 3: 367–387.
Lindsted, K., Tonstad, S. and Kuzma, J. (1991) Body mass index and patterns of mortality among seventh-day adventist men. *Int J Obes* 15: 397–406.
Logan, T.D. (2006) Food, nutrition, and substitution in the late nineteenth century. *Explorations in Economic History* 43: 527–545.
Logan, T.D. (2009) The transformation of hunger: the demand for calories past and present. *The Journal of Economic History* 69: 388–408.
Lumey, L. (1998) Reproductive outcomes in women prenatally exposed to undernutrition: a review of findings from the Dutch famine birth cohort. *Proceedings of the Nutrition Society* 57: 129–135.
Lumey, L. and Van Poppel, F. (1994) The Dutch famine of 1944–45: mortality and morbidity in past and present generations. *Social History of Medicine* 7: 229–246.
Lumey, L.H., Stein, A.D. and Susser, E. (2011) Prenatal famine and adult physical and mental health. *Annual Review of Public Health*, forthcoming.
Martin, R.M., Gunnell, D., Pemberton, J., Frankel, S. and Davey Smith, G. (2005) Cohort profile: the Boyd Orr cohort—an historical cohort study based on the 65 year follow-up of the Carnegie Survey of Diet and Health (1937–39). *International Journal of Epidemiology* 34: 742–749.

Mazumder, B., Almond, D., Park, K., Crimmins, E.M. and Finch, C.E. (2009) Lingering prenatal effects of the 1918 influenza pandemic on cardiovascular disease. *Journal of Developmental Origins of Health and Disease* 1: 1–9.

McCalman, J., Morley, R. and Mishra, G. (2008) A health transition: Birth weights, households and survival in an Australian working-class population sample born 1857–1900. *Social Science and Medicine* 66: 1070–1083.

McEvoy, B.P. and Visscher, P.M. (2009) Genetics of human height. *Economics and Human Biology* 7: 294–306.

McGee, D.L. and Diverse Population Collaboration (2005) Body mass index and mortality: a meta-analysis based on person-level data from twenty-six observational studies. *Annals of Epidemiology* 15: 87–97.

Mednick, S.A. and Mednick, B. (1984) A brief history of North American longitudinal research. In A.M. Sarnoff, M. Harway and K.M. Finello (eds), *Handbook of Longitudinal Research* (pp. 19–21), New York: Praeger.

Mehta, N.K. and Chang, V.W. (2009) Mortality attributable to obesity among middle-aged adults in the United States. *Demography* 46: 851–872.

Mei, Z., Grummer-Strawn, L.M., Thompson, D. and Dietz, W.H. (2004) Shifts in percentiles of growth during early childhood: analysis of longitudinal data from the California Child Health and Development Study. *Pediatrics* 113: e617–e627.

Moradi, A. and Baten, J. (2005) Inequality in Sub-Saharan Africa: new data and new insights from anthropometric estimates. *World Development* 33: 1233–1265.

Murphy, M. (2009) Where have all the children gone? Women's reports of more childlessness at older ages than when they were younger in a large-scale continuous household survey in Britain. *Population Studies* 63: 115–133.

Murray, J.E. (1997) Standards of the present for people of the past: Height, weight, and mortality among men of Amherst College, 1834–1949. *Journal of Economic History* 57: 585–606.

Murray, J.E. (2007) *Origins of American Health Insurance: A History of Industrial Sickness Funds*. New Haven: Yale University Press.

Must, A., Spadano, J., Coakley, E.H., Field, A.E., Colditz, G. and Dietz, W.H. (1999) The disease burden associated with overweight and obesity. *Journal of the American Medical Association* 282: 1523–1529.

Nelson, R.E. (forthcoming) Testing the fetal origins hypothesis in a developing country: evidence from the 1918 Influenza Pandemic. *Health Economics*.

Nettle, D. (2002) Women's height, reproductive success and the evolution of sexual dimorphism in modern humans. *Proceedings of the Royal Society of London. Series B: Biological Sciences* 269: 1919–1923.

Nicholas, S. and Oxley, D. (1993) The living standards of women during the industrial revolution, 1795–1820. *Economic History Review New Series* 46: 723–749.

North, K.E. and Martin, L.J. (2008) The importance of gene–environment interaction: implications for social scientists. *Sociological Methods & Research* 37: 164–200.

Oddy, D.J. (1970) Working-class diets in late nineteenth-century Britain. *The Economic History Review* 23: 314–323.

Osler, M., Godtfredsen, N. and Prescott, E. (2008) Childhood social circumstances and health behaviour in midlife: the Metropolit 1953 Danish male birth cohort. *International Journal of Epidemiology* 37: 1367–1374.

Owen, C., Whincup, P., Orfei, L., Chou, Q., Rudnicka, A., Wathern, A., Kaye, S., Eriksson, J., Osmond, C. and Cook, D. (2009) Is body mass index before middle age related to coronary heart disease risk in later life? Evidence from observational studies. *International Journal of Obesity* 33: 866–877.

Parman, J. (2009) *Childhood Health and Educational Attainment: Evidence from (Genetic) Brothers in Arms*. Davis: Department of Economics, University of California, Davis.

Philipson, T. and Posner, R. (2003) The long-run growth in obesity as a function of technological change. *Perspectives in Biology and Medicine* 46: 87–107.
Pierce, J. (1989) International comparisons of trends in cigarette smoking prevalence. *American Journal of Public Health* 79: 152–157.
Pool, I. (1991) *Te Iwi Maori : a New Zealand Population Past Present & Projected*. Auckland: Auckland University Press.
Power, C. and Elliott, J. (2006) Cohort profile: 1958 British birth cohort (National Child Development Study). *Int. J. Epidemiol.* 35: 34–41.
Preston, S. and Wang, H. (2006) Sex mortality differences in the United States: the role of cohort smoking patterns. *Demography* 43: 631–646.
Riley, J.C. (1990) The risk of being sick: morbidity trends in four countries. *Population and Development Review* 16: 403–432.
Roberts, C. (1879) *A Manual of Anthropometry*. London: J&A Churchill.
Rogers, A.R. and Mukherjee, A. (1992) Quantitative genetics of sexual dimorphism in human body size. *Evolution* 46: 226–234.
Rosengren, A., Wedel, H. and Wilhelmsen, L. (1999) Body weight and weight gain during adult life in men in relation to coronary heart disease and mortality: a prospective population study. *European Heart Journal* 20: 269–277.
Sach, T., Barton, G., Doherty, M., Muir, K., Jenkinson, C. and Avery, A. (2006) The relationship between body mass index and health-related quality of life: comparing the EQ-5D, EuroQol VAS and SF-6D. *International Journal of Obesity* 31: 189–196.
Shlomowitz, R. (2007) Did the mean height of Australian-born men decline in the late nineteenth century? A comment. *Economics and Human Biology* 5: 484–488.
Silventoinen, K. (2003) Determinants of variation in adult body height. *Journal of Biosocial Science* 35: 263–285.
Silventoinen, K., Zdravkovic, S., Skytthe, A., McCarron, P., Herskind, A.M., Koskenvuo, M., de Faire, U., Pedersen, N., Christensen, K., Kaprio, J., Genom, E.P., Silventoinen, K., Zdravkovic, S., Skytthe, A., McCarron, P., Herskind, A.M., Koskenvuo, M., de Faire, U., Pedersen, N., Christensen, K. and Kaprio, J. (2006) Association between height and coronary heart disease mortality: a prospective study of 35,000 twin pairs. [see comment]. *American Journal of Epidemiology* 163: 615–621.
Singh, P., Lindsted, K. and Fraser, G. (1999) Body weight and mortality among adults who never smoked. *American Journal of Epidemiology* 150: 1152–1164.
Solomon, C. and Manson, J. (1997) Obesity and mortality: a review of the epidemiologic data. *American Journal of Clinical Nutrition* 66: 1044S–1050S.
Song, S. (2009) Does famine have a long-term effect on cohort mortality? Evidence from the 1959–1961 Great Leap forward famine in China. *Journal of Biosocial Science* 41: 469–461.
Song, Y., Smith, G. and Sung, J. (2003) Adult height and cause-specific mortality: a large prospective study of South Korean men. *American Journal of Epidemiology* 158: 479–485.
Sontag, L.W. (1971) The history of longitudinal research: Implications for the future. *Child Development* 42: 987–1002.
Starr, J.M., Taylor, M.D., Hart, C.L., Davey Smith, G., Whalley, L.J., Hole, D.J., Wilson, V. and Deary, I.J. (2004) Childhood mental ability and blood pressure at midlife: linking the Scottish Mental Survey 1932 and the Midspan studies. *Journal of Hypertension* 22: 893–897.
Steckel, R.H. (1979) Slave height profiles from coastwise manifests. *Explorations in Economic History* 16: 363–380.
Steckel, R.H. (1986) A peculiar population: the nutrition, health, and mortality of American slaves from childhood to maturity. *The Journal of Economic History* 46: 721–741.

Steckel, R.H. (1995) Stature and the standard of living. *Journal of Economic Literature* 33: 1903–1940.

Steckel, R.H. (1998) Strategic ideas in the rise of the new anthropometric history and their implications for interdisciplinary research. *Journal of Economic History* 58: 803– 821.

Steckel, R.H. (2000) Diets versus diseases in the anthropometrics of slave children: a reply. *The Journal of Economic History* 60: 247–259.

Steckel, R.H. (2005) Young adult mortality following severe physiological stress in childhood: skeletal evidence. *Economics and Human Biology* 3: 314–328.

Steckel, R.H. (2008) Biological measures of the standard of living. *Journal of Economic Perspectives* 22: 129–152.

Steckel, R.H. (2009a) *Children of Adversity: The Care and Feeding of Slave Children.* Columbus: Department of Economics, Ohio State University.

Steckel, R.H. (2009b) Heights and human welfare: recent developments and new directions. *Explorations in Economic History* 46: 1–23.

Steckel, R.H. and Haurin, D.R. (1995) Health and nutrition in the American Midwest: evidence from the height of Ohio National Guardsmen, 1850–1910. In J. Komlos (ed), *Stature, Living Standards, and Economic Development* (pp. 117–128). Chicago: University of Chicago Press.

Steckel, R.H. and Rose, J.C. (2002) *The Backbone of History : Health and Nutrition in the Western Hemisphere*. Cambridge, UK; New York: Cambridge University Press.

Stenberg, S. and Vagero, D. (2006) Cohort profile: the Stockholm birth cohort of 1953. *International Journal of Epidemiology* 35: 546–548.

Stevens, J. (2000) Impact of age on associations between weight and mortality. *Nutrition Reviews* 58: 129–137.

Stewart, S.T., Cutler, D.M. and Rosen, A.B. (2009) Forecasting the effects of obesity and smoking on U.S. Life Expectancy. *New England Journal of Medicine* 361: 2252–2260.

Sturm, R. and Wells, K. (2001) Does obesity contribute as much to morbidity as poverty or smoking? *Public Health* 115: 229–235.

Su, D. (2005) Body mass index and old-age survival: a comparative study between the Union Army Records and the NHANES-I epidemiological follow-up sample. *American Journal of Human Biology* 17: 341–354.

Symmons, D.P.M., Bankhead, C.R., Harrison, B.J., Brennan, P., Silman, A.J., Barrett, E.M. and Scott, D.G.I. (2005) Blood transfusion, smoking, and obesity as risk factors for the development of rheumatoid arthritis. Results from a primary care-based incident case-control study in Norfolk, England. *Arthritis & Rheumatism* 40: 1955–1961.

Tanner, J.M. (1978) *Foetus into man: physical growth from conception to maturity.* Cambridge, Harvard University Press.

Tanner, J.M. (1981) *A History of the Study of Human Growth.* Cambridge: Cambridge University Press.

Thernstrom, S. (1964) *Poverty and Progress; Social Mobility in a Nineteenth Century City.* Cambridge: Harvard University Press.

Thomas, D. and Frankenberg, E. (2002) The measurement and interpretation of health in social surveys. In C.J.L. Murray, J.A. Salomon, C.D. Mathers and A.D. Lopez (eds), *Summary Measures of Population Health: Concepts, Ethics, Measurement and Applications*. Geneva: World Health Organization.

Trussel, J. and Steckel, R. (1978) The age of slaves at menarche and their first birth. *Journal of Interdisciplinary History* 8: 477–505.

Van Den Berg, B.J., Christianson, R.E. and Oechsli, F.W. (1988) The California Child Health and Development Studies of the School of Public Health, University of California at Berkeley. *Paediatric and Perinatal Epidemiology* 2: 265–282.

Viswanathan, B. and Sharma, V. (2009) Socio-economic differences in heights of adult Indian women. *Journal of Developing Societies* 25: 421–455.
Voth, H.-J. (1996) Physical exertion and stature in the Habsburg Monarchy, 1730–1800. *Journal of Interdisciplinary History* 27: 263–275.
Waaler, H. (1984) Height, weight and mortality. The Norwegian experience. *Acta Medica Scandinavica* Supplementum 679: 1–56.
Wadsworth, M., Kuh, D., Richards, M. and Hardy, R. (2006) Cohort profile: the 1946 national birth cohort (MRC national survey of health and development). *International Journal of Epidemiology* 35: 49–54.
Wall, W.D. and Williams, H.L. (1970) *Longitudinal Studies & the Social Sciences*. London: Heinemann Educational Publishers.
Wannamethee, S.G., Shaper, A.G. and Walker, M. (2005) Overweight and obesity and weight change in middle aged men: impact on cardiovascular disease and diabetes. *Journal of Epidemiology and Community Health* 59: 134–139.
Ward, W.P. (1993) *Birth Weight and Economic Growth: Women's Living Standards in the Industrializing West*. Chicago: University of Chicago Press.
Wells, J.C.K. (2007) Sexual dimorphism of body composition. *Best Practice & Research Clinical Endocrinology & Metabolism* 21: 415–430.
Whincup, P.H., Cook, D.G. and Geleijnse, J.M. (2004) A life course approach to blood pressure. In D. Kuh and Y. Ben-Shlomo (eds), *A Life Course Approach to Chronic Disease Epidemiology*. Oxford: Oxford University Press: 218–239.
Whitwell, G. and Nicholas, S. (2001) Weight and welfare of Australians, 1890–1940. *Australian Economic History Review* 41: 159–175.
World Health Organization (1999) *Obesity: Preventing and Managing the Global Epidemic*. Geneva: World Health Organization.
Young, C.H., Savola, K.L. and Phelps, E. (1991) *Inventory of Longitudinal Studies in the Social Sciences*. Newbury Park: Sage Publications.

4

IMPROVING HUMAN DEVELOPMENT: A LONG-RUN VIEW

Leandro Prados de la Escosura

Readers of the *Human Development Report* (HDR), published periodically by the United Nations Development Programme (UNDP), tend to have mixed feelings. The pessimistic rhetoric of the HDR seems to be contradicted by its own numbers. In fact, when weighed up in human development terms, developing countries tend to fare better relative to advanced countries than in per capita income terms.

It is the purpose of this chapter to bridge the gap between the empirical evidence on human development and the HDR rhetoric by providing a new, 'improved' index (IHDI, hereafter), informed by welfare economics.[1] The IHDI is presented here along the UNDP's HDI (UNHDI, henceforth) for the world and its main regions over the period 1870–2005.

What defines the new human development index? In the first place, its social, non-income dimensions are derived using a convex achievement function as an alternative to the linear transformation employed in the UNHDI. Thus, in the new index, as a social indicator reaches higher levels, its increases represent higher achievements than if the same increase would take place at a lower level, whereas in the UNDP linear transformation the same change results regardless of the starting level. Second, in an attempt to reduce substitutability among the index components, its three dimensions (longevity, access to knowledge and average incomes) are combined into the new IHDI using a geometric average, rather than the arithmetic average used in the UNHDI. The final outcome is a new human development index which, by not concealing the gap between rich and poor countries, casts a much less optimistic view than the one provided by conventional UNDP index while satisfying the HDR concern for international differences.

The chapter is organized in four sections. Section 1 assesses the UNHDI and exposes its main shortcomings. In an attempt to provide a response to these objections Section 2 presents the new IHDI. Then, world trends in human development since the late 19th century, derived from both the IHDI and the UNHDI, are compared in Section 3. Some concluding remarks complete the chapter.

Economics and History, First Edition. David Greasley and Les Oxley

1. Assessing the Human Development Index

Challenging GDP (or GNP) per head as a measure of welfare, in spite of its advantage as a synthetic index and the observed association between economic growth and welfare (Lewis, 1955; Beckerman, 1993), has been recurrent since the spread of national accounts more than half a century ago (United Nations, 1954; Dasgupta, 1993; Engerman, 1997; Fleurbaey, 2009). Different socio-economic indicators have been explored as an alternative to GDP per head among which the basic needs approach and the physical index of quality of life are widely known.[2] The UNHDI, a synthetic product of the UNDP, published annually since 1990, has been the latest addition to these social welfare measures. Although, on this occasion, the index has reached beyond academic borders, as a measure of well-being the UNHDI has not escaped strong criticism.[3]

Human development was originally defined as ‘a process of enlarging people's choices’ that enables them ‘to lead a long and healthy life, to acquire knowledge and to have access to resources needed for a decent standard of living’ (UNDP, 1990, p. 10). In other words, human development emphasizes positive freedom (Desai, 1991, p. 356). As a synthetic measure of human development, the UNHDI tries to capture a country's achievements in longevity, knowledge and standard of living through various indices: the relative achievement in life expectancy at birth, in education and in ‘all dimensions of human development not reflected in a long and healthy life and in knowledge’ for which the adjusted *per capita* GDP (its logarithm) is a surrogate (UNDP, 2001, p. 240). These achievements provide individuals the freedom to choose (Kakwani, 1993; Fleurbaey, 2009) and, thus, the opportunity ‘to lead lives they have reasons to value’ (Sen, 1997).

Indices for each dimension (I) are computed according to the following formula,

$$I = (x - Mo)/(M - Mo) \qquad (1)$$

where x is the observed value of a given dimension of welfare, and Mo and M represent the maximum and minimum values, or goalposts. Goalposts representing levels not reached yet and below the present's lowest level, respectively, were chosen for each indicator in order to make possible comparisons over time.[4] Each dimension ranges, thus, between 0 and 1. The UNHDI is obtained as the unweighted arithmetic average of the three dimension indices.

Reactions to non-conventional indicators of well-being have always been critical. One of the most popular synthetic indices, Morris's (1979) physical quality of life index (PIQL; an unweighted average of normalized indices of infant mortality, life expectancy and literacy) was seriously questioned on the basis of the high collinearity between its first two components (Hopkins, 1991) and has only made an uncritical comeback in the historical literature (Federico and Toniolo, 1991; Domínguez and Guijarro, 2000).[5]

The UNHDI, presumably an improvement on Morris's PIQL, has been seriously questioned (Dasgupta, 1993, p. 77).[6] Srinivassan (1994, p. 240), for example, described the new index as ‘conceptually weak and empirically unsound, involving serious problems of non-comparability over time and space’, whereas Dowrick *et al.* (2003) stressed its lack of welfare economics foundations. Moreover, the distribution of each dimension of the index is not taken into account.[7] Furthermore, the weakness of the data underlying UNHDI (incomplete coverage, measurement errors and biases) has been highlighted as a major shortcoming of the new index (Srinivassan, 1994).[8] GDP per head estimates for developing countries are highly questionable (Heston, 1994). Moreover, literacy and enrolment data are frequently non-homogeneous making comparisons difficult.[9] Lastly life expectancy data tend to be interpolated and often obtained through life tables' projection rather than through direct estimation.[10].

Major critical issues of the human development index are: How to transform the original values of social dimensions into indices? Should a linear or a non-linear transformation be used? Do human development dimensions (longevity, education and income) provide different insights of welfare, or are they simply redundant? If they capture different welfare dimensions, should equal weights be allocated to each dimension and kept unaltered over time? How to combine the main dimensions of well-being? Is an arithmetic average the appropriate procedure?[11]

The choice of UNHDI's components has provoked an endless debate. For example, the inclusion of average incomes in the index of human development raises two distinctive issues. On the one hand, if those dimensions of human development 'not reflected in a long and healthy life and in knowledge' need to be considered, why is income per head chosen as a proxy? Is it just because of its availability? On the other hand, why imposing a diminishing marginal utility on income? Against the view that a decent standard of living does not require unlimited income it has been opposed that 'additional income above the threshold can allow more human development' (Gormely, 1995, p. 264) and that it is only above a given threshold that per capita income becomes relevant for human development (Sagar and Najam, 1998, pp. 253–254). Furthermore, it has been argued that a non-modified GDP per head 'may be appropriate for long run welfare comparisons if the focus is broader than just the escape from poverty' (Crafts, 1997, p. 304). In the case of education, it is commonly accepted that, for developing countries, literacy is an essential element of human development, but it becomes meaningless for developed countries, when literacy rates are close to 100% (see, for example, Lindert, 2004). Fortunately, a wider range of variation is permitted by the aggregate enrolment rate for primary, secondary and tertiary education, also a component of the UNHDI educational dimension.

The aggregation of each dimension into a synthetic index has provoked some adverse reactions. For example, Kakwani (1993) and Aturupane *et al.* (1994) suggested the use of socio-economic indicators separately, whereas Dasgupta and Weale (1992) proposed an ordinal rather than cardinal measure of well-being, which was also made more inclusive by incorporating civil and political liberties.

Does each UNHDI component measure a different aspect of well-being, or is it highly correlated to the rest of them?[12] Previous attempts to derive alternative welfare indices to conventional GDP per head suffered from either a high correlation with GDP, or were obtained from highly correlated components that rendered them redundant. There has been some outright rejection of the UNHDI. For example, McGillivray (1991, p. 1467), after stressing the positive correlation among the index's individual components, concluded that the UNHDI was 'yet another redundant composite intercountry development indicator'. A way of establishing whether the indicators included under the umbrella of human development did capture different aspects of well-being has been to use principal components analysis (PCA).[13] PCA allows one to establish whether the human development index attributes are redundant or add information on different facets of well-being.[14] This way it was found that the three dimensions contained in the UNHDI belonged to the same component and, therefore, the simultaneous use of the three attributes is justified despite its high cross-correlation (UNDP, 1993, pp. 109–110).[15]

The weighting system is a major objection to the UNHDI (Hopkins, 1991; Booysen, 2002). Should each dimension (longevity, education and income) receive the same weights in the index over space and time?[16] This choice finds support in the notion that each of them is equally essential in determining its level, a feature considered to be a main attribute of the human development concept (Sagar and Najam, 1998, p. 251).[17] However, it has been argued, UNHDI weights are based on judgment rather than on welfare economics (Dowrick *et al.*, 2003, p. 504). A substantive objection to the use of fixed weights is that the relative values of the index components are not necessarily the same across countries (or individuals) and over time (Srinivassan, 1994, p. 240). Historical evidence on the relationship between life expectancy and *per capita* income lends support to this assertion (Preston, 1975).[18] Modern economic growth predated improvements in life expectancy but the latter spread more rapidly (Easterlin, 1999). A technical solution is offered by PCA. Its results provide optimal weights for each HDI component over time by weighting attributes by their variance[19] and, counter-intuitively, suggest stable one-third weights for each dimension of the index.[20]

An additional difficulty is that attainments in each component are traded off against each other but these tradeoffs are not explicit. A close examination of the implicit tradeoffs offers some surprising results. For example, the implicit monetary valuation of an extra year of life expectancy rises dramatically with income as, by construction, the UNHDI implicitly values life relatively less in poor than in rich countries.[21]

Is the unweighted arithmetic average of all dimensions (longevity, education and income) an acceptable way to derive a synthetic human development index? It has been noted that additivity over these attributes implies perfect substitution, which contradicts the notion that each dimension is equally crucial in determining the level of human development. Hence, it has been suggested that the substitutability among the index components should be restricted through their geometric average (Desai, 1991, p. 356; Sagar and Najam, 1998, pp. 251–252) since with a multiplicative procedure the human development index will only experience a significant improvement if each of its dimensions does it.

How should the original values of social dimensions be transformed into well-being indices? An objection to the linear transformation of the original values in the UNDP approach to human development was made by Srinivassan (1994, p. 240) who pointed out that 'the "intrinsic" value of a single "functioning", namely, the ability to live a healthy life, is not captured by its linear deprivation measure in UNHDI, since a *unit* decrease in the deprivation in life expectancy at an initial life expectancy of, say, 40 years is not commensurate with the same unit decrease at 60 years'.

The nonlinearity of the relationship between the value of each social indicator and its achievement, so that the observed differences in the levels of social indicators do not reflect their true achievement, has been thoroughly explored by Kakwani (1993), who stressed that social indicators such as life expectancy, infant mortality or literacy have, in opposition to GDP per head, asymptotic limits, reflecting physical and biological maxima.

Using an axiomatic approach Kakwani (1993) constructed a normalized index from an achievement function in which an increase in the standard of living of a country at a higher level implies a greater achievement than would have been the case if it occurred at a lower level:[22]

$$\mathrm{f}(x, M_0, M) = ((M - M_0)^{1-\varepsilon} - (M - x)^{1-\varepsilon})/(M - M_0)^{1-\varepsilon} \quad \text{for } 0 < \varepsilon < 1$$

$$= \mathrm{f}(x, M_0, M) \tag{2}$$

$$= (\log(M - M_0) - \log(M - x))/\log(M - M_0) \quad \text{for } \varepsilon = 1 \tag{3}$$

where x is an indicator of a country's standard of living, M and M_0 are the maximum and minimum values, respectively, and log stands for the natural logarithm. The achievement function proposed by Kakwani (1993, p. 314) is a convex function of x, and it is equal to 0 if $x = M_0$, and equal to 1 if $x = M$, ranging, then, between 0 and 1.

In fact, the UNHDI represents a particular case, for $\varepsilon = 0$, which yields expression (1) for each dimension of the index. Such particular case does not satisfy, however, one of the axioms of the achievement index defined by Kakwani, namely, that the index should give greater weight to the improvement of a country which has higher level for each social indicator. This axiom follows 'from the belief that as the standard of living reaches progressively higher limits, incremental improvement should require much greater resources than similar incremental improvements from a lower base' (Kakwani, 1993, p. 312).

Nonetheless, Kakwani's rationale can be challenged, for example, on the basis that an 'improvement in education attainment may not be more difficult as the level of education becomes higher and higher' (Tsui, 1996, p. 302). In fact, Noorbakhsh (1998) modified the human development index by extending the principle of diminishing returns to education (but not to longevity). The rationale is that 'under similar conditions the early "units" of educational attainments to a country should be of much higher value than the last ones' (Noorbakhsh, 1998, p. 519). Such assertion implies that the ethical and measurement aspects seem to be at odds in the human development index. However, as Dasgupta (1990, p. 23) rightly pointed out,

> Equal increments are possibly of less and less ethical worth as life expectancy rises to 65 or 70 years and more. But we are meaning performance here. So it would seem that it becomes more and more *commendable* if, with increasing life

expectancy, the index were to rise at the margin. The idea here is that it becomes more and more difficult to increase life expectancy as life expectancy rises.[23]

Therefore, the acceptance of Noorbakhsh's ethical argument for a 'modified' index would distort the measurement of performance, which is my main purpose here, by reducing the index variance of across countries and imposing, hence, artificial convergence across countries.[24] Such a constraint on the index dispersion would only make sense if the single goal of the UNHDI were just measuring *basic* human development and not, as in our case, assessing the evolution of well-being over time.

2. Introducing the 'Improved' Index of Human Development

As a way to answering some of these queries I have constructed the IHDI in which its non-income dimensions are derived with a convex achievement function (i.e. using expression (3)). Thus, in the alternative human development index, IHDI, as a social indicator reaches higher levels, its increases represent higher achievements than had the same increase taken place at a lower level, whereas in the UNHDI they reflect the same change regardless its starting level.

Some minor changes have been introduced in the conventional goalposts so the maximum and minimum represent levels above the highest and below the lowest, respectively.[25] For life expectancy at birth, although the conventional maximum, M, of 85 years has been kept, a minimum, M_0, of 24 years has been chosen, whereas 25 years has been accepted as the lowest historical level.[26] For the education indicators (literacy and enrolment), although UNDP values of $M = 100$ and $M_0 = 0$ have been kept, the highest and lowest historical values have been set at 99% and 1%, respectively.[27]

As regards per capita income, it is worth noting that, in international comparisons, dissatisfaction with *nominal* income (i.e. national GDP per head converted into a common currency using the trading exchange rate) has led to an almost generalized use of *real* income (the conversion per capita GDP into a common currency using a purchasing power parity (PPP) exchange rate).[28] Unfortunately, the construction of PPP converters involves high costs in terms of time and resources. Only PPPs for a restricted country sample have been constructed for earlier periods, and most of them for output components.[29]

An indirect method to derive historical estimates of real per capita income levels for a large sample of countries is the backward projection of PPP-adjusted GDP per capita for a given benchmark with volume indices derived from national accounts data.[30] It is worth noting that fixed-base *real* (PPP-adjusted) product data represent a most convenient alternative to carrying out painstaking direct comparisons across space and time and have the presentation advantage that their growth rates are identical to those calculated from national accounts.[31] Alas, a distant PPP benchmark introduces distortions in inter-temporal comparisons because its validity depends on how stable the basket of goods and services used to construct the original PPP converters remains over time. As growth occurs over time the composition of output, consumption and relative prices all vary, and the economic meaning of comparing real product per head based upon remote PPPs becomes entirely questionable. Hence, using a single PPP benchmark for long-run comparisons implies a hardly realistic assumption: that no changes in relative prices (and, hence, no technological change) takes place over time.

Unfortunately, in the current state of research there is no alternative to the use of this approach, especially when a world country sample over one and a half centuries is considered.

Then, the UNHDI assumption that the marginal utility of per capita income declines as it reaches higher levels has been accepted. The reason to keep such an astringent assumption is that, following the UNDP proposal, this transformed measure is taken as a proxy for any well-being dimension outside health and education, and not for income per head. Therefore, the log of GDP per head is employed in expression (1) with a maximum of 40,000 Geary–Khamis 1990 dollars and a minimum of 100 dollars. Similar to the cases of social indicators, I have assumed a lower bound for per capita GDP, 300 Geary–Khamis 1990 dollars, which represents a basic level of physiological subsistence (Sagar and Najam, 1998, p. 254; Milanovic *et al.*, 2007), which is below the World Bank's extreme poverty measure of one dollar a day/person and Maddison's (2006) 400 dollars per head.[32]

Finally, the three main dimensions of human development (longevity, knowledge and income) have been combined using a geometric average to derive the new IHDI. A geometric average of the human development attributes has the advantage of reducing their substitutability, precluding the chance that one attribute's improvement offsets another's worsening, as is the case with its arithmetic average employed in the UNHDI. Under the geometric average alternative, instead, only if all dimensions improve will an improvement in the human development index take place. Thus, if we denote by L and E the non-linearly transformed values of life expectancy and education, and by Y_{un} the adjusted per capita income, the IHDI can be expressed as

$$\text{IHDI} = L^{1/3} E^{1/3} Y_{\text{un}}^{1/3} \tag{4}$$

3. Trends in Human Development

Trends in aggregate human development have been computed for four different country samples for which time and spatial coverage are inversely related. Thus although only 88 countries are considered for the entire time span, 1870–2005, the number rises to 99, 134 and 156 countries for those samples starting in 1913, 1950 and 1990, respectively. Fortunately these samples represent more than 90% of the world population (and practically all since 1950). Interestingly, the results for regional aggregates in each of these samples are highly coincidental so the different indices can be spliced into a single one for each main world region.[33]

A substantial improvement in world human development is observed since 1870 – and especially over 1913–1960, multiplying by seven its initial level. When the

Table 1. Human Development in the World, 1870–2005: Alternative Estimates.

	Levels			Annual growth rates	
Panel A	IHDI	UNHDI	Panel B	IHDI	UNHDI
1870	0.064	0.196	1870–1880	1.2	0.7
1880	0.072	0.211	1880–1890	1.6	0.9
1890	0.085	0.231	1890–1900	1.5	0.9
1900	0.098	0.253	1900–1913	1.2	0.7
1913	0.115	0.278	1913–1929	2.1	1.1
1929	0.159	0.333	1929–1938	1.8	1.3
1938	0.187	0.375	1938–1950	1.8	1.2
1950	0.232	0.433	1950–1960	2.0	1.6
1960	0.283	0.507	1960–1970	1.3	1.1
1970	0.323	0.565	1970–1980	0.8	0.6
1980	0.349	0.601	1980–1990	0.9	0.6
1990	0.380	0.639	1990–2000	1.2	0.7
2000	0.427	0.684	2000–2005	1.3	0.8
2005	0.455	0.711			
			1870–1913	1.4	0.8
			1913–1950	1.9	1.2
			1950–1970	1.7	1.3
			1970–1990	0.8	0.6
			1990–2005	1.2	0.7
			1870–2005	1.5	1.0

results for the IHDI and the UNHDI are compared, the same trend is confirmed, but for a significant difference in initial levels and an absolute gap widening between them as the IHDI lagged behind (Table 1 and Figure 1). In terms of the conventional HDR categories – 'low' (<0.5), 'medium' (0.5) and 'high' (0.8) levels – the average human development in the world, according to the IHDI, would still remain today in the 'low' category, whereas, for the UNHDI, the world belonged to the 'medium' level since 1960 and it is getting closer to the 'high' level. Thus, over 1870–2005 the gain in the UNHDI represented almost two-thirds of its potential maximum (i.e. 1 less its initial level) whereas it was only two-fifths for the IHDI. Nonetheless, the UNHDI improvement was slower, at 0.9% yearly, against 1.4% for the IHDI.

Trends in world human development are affected by its regional evolution, particularly by that of large regions exhibiting idiosyncratic behaviour such as, for example, China and India or Africa. It can be noticed that their exclusion increases human development over 1870–2005 (Figure 2 and Table 2). However, while including Africa worsens the world level since 1950 and, especially, since 1990, in the case of China and India, from 1980 onwards, their inclusion has a less negative impact on the world level as they (and especially China) have experienced substantial gains in human development.

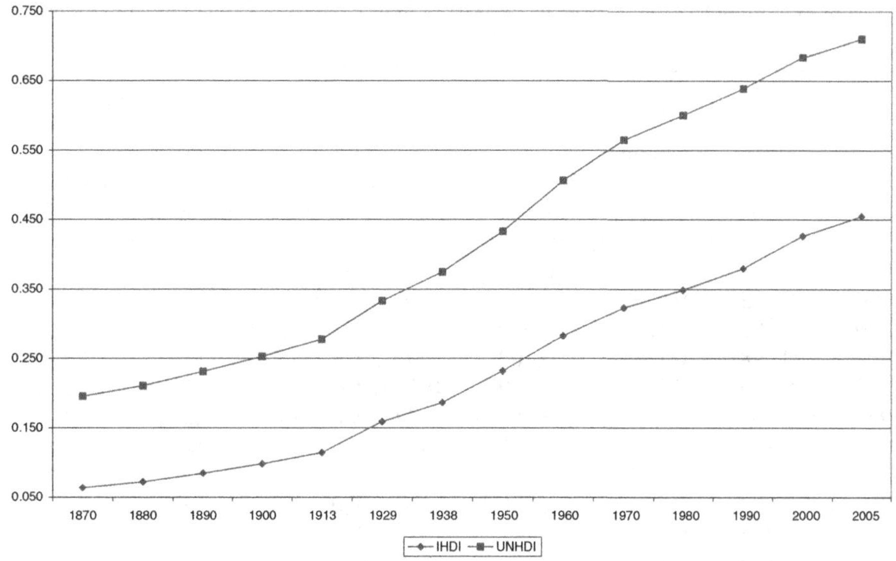

Figure 1. Human Development in the World, 1870–2005: UNHDI and IHDI Estimates.

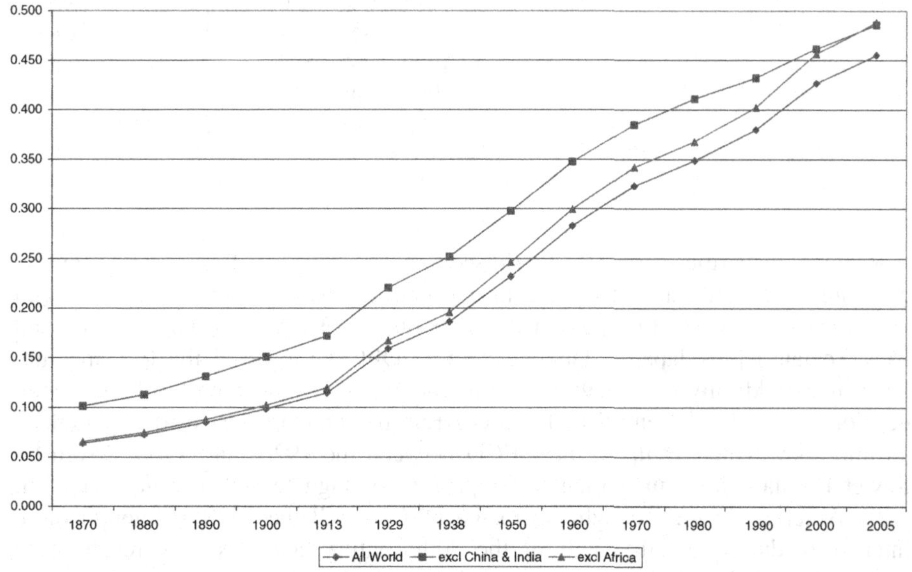

Figure 2. Human Development in the World, and excluding China and India and Africa, 1870–2005.

Table 2. Human Development in the World, and excluding China and India, and Africa, 1870–2005.

	Levels				Annual growth rates		
Panel A	All	Excluding China and India	Excluding Africa	Panel B	All	Excluding China and India	Excluding Africa
1870	0.064	0.101	0.066	1870–1880	1.2	1.1	1.3
1880	0.072	0.113	0.074	1880–1890	1.6	1.5	1.6
1890	0.085	0.131	0.088	1890–1900	1.5	1.4	1.5
1900	0.098	0.151	0.102	1900–1913	1.2	1.0	1.2
1913	0.115	0.172	0.119	1913–1929	2.1	1.6	2.1
1929	0.159	0.221	0.167	1929–1938	1.8	1.5	1.8
1938	0.187	0.252	0.196	1938–1950	1.8	1.4	1.9
1950	0.232	0.298	0.246	1950–1960	2.0	1.6	2.0
1960	0.283	0.348	0.300	1960–1970	1.3	1.0	1.3
1970	0.323	0.385	0.342	1970–1980	0.8	0.7	0.7
1980	0.349	0.411	0.368	1980–1990	0.9	0.5	0.9
1990	0.380	0.432	0.402	1990–2000	1.2	0.7	1.3
2000	0.427	0.461	0.456	2000–2005	1.3	1.0	1.4
2005	0.455	0.486	0.488				
				1870–1913	1.4	1.2	1.4
				1913–1950	1.9	1.5	2.0
				1950–1970	1.7	1.3	1.6
				1970–1990	0.8	0.6	0.8
				1990–2005	1.2	0.8	1.3
				1870–2005	1.5	1.2	1.5

Regional disparities across the world seem, hence, relevant. Table 3 and Figure 3 compare levels and rates of change in the main regions. It appears that advanced countries, i.e. Western Europe and its offshoots (the USA, Canada, Australia and New Zealand) plus Japan – labelled here as OECD – crossed the 0.5 'medium level' threshold only in the 1950s, and are about to reach a 'high level' of human development (0.8).[34] Central and Eastern Europe (including Russia) experienced an impressive catching up to the OECD between the 1920s and 1960, driven by Soviet Russia's gains in human development, to stagnate and diverge thereafter. Latin America, in turn, caught up to the OECD until the 1970s, although more intensively during the first half of the 20th century, and has only reached the 'medium level' lately. Asia, starting from low levels – similar to those of Africa up to the early 1920s – improved significantly until 1970 and, again, at the turn of the century. A sustained improvement took place in Africa between the 1920s and the 1970s – with special intensity in the 1930s and 1950s – but has slowed down since 1980. Thus, Asia's catching up and Eastern Europe's falling behind led these

Table 3. Human Development across World Regions, 1870–2005.

	Levels					
Panel A	World	OECD	Central and and Eastern Europe (w/Russia)	Latin America	Asia (excluding Japan)	Africa
1870	0.064	0.180	0.074	0.044	0.024	0.020
1880	0.072	0.200	0.085	0.049	0.026	0.021
1890	0.085	0.235	0.099	0.061	0.028	0.022
1900	0.098	0.269	0.122	0.076	0.029	0.026
1913	0.115	0.305	0.141	0.106	0.032	0.030
1929	0.159	0.379	0.209	0.141	0.067	0.043
1938	0.187	0.414	0.280	0.163	0.087	0.058
1950	0.232	0.468	0.399	0.234	0.118	0.074
1960	0.283	0.531	0.495	0.281	0.170	0.116
1970	0.323	0.591	0.527	0.328	0.221	0.147
1980	0.349	0.636	0.541	0.383	0.253	0.185
1990	0.380	0.684	0.542	0.414	0.302	0.209
2000	0.427	0.746	0.536	0.485	0.369	0.228
2005	0.455	0.779	0.557	0.510	0.406	0.245

	Average growth rates (%)					
Panel B	World	OECD	Central and and Eastern Europe (w/Russia)	Latin America	Asia (excluding Japan)	Africa
1870–1880	1.2	1.1	1.4	1.1	0.7	0.5
1880–1890	1.6	1.6	1.5	2.2	0.8	0.6
1890–1900	1.5	1.3	2.1	2.2	0.3	1.6
1900–1913	1.2	1.0	1.1	2.6	0.8	0.9
1913–1929	2.1	1.4	2.5	1.8	4.5	2.3
1929–1938	1.8	1.0	3.3	1.6	2.9	3.4
1938–1950	1.8	1.0	2.9	3.0	2.6	2.0
1950–1960	2.0	1.3	2.1	1.8	3.6	4.6
1960–1970	1.3	1.1	0.6	1.6	2.6	2.4
1970–1980	0.8	0.7	0.3	1.5	1.3	2.3
1980–1990	0.9	0.7	0.0	0.8	1.8	1.2
1990–2000	1.2	0.9	−0.1	1.6	2.0	0.9
2000–2005	1.3	0.9	0.8	1.0	1.9	1.4
1870–1913	1.4	1.2	1.5	2.1	0.7	0.9
1913–1950	1.9	1.2	2.8	2.1	3.5	2.5
1950–1970	1.7	1.2	1.4	1.7	3.1	3.5
1970–1990	0.8	0.7	0.1	1.2	1.6	1.8
1990–2005	1.2	0.9	0.2	1.4	2.0	1.1
1870–2005	1.5	1.1	1.5	1.8	2.1	1.9

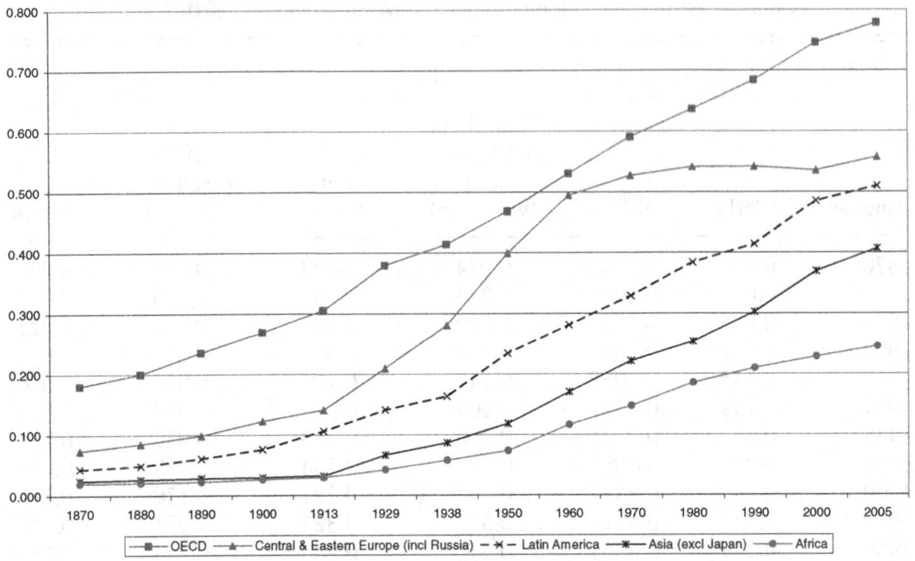

Figure 3. Human Development Across World Regions, 1870–2005.

two regions to converge with Latin America, whereas Africa and the OECD tend to diverge at low and high levels of human development.

All this leads to the issue of whether the human development gap between the 'core' – OECD – and the 'periphery' – all other countries, labelled the *Rest* henceforth – deepened over time. I have carried out comparisons between OECD and the *Rest* in which China and India and Africa have been successively excluded (Table 4). It appears that the absolute gap – i.e. the difference in human development values – increased over time, although at a more intense pace until 1929 (Figure 4). The inclusion of either China and India or Africa increased the gap but, since the 1980s, the human development improvement in these Asian countries made the gap between OECD and the *Rest*, with and without China and India, converge. The absolute gap between 'core' and 'periphery' results from differentials between OECD and each of the components of the *Rest*. A closer look at different developing regions reveals that most of the OECD absolute gap with Latin America and Asia (excluding Japan) originated in the late 19th and the first half of the 20th century, becoming relatively stable since the 1950s. This is not the case, however, for the absolute gap between OECD and Africa which increased steadily throughout the 20th century, accelerating since 1980 (Figure 5). Central and Eastern Europe represent an outlier, with its gap to OECD closing between 1929 and 1960 to widen dramatically thereafter, converging towards the OECD–Latin America gap.

However, in relative terms, the gap – namely, the ratio between OECD and the *Rest* – fell from 5.8 in 1900 to 2.4 in 1960 (and when China and India are

Table 4. Human Development in OECD and the *Rest*, 1870–2005.

Levels					Annual growth rates				
			The *Rest* without					The *Rest* without	
Panel A	OECD	The *Rest*	China and India	Africa	Panel B	OECD	The *Rest*	China and India	Africa
1870	0.180	0.032	0.043	0.032	1870–1880	1.1	1.1	1.3	1.2
1880	0.200	0.036	0.049	0.036	1880–1890	1.6	1.3	1.5	1.3
1890	0.235	0.041	0.057	0.041	1890–1900	1.3	1.4	1.9	1.4
1900	0.269	0.046	0.069	0.048	1900–1913	1.0	1.3	1.5	1.4
1913	0.305	0.055	0.083	0.057	1913–1929	1.4	3.2	2.4	3.3
1929	0.379	0.093	0.122	0.097	1929–1938	1.0	3.0	2.9	3.0
1938	0.414	0.121	0.158	0.127	1938–1950	1.0	2.5	2.2	2.6
1950	0.468	0.163	0.206	0.174	1950–1960	1.3	2.9	2.3	2.9
1960	0.531	0.217	0.259	0.231	1960–1970	1.1	1.8	1.4	1.8
1970	0.591	0.261	0.297	0.276	1970–1980	0.7	1.1	1.0	1.0
1980	0.636	0.290	0.328	0.305	1980–1990	0.7	1.2	0.7	1.2
1990	0.684	0.326	0.352	0.344	1990–2000	0.9	1.4	0.7	1.5
2000	0.746	0.374	0.380	0.400	2000–2005	0.9	1.5	1.3	1.6
2005	0.779	0.404	0.405	0.434					
					1870–1913	1.2	1.3	1.5	1.3
					1913–1950	1.2	2.9	2.4	3.0
					1950–1970	1.2	2.3	1.8	2.3
					1970–1990	0.7	1.1	0.9	1.1
					1990–2005	0.9	1.4	0.9	1.5
					1870–2005	1.1	1.9	1.7	1.9

excluded, from 4.1 in 1890 to 2.0 in 1960) and stabilized for the last half a century (Figure 6). The relative gap between OECD and each of the developing regions shrank over time, but while by mid-20th century the main reduction had already taken place in Latin America (from a ratio of 4.1 to 2 over 1880–1950, to represent 1.5 in 2005) and Asia (excluding Japan) (from 9.4 to 2.7 over 1913–1970, and was still 1.9 by 2005) to stabilizing thereafter, the gap between OECD and Africa declined more gradually over 1913–1980 (from 10.3 to 3.4, and remained at 3.2 in 2005). Meanwhile, the OECD gap with Eastern Europe (including Russia), after falling to a minimum by 1960, provided the exception by increasing to return to its pre-World War II size (Figure 7). It is worth noting that the declining relative gap in human development contrasts with the increasing gap in per capita income (Figure 8).

At this point it is worth focusing on how the absolute and relative differentials between OECD and the *Rest* resulting from the IHDI compare to those from the

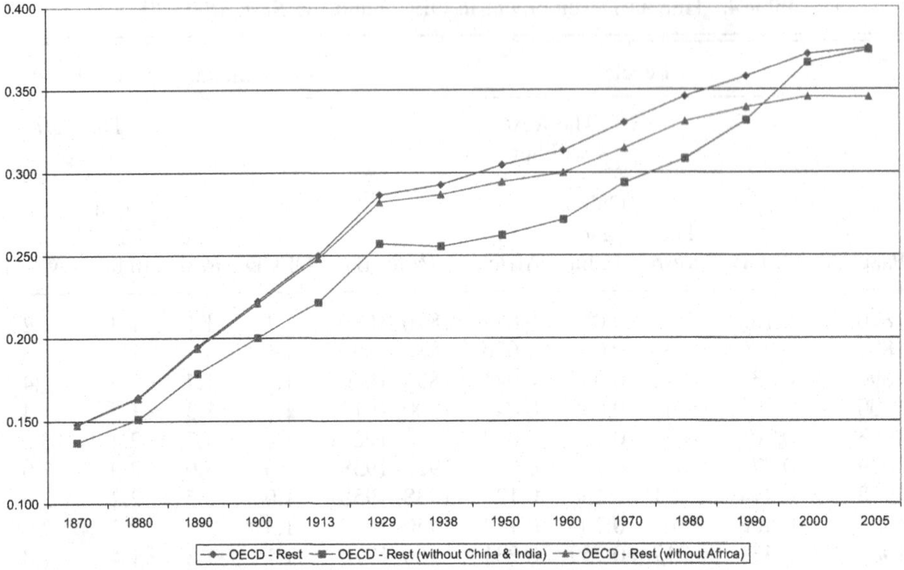

Figure 4. Absolute Gap in Human Development between OECD and the *Rest*, 1870–2005.

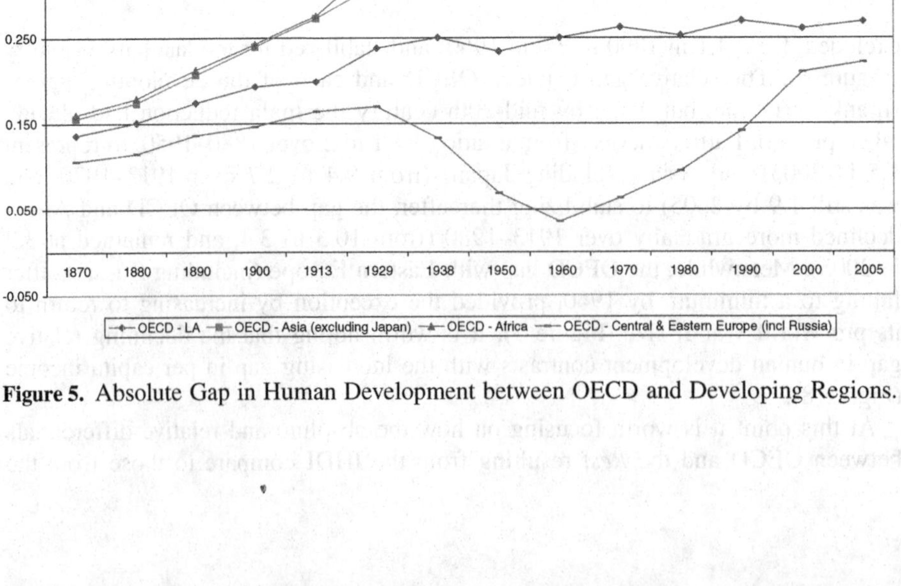

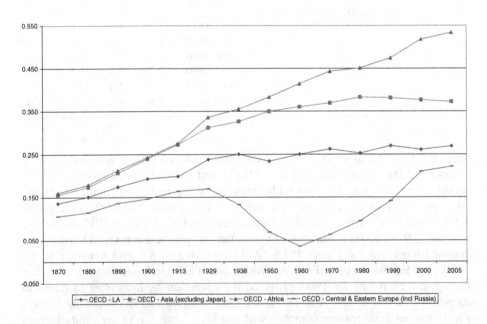

Figure 5. Absolute Gap in Human Development between OECD and Developing Regions.

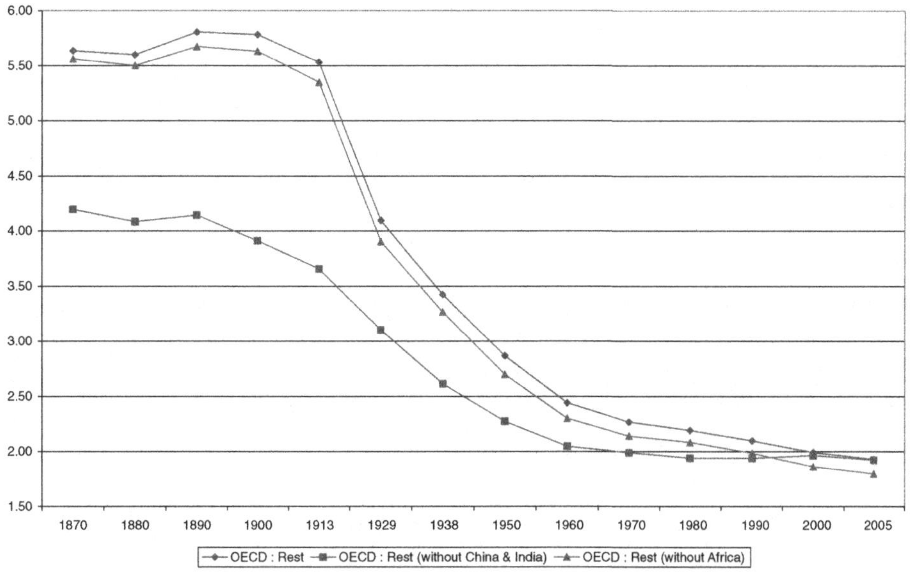

Figure 6. Relative Gap in Human Development between OECD and the *Rest*, 1870–2005.

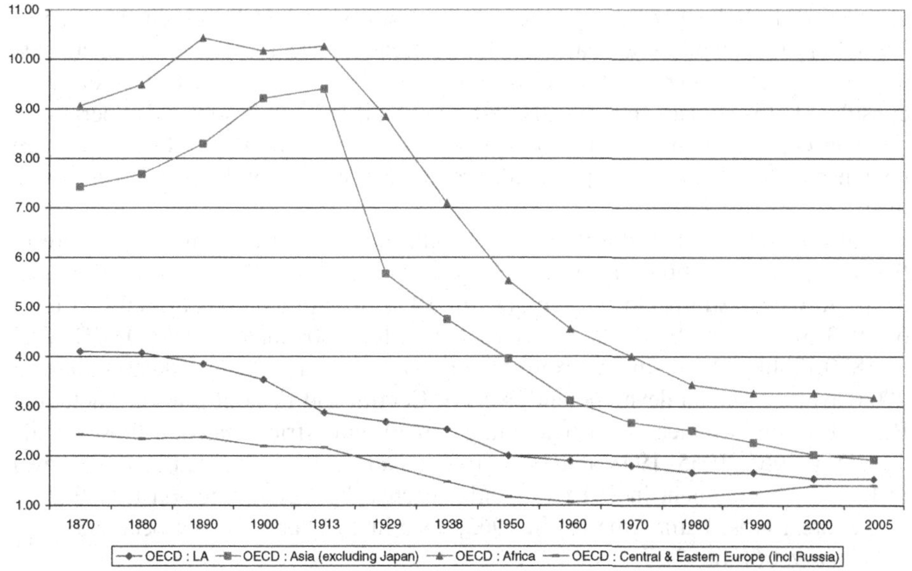

Figure 7. Relative Gap in Human Development between OECD and Developing Regions.

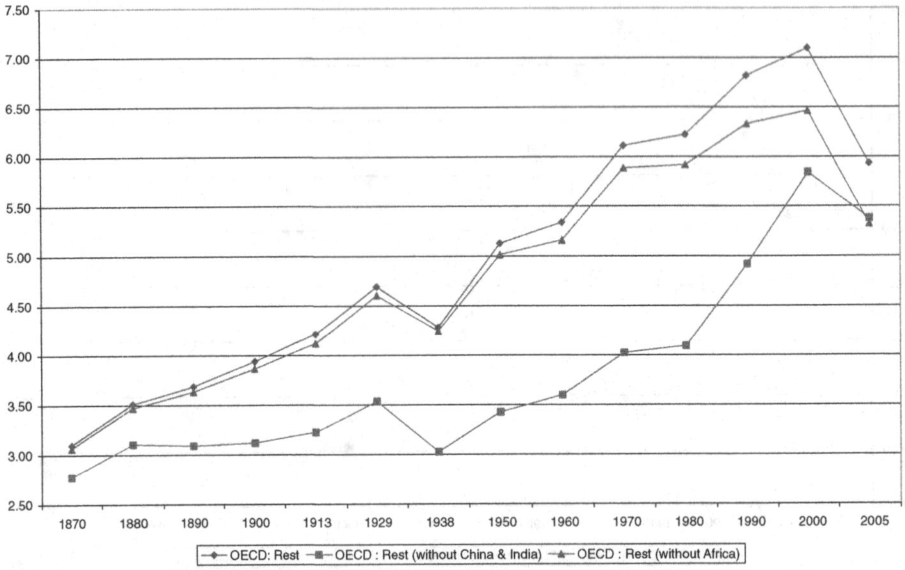

Figure 8. Relative Gap in Real Per Capita GDP between OECD and the *Rest*, 1870–2005.

conventional UNHDI. Although the absolute gap is initially larger in the case of the UNHDI, it exhibits an early declining trend (since the late 1920s), against a steady widening gap for the IHDI (Figure 9). When the relative differential is considered, it is appears that the UNHDI gap is substantially lower and experienced a milder contraction over 1900–1960 (Figure 10). Thus, the UNHDI offers a more benign view of the core–periphery differentials than the new human development index.

And how does human development in today's developing countries compare to that of advanced nations in the past? By 2005, the level of human development in the *Rest* was similar to the OECD's in 1938, it had achieved the OECD level of 1913 by the mid-1980s, and only by the early 1950s matched the OECD level in 1870 (Table 4). A similar exercise for major world regions indicates that, in 2005, average human development levels in Central and Eastern Europe (including Russia), Latin America, Asia (excluding Japan) and Africa matched those of the OECD in 1965, 1955, 1938 and 1890, respectively. Alternatively, the OECD level of human development in 1913 was only reached by Central and Eastern Europe in the late 1940s, Latin America in 1965, Asia in 1990 and has not been achieved in Africa yet (Table 3).[35]

But, do regional differentials with the OECD in terms of human development match those in per capita GDP? In general, developing countries perform better in human development than in income per head terms – although not to the extent suggested by the conventional UNHDI (Crafts, 2002). Thus, in 2005, real per capita

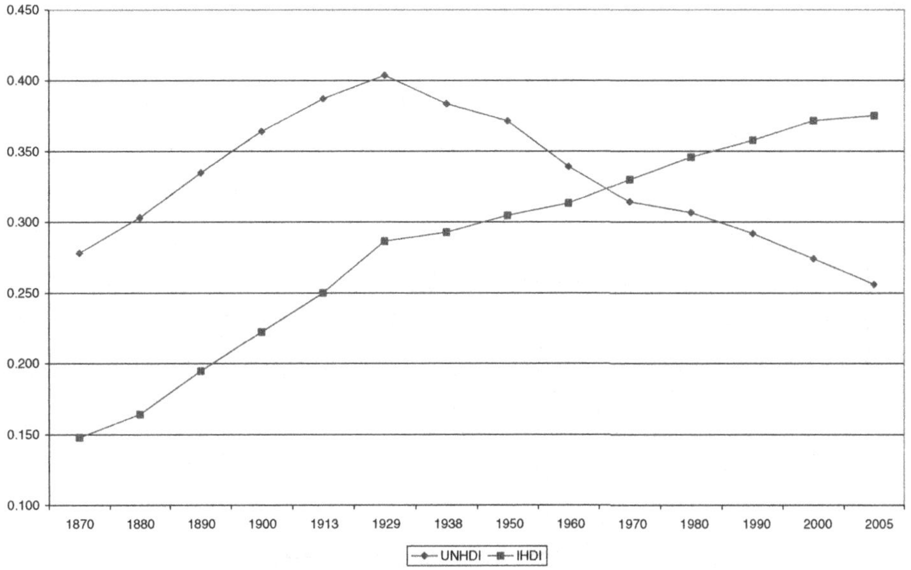

Figure 9. Absolute Human Development Gap between OECD and the *Rest*: UNHDI and IHDI.

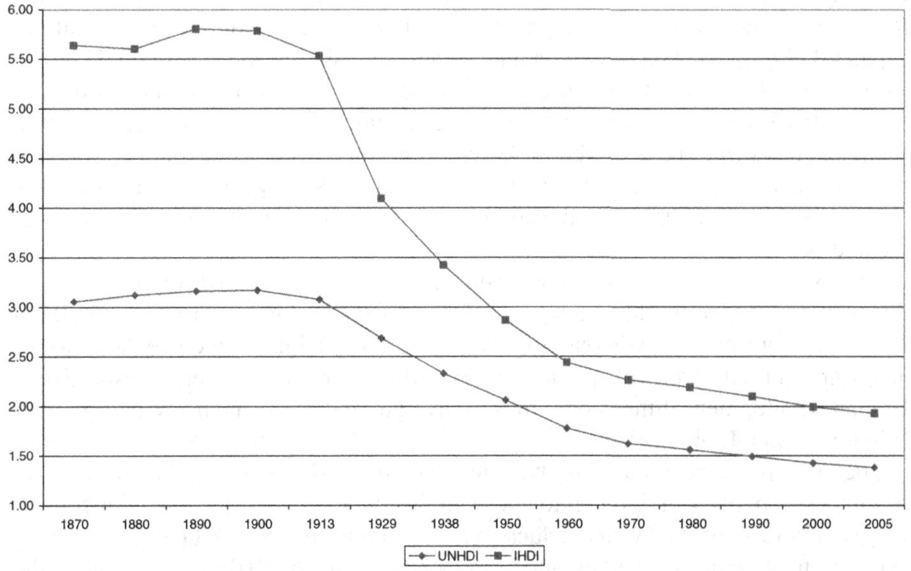

Figure 10. Relative Human Development Gap between OECD and the *Rest*: UNHDI and IHDI.

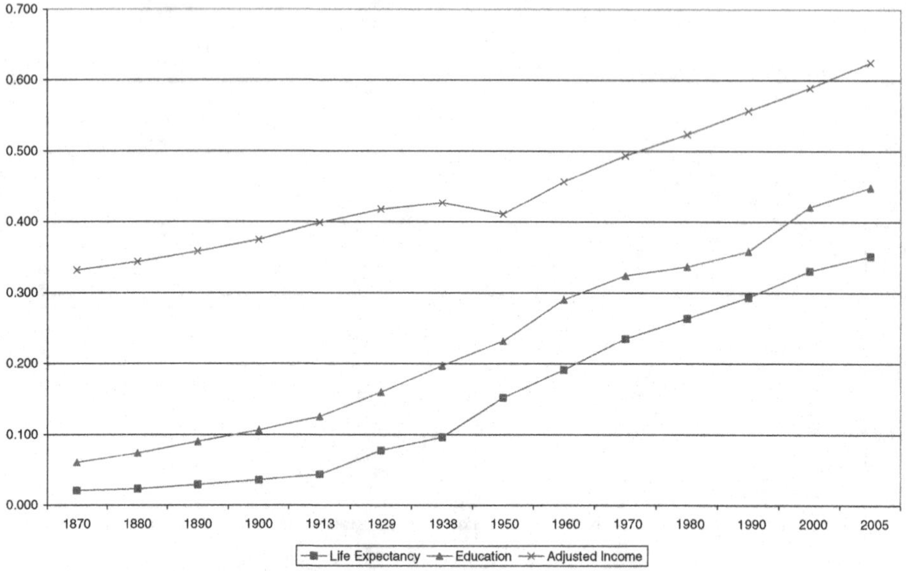

Figure 11. Dimensions of Human Development in the World, 1870–2005.

GDP for the *Rest* was similar to that of OECD by 1925, and only in 1970 did the *Rest* achieve the OECD income per head by 1870. Furthermore, in 2005, real per capita GDP in Latin America, Asia and Africa were similar to that of OECD by the early 1950s, 1920 and mid-19th century, respectively, whereas OECD income per head in 1913 was not reached in Latin America until the late 1960s, up to 2000 in Asia, and has still to be achieved in Africa. This is the result of the public provision of health (McKeown *et al.*, 1975; McKinley and McKinley, 1977; Loudon, 2000; Cutler and Miller, 2005) and education that increased more than proportionally to income per head.

Trends in human development result from those exhibited by each of its dimensions. For the world as a whole, education is the dimension which fits IHDI evolution more closely, whereas life expectancy and adjusted income, with lower and higher initial levels, experience faster and slower improvements, respectively. Human development dimensions, thus, converge, and more intensely before 1970 (Figure 11 and Table 5, Panel A).

The multiplicative nature of the new human development index allow us to decompose changes in IHDI into those of its dimensions – i.e. the transformed values of life expectancy and education, and adjusted per capita income. Thus, expression (4) can be differentiated, and changes in the IHDI expressed as the equally weighted average of the variation rates of its components. Thus, denoting rates of variation as lower case,

$$\text{IHDI} = 1/3l + 1/3e + 1/3y_{\text{un}} \tag{5}$$

Table 5. Human Development and Its Dimensions: the World, 1870–2005.

	Levels					Annual IHDI growth and its decomposition (%)			
Panel A	IHDI	Life expectancy	Education	Adjusted income	Panel B	IHDI	Life expectancy	Education	Adjusted income
1870	0.064	0.021	0.061	0.332	1870–1880	1.2	0.32	0.58	0.10
1880	0.072	0.023	0.074	0.344	1880–1890	1.6	0.49	0.42	0.09
1890	0.085	0.029	0.090	0.358	1890–1900	1.5	0.50	0.39	0.11
1900	0.098	0.036	0.106	0.375	1900–1913	1.2	0.47	0.38	0.14
1913	0.115	0.044	0.125	0.399	1913–1929	2.1	0.67	0.28	0.05
1929	0.159	0.077	0.159	0.418	1929–1938	1.8	0.48	0.47	0.05
1938	0.187	0.096	0.197	0.427	1938–1950	1.8	0.79	0.28	−0.07
1950	0.232	0.152	0.232	0.411	1950–1960	2.0	0.41	0.40	0.19
1960	0.283	0.191	0.290	0.457	1960–1970	1.3	0.53	0.28	0.19
1970	0.323	0.235	0.324	0.494	1970–1980	0.8	0.54	0.18	0.28
1980	0.349	0.264	0.337	0.524	1980–1990	0.9	0.46	0.27	0.27
1990	0.380	0.294	0.358	0.557	1990–2000	1.2	0.35	0.48	0.17
2000	0.427	0.331	0.421	0.589	2000–2005	1.3	0.33	0.34	0.32
2005	0.455	0.352	0.449	0.625					
					1870–1913	1.4	0.45	0.44	0.11
					1913–1950	1.9	0.66	0.33	0.02
					1950–1970	1.7	0.46	0.35	0.19
					1970–1990	0.8	0.50	0.23	0.27
					1990–2005	1.2	0.35	0.43	0.22
					1870–2005	1.5	0.52	0.37	0.12

It can be observed that gains in the IHDI are driven by improvements in its social indicators (Table 5, Panel B, and Figure 12). Life expectancy is the main contributor to improving world human development over the long run, and specifically between 1880 and 1990. This fact is associated with the diffusion of new methods of preventing the disease transmission, including low cost improvements in public health and knowledge dissemination through schooling (Riley, 2005a) and to the introduction of new vaccines (since the 1890s) and drugs to cure infectious diseases (sulpha drugs since the late 1930s and, since the 1950s, antibiotics) (Easterlin, 1999, p. 270; Jayachandran *et al.*, 2010). A closer look highlights the contribution of education prior to 1913 and, again, since 1990.

When a similar exercise is carried out for the advanced and the developing countries and IHDI is decomposed into its dimensions (Figures 13 and 14), it emerges that, in the OECD, life expectancy made a significant contribution to the improvement of human development, especially during the first half of the 20th century and since 1970 (Table 6 and Figure 15). Also education did it in the late 19th and early 20th century and, again, in the 1960s. Meanwhile, in the *Rest*, education improvement was significant in the late 19th century and during the 1930s and, once more, since 1990; increasing longevity, however, only represented the main contribution to human development gains between 1913 and 1950 (even if

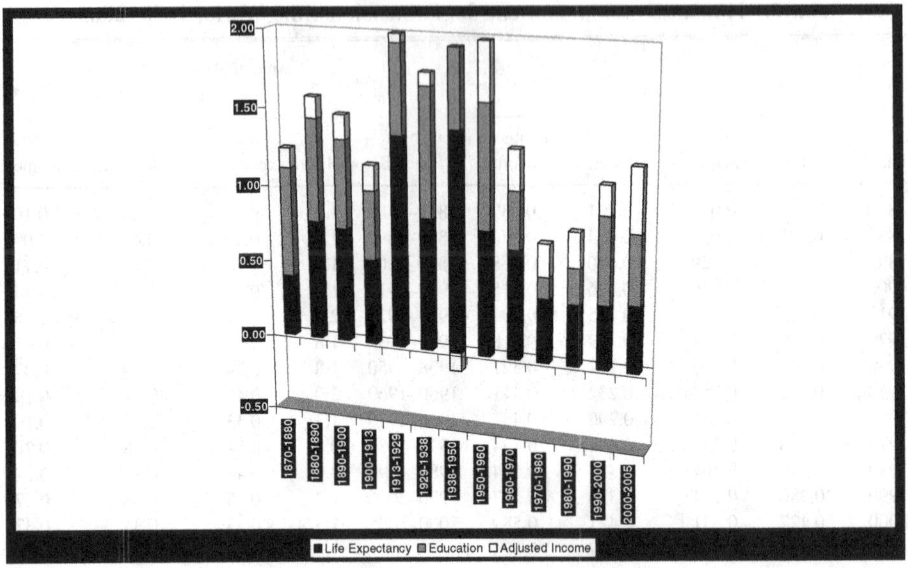

Figure 12. Decomposing IHDI Average Yearly Variation into its Dimensions in the World.

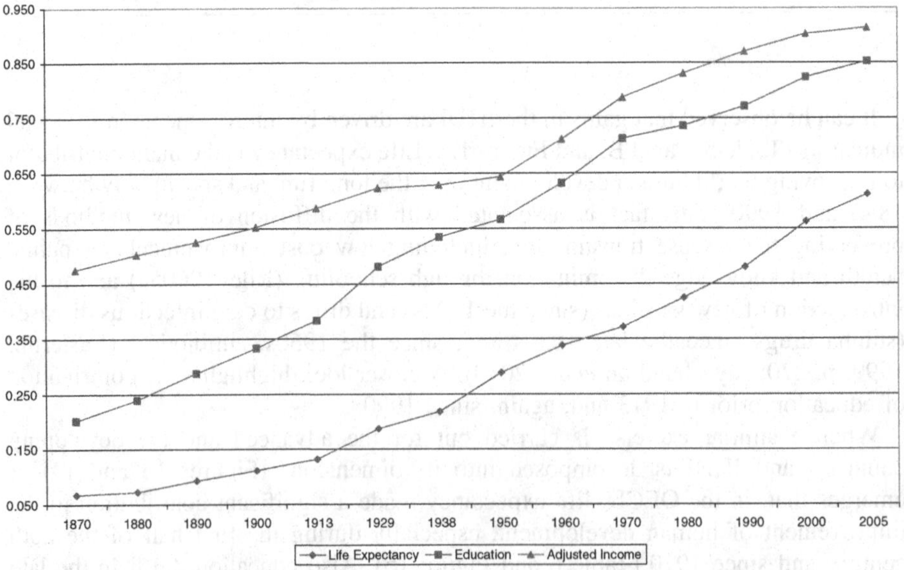

Figure 13. Dimensions of Human Development in the OECD, 1870–2005.

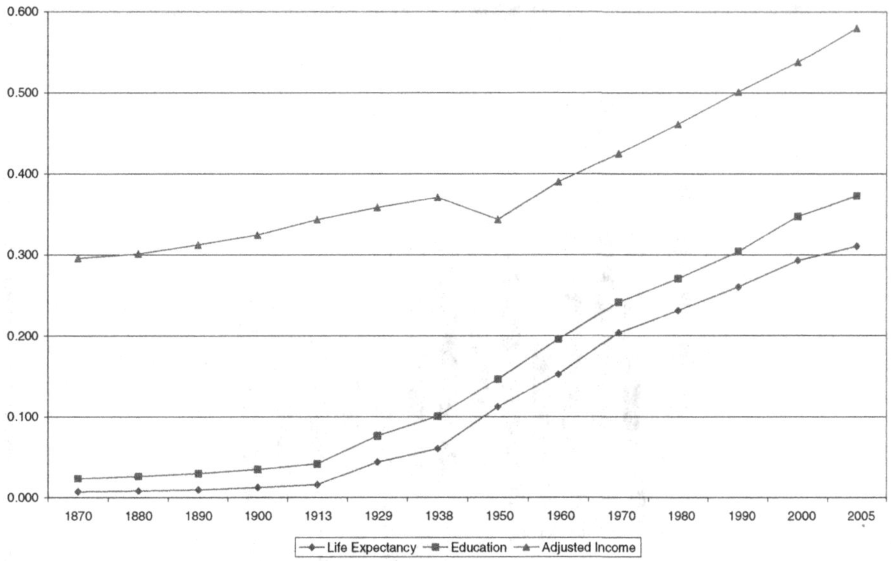

Figure 14. Dimensions of Human Development in the *Rest*, 1870–2005.

Table 6. Human Development and its Dimensions: OECD, 1870–2005.

	Levels					Annual IHDI growth and its decomposition			
Panel A	IHDI	Life expectancy	Education	Adjusted income	Panel B	IHDI	Life expectancy	Education	Adjusted income
1870	0.180	0.068	0.202	0.476	1870–1880	1.1	0.25	0.57	0.19
1880	0.200	0.073	0.240	0.503	1880–1890	1.6	0.52	0.39	0.09
1890	0.235	0.093	0.288	0.526	1890–1900	1.3	0.48	0.39	0.13
1900	0.269	0.111	0.333	0.553	1900–1913	1.0	0.46	0.38	0.16
1913	0.305	0.132	0.383	0.587	1913–1929	1.4	0.55	0.36	0.09
1929	0.379	0.188	0.481	0.623	1929–1938	1.0	0.57	0.40	0.03
1938	0.414	0.218	0.535	0.629	1938–1950	1.0	0.77	0.16	0.06
1950	0.468	0.288	0.566	0.643	1950–1960	1.3	0.43	0.30	0.27
1960	0.531	0.338	0.632	0.712	1960–1970	1.1	0.30	0.38	0.32
1970	0.591	0.371	0.713	0.787	1970–1980	0.7	0.61	0.14	0.24
1980	0.636	0.424	0.736	0.831	1980–1990	0.7	0.57	0.22	0.21
1990	0.684	0.480	0.771	0.870	1990–2000	0.9	0.61	0.25	0.14
2000	0.746	0.562	0.824	0.903	2000–2005	0.9	0.64	0.26	0.10
2005	0.779	0.611	0.852	0.914					
					1870–1913	1.2	0.44	0.42	0.14
					1913–1950	1.2	0.62	0.31	0.07
					1950–1970	1.2	0.37	0.34	0.30
					1970–1990	0.7	0.59	0.18	0.23
					1990–2005	0.9	0.62	0.26	0.13
					1870–2005	1.1	0.51	0.34	0.15

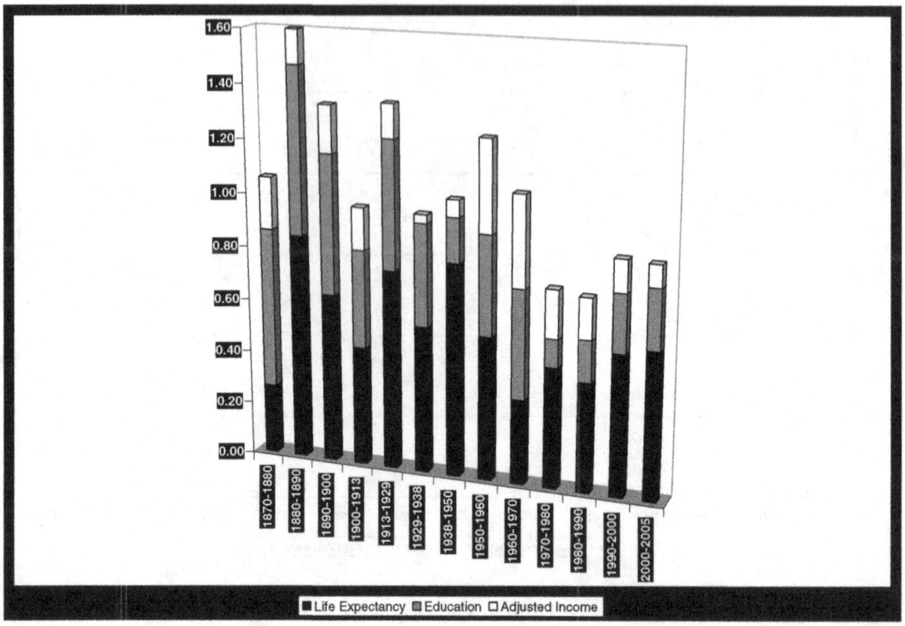

Figure 15. Decomposing IHDI Average Yearly Variation into its Dimensions in OECD.

it weakened during the Great Depression) (Table 7 and Figure 16). The stagnation of life expectancy in Eastern Europe, especially in Russia, since 1960 (and its decline in the 1990s), which converged to Asian levels, together with the remarkable slowdown since 1990 in Africa, as a result of HIV/AIDS, helps to explain it (Figure 17). Meanwhile, wide differences in education between Central and Eastern Europe and the developing world persisted over time (Figure 18).

In our previous discussion it was found that the human development gap between OECD and the *Rest* increased in absolute terms over the long run, whereas the opposite occurred in relative terms, but what role did each of its different dimensions play in it? In absolute terms, up to 1929, the larger gap was in terms of education; then, life expectancy took over doubling its gap over 1929–2005 (Figure 19). In relative terms, a dramatic contraction in the life expectancy gap took place between 1913 and 1970 – especially during the first half of the 20th century – which then stagnated and only increased slightly since 1990, as a result of the growing OECD differential with Russia and Africa. The relative gap in education fell throughout the 20th century and at a remarkable pace over 1929–1960. In turn, the adjusted income gap, which arguably captures any other dimension of well-being, remained flat (Figure 20).

If we now try to ascertain which share in the reduction of the relative gap in human development between the OECD and the *Rest* is attributable to each of its dimensions, it appears that, during the phase of deeper decline, 1913–1960,

Table 7. Human Development and its Dimensions: the *Rest*, 1870–2005.

	Levels					Annual IHDI growth and its decomposition			
Panel A	IHDI	Life expectancy	Education	Adjusted income	Panel B	IHDI	Life expectancy	Education	Adjusted income
1870	0.032	0.007	0.024	0.296	1870–1880	1.1	0.48	0.45	0.07
1880	0.036	0.008	0.027	0.301	1880–1890	1.3	0.47	0.41	0.12
1890	0.041	0.010	0.030	0.312	1890–1900	1.4	0.57	0.34	0.09
1900	0.046	0.013	0.035	0.324	1900–1913	1.3	0.51	0.37	0.12
1913	0.055	0.016	0.042	0.343	1913–1929	3.2	0.61	0.36	0.03
1929	0.093	0.044	0.076	0.358	1929–1938	3.0	0.50	0.44	0.06
1938	0.121	0.061	0.101	0.371	1938–1950	2.5	0.68	0.41	−0.08
1950	0.163	0.112	0.146	0.343	1950–1960	2.9	0.42	0.40	0.18
1960	0.217	0.152	0.196	0.390	1960–1970	1.8	0.49	0.36	0.15
1970	0.261	0.204	0.242	0.425	1970–1980	1.1	0.40	0.35	0.25
1980	0.290	0.231	0.271	0.461	1980–1990	1.2	0.37	0.37	0.26
1990	0.326	0.261	0.304	0.501	1990–2000	1.4	0.37	0.41	0.22
2000	0.374	0.293	0.347	0.538	2000–2005	1.5	0.29	0.35	0.37
2005	0.404	0.311	0.373	0.580					
					1870–1913	1.3	0.51	0.38	0.10
					1913–1950	2.9	0.61	0.39	0.00
					1950–1970	2.3	0.45	0.38	0.16
					1970–1990	1.1	0.38	0.36	0.26
					1990–2005	1.4	0.34	0.39	0.28
					1870–2005	1.9	0.52	0.38	0.09

although life expectancy accounted for most of it over 1913–1929 and 1938–1950, education was the main dimension responsible during the Depression years and in the 1950s. Since 1970, closing the gap slowed down, with education as the leading contributor (Figure 21). It can be suggested, therefore, that the human development gap between OECD and the *Rest* has not closed as the catching up in life expectancy has stopped, largely due to the behaviour of Russia and Africa, although it has weakened in terms of education.

4. Concluding Remarks

For many developing countries the usual pessimistic overtones of the *Human Development Reports* are contradicted by the rosy picture that emerges from their figures when compared with their own economic growth record. In an attempt to explain such a contradiction this chapter offers a new IHDI in which social dimensions are obtained using a convex achievement function and the index's dimensions are combined multiplicatively.

A long-run improvement in world human development is found for the last 135 years that, nonetheless, fell short of its maximum potential. Regional variance emerges an important feature of human development. In particular, although the

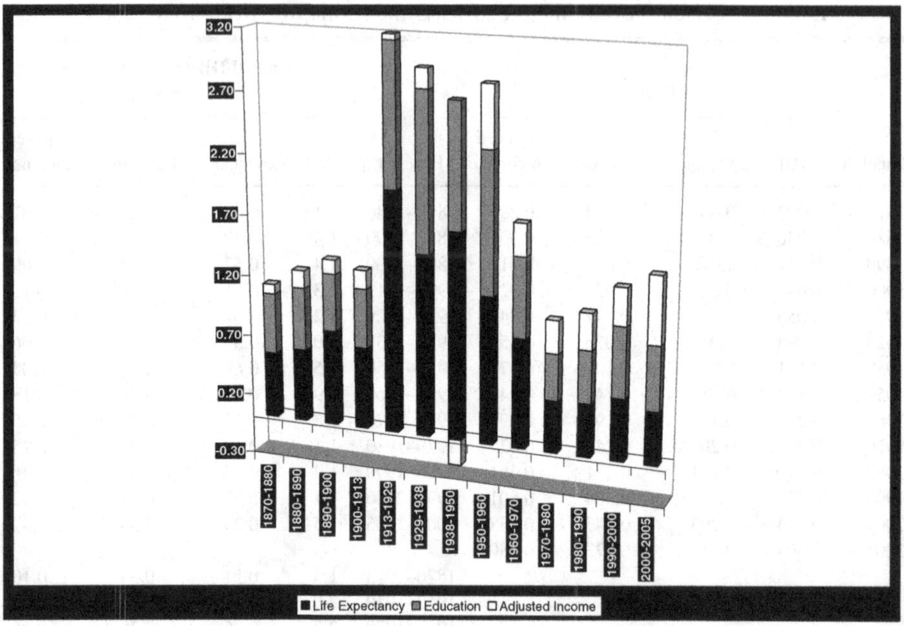

Figure 16. Decomposing IHDI Average Yearly Variation into its Dimensions in the *Rest*.

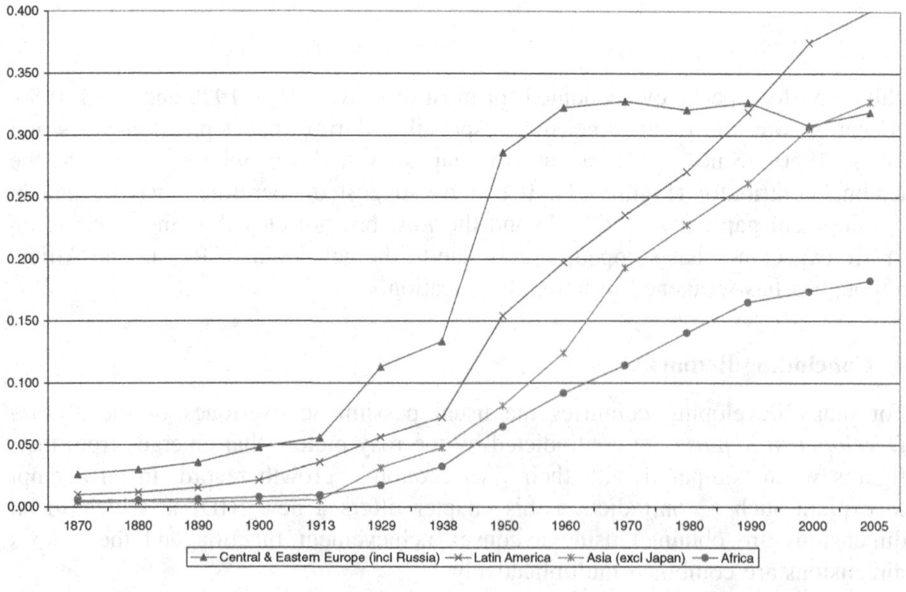

Figure 17. Life Expectancy in the *Rest*: Regional Composition.

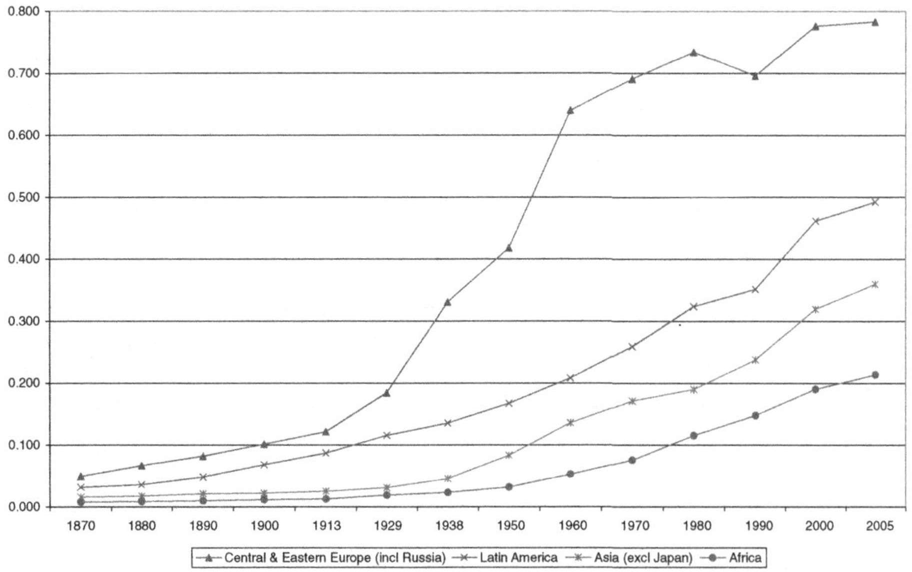

Figure 18. Education in the *Rest*: Regional Composition.

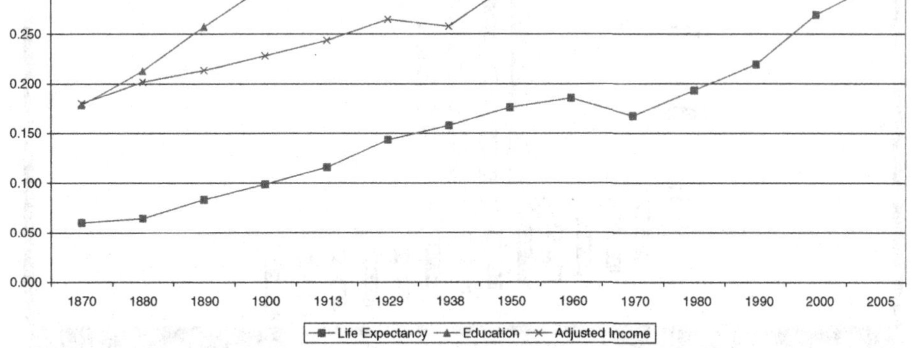

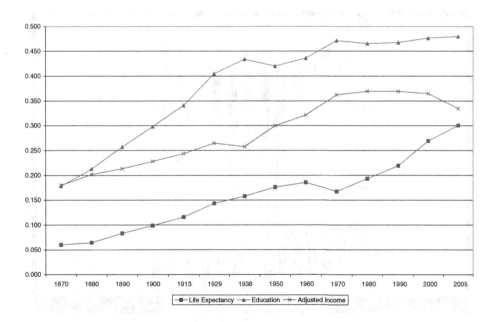

Figure 19. Human Development Dimensions: Absolute Gap between OECD and the *Rest*.

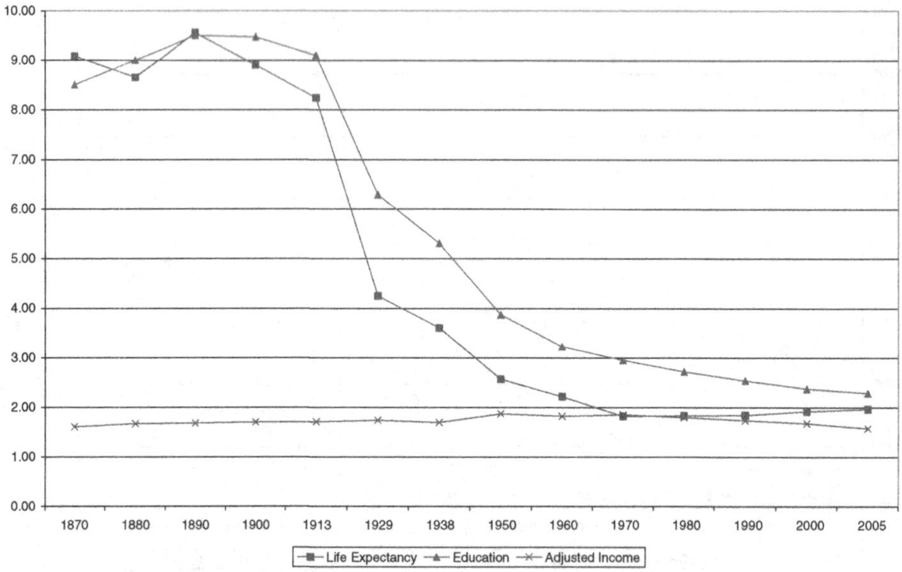

Figure 20. Human Development Dimensions: Relative Gap between OECD and the *Rest*.

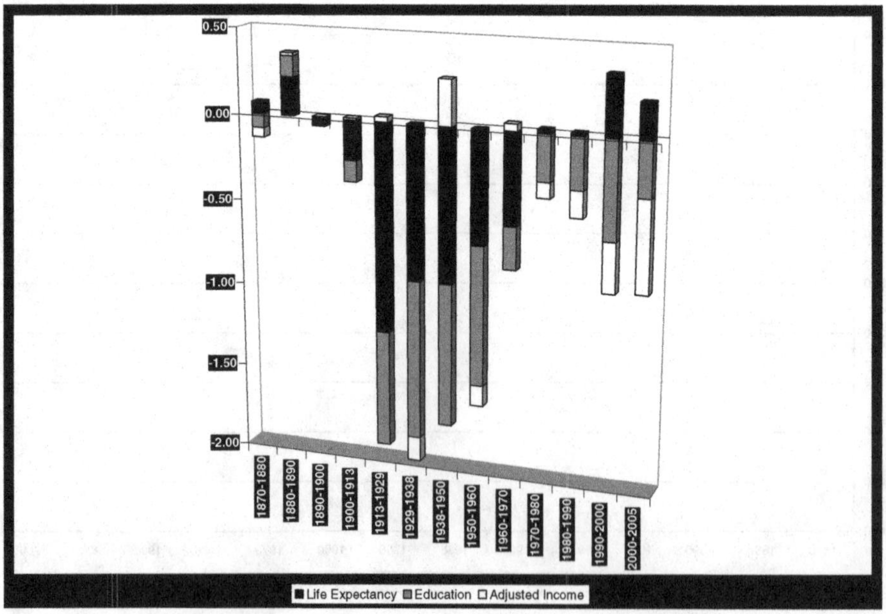

Figure 21. Decomposing Average Yearly Variation in the Relative OECD–*Rest* IHDI Gap into its Dimensions.

absolute gap between rich and poor countries widened, the relative gap in human development, contrary to the observed trend in real income per head, fell over time. However, closing the gap has slowed down its pace significantly since 1970 due to the behaviour of Africa and Central and Eastern Europe, especially Russia. Gains in life expectancy provide the main contribution to improving human development over the long run. However, the gap has failed to close largely as a result of the stagnation of life expectancy in Russia since 1960 and more recently as a consequence of the impact of HIV/AIDS in Sub-Saharan Africa.

When compared to the conventional UNDP index, the IHDI provides systematically lower levels of human development for the developing countries. As a result the gap between rich and poor countries is highlighted and a much less optimistic view than the conventional UNHDI results, justifying the concern for international differences expressed in *Human Development Reports*. These sobering new findings highlight the need to increase levels of human development in developing countries while suggesting some weaknesses that required to be addressed, in particular, health improvements to enhance life expectancy and further stress on secondary and tertiary education.

Acknowledgements

Earlier versions of this chapter were presented at the Copenhagen Institute of Economics and the European University Institute, Florence. I am indebted to Giovanni Federico, Christian Morrisson, Jim Riley, Joan Rosés, Isabel Sanz-Villarroya and Giovanni Vecchi for their suggestions. I am most grateful to Alexander Apostolides, Pablo Astorga, Facundo Alvaredo, Luis Bértola, Peter Boomgaard, Victor Bulmer-Thomas, Joaquim da Costa Leite, Mark Harrison, Salomón Kalmanovitz, Bruno Monasterio, Christian Morrisson, Fabrice Murtin, Les Oxley, Sevket Pamuk, David Reher, Alvaro Ferreira da Silva, Jan-Pieter Smits, Socrates Petmetzas and Marianne Ward for kindly sharing their data. Financial support from the Spanish Ministry of Science and Innovation (Research Project 'Consolidating Economics', Consolider-Ingenio 2010 Programme), the HI-POD Project, Seventh Research Framework Programme Contract no. 225342, and Fundación Rafael del Pino's Research Project on 'Economic Freedom in History' is highly appreciated. The usual disclaimer applies.

Notes

1. Welfare economics is meant here in a broad sense and not restricted to conventional 'welfare economics'.
2. Cf. Adelman and Morris (1967), Beckerman (1966), Beckerman and Bacon (1966), Ehrlich (1969), Heston (1973), Hicks and Streeten (1979), Larson and Wilford (1979), Morris (1979), Streeten *et al.* (1981), McGranahan *et al.* (1985) and Ram (1982).
3. The human development index has been received favourably, though uncritically, among economic historians who perceive it as a 'retrospective index of welfare' (Costa and Steckel, 1997, pp. 73–74) and have been adapted it imaginatively to the available evidence (Steckel and Floud, 1997a; Astorga and Fitzgerald, 1998; Astorga *et al.*, 2005).
4. For life expectancy at birth the maximum and the minimum values are established at 85 and 25 years, respectively. For education, the maximum and minimum are 100

and 0. The education index combines adult literacy and gross enrolment (primary, secondary and tertiary), with two-thirds and one-third weights, respectively. In the case of per capita GDP, a logarithmic transformation is imposed to allow for its assumed diminishing returns in terms of human development, and the maximum and minimum values are the logarithms of 40,000 and 100 dollars, respectively.

5. Mazumdar (1999) has, nonetheless, widened the PIQL index to include other social dimensions in an attempt to measure the quality of life.
6. The nature of its sponsor, its world coverage and its annual availability suggest, however, that the HDI may last longer than previous attempts at assessing well-being.
7. Thus, the HDI adds up social indicators for various domains of individual well-being but does not derive an aggregate of individual indices (Fleurbaey, 2009, p. 1055). Hicks (1997), Grimm *et al.* (2008), and Bértola *et al.* (2008) provide alternative human development measures allowing for income distribution.
8. Unfortunately, most of these shortcomings tend to be unavoidable in historical studies.
9. That is, the age coverage differs widely (figures for population above 7, 10 or 15 years old are simultaneously used) and often the literate population includes those who can read but cannot write. Similarly, enrolment figures are incomplete as the non-public sector is usually neglected. Moreover, comparability between very different writing systems (Chinese ideograms versus western alphabet, for example) is fraught with difficulties (Lind, 2004).
10. It can be argued, however, that life tables' projections can be superior to imperfectly collected data on life expectancy.
11. An additional worry derives from the fact that the HDI combines stock and flow variables. It has been suggested that if an annual index is required as a measure of progress, it should be computed on annual basis with flow data and preferably taking into account yearly changes in *per capita* income, in infant mortality and in school enrolment (Aturupane *et al.*, 1994, p. 246).
12. 'If they are *mutually orthogonal*, then each measures an aspect of development unrelated to that measured by any other. At the other extreme, if they *perfectly correlate* with each other, then all indicators measure the same aspect' (Srinivasan, 1994, p. 240).
13. PCA is a statistical technique for transforming a large set of variables into a smaller set of uncorrelated variables that accounts for most of the variation in the original variables. The principal components are linear combinations of the original variables with characteristic vectors of the correlation matrix of original variables as weights. The first principal component captures the largest proportion of the variation in the original set of variables.
14. See Ram (1982) for a pioneering use of PCA to computing the physical index of quality of life. Also, see Ogwang (1994), Ogwang and Abdou (2003) and Lai (2000).
15. Cf. Chakravarty (2003). This conclusion contradicts Ogwang (1994) who used PCA to identify a single variable (life expectancy) which best represents the three constituent elements of the HDI and, hence, to eliminate the problem of arbitrary choice of weights.
16. Kelley (1991, p. 319) argued that the 'production-transformation between income per capita and other human development indicators may be nonlinear, and thus might justify unequal or even variable weights by income level'.

17. This choice has been justified as human development is a concept that goes beyond the utilitarian calculus deliberately (Desai, 1991, p. 354).
18. Preston (1975, pp. 236–237) stressed that the relationship between life expectancy and GDP per head shifted upwards over the 20th century, and countries attained higher life expectancy at lower income levels as time went by.
19. The variances of the principal components are equal to the associated characteristic roots. The proportion of the variation ascribed to a particular principal component is obtained by dividing the associated characteristic root by the sum of all the characteristic roots.
20. Cf. UNDP (1993) and Ogwang (1994).
21. The striking trade off between per capita income and longevity arises 'from the fact that the marginal effect on the HDI of longer life is a constant', while at the same time, 'the marginal effect of extra income falls very sharply as income increases' (Ravallion, 1997, p. 633). Such a result is supported by the results obtained by Dowrick *et al.* (2003, p. 525) who argue that 'life expectancy in many parts of the world could be extended at a surprisingly low cost'. However, they criticize the UNHDI for implicitly valuing 'life expectancy above its opportunity cost'.
22. For example, in the case of longevity, 'a further increase must be regarded as a greater achievement than an equal increase at lower levels of longevity, . . . the achievement must increase at a faster rate than the longevity' (Kakwani, 1993, p. 313).
23. The same reasoning is reproduced in Dasgupta and Weale (1992, p. 125) who, nonetheless, make an exception in the case of literacy: 'It is not immediately apparent why it should be a lot less or a lot more difficult to increase the literacy rate when people are more literate'.
24. The fact that the human development index aims at reflecting human needs does not necessarily imply that differences across countries should be forced to narrow down. On the contrary, the reader will notice the stress HDR place on such differences in sharp contrast with the evidence provided by the UNHDI.
25. Altering goalposts is not new. For example, Dasgupta (1990) and Kakwani (1993) used 80 years as the maximum goalpost for life expectancy at birth in present time developing countries.
26. Truncating the lower part of the distribution by assuming a 'floor' of 25 years of life expectancy, which is not far from the actual value in the poorest developing countries, both in the present and in the past, has the advantage of allowing one to consider countries for which no data exist. The alternative option would be to reduce the country sample. Moreover, accepting a minimum value, M_0, of 24 years precludes a zero value for the transformed life expectancy.
27. The assumption of 1% as the lowest historical value for literacy and enrolment seems more reasonable than accepting zero as in the UNHDI, although a historical maximum of 99% is also accepted in the UNHDI. The consequence of assuming a historical lower bound of 1% is preventing zero values for the transformed variables.
28. Empirical evidence strongly rejects the conventional results obtained through the trading exchange rate converter (Summers and Heston, 1991; van Ark, 1993).
29. See the discussion in Prados de la Escosura (2000). Ward and Devereux (2003) have accepted the challenge to build direct PPP estimates from the expenditure side for 12 western economies at five benchmarks (1872, 1884, 1905, 1930 and 1950).
30. Maddison (2009) and Conference Board (2010) estimates era provide the best and most recent examples.

31. A significant strand of the literature defends the view defends that the best estimates of growth rates are those obtained from national accounts (Bhagwati and Hansen, 1973; Isenman, 1980; Kravis and Lipsey, 1991; Maddison, 1991, 1995) on the grounds that 'using domestic prices to measure growth rates is more reliable, because those prices characterize the trade offs faced by the decision making agents' (Nuxoll, 1994).
32. This lower bound for per capita income which, no doubt, truncates the data set at the bottom, allows me to consider countries in earlier periods for which no data exist and that, otherwise, would reduce the country sample considered here.
33. Thus, I have spliced the four sample estimates into a single one in which the levels for each world region i in the larger country sample (X_{i1990}) are accepted and earlier benchmark estimates (X_{it}, for $t = 1870, 1913, 1950$) are successively re-scaled up to match the new benchmark level X' for the year (o) in which each pair of benchmark estimates overlap, $X'_{it} = (X'_{io}/X_{io}) * X_{it}$.
34. The Organization for Economic Cooperation and Development (OECD), created in Paris on 14th December 1960, included 20 countries from Western Europe and the Western Offshoots (Australia, Canada, New Zealand and the USA). Today it includes 32 countries. In this paper OECD refers to its pre-1995 membership: Australia, Austria, Belgium, Canada, Denmark, Finland, France, Germany, Greece, Iceland – only since 1990, Ireland, Italy, Japan, Luxembourg, Netherlands, New Zealand, Norway, Portugal, Spain, Sweden, Switzerland, Turkey, the UK and the USA. Luxembourg has been excluded due to lack of data. Turkey has also been excluded in order to have a more homogeneous group in terms of economic and social development and was allocated to the Asia group. New members since 1995: Czech Republic, Hungary and Slovakia, are included in Eastern Europe; South Korea, in Asia; and Mexico, in Latin America.
35. Nonetheless, these results support the view that human development in today's less developed countries compare favourably with that of developed countries in the late 19th century (Crafts, 2002).

References

Adelman, I. and Morris, C.T. (1967) *Society, Politics and Economic Development*. Baltimore, MD: Johns Hopkins University Press.

Altug, S., Filiztekin, A. and Pamuk, S. (2008) Sources of long-term growth for Turkey, 1880-2005. *European Review of Economic History* 12(3): 393–430.

Alvaredo, F. and Atkinson, A.B. (2010) Colonial rule, apartheid and natural resources: top incomes in South Africa 1903-2005. Mimeo, Department of Economics, University of Oxford.

van Ark, B. (1993) The ICOP approach. Its implications and applicability. In A. Szirmai, B. van Ark and D. Pilat (eds), *Explaining Economic Growth* (pp. 375–398). Amsterdam: North-Holland.

Arriaga, E.E. (1968) *New Life Tables for Latin American Populations in the Nineteenth and Twentieth Centuries*. Population Monographs Series No. 3. Berkeley, CA: Institute of International Studies, University of California.

Astorga, P. and Fitzgerald, V. (1998) Statistical appendix. In R. Thorp (ed.), *Progress, Poverty and Exclusion: An Economic History of Latin America in the 20th Century* (pp. 307–365). Washington, DC: Inter-American Development Bank.

Astorga, P., Bergés, A.R. and FitzGerald, E.V.K. (2003) The Oxford Latin American Economic History Database (OxLAD). Oxford: Latin American Centre, Oxford University. Available at http://oxlad.qeh.ox.ac.uk/ (last accessed 19 April 2010).

Astorga, P., Berges, A.R. and Fitzgerald, E.V.K. (2005) The standard of living in Latin America during the twentieth century. *Economic History Review* 63(4): 765–796.

Aturupane, H., Glewwe P. and Isenman P. (1994) Poverty, human development, and growth: an emerging consensus? *American Economic Review, Papers and Proceedings* 84(2): 244–249.

Ayeni, O. (1976) Retrospective estimates of mortality from the Nigerian medical censuses of 1930–1932: a research note. *Nigerian Journal of Economic and Social Studies* 18: 461–469.

Bakker, G.P., den Huitker, T.A. and van Bochove, C.A. (1990) The Dutch economy 1921–1938: revised macroeconomic data for the interwar period. *Review of Income and Wealth* 36: 187–206.

Banks, A.S. (2010) *Cross-National Time-Series Data Archive*, http://www.databanksinternational.com/ (last accessed 3 May 2010).

Baptista, A. (1997) *Bases Cuantitativas de la Economía Venezolana, 1830–1995*. Caracas: Fundación Polar.

Barro, R. and Lee, J.W. (2002) International data on educational attainment: updates and implications. Working Paper 42, Harvard University Center for International Development CID. Accompanying dataset available at http://www.ksg.harvard.edu/CID (last accessed 15 April 2009).

Batista, D., Martins, C., Pinheiro, M. and Reis, J. (1997) *New Estimates of Portugal's GDP 1910–1958*. Lisbon: Banco de Portugal.

Beckerman, W. (1966) *International Comparisons of Real Incomes*. Paris: OECD Development Centre.

Beckerman, W. (1993) Is economic growth still desirable?. In A. Szirmai, B. van Ark and D. Pilat (eds), *Explaining Economic Growth. Essays in Honour of Angus Maddison* (pp. 77–100). Amsterdam: North-Holland.

Beckerman, W. and Bacon, R. (1966) International comparisons of income levels: a suggested new measure. *Economic Journal* 76(303): 519–536.

Benavot, A. and Riddle P. (1988) The expansion of primary education, 1870–1940: trends and issues. *Sociology of Education* 61(3): 191–210.

Bértola, L. (1998) *El PBI de Uruguay, 1870–1936 y Otras Estimaciones*. Montevideo: Universidad de la República.

Bértola, L., M. Camou, S. Maubrigades, and N. Melgar (2008), "Human Development and Inequality in the 20th Century: the Mercosur Countries in a Comparative Perspective", Universidad Carlos III Working Papers in Economic History 08-06.

Bhagwati, J.N. and Hansen, B. (1973) Should growth rates be evaluated at international prices? In J.N. Bhagwati and R.S. Eckaus (eds), *Development and Planning: Essays in Honour of Paul Rosenstein-Rodan* (pp. 53–68). Cambridge, MA: MIT Press.

Booysen, F. (2002) An overview and evaluation of composite indices of development. *Social Indicators Research* 59(2): 115–151.

Bourbeau, R., Légaré, J. and Émond, V. (1997) *New Birth Cohort Life Tables for Canada and Quebec,1801–1991*. Research Paper No. 3, Statistics Canada, Demographic Division. Available at www.statcan.ca (last accessed 8 May 2008).

Bourguignon, F. and Morrisson, C. (2002) Inequality among world citizens. *American Economic Review* 92(4): 727–744.

Braun, J., Braun, M., Briones, I. and Díaz, J. (2000) Economía chilena, 1810–1995. Estadísticas históricas. Pontificia Universidad Católica de Chile, Instituto de Economía, Documento de Trabajo no. 187.

Brundenius, C. and Zimbalist, A. (1989) *The Cuban Economy: Measurement and Analysis of Socialist Performance*. Baltimore, MD: Johns Hopkins University Press.

Bureau of Economic Analysis (2010) *GDP by Industry, 1910 to 2009*. Available at http://www.bea.gov/industry/iotables/prod/table_list.cfm?anon=56082 (last accessed 5 May 2010).

Buyst, E. (1997) New GNP estimates for the Belgian economy during the interwar period. *Review of Income and Wealth* 43: 357–375.

Caldwell, J., Bracher, M., Santow, G. and Caldwell P. (1986) Population trends in China – a perspective provided by the 1982 census. In C. Li (ed.), *A Census of One Billion People* (pp. 352–391). Hong Kong: Republic of China Population Census Office.

CEPAL (2009) América Latina y el Caribe. Series históricas de estadísticas económicas 1950–2008. *Cuadernos Estadísticos* 37, Comisión Económica para América Latina y el Caribe. Available at http://www.eclac.cl/deype/cuaderno37/index.htm (last accessed 5 February 2010).

Cha, M.S. and Kim, N.N. (2006) Korea's first industrial revolution, 1911–40. Naksungdae Institute of Economic Research (NIER) Working Papers Series 2006-3. Available at http://www.naksung.re.kr/papers/wp2006-3.pdf (last accessed 17 March 2010).

Cha, M.S. and Wu, T.M. (2002) Colonial transition to modern economic growth in Korea and Taiwan. Mimeo, Yeungnam University and National Taiwan University.

Chakravarty, S.R. (2003) A generalized human development index. *Review of Development Economics* 7(1): 99–114.

Coatsworth, J.H. (1989) The decline of the Mexican economy, 1800–1860. In R. Liehr (ed.), *América Latina en la época de Simón Bolívar. La formación de las economías nacionales y los intereses económicos europeos 1800–1850* (pp. 27–53). Berlin: Colloquium.

Cohen, D. and Soto, M. (2007) Growth and human capital: good data, good results. *Journal of Economic Growth* 12(1): 51–76.

Conference Board (2010) *Total Economy Database, January 2010*. Available at http://www.conference-board.org/economics/database.cfm (last accessed 15 April 2010).

Conte, L., della, Torre G. and Vasta, M. (2007) The human development index in historical perspective: Italy from political unification to the present day. Quaderni Università degli Studi di Siena, Dipartimento di Economia Politica No. 491.

Cortés Conde, R. (1997) *La economía argentina en el largo plazo*. Buenos Aires: Editorial Sudamericana/ Universidad de San Andrés.

Costa, D.L. and Steckel, R.H. (1997) Long-term trends in health, welfare, and economic growth in the United States. In R.H. Steckel and R. Floud (eds), *Health and Welfare during Industrialization* (pp. 47–89). Chicago, IL: University of Chicago Press.

Crafts, N. (1997) The human development index and changes in standards of living: some historical comparisons. *European Review of Economic History* 1(3): 299–322.

Crafts, N. (2002) The human development index, 1870–1999: some revised estimates. *European Review of Economic History* 6(3): 395–405.

Cutler, D. and Miller, G. (2005) The role of public health improvements in health advance: the twentieth century United States. *Demography* 42(1): 1–22.

Dasgupta, P. (1990) Well-being and the extent of its realization in poor countries. *Economic Journal* 100(400): 1–32.

Dasgupta, P. (1993) *An Inquiry into Well-Being and Destitution*. Oxford: Clarendon Press.

Dasgupta, P. and Weale, M. (1992) On measuring the quality of life. *World Development* 20(1): 119–131.

Della Paolera, G., Taylor, A.M. and Bozolli, C.G. (2003) Historical statistics. In G. Della Paolera and A.M. Taylor (eds), *A New Economic History of Argentina* (pp. 376–385). New York: Cambridge University Press (with CD-ROM).

Deprez, P. (1979) The low countries. In W.R. Lee (ed.), *European Demography and Economic Growth* (pp. 236–283). London: Croom Helm.

Desai, M. (1991) Human development: concept and measurement. *European Economic Review* 35: 350–357.

Díaz, J., Lüders, R. and Wagner, G. (2007) Economía Chilena 1810–2000. Producto total y sectorial. Una nueva mirada. Pontificia Universidad Católica de Chile, Documento de trabajo 315.

Domínguez, R. and Guijarro, M. (2000) Evolución de las disparidades espaciales del bienestar en España, 1860–1930: El Índice Físico de Calidad de Vida. *Revista de Historia Económica* 18(1): 109–137.

Dopico, F. and Reher, D.S. (1998) *El declive de la mortalidad en España, 1860–1930*. Asociación de Demografía Histórica, Monografía No. 1.

Dowrick, S., Dunlop, Y. and Quiggin, J. (2003) Social indicators and comparisons of living standards. *Journal of Development Economics* 70: 501–529.

Easterlin, R. (1999) How beneficent is the market? A look at the modern history of mortality. *European Review of Economic History* 3(3): 257–294.

Easterly, W. (1999) Life after growth. *Journal of Economic Growth* 4(3): 239–276. Underlying data available at http://www.worldbank.org/html/prdmg/grthweb/growtht.htm (last accessed 13 March 2009).

Eckstein, A. (1955) National income and capital formation in Hungary, 1900–1950. *Income and Wealth*, 5: 150–223.

Ehrlich, E. (1969) Dynamic international comparisons of national incomes expressed in terms of physical indicators. *Osteuropa Wirtschaft* 14: 1–25.

Eisner, G. (1961) *Jamaica, 1830–1930: A Study in Economic Growth*. Manchester: Manchester University Press.

Engerman, S.L. (1997) The standard of living debate in international perspective: measures and indicators. In R.H. Steckel and R. Floud (eds), *Health and Welfare during Industrialization* (pp. 17–45). Chicago, IL: University of Chicago Press.

Fargues, P. (1986) Un siècle de transition démographique en Afrique méditerranéenne 1885–1985. *Population* 41(2): 205–232.

Federico, G. and Toniolo, G. (1991) Italy. In R. Sylla and G. Toniolo (eds), *Patterns of European Industrialization. The Nineteenth Century* (pp. 197–217). London: Routledge.

Feinstein, C.H. (2005) *An Economic History of South Africa. Conquest, Discrimination and Development*. Cambridge: Cambridge University Press.

Fenoaltea, S. (2005) The growth of the Italian economy, 1861–1913: preliminary second-generation estimates. *European Review of Economic History* 9: 273–312.

Fleurbaey, M. (2009) Beyond GDP: the quest for a measure of social welfare. *Journal of Economic Literature* 47(4): 1029–1075.

Flora, P. (1973) Historical processes of social mobilization: urbanization and literacy, 1850–1965. In S.N. Eisenstadt and S. Rokkan (eds), *Building States and Nations: Models and Data Resources* (pp. 213–258). London: Sage.

Flora, P. (1983) *State, Economy, and Society in Western Europe 1815–1975. A Data Handbook in Two Volumes*. Frankfurt: Campus Verlag.

Floud, R. and Harris, B. (1997) Health, height, and welfare: Britain, 1700–1980. In R.H. Steckel and R. Floud (eds), *Health and Welfare during Industrialization* (pp. 91–126). Chicago, IL: University of Chicago Press.

Glass, D.V. and Grebenik, E. (1967) World population, 1800–1950. In H.J. Habakkuk and M. Postan (eds), *Cambridge Economic History of Europe*. Vol. VI: *The Industrial Revolutions and After: Incomes, Population, and Technological Change (I)* (pp. 56–138). Cambridge: Cambridge University Press.

Goerlich Gisbert, F. and Pinilla Pallejá, R. (2005) Esperanza de vida y potencial de vida a lo largo del siglo XX en España. *Revista de Demografía Histórica* 23(2): 79–109.

Goldsmith, R.W. (1961) The economic growth of Tsarist Russia: 1860–1913. *Economic Development and Cultural Change* 9: 441–475.

Goldsmith, R.W. (1986) *Desenvolvimento Financeiro Sob Um Século de Inflaçao*. Rio de Janeiro: Harper & Row do Brasil.

Good, D.F. (1994) The economic lag of Central and Eastern Europe: income estimates for the Habsburg successor states, 1870–1910. *Journal of Economic History* 54(4): 869–891.

Gormely, P.J. (1995) The human development index in 1994: impact of income on country rank. *Journal of Economic and Social Measurement* 21: 253–267.

Greasley, D. and Oxley, L. (2000a) Measuring New Zealand's GDP 1865–1933. *Review of Income and Wealth* 46, 351–368.

Greasley, D. and Oxley, L. (2000b) Outside the club: New Zealand's economic growth 1870–1993. *International Review of Applied Economics* 14: 173–192.

GRECO (Grupo de Estudios de Crecimiento Económico) (2002) *El Crecimiento Económico Colombiano en el Siglo XX*. Bogotá: Banco de la República – Fondo de Cultura Económica.

Gregory, P. (1982) *Russian National Income*. Cambridge: Cambridge University Press.

Grimm, M., Harttgen, K., Klasen, S. and Misselhorn, M. (2008) A human development index by income groups. *World Development* 36(12): 2527–2546.

Grytten, O.H. (2004) The gross domestic product for Norway 1830–2003. In Ø. Eitrheim, J.T. Klovland and J.F. Qvigstad (eds), *Historical Monetary Statistics for Norway 1819–2003* (pp. 241–288). Oslo: Norges Bank, Norges Bank Occasional Papers no. 35.

Haines, M. (1994) Estimated life tables for the United States, 1850–1900. National Bureau of Economic Research Working Paper Series 15 on Historical Factors in Long Run Growth.

Hanley, S.B. (1990) The relationship between education and economic growth. In G. Tortella (ed.), *Education and Economic Development since the Industrial Revolution* (pp. 69–87). Valencia: Generalitat Valenciana.

Hansen, S.A. (1974) *Økonomisk vækst i Danmark*. Copenhagen: Akademisk Forlag.

Hayami, Y. and Ruttan, V.W. (1985) *Agricultural Development: An International Perspective*. Baltimore, MD: Johns Hopkins University Press.

Helczmanovski, H. (1979) Austria–Hungary. In W. R. Lee (ed.), *European Demography and Economic Growth* (pp. 27–78). London: Croom Helm.

Heston, A. (1973) A comparison of some short-cut methods of estimating real product per capita. *Review of Income and Wealth* 19(1): 79–104.

Heston, A. (1994) A brief review of some problems in using national accounts data in level of output comparisons and growth studies. *Journal of Development Economics* 44: 29–52.

Hicks, D.A. (1997) The inequality-adjusted human development index: constructive proposal. *World Development* 28(8): 1283–1298.

Hicks, N. and Streeten, P. (1979) Indicators of development: the search for a basic needs yardstick. *World Development* 7: 567–580.

Hjerppe, R. (1996) *Finland's Historical National Accounts 1860–1994: Calculation Methods and Statistical Tables*. Jyväskylä: J.Y.H.L.

Hoffmann, W.G., Grumbach, F. and Hesse, H. (1965) *Das Wachstum der Deutschen Wirtschaft seit der Mitte des 19.Jahrhunderts*. Berlin: Springer.

Honda, G. (1997) Differential structure, differential health: industrialization in Japan, 1868–1940. In R.H. Steckel and R. Floud (eds), *Health and Welfare during Industrialization* (pp. 251–284). Chicago, IL: University of Chicago Press.

Hopkins, M. (1991) Human development revisited: a new UNDP report. *World Development* 19(10): 1469–1473.

Horlings, E. (1997) The contribution of the service sector to gross domestic product in Belgium, 1835–1990. Mimeo, Universiteit Utrecht, Utrecht.

INEGI (1995) *Estadísticas históricas de México*. México DF: INEGI.

International Monetary Fund (IMF) (2010) *International Financial Statistics*. Washington, DC: IMF.

Isenman, P. (1980) Inter-country comparison of 'real' (PPP) incomes: revised estimates and unresolved questions. *World Development* 8(1): 61–72.
Jannetta, A.B. and Preston, S.H. (1991) Two centuries of mortality change in central Japan: the evidence from a temple death register. *Population Studies* 45(3): 417–436.
Jayachandran, S., Lleras-Muney, A. and Smith, K.V. (2010) Modern medicine and the twentieth century decline in mortality: evidence on the impact of sulfa drugs. *American Economic Journal: Applied Economics* 2(2): 118–146.
Johansson, S.R. and Mosk, C. (1987) Exposure, resistance and life expectancy: disease and death during the economic development of Japan, 1900–1960. *Population Studies* 41(2): 207–235.
Kakwani, N. (1993) Performance in living standards. An international comparison. *Journal of Development Economics* 41: 307–336.
Kalmanovitz Krauter, S. and López Rivera, E. (2009) *Las Cuentas Nacionales de Colombia en el Siglo XIX*. Bogotá: Universidad de Bogotá Jorge Tadeo Lozano.
Kannisto, V., Nieminen, M. and Turpeinen, O. (1999) Finnish life tables since 1751. *Demographic Research* 1, 1. Available at www.demographic-research.org/Volumes/Vol1/1 (last accessed in 27 February 2009).
Kelley, A.C. (1991) The human development index: 'handle with care'. *Population and Development Review* 17: 315–324.
Kendrick, J.W. (1961) *Productivity Trends in the United States*. Princeton, NJ: National Bureau of Economic Research.
Keyfitz, N. and Fleiger, W. (1968) *World Population: An Analysis of Vital Data*. Chicago, IL: University of Chicago Press.
Kimura, M. (1990) Diffusion of primary education in Korea. In G. Tortella (ed.), *Education and Economic Development since the Industrial Revolution* (pp. 337–353). Valencia: Generalitat Valenciana.
Kostelenos, G. and Associates (2007) *Gross Domestic Product, 1830–1939* (in Greek). Athens: Centre of Planning and Economic Research (KEPE).
Krantz, O. and Schön, L. (2007) *Swedish Historical National Accounts 1800–2000. Aggregate Output Series*. Lund: Lund University.
Kravis, I.B. and Lipsey, R.E. (1991) The international comparison program: current status and problems. In P.E. Hooper and J.D. Richardson (eds), *International Economic Transactions: Issues in Measurement and Empirical Research* (pp. 437–464). Studies in Income and Wealth 55. Chicago, IL: NBER and University of Chicago Press.
Lai, D. (2000) Temporal analysis of human development indicators: principal component approach. *Social Indicators Research* 51(3): 331–366.
Lains, P. (2006) Growth in a protected environment: Portugal, 1850–1950. *Research in Economic History* 24: 121–163.
Langford, C., and Storey, P. (1993) Sex differentials in mortality early in the twentieth century: Sri Lanka and India compared. *Population and Development Review* 19(2): 263–282.
Larson, D.A. and Wilford, W.T. (1979) The physical quality of life index: a useful social indicator? *World Development* 7: 581–584.
Lavely, W. and Wong, R.B. (1998) Revising the Malthusian narrative: the comparative study of population dynamics in late imperial China. *Journal of Asian Studies* 57(3): 714–748.
Leite, J. da Costa (2005) Populaçao e crescimento económico. In P. Lains and A. Ferreira da Silva (eds.), *História Económica de Portugal 1700–2000* (Vol. II, O Século XIX, pp. 43–81). Lisboa: Impresa de Ciências Sociais.
Lewis, W.A. (1955) *The Theory of Economic Growth*. London: George Allen and Unwin.
Lindert, P.H. (2004) *Growing Public. Social Spending and Economic Growth since the Eighteenth Century* (2 vols). Cambridge: Cambridge University Press.
Loudon, I. (2000) Maternal mortality in the past and its relevance to developing countries today. *American Journal of Clinical Nutrition* 72, 1 (supplement): 241S–246S.

Maddison, A. (1991) *Dynamic Forces in Capitalist Development. A Long-run Comparative View*. Oxford: Oxford University Press.

Maddison, A. (1995) *Monitoring the World Economy, 1820–1992*. Paris: OECD Development Centre.

Maddison, A. (2006) *The World Economy*. Paris: OECD Development Centre.

Maddison, A. (2009) *Statistics on World Population, GDP and Per Capita GDP, 1–2006 AD*. Last update: March 2009, horizontal file. Available at http://www.ggdc.net/maddison/ (last accessed 27 July 2009).

Markevich, A. and Harrison, M. (2009) Russia's real national income: the Great War, Civil War, and Recovery, 1913 to 1928. Warwick Economic Research Papers 911.

Markussen, I. (1990) The development of writing ability in Nordic countries in the eighteenth and nineteenth centuries. *Scandinavian Journal of History* 15: 37–63.

Mazumdar, K. (1999) Measuring the well-beings of the developing countries: achievement and improvement indices. *Social Indicators Research* 47(1): 1–60.

Mazur, D.P. (1969) Expectancy of life at birth in 36 nationalities of the Soviet Union: 1958–60. *Population Studies* 23(2): 225–246.

McAlpin, M.B. (1983) Famines, epidemics, and population growth: the case of India. *Journal of Interdisciplinary History* 14(2): 352–366.

McGillivray, M. (1991) The human development index: yet another redundant composite development indicator? *World Development* 19(10): 1461–1468.

McGranahan, D.V., Pizarro, P. and Richard, C. (1985) *Measurement and Analysis of Socio-Economic Development*. Geneva: United Nations Research Institute for Social Development (UNRISD).

McKeown, T., Record, R.G. and Turner, R.D. (1975) An interpretation of the decline of mortality in England and Wales during the twentieth century. *Population Studies* 29(3): 391–422.

McKinlay, J.B. and McKinlay, S.M. (1977) The questionable contribution of medical measure to the decline of mortality in the United States in the twentieth century. *Milbank Memorial Fund Quarterly. Health and Society* 55(3): 405–428.

Milanovic, B., Lindert, P.H. and Williamson, J.G. (2007) Measuring ancient inequality. Working Paper 13550, National Bureau of Economic Research. Available at http://www.nber.org/papers/w13550 (last accessed 29 June 2009).

Ministerio de Salud Pública (2001) *Tablas de Mortalidad del Uruguay por sexo y edad 1908–1999*. Montevideo: Ministerio de Salud Pública, Dirección General de la Salud, Departamento de Estadística.

Mironov, B.N. (1991) The development of literacy in Russia and the USSR from the tenth to the twentieth centuries. *History of Education Quarterly* 31(2): 229–252.

Mironov, B.N. (1993) Educación y desarrollo económico en Rusia, siglos XIX y XX. In C.E. Núñez and G. Tortella (eds), *La maldición divina. Ignorancia y atraso en perspectiva histórica* (pp. 271–306). Madrid: Alianza.

Mitchell, B.R. (1988) *British Historical Statistics*. Cambridge: Cambridge University Press.

Mitchell, B.R. (2003a) *International Historical Statistics: Africa, Asia, and Oceania 1750–2000*. New York: Palgrave Macmillan.

Mitchell, B.R. (2003b) *International Historical Statistics: The Americas, 1750–2000*, 5th edn. New York: Palgrave Macmillan.

Mitchell, B.R. (2003c) *International Historical Statistics: Europe 1750–2000*. New York: Palgrave Macmillan.

Morris, M.D. (1979) *Measuring the Condition of the World's Poor: The Physical Quality of Life Index*. New York: Pergamon.

Morrisson, C. and Murtin, F. (2007) Education inequalities and the Kuznets curves: a global perspective since 1870. Paris School of Economics Working Papers 2007-2012.

Morrisson, C. and Murtin, F. (2009) The century of education. *Journal of Human Capital* 3(1): 1–42 (and data appendix)
Myllantaus, T. (1990) Education in the making of modern Finland. In G. Tortella (ed.), *Education and Economic Development since the Industrial Revolution* (pp. 153–171). Valencia: Generalitat Valenciana.
Newland, C. (1991) La educación elemental en Hispanoamérica: desde la independencia hasta la centralización de los sistemas educativos nacionales. *Hispanic American Historical Review* 71(2): 335–364.
Nicolau, R. (2005) Población, salud y actividad. In A. Carreras and X. Tafunell (eds), *Estadísticas Históricas de España. Siglos XIX–XX*, 3 vols (Vol. II, pp. 77–154). Madrid: Fundación BBVA.
Nilsson, A. (1999) What do literacy rates in the 19th century really signify? New light on an old problem from unique Swedish data. *Paedagogica Historica* 35(2): 275–296.
Noorbakhsh, F. (1998) A modified human development index. *World Development* 26(3): 517–528.
Notkola, V., Timaeus, I.M. and Siiskonen, H. (2000) Mortality transition in the Ovamboland region of Namibia, 1930–1990. *Population Studies* 54(2): 153–167.
Nunes, A.B. (1993) Education and economic growth in Portugal: a simple regression approach. *Estudos de Economia* 13(2): 181–205.
Núñez, C.E. (2005) Educación. In A. Carreras and X. Tafunell (eds), *Estadísticas Históricas de España, Siglos XIX y XX*. Bilbao: Fundación BBBV.
Núñez, J. (2005) Signed with an X: methodology and data sources for analyzing the evolution of literacy in Latin America and the Caribbean, 1900–1950. *Latin American Research Review* 40(2): 117–135.
Nuxoll, D.A. (1994) Differences in relative prices and international differences in growth rates. *American Economic Review* 84: 1423–1436.
Ogwang, T. (1994) The choice of principal components for computing the human development index. *World Development* 19: 1461–1468.
Ogwang, T. and Abdou, A. (2003) The choice of principal variables for computing some measures of human well-being. *Social Indicators Research* 64: 139–152.
Ouane, A. and Amon-Tanoh, Y. (1990) Literacy in French-speaking Africa: a situational analysis. *African Studies Review* 33(3): 21–38.
Pamuk, S. (2006) Estimating economic growth in the Middle East since 1820. *Journal of Economic History* 66(3): 809–828.
Pamuk, S. (2007) Economic change in twentieth century Turkey: is the glass more than half full? American University of Paris Working Paper 41.
Prados de la Escosura, L. (2000) International comparisons of real product, 1820–1990: an alternative data set. *Explorations in Economic History* 37(1): 1–41.
Prados de la Escosura, L. (2003) *El progreso económico de España. 1850–2000*. Madrid: Fundación BBVA, updated.
Pressat, R. (1985) Historical perspectives on the population of the Soviet Union. *Population and Development Review* 11(2): 315–334.
Preston, S.H. (1975) The changing relationship between mortality and level of economic development. *Population Studies* 29(2): 231–248.
Ram, R. (1982) Composite indices of physical quality of life, basic needs fulfilment, and income. A principal component representation. *Journal of Development Economics* 11: 227–247.
Ravallion, M. (1997) Good and bad growth: the human development reports. *World Development* 25(5): 631–638.
Recchini de Lattes, Z. and Lattes, A.E. (eds) (1975) *La población de Argentina*. Buenos Aires: Instituto Nacional de Estadística y Censos.

Reis, J. (1993) El analfabetismo en Portugal en el siglo XIX: una interpretación. In C.E. Núñez and G. Tortella (eds), *La maldición divina. Ignorancia y atraso en perspectiva histórica* (pp. 237–269). Madrid: Alianza.

Riley, J.C. (2005a) Estimates of regional and global life expectancy, 1800–2001. *Population and Development Review* 31(3): 537–543.

Riley, J.C. (2005b) The timing and pace of health transitions around the world. *Population and Development Review* 31(4): 741–764.

Riley, J.C. (2005c) Bibliography of works providing estimates of life expectancy at birth and estimates of the beginning period of health transitions in countries with a population in 2000 of at least 400,000. Available at www.lifetable.de/RileyBib.htm (last accessed 15 February 2010).

Ritschl, A. and Spoerer, M. (1997) Das bruttosozialprodukt in Deutschland nach den amtlichen Volseinkommes- und Sozialproduktsstatistiken 1901–1995. *Jahrbuch für Wirtschaftsgeschichte* 2: 27–54.

Sagar, A.D. and Najam, A. (1998) The human development index: a critical review. *Ecological Economics* 25: 249–264.

Sandberg, L.G. and Steckel, R.H. (1997) Was industrialization hazardous to your health? Not in Sweden. In R.H. Steckel and R. Floud (eds), *Health and Welfare during Industrialization* (pp. 127–159). Chicago, IL: University of Chicago Press.

Santamaría, A. (2005) Las cuentas nacionales de Cuba, 1690–2005. Mimeo, Centro de Estudios Históricos, Centro Superior de Investigaciones Científicas.

Sarkar, N.K. (1951) A note on abridged life tables for Ceylon, 1900–1947. *Population Studies* 4(4): 439–443.

Schulze, M.S. (2000) Patterns of growth and stagnation in the late nineteenth century Habsburg economy, *European Review of Economic History* 4(3): 311–340.

Sen, A. (1997) Human capital and human capability. *World Development* 25(12): 1959–1961.

Shorter, F.C. and Macura, M. (1982) *Trends in Fertility and Mortality in Turkey 1935–1975*. Washington, DC: National Academy Press.

Siampos, G.S. (1970) The population of Cambodia, 1945–1980. *Milbank Memorial Fund Quarterly* 48: 317–360.

Simkins, C. and van Heyningen, E. (1989) Mortality, and migration in the Cape Colony, 1891–1904. *International Journal of African Historical Studies* 22(1): 79–111.

Smits, J.P. (2006) Economic growth and structural change in Sub Saharan Africa during the twentieth century: new empirical evidence. Unpublished paper presented at the International Economic History Association Conference, Helsinki.

Smits, J.P., Horlings, E. and van Zanden, J.L. (2000) *Dutch GNP and its Components, 1800–1913*. Groningen: Groningen Growth and Development Centre Research Monograph no. 5.

Srb, V. (1962) Population development and population policy in Czechoslovakia. *Population Studies* 16(2): 147–159.

Srinivassan, T.N. (1994) Human development: a new paradigm or reinvention of the wheel? *American Economic Review, Papers and Proceedings* 84(2): 238–243.

Stadler, J.J. (1963) The gross domestic product of South Africa 1911–1959. *South African Journal of Economics* 31(3): 185–208.

Statistics Canada (2004) *Historical Statistics of Canada*. Available at http://www.statcan.ca/ (last accessed 25 July 2009).

Steckel R.H. and Floud R. (eds) (1997a) *Health and Welfare during Industrialization*. Chicago, IL: University of Chicago Press.

Steckel, R.H. and Floud, R. (1997b) Conclusions. In R.H. Steckel and R. Floud (eds), *Health and Welfare during Industrialization* (pp. 423–449). Chicago, IL: University of Chicago Press.

Streeten, P., Burki, S., Haq, M., Hicks, N. and Stewart, F. (1981) *First Things First: Meeting Basic Human Needs in Developing Countries*. New York: Oxford University Press.

Summers, R. and Heston, A. (1991) The Penn World Table (mark 5): an expanded set of international comparisons, 1950–1988. *Quarterly Journal of Economics* 106: 327–368.

Taira, K. (1971) Education and literacy in Meiji Japan: an interpretation. *Explorations in Economic History* 8: 371–394.

Tomlinson, B.R. (1993) *The Economic History of Modern India, 1860–1970*. Cambridge: Cambridge University Press.

van Tonder, J.L. and van Eeden, I.J. (1975) *Abridged Life Tables for All the Population Groups in the Republic of South Africa (1921–70)*. Pretoria: Institute for Sociological, Demographic and Criminological Research, Human Sciences Research Council.

Toutain, J.C. (1997) Le produit intérieur brut de la France, 1789–1990. *Economies et Societés. Histoire Economique Quantitative* 1(11): 5–136.

Tsai, W.-H. (2008) The growth of Taiwan's aging population and its socio-economic consequences. *Taiwanese Gerontological Forum* 1(1): 1–10; http://www.ncku.edu.tw/forum/vol1/article1 (last accessed 13 March 2010).

Tsui, K.-Y. (1996) Improvement indices of well-being. *Social Choice and Welfare* 13(3): 291–303.

UNESCO (1953) *Progress of Literacy in Various Countries. A Preliminary Statistical Study of Available Census Data since 1900*. Paris: UNESCO.

UNESCO (1957) *World Illiteracy at Mid-Century. A Statistical Study*. Paris: UNESCO.

UNESCO (1970) *Literacy 1967–1969: Progress Achieved in Literacy throughout the World*. Paris: UNESCO.

UNESCO (2002) *Estimated Illiteracy Rate and Illiterate Population Aged 15 Years and Older by Country, 1970–2015*. Paris: UNESCO.

UNESCO (2010) *Total Enrolment, School Life Expectancy, and Expenditure on Education 1970–2005*. Paris: UNESCO.

United Nations (1954) *Report on International Definition and Measurement of Standards and Levels of Living*. New York: United Nations.

United Nations (1993) *Demographic Yearbook 1991 Special Issue: Population Ageing and the Situation of Elderly Persons*. New York: United Nations.

United Nations (2000) *Demographic Yearbook Historical Supplement 1948–1997*. New York: United Nations.

United Nations Development Programme (UNDP) (1990) *Human Development Report*. New York: Oxford University Press.

United Nations Development Programme (UNDP) (1993) *Human Development Report*. New York: Oxford University Press.

United Nations Development Programme (UNDP) (2001) *Human Development Report*. New York: Oxford University Press.

United Nations Development Programme (UNDP) (2009) *Human Development Report*. New York: Oxford University Press.

Urquhart, M.C. (1993) *Gross National Product, Canada 1870–1926: The Derivation of the Estimates*. Kingston: McGill-Queen's University Press.

Valaoras, V. (1960) A reconstruction of the demographic history of modern Greece. *Miliband Memorial Fund Quarterly* 38: 114–139.

Valério, N. (2001) *Estatísticas Históricas Portuguesas*, 2 vols. Lisboa: Instituto Nacional de Estatística

Vallin, J. (1976) La population de la Thailande. *Population* 31(1): 153–175.

Vamplew W. (ed.) (1987) *Australians. Historical Statistics*. Broadway: Fairfax, Syme, and Weldon.

Veiga, R.T. (2005) A transiçao demográfica. In P. Lains and A. Ferreira da Silva (eds), *História Económica de Portugal 1700–2000.* Vol. III: *O Século XX* (pp. 37–63). Lisboa: Impresa de Ciências Sociais.
Viñao Frago, A. (1990) The history of literacy in Spain: evolution, traits, and questions. *History of Education Quarterly* 30(4): 573–599.
Visaria, L. and Visaria, P. (1982) Population (1757–1947). In D. Kumar (with M. Desai) (ed.), *Cambridge Economic History of India*, 2 vols. (Vol. II), pp. 463–532. Cambridge: Cambridge University Press.
Ward, M. and Devereux, J. (2003) New evidence on catch-up and convergence after 1870. Mimeo, Department of Economics, Loyola College, Baltimore, MD.
Ward, M. and Devereux, J. (2009) The road not taken: pre-revolutionary Cuban living standards in comparative perspective. Mimeo, Department of Economics, Loyola College, Baltimore, MD.
Whitwell, G., de Souza, C. and Nicholas, S. (1997) Height, health, and economic growth in Australia. In R.H. Steckel and R. Floud (eds), *Health and Welfare during Industrialization* (pp. 379–422). Chicago, IL: University of Chicago Press.
World Bank (2010) World Development Indicators Database, Washington, DC: World Bank; http://data.worldbank.org/data-catalog (last accessed 5 June 2010).
Yousef, T.M. (2002) Egypt's growth performance under economic liberalism: a reassessment with new GDP estimates. *Review of Income and Wealth* 48(4): 561–579.
Zamagni, V. (1990) *Dalla Periferia al Centro. La seconda rinascita economica dell'Italia 1861–1981.* Bologna: Il Mulino.

Data Appendix

Life Expectancy at Birth

Life expectancy is defined in the 'Technical Notes' to the United Nations (2000), *Demographic Yearbook Historical Supplement 1948–1997*, as 'the average number of years of life which would remain for males and females reaching the ages specified if they continued to be subjected to the same mortality experienced in the year(s) to which these life expectancies refer'. In the Life Tables, estimates are based on the assumption that 'the theoretical cohort is subject, throughout its existence, to the age-specific mortality rates observed at a particular time. Thus levels of mortality prevailing at the time a life table is constructed are assumed to remain unchanged into the future until all members of the cohort have died'.

Unless reference is made to a specific country's sources, UNDP *Human Development Report* (2009) provides the data for most countries over 1980–2005. The United Nations (2000), *Demographic Yearbook Historical Supplement*, provides the data from 1950 onwards. Pre-1950 data come from Flora (1983), vol. II, for Western Europe, and for Latin America from Astorga *et al.* (2003) OxLAD database (which Pablo Astorga kindly supplemented with the working sheets prepared by Shane and Barbara Hunt), completed for the 19th century with Arriaga (1968). Riley (2005c) has proved to be extremely useful both for the references it provides as for the data included in it.

Exceptionally, in the absence of life expectancy estimates for early years, its level has been obtained by projecting available data with infant survival rates.

This is the procedure was used to distribute the average life expectancy estimate for Argentina, 1869–1894; and to derive life expectancy for Jamaica, 1880–1900; Panama, 1900–1929; Guyana, 1950–1960; and Yugoslavia, 1929–1950.

Africa

Most pre-1950 estimates come from Riley (2005b) who points out that the earliest health transition started in the 1920s when mean and median values were 26.4 and 25.4 years, respectively. Strong assumptions were needed. Lower bound estimates for 1950 or 1940s levels were used for 1938, whereas prior to 1929 life expectancy at birth was assumed to be 25 years (the minimum goalpost) for Sub Saharan Africa unless specified below:

- Algeria, 1930s, Riley (2005b); 1920s, assumed to be the same as Tunisia's.
- Angola, 1938, Riley (2005b).
- Benin, 1938, Riley (2005b).
- Cameroon, 1929 and 1933, and 1938 (assumed to be equal to the lower bound estimate for 1950), Riley (2005b).
- Angola, Benin, Chad, Eritrea, Ethiopia, Gabon, Gambia, Niger, Sudan, Togo, 1929–1933, assumed to be as Nigeria's.
- Burkina Faso, Burundi, CAR, Congo, Congo Dem. Rep., Côte d'Ivoire, Liberia, Mali, Mauritania, Rwanda, Tanzania, 1929–1933, assumed to be as in Ghana.
- Côte d'Ivoire, 1938, Riley (2005b).
- Egypt, 1929–1938, Fargues (1986); 1925, assumed to be similar to Tunisia's.
- Ethiopia, 1938, Riley (2005b).
- Ghana, 1920, Riley (2005b); 1933, Bourguignon and Morrison (2002).
- Kenya, Riley (2005b) provides an estimate of 23.5 years for the 1930s. Thus, the minimum goalpost of 25 years was assigned to the pre-1938 period.
- Lesotho, Madagascar and Malawi, 1925–1933, assumed to be as in Mauritius.
- Mauritius, 1920s, Riley (2005b); 1930s, assumed to be the same as in 1942–1946, United Nations (1993).
- Morocco, 1925–1938, assumed to be as Tunisia's.
- Mozambique, 1929–1938, assumed to be as in Angolas.
- Namibia, 1870–1900, assumed it evolves as South Africa; 1900, assumed to be the same as for blacks in Cape Colony from Simkins *et al.* (1989); 1938, Notkola *et al.* (2000, p. 161). Northern Namibia figure adjusted with the ratio all Namibia to Northern Namibia c. 1960. It does not change over 1900–1938.
- Nigeria, 1929–1933, average of Ayeni (1976) for 1931, cited in Riley (2005b).
- Senegal, 1938, average of Riley (2005b).
- South Africa, 1880–1925, Simkins *et al.* (1989); 1929–1938, van Tonder and van Eeden (1975), cited in Riley (2005b).
- Tunisia, 1920s, Riley (2005b); 1930s, assumed to be the same as Algeria's.
- Uganda, 1930s (c. 1935), 23.9 (Riley, 2005b), so I have assigned the minimum goalpost for 1850–1938.

- Zambia, 1929–1938, assumed to be the same as Zimbabwe's.
- Zimbabwe, 1930s, 26.4 (Riley, 2005b). I have assigned the minimum goalpost over 1850–1929.

The Americas

- Argentina, 1870–1890, Recchini de Lattes and Lattes (1975).
- Canada, United Nations (2000) level for 1938 backwards projected for pre-1938 period with Bourbeau *et al.* (1997) in order to maintain consistency over time.
- Chile, 1890–1900, and Uruguay, 1870–1900, assumed to have evolved along Argentina.
- Uruguay, 1900–1938, Ministerio de Salud Pública (2001),
- Life expectancy in Columbia, 1870–1900, and Cuba, 1860–1900, Panama, 1880–1900, Honduras, 1890–1900, Puerto Rico, 1860–1890 and Venezuela, 1880–1900, has been assumed to evolve along Costa Rica's.
- Paraguay, 1900, Arriaga (1968).
- Peru, 1913–1938, has been assumed to evolve along Bolivia's and Puerto Rico, 1900–1950 along Cuba's.
- Puerto Rico, 1860–1890, assumed it evolves along Costa Rica; 1890, Riley (2005b); 1900–1938, United Nations (1993).
- Trinidad and Tobago, 1860–1900, assumed to have evolved along Jamaica's.
- USA, up to 1890, Haines (1994).
- Uruguay, 1913–1938, Ministerio de Salud Pública (2001).

Asia

Most pre-1950 estimates come from Riley (2005b) who claims that the earliest health transition started in the 1870/1890s when mean and median values were 27.5 and 25.1 years, respectively. Strong assumptions were have been accepted. Lower bound estimates for 1950 or 1940s levels were used for 1938, whereas prior to 1929 life expectancy at birth was assumed to be 25 years (the minimum goalpost) unless specified below:

- Cambodia, 1938, Siampos (1970), cited in Riley (2005b); 1929–1933, assumed it evolved along China as they had similar levels in 1925 and 1938.
- China, 1938 and 1925, upper and lower bound in 1925–1936, respectively, Riley (2005b); 1929–1933, Caldwell *et al.* (1986), cited in Lavely and Wong (1998).
- Hong Kong SAR, assumed to have evolved at the same rate of variation as Taiwan's, 1900–1938.
- Cyprus, up to 1933, since in Cyprus and Greece life expectancy levels were identical in 1890 and very close in 1938, I assumed they were the same over the period. Figures for 1890, from Riley (2005b).
- India, 1890–1938, McAlpin (1983); extrapolated to 1880 with Visaria and Visaria (1982).

- Indonesia, 1920s, Riley (2005b).
- Japan, 1870, Riley (2005b); 1880, Janetta and Preston (1991); 1890–1900, Johansson and Mosk (1987).
- Korea, 1913, Riley (2005b) for 1915, 23.5 years. Since I assumed the historical lower bound to be 25 years, this value was assigned to the pre-1913 era; 1920s-1933, adding 0.87 years per annum as suggested by Riley (2005b); 1938, United Nations (1993).
- Lao PDR, 1929–1933, assumed to evolve as Vietnam's.
- Malaysia, 1929–1938, 1950 level backwards projected with the infant survival rate.
- Nepal, 1925–1933, assumed to evolve as India.
- Singapore, 1929–1938, 1950 level backwards projected with the infant survival rate; 1870–1925, assumed to evolve at the same pace as Malaysia's.
- Sri Lanka, 1890–1925, 1938, Langford and Storey (1993); 1929, Sarkar (1951), 1929–1933.
- Taiwan, 1890–1938, 1955, Cha and Wu (2002); 1950, Glass and Grebenik (1967); 1980–2005, english.moe.gov.tw/public/Attachment/9101916565871.pdf; 2000–2005, Tsai (2008).
- Thailand, 1938, Vallin (1976).
- Turkey, pre-1913, 1920s and 1930s, assumed it evolved at the same rate of change as Greece's; 1913, Pamuk (2007); 1938, Shorter and Macura (1982).

Oceania

- Australia, 1870–1900, Whitwell *et al.* (1997).
- New Zealand (adjusted for Maori population), 1870, Riley (2005b); 1880–1890, Glass and Grebenik (1967).

Europe

- Austria, 1870, Helczmanovski (1979); 1880–1890, interpolated from Helczmanovski (1979), Glass and Grebenik (1967, p. 82) and the United Nations (1993).
- Belgium, Deprez (1979), 1870, and Flora (1983), 1880–1900. Interpolation with United Nations (1993) for 1928/1932.
- Bulgaria, 1870–1890, assumed to move along Greece's.
- Cyprus, since in Cyprus and Greece the levels in 1890 were identical and in 1950 very close, I assumed they were the same over the period up to 1938.
- Czechoslovakia, 1870–1913, Sbr (1962); for 1890, Riley (2005b).
- Finland, up to 1990, Kannisto *et al.* (1999).
- France, 1870–1900, Flora (1983).
- Germany, 1870–1890, Flora (1983).
- Greece, pre-1913, Valaoras (1960).
- Hungary, 1870–1900, assumed to evolve along Austria's.
- Ireland, 1850–1900, assumed to evolve along the UK's.

- Italy, 1881 and 1901, Zamagni (1990); 1870–1938, Conte *et al.* (2007).
- Poland, 1870–1913, assuming it evolved as Czechoslovakia's.
- Portugal, 1850–1933, Leite (2005); 1920–1930, Veiga (2005); 1925–1929, Valèrio (2001).
- Romania, assumed to evolve along Greece, 1870–1890, and along Bulgaria's, 1890–1929.
- Russia, Pressat (1985), European Russia, 1870–1913; European Soviet Union, 1925–1933; Soviet Union, 1938.
- Baltic Republics, Ukraine, 1900, 1935, Riley (2005b), Mazur (1969).
- Spain, Dopico and Reher (1998), 1870–1938; 1950–2000, Nicolau (2005) and Goerlich and Pinilla (2005).
- Sweden, 1870–1965, Sandberg and Steckel (1997), taken from Keyfitz and Fleiger (1968).
- UK, 1850–1900, Floud and Harris (1997).
- Yugoslavia, assumed to evolve along Greece's, 1870–1890, and along Bulgaria's, 1890–1929.

Literacy

The rate of adult literacy is defined as the percentage of population aged 15 years or over who is able to read and write. Although from a conceptual point of view there are no objections to the UNESCO definition of literate person, namely, 'who can, with understanding, both read and write a short simple statement on his everyday life' (quoted in Nilsson, 1999, p. 278), assessing a person's literacy is quite a different issue. Empirically, literacy is a far from uniform a concept. On the one hand, reading and writing do not necessarily go together in developing countries and it has been shown that, prior to the diffusion of the schooling system, the lag between acquiring the ability to read and to write can be as wide as a century or more (Markussen, 1990; Nilsson, 1999) and, therefore, the estimated literacy rate would vary wildly depending on whether a wide (read ability only) or a narrow (reading and writing skills) definition of literacy is used, and how it is actually measured (with marriage signatures being particularly misleading in pre-industrial societies). Moreover, becoming literate is far more difficult and time intensive in countries which languages employ Chinese characters (Taira, 1971; Honda, 1997). In practice, although classifying a person as truly literate should imply that she is able to read and write, it not always possible make such a precise distinction for the past (Nilsson, 1999, p. 279). This has led to historians to focus on estimating the share of illiterate population (Flora, 1973). Unfortunately, historical data are far from homogeneous and, therefore, the results will suffer from biases which, nonetheless, will not condition long run trends.

The UNDP *Human Development Report* (2009) provides most of the data for 1980–2005. Unless reference is made to a specific country's sources, data from 1950 onwards come from the UNESCO (1953, 1957, 1970, 2002) and World Bank (2010), completed with data from Banks (2010), Hayami and Ruttan (1985) and Easterly (1999), and additional data for 1850–1965 come from Flora (1973). As regards different world regions, Flora (1983) provides data for Western Europe, whereas data for Latin America in the 20th century come from Astorga and Fitzgerald (1998) and Astorga *et al.* (2003) OxLAD database (which Pablo Astorga kindly supplemented with their working sheets prepared by Shane and Barbara Hunt), completed with Newland (1991) for the 19th century.

Exceptionally, in the absence of estimates, literacy rates have been backwards projected with the rate of primary enrolment or the years of primary education (Morrisson and Murtin, 2009). Also, for the post-1960, in its absence, it has been derived by assuming the illiteracy rate to be identical to the share of population without any schooling from data in Barro and Lee (2002) and Cohen and Soto (2007).

Africa

There is uncertainty about literacy rates even in recent times as evidenced by the wide discrepancies between UNESCO and UNDP figures for 16 countries out of 53 over the years 1980–1995. In order to keep consistency with UNDP's HDR I have opted for the latter with a few exceptions (Algeria 1990–1995, Botswana 1980–1985).

- Guinea, Madagascar, Mali, Mauritius, Niger, Senegal and Togo, 1970–1980, Ouane and Amon-Tanoh (1990).
- Literacy rates have been projected backwards with the rate of primary enrolment for Algeria, 1870–1880, 1930s; Burundi, 1929; Cape Verde, Equatorial Guinea, Guinea, Zambia, 1929–1938; Ghana 1880–1938; Kenya, Sudan and Tanzania,1920–1938; Lesotho and Liberia, 1890–1938; Mauritius, 1870–1933; Namibia, Nigeria, Togo and Zimbabwe, 1913–1938; Seychelles and Sierra Leone, 1900–1938; South Africa, 1925–1933; Uganda, 1920–1938.
- Literacy rates have been backwards projected with years of primary education for the population above 15 years (Morrisson and Murtin (2009) for Angola, Cameroon, Côte d'Ivoire, Madagascar, Malawi, Mali, Mozambique and Senegal 1870–1938; Eritrea and Ethiopia, 1870–1933; Kenya and Uganda, 1870–1913; Sierra Leone and Tunisia, 1870–1890).
- Namibia, 1870–1913, assumed to evolve along South Africa; Botswana and Swaziland, 1870–1938, assumed to be the same as Namibia's. Libya, 1870–1900, assumed to be as Morocco's.

The Americas

- Chile, 1870, Braun *et al.* (2000).
- Cuba, 1870–1890, Newland (1991).
- Nicaragua, 1900, Núñez (2005).
- USA, 1870–1890, 1960–1970, Costa and Steckel (1997).
- Literacy rates have been backwards projected with the rate of primary enrolment for Bahamas, 1890–1900; Barbados, 1870–1938; Belize,

1870–1900; Bolivia, 1870–1890; Guyana, 1870–1900; Puerto Rico, 1870–1890.

- Literacy rates have been backwards projected with years of primary education for the population above 15 years (Morrisson and Murtin (2009) for Dominican Republic, 1870–1900; El Salvador, 1870–1890; Uruguay, 1870–1890; Venezuela, 1870–1880).
- Trinidad and Tobago, St. Kitts, St. Lucia, St. Vincent and the Grenadines, and Surinam, assumed to evolve along Jamaica over 1870–1890.

Asia

- China, 1870, 1913, Morrisson and Murtin (2007).
- India, 1890, 1938, Tomlinson (1993).
- Japan, 1870, Steckel and Floud (1997b); 1880–1890 (assuming the rate of primary enrolment was a good approximation), Hanley (1990); 1900–1938, Honda (1997).
- Korea, 1929–1933, Kimura (1990).
- Australia, 1870, Vamplew (1987) 1890–1900, Steckel and Floud (1997b).
- Literacy rates have been projected backwards with the rate of primary enrolment for Cambodia and Laos, 1913–1938; China, 1929–1933; Hong Kong, 1870–1925; India, 1870–1880, 1920s; Indonesia, Taiwan and Vietnam, 1900–1938; Iran, Jordan, Malaysia and Myammar, 1920s; Israel, Lebanon, Sri Lanka and Syria, 1920–1938; Korea, 1913–1925; Fiji, 1900–1913, 1925–1938.
- Literacy rates have been backwards projected with years of primary education for the population above 15 years (Morrisson and Murtin (2009) for Iraq, 1870–1938; Malaysia, 1870–1900; Myammar, 1870–1880; Philippines, 1870–1913; Syria, 1870–1900; Thailand, 1880–1920, 1929).

Europe

- Austria, 1880–1913, Flora (1983).
- Belgium, 1938, 1955, Banks (2010).
- Bulgaria, 1955, 1965, Banks (2010).
- Czechoslovakia, 1880–1900, Flora (1983); 1938, 1955, 1965, Banks (2010).
- Finland, 1870, Crafts (1997); 1880–1890, Myllantaus (1990); 1900, Flora (1983); 1925–1960, Banks (2010).
- Germany, 1950, 1955, Banks (2010).
- Greece, 1925–1955, Banks (2010).
- Ireland, 1870–1900, Flora (1983); 1913, Crafts (1997).
- Italy, 1870–1880, Flora (1983); 1890, 1960, Conte *et al.* (2007); 1925, 1938, 1955, Banks (2010).
- Poland, 1870–1890, assumed to evolve along Hungary's; 1900, Flora (1983); 1920–1965, Banks (2010).
- Portugal, 1880, Reis (1993); 1880–1890, 1913–1938, 1955–1965, Nunes (1993).

- Romania, 1920–1965, Banks (2010).
- Russia, 1870–1960, Mironov (1991, 1993).
- Spain, 1870–1880, Núñez (2005); 1890–1930, Reher (personal communication); Viñao Frago (1990).
- Sweden, 1870–1965, Banks (2010).
- Yugoslavia//Serbia, 1920–1990, Banks (2010).
- UK, 1870–1965, Banks (2010).
- Literacy rates have been backwards projected with the rate of primary enrolment for Albania, 1920–1938; Cyprus, 1880–1900; Estonia, 1938–1965; Luxembourg, 1929–1938; Malta, 1890–1900.
- Literacy rates have been backwards projected with years of primary education (Morrisson and Murtin (2009) for Bulgaria, 1870–1880).

Enrolment

The enrolment ratio is computed by referring the number of students, at a particular education level, to the relevant school age population. Historical evidence allows one to estimate the rate of unadjusted enrolment defined as the percentage of population aged 5–24 enrolled in primary, secondary and tertiary education. Enrolment rates basically capture the expansion of formal education and do not inform about the length of the academic year, students' attendance, the content and quality of education or students' performance and completion (see Benavot and Riddle (1988) for a detailed discussion of its shortcomings and biases). Figures on enrolment, apparently straight forward, present difficulties of interpretation. The usual measurement procedure is to divide the number of students by the relevant school-age population cohort, for example, primary enrolment rate as the share of children receiving primary education over population aged 5 to 14 years, keeping this yardstick fixed over time (namely, the *unadjusted* enrolment rate). Usually, however, such age span is longer that primary schooling, leading to an underestimate and, even worse, comparability is fraught with difficulties as the length of primary or secondary schooling changes across countries and over time and, therefore, biases of unknown sign are introduced (Benavot and Riddle, 1988, p. 195; Nilsson, 1999, p. 282). Alas, up to the mid-20th century, the only kind of enrolment rate that can be easily computed for a large number of countries and over a long time span is the unadjusted one. Later, international organizations (UNESCO, OECD, World Bank) have provided gross enrolment rates, in which the denominator is adjusted to the age bracket for which each type of schooling (primary, secondary etc) is provided. Here the difficulty is that enrolment rates above 100% can appear as under- and/or over-age students are included in the numerator. Eliminating them is thus required, and the result is the unusually available net enrolment rate. In the present case, since the numerator includes primary, secondary and tertiary enrolment numbers and the denominator, population aged 5–24, the differences between gross and net rates tend to be negligible. However, the unadjusted rate will usually underestimate the actual enrolment rate as in the past hardly any country's education extended to those age 24 years. Thus, I have corrected the bias in my historical estimates (here, pre-1980) with the ratio for 1980 between gross all enrolment rates and the unadjusted rates I computed from historical sources.

The UNDP *Human Development Report* (2009) provides most of the data from 1980 onwards. Unless reference is made to a specific country's sources, enrolment estimates come from Banks (2010) and Mitchell (2003a, b, c) completed with UNESCO (2010) for the period 1970–2005; additional data for Western Europe come from Flora (1983), whereas for Latin America most estimates come from Astorga and Fitzgerald (1998) and Astorga *et al.* (2003) OxLAD database (which Pablo Astorga kindly supplemented with their working sheets prepared by Shane and Barbara Hunt), completed with Newland (1991) for the 19th century.

As regards the relevant population, I have computed the share of population aged 5–24 (and 5–14) over total population at census years from Mitchell (2003a, b, c) and interpolated them log linearly to derive yearly series that have been, then, multiplied by total population figures, provided by Mitchell (2003a, b, c), and supplemented with those by Banks (2010) and Maddison (2009). The population share of those aged 5–24 years for missing African and Asian countries have been replaced with the one from a neighbour country with a similar demographic transition.

For the pre-World War II era, Benavot and Riddle (1988) and Lindert (2004) provide useful estimates of primary and primary and secondary education enrolment rates, respectively, that in the absence of direct sources, have been used.

Occasionally, the all (i.e. primary, secondary and tertiary) enrolment rate for 19th and early 20th century Asian and African countries has been obtained by adjusting the primary or primary and secondary enrolment ratio with the ratio resulting of dividing the share of population aged 5–14 years by the share of population aged 5–24. This crude procedure implies the assumption that secondary and tertiary enrolment numbers represent a tiny proportion of the relevant population cohort.

Africa

- Algeria, 1870–1960, Fargues (1986).
- Tunisia, 1925–1938, 1960, Fargues (1986).

Population aged 5–24 (and 5–14) share in total population for missing countries. Nigeria's has also been accepted for Benin, Cameroon, Equatorial Guinea and Togo. South Africa's has been adopted for Botswana, Lesotho, Namibia and Swaziland. Mali's for Burkina Faso, CAR, Chad, Congo, Gambia, Guinea, Guinea-Bissau, Mauritania, Niger and Senegal. Uganda's for Burundi, Congo D.R. and Rwanda. Ghana's for Cape Verde, Côte d'Ivoire, Gabon, Liberia and Sierra Leone. Kenya's for Somalia. Mozambique's for Comoros and Madagascar. Egypt's for Djibuti, Ethiopia and Sudan. Algeria's for Lybia. Tanzania's for Malawi.

All enrolment derived with primary enrolment in Benavot and Riddle (1988), adjusted to all enrolment with the ratio of those aged 5–14 years to those aged 5–24 years, for Benin, Sudan, 1925–1933; Cameroon, 1890–1933; Congo, Madagascar, Tanzania and Uganda 1920–1938; Côte d'Ivoire, 1938; Egypt, 1890–1913; Gabon, 1925–1938; Gambia, 1900–1929; Kenya, 1920, 1938; Lesotho, 1890–1938;

Mauritius, 1880, 1929, 1938; Mozambique and Zambia, 1938; Namibia, Togo, 1913–1938; Reunion and Seychelles, 1900–1938; Senegal, 1929–1933; Botswana, 1955–1960; Swaziland, 1955–1965; Namibia, 1870–1913, 1950–1980, assumed to evolve along South Africa; Zambia, assumed to evolve along Zimbabwe, 1870–1925. Botswana and Swaziland, 1870–1938, assumed to be the same as Namibia's. Libya, 1920–1938, assumed to be as Morocco's. Bahrain, 1950–1970, and Brunei-Darussalam, Oman, Qatar and UAE, 1950–1980, assumed to evolve along Kuwait's.

All enrolment rates have been backwards projected with years of primary education for the population above 15 years (Morrisson and Murtin (2009) for Angola, 1870–1950; Egypt, 1870–1880; Kenya, 1870–1913; Madagascar and Zimbabwe, 1870–1900; Malawi, 1870–1890; Mali, 1890–1938; Mozambique, 1870–1920; Tunisia, 1870–1890; Uganda, 1870–1913).

The Americas

- Puerto Rico, 1870–1880, Newland (1991).
- Venezuela, 1870–1890, Newland (1991).
- All enrolment derived with primary enrolment in Benavot and Riddle (1988) adjusted to all enrolment with the ratio of those aged 5–14 years to those aged 5–24 years, for Bahamas, Barbados, Belize, St Kitts, St Lucia, St Vincent and Surinam, 1890–1938; Dominican Rep., 1870–1913; Ecuador, 1870–1880; Guyana, 1870–1900.
- All enrolment rates have been backwards projected with years of primary education for the population above 15 years (Morrisson and Murtin (2009) for Cuba, 1870–1890; Honduras, 1870–1880; Panama, 1870–1890; Paraguay, 1870–1880).
- Trinidad and Tobago, St. Kitts, St. Lucia, St. Vincent and the Grenadines, and Surinam, assumed to evolve along Jamaica's over 1870–1890.

Asia

- China, 1890–1913, assumes it evolved at the same pace as Hong Kong.
- Population aged 5–24 (and 5–14) share in total population for missing countries. Syria's for Lebanon. China's for Nepal.
- All enrolment derived with primary enrolment in Benavot and Riddle (1988) adjusted to all enrolment with the ratio of those aged 5–14 years to those aged 5–24 years, for Cambodia, 1920–1938; Iraq, 1913–1925; Israel and Laos, 1920–1938; Lebanon, 1920; Philippines, Taiwan and Fiji, 1900; Syria, 1900–1920.
- All enrolment rates have been backwards projected with years of primary education for the population above 15 years (Morrisson and Murtin (2009) for India and Myanmar, 1870; Iran and Iraq, 1870–1900; Philippines and Syria, 1870–1890; Thailand, 1800–1900; Turkey, 1870–1880).

- Hong Kong assumed to have evolved as China, 1955–1980, and Kuwait as Iraq, 1950–1960.

Europe

- Italy, 1870, 1913, 1929, Conte *et al.* (2007).
- Portugal, 1880–1913, Reis (1993), primary enrolment.
- Spain, 1870–1985, Núñez (2005).
- Population aged 5–24 (and 5–14) share in total population for Cyprus, Turkey's and Greece's, weighted by the shares of Turkish and Greek in total population.
- All enrolment derived with primary enrolment in Benavot and Riddle (1988) adjusted to all enrolment with the ratio of those aged 5–14 years to those aged 5–24 years, for Czechoslovakia, 1913; Denmark, 1870; Estonia, Latvia, Lithuania, 1920–1938; Luxembourg, 1929–1950; Malta, 1890–1950; Romania, 1870.
- All enrolment derived with primary and secondary enrolment in Lindert (2004) adjusted to all enrolment with the ratio of those aged 5–14 years to those aged 5–24 years (Mitchell, 2003c), for Ireland, 1870–1900; Italy, 1870; Portugal, 1920; Switzerland, 1870; UK, 1870–1900.
- All enrolment rates have been backwards projected with years of primary education for the population above 15 years (Morrisson and Murtin (2009) for Bulgaria, 1870–1880).

Per Capita GDP

Most data come from Maddison (2006, 2009) up to 1990, and Conference Board (2010), since 1995 (although sometimes for the post-1950 period as it is in the case of China, since Conference Board has adjusted the estimates to the recent findings in the 2005 PPP round), and are expressed in 1990 Geary–Khamis dollars. Otherwise, for specific countries shown below, Maddison's per capita GDP levels (usually for 1950) are projected backwards with volume indices of real per capita GDP.

Africa

Estimates for Sub Saharan Africa, West, East and Central-South regions, 1913–1938, come from Smits (2006). The West includes Benin, Burkina Faso, Cape Verde, Côte d'Ivoire, Gambia, Ghana, Guinea, Guinea-Bissau, Liberia, Mali, Mauritania, Niger, Nigeria, Senegal, Sierra Leone and Togo. The East, Burundi, Comoro Islands, Djibouti, Eritrea and Ethiopia, Kenya, Madagascar, Malawi, Mauritius, Mozambique, Reunion, Rwanda, Seychelles, Somalia,Tanzania, Uganda, Zambia and Zimbabwe. Central-South, Angola, Cameroon, Central African Republic, Chad, Congo, Congo D.R., Equatorial Guinea, Gabon, São Tomé and Principe, Sudan, Botswana, Lesotho, Namibia, South Africa and Swaziland.

Levels for each country within each Sub-Saharan region over 1913–1938 were derived by projecting backward per capita GDP in 1950 (from Maddison, 2009) with Smits (2006) regional aggregate volume series. For the period 1870–1913, I assumed Benin, Côte d'Ivoire, Gabon, Liberia and Senegal evolved along Ghana's. For the rest of the countries I assigned the lower bound for per capita income (1990 $300) as their levels were around or below such level by 1913. This way I was able to derive income levels to combine with education and life expectancy indices into a human development index for each country. Once national HDI were obtained, I aggregated them again into Smits' defined three regions, West, East and Central-South, as the individual country values would obviously be highly arbitrary and conjectural.

- For Nigeria, 1870–1913, Bourguignon and Morrisson (2002).
- For Algeria and Egypt, 1870–1950, and Ghana, 1870–1913, estimates come from Maddison (2006, pp. 577–578). I interpolated levels for 1890, 1900, 1925 and 1938 for Algeria. I interpolated levels for Morocco and Tunisia in the years 1880, 1890 and 1900, and then, 1925, 1929, 1933 and 1938 by assuming that these two countries grew at the same pace as Algeria.
- For Egypt, 1870–1950, Maddison (2006, p. 577). Pamuk (2006) and Yousef (2002) also provide estimates. The former figures match closely Maddison's estimates. The latter suggest too low levels for 1870–1913.
- For South Africa, 1913–1950, nominal GDP, Stadler (1963); deflator, Alvaredo and Atkinson (2010). Population comes from Feinstein (2005, pp. 257–258). 1870–1913, estimates for 1913 projected backwards with Bourguignon and Morrisson (2002) levels.

The Americas

Data for 20th century Latin America comes from CEPAL (2009), from 1950 onwards, and from Astorga and Fitzgerald (1998) and Astorga *et al.* (2003). Otherwise the sources are:

- Argentina, Della Paolera *et al.* (2003), 1884–1950, assuming the rate of growth over 1870–1884 was identical to that for 1884–1890. The alternative option of projecting backwards the level for 1884 to 1875 with Cortés Conde (1997) casts too low a figure. I assumed the level for 1870 was identical to that of 1875.
- Brazil, Goldsmith, (1986), up to 1950.
- Chile, Díaz, Lüders and Wagner (2007), up to 1950.
- Colombia, Kalmanovitz and López Rivera (2009) and data kindly provided by Salomón Kalmanovitz in private communication, up to 1905; GRECO (2002), 1905–1950.
- Cuba, Santamaría (2005), up to 1902; Ward and Devereux (2009), 1902–1958; Maddison (2009), volume series from 1958 onwards. An important caveat is that Maddison (2006) level for 1990 has not been accepted. The reason is that given the lack of PPPs for Cuba in 1990 Maddison (2006, p. 192)

assumed its per capita GDP was 15% below the Latin American average. Since this is an arbitrary assumption, I started from Brundenius and Zimbalist's (1989) estimate of Cuba's GDP per head relative to six major Latin American countries (Argentina, Brazil, Chile, Colombia, Mexico and Venezuela, LA6) in 1980 (provided in Astorga and Fitzgerald, 1998) and applied this ratio to the average per capita income of LA6 in 1980 Geary–Khamis dollars to derive Cuba's level in 1980. Then, following Maddison (1995, p. 166), I derived the level for 1990 with the growth rate of real per capita GDP at national prices over 1980–1990 and reflated the result with the US implicit GDP deflator to arrive to an estimate of per capita GDP in 1990 at 1990 Geary–Khamis dollars. Interestingly, the position of Cuba relative to the USA in 1929 and 1955 is very close to the one derived with a different approach by Ward and Devereux (2009).

- Ecuador, 1870–1890, I assumed it evolved as Peru over 1890–1900 yielding $470 for 1890 and I arbitrarily assumed a per capita GDP of $400 for 1870–1880.
- Mexico, Coatsworth (1989, p. 41) for the 19th century. INEGI (1995), 1896–1950.
- Peru, Monasterio (private communication), 1896–1950. I assumed the level for 1890 was the same as for 1896. I also arbitrarily assumed GDP per head for 1870–1880 was $400.
- Uruguay, Bértola (1998), 1870–1938.
- Venezuela, Baptista (1997), up to 1950.
- Central America (Costa Rica, El Salvador, Guatemala, Honduras and Nicaragua): I derived the level for 1913 by assuming the growth over 1913–1920 was identical to that of 1920–1925, the latter derived from OxLAD database (Astorga *et al.*, 2003).
- Caribbean, Bahamas, Barbados, Belize, Guyana, St. Kitts and Nevis, St. Lucia, St. Vincent and the Grenadines and Suriname, Maddison (2006, 2009), Conference Board (2010), and Bulmer-Thomas (personal communication), 1950 onwards.
- Trinidad and Tobago, Maddison (2009), 1950–1970.
- Jamaica, Eisner (1961), 1850–1930; Maddison (2009), 1938 onwards.
- Puerto Rico, Maddison (2009), since 1950.
- Canada, Urquhart (1993), 1870–1926; Statistics Canada (2004), 1926–1976.
- USA, Kendrik (1961), 1869–1953; Bureau of Economic Analysis, since 1953.

Asia

- Estimates for the Middle East, 1870–1913, Pamuk (2006). The countries included are Iran, Iraq, Jordan, Lebanon, Palestine (Israel), Saudi Arabia, Syria, Yemen and the Gulf (Bahrain, Kuwait, Oman, Qatar, UAE) countries.
- Bhutan, Brunei and Maldives, Maddison (2006).
- Korea, 1913–1938, Cha and Kim (2006). 1890, Bourguignon and Morrisson (2002).

- Myammar, 1880–1890, assumed to evolve along India.
- Philippines, 1890, Bourguignon and Morrisson (2002).
- Turkey, 1880, Altug *et al.* (2008); 1890, Bourguignon and Morrisson (2002).
- Taiwan, 1880–1890, assumed to evolve as China's; 1900, Cha and Wu (2002).

Oceania

- New Zealand, 1870–1938, Greasley and Oxley (2000a, b).

Europe

- Austria, 1870–1913, Maddison (2009) level for 1913 projected backwards with Schulze (2000) estimates for Imperial Austria under the assumption that real output per head in Modern Austria moved along Imperial Austria's.
- Belgium, up to 1913, Horlings (1997); 1925–38, average of GDP estimates of income and expenditure approaches, Buyst (1997) and Horlings (1997), output.
- Czechoslovakia, Poland, Yugoslavia and Romania, 1880, computed with Good (1994) ratio of 1880 GDP per head to the average GDP per head of 1870 and 1890 applied to Maddison's average levels for 1870 and 1890.
- Cyprus, 1921–1950, Apostolides (private communication). I assumed the level for 1913 was identical to that for 1921.
- Denmark, Hansen (1974), 1850–1938.
- France, Toutain (1997), Yemen.
- Finland, up to 1990, Hjerppe (1996).
- Germany, nominal GDP, 1950–2000, International Monetary Fund (2010); 1901–1913, 1925–1949, Spoerer and Ritschl (1997); 1901 level backwards projected with Hoffmann *et al.* (1965) to 1870. Real GDP derived by deflating nominal GDP. The deflator comes from International Monetary Fund, 1960–2000; Spoerer and Ritschl (1997), 1901–1960; 1870–1901, Hoffmann *et al.* (1965).
- Greece, up to 1938, Kostelenos *et al.* (2007), moving base series.
- Hungary, 1870–1913, Maddison (2009) level for 1913 projected backwards to 1870 with Schulze (2000) estimates for Imperial Hungary, under the assumption that movements in real output per head in Modern Hungary reflected those in Imperial Hungary; Modern (Republic of), as defined by the Treaty of Trianon (1919) 1913–1938, Eckstein (1955, p. 175).
- Italy, 1850–1913, Fenoaltea (2005).
- Netherlands, up to 1913, Smits *et al.* (2000), average of income, output and expenditure estimates; 1921–1938, Bakker *et al.* (1990).
- Norway, Grytten (2004).
- Portugal, 1850–1910, Lains (2006); 1910–1950, Batista *et al.* (1997).
- Russia, Imperial, 1870–1885, Goldsmith (1961), agricultural and industrial output weighted with Gregory (1982) weights for 1883–1887; 1885–1913, Gregory (1982), Table 3.1; 1913–1928, Markevich and Harrison (2009), Table

C-1. Since 1990, Russian Federation.
- Spain, Prados de la Escosura (2003, updated).
- Sweden, Krantz and Schön (2007).
- United Kingdom, 1850–1985, Mitchell (1988).

Population

All figures are adjusted to refer mid-year and to take into account the territorial changes and are derived from Maddison (2009) and Mitchell (2003a, b, c), completed with Astorga *et al.* (2003) OxLAD database and CEPAL (2009), for Latin America and the Caribbean, 1900–1938 and 1950–2008, respectively; Banks (2010), for Liberia, Sierra Leone, Ethiopia and Malawi; Fargues (1986), for Algeria and Tunisia; and Nicolau (2005) for Spain. Turkey, 1870–1913, Pamuk (2006, 2007), Cyprus, 1925–1938, Apostolides (private communication).

5

A PATCHWORK SAFETY NET: A SURVEY OF CLIOMETRIC STUDIES OF INCOME MAINTENANCE PROGRAMS IN THE UNITED STATES IN THE FIRST HALF OF THE TWENTIETH CENTURY

Price Fishback, Samuel Allen,
Jonathan Fox and Brendan Livingston

The USA has always had a much larger safety net than most people realize. In the current era the USA is considered a laggard among the world's developed economies in terms of social welfare expenditures. Part of this image is driven by the fact that many developed nations have adopted a strategy of universal programs where all receive health care and family support payments. Meanwhile, the USA follows a safety net strategy, in which private purchases of insurance and private charities play a much larger role and people typically do not receive payments until their income drops below specified levels. As a result, gross government expenditures on social welfare in the USA circa 2000 are much smaller as a share of GDP than in Sweden, Norway, Finland and Denmark. Once adjustments for taxation of benefits and purchases and unfunded mandates are taken into account, however, the gap narrows considerably. In 1990 purchasing power dollars, net government expenditures by the USA in 2003 were $5408 per capita, which was lower than Sweden's per capita spending of $6259 and Norway's $5901, about the same as Denmark's $5472 and higher than Finland's $4232. Once private social welfare expenditures are included in the totals, the US per capita net public and private social welfare spending rises to $7850, which is substantially higher than Sweden's $6715, Norway's $6315, Denmark's $5818 and Finland's $4920.[1]

One reason that the extent of the US social safety net is underestimated is that it is composed of a large patchwork system of programs. Anybody reading the House of Representative's Ways and Means Committee's *Green Book*, a massive volume providing an overview of social welfare programs, will by struck by the broad range of programs available for the poor in the USA. Another reason that the volume is so large is that the benefits in a number of programs often vary

Economics and History, First Edition. David Greasley and Les Oxley

substantially across states. The responsibility for income maintenance programs has been centred in local and state governments since colonial times. Until the New Deal during the Great Depression of the 1930s, the federal government provided disability aid and pensions only to families of veterans of the military and its own employees on the grounds that problems related to unemployment and injury were local affairs.[2] Franklin Roosevelt's administration argued for the expansion of federal involvement during the New Deal by claiming that the Great Depression was a nationwide problem that needed to be dealt with by a national government.

We seek to make sense of the broad array of social welfare programs at all levels of government across the USA and over time by surveying the cliometric literature on the history of poverty and social insurance programs during the early 20th century. Cliometrics applies economic and statistical analysis to the study of history, represented by the muse Clio, and thus is particularly well suited to the measurement of the extent of the programs in the economy. In Section 1, we discuss the shifts in responsibility for public social welfare programs between the local, state and federal governments and the difficulties these shifts present for collecting data that fully describe the patchwork system of programs in the USA over time. The benefits offered in the programs varied a great deal across the USA in the early 20th century and we explore the degree to which the relative rankings of benefits across the states remained stable over the course of the 20th century in Section 2. After summarizing the existing studies that examine the determinants of benefits across locations prior to 1940, in Section 3 we offer some preliminary analysis of the political and economic determinants of benefits from 1940 through 2000. Finally, we survey a group of studies that have examined the impact of poverty and social insurance programs on socio-economic outcomes in Section 4.

1. The Development of the Patchwork System and the Challenges Created for Data Collection

The local and state focus of social welfare spending has played havoc with the collection of quantitative evidence on income maintenance during the 18th, 19th and early 20th centuries in the USA. Ziliak and Hannon (2006), who are among the few cliometricians who have performed quantitative analysis of US poverty programs during that period, searched high and low to put together time series and cross-sections on welfare spending prior to 1929 for the *Millennial Edition of the Historical Statistics of the United States*. They could only find long time series for a handful of large cities and eastern seaboard states, state level cross-sections of pauper support from the 1850, 1860 and 1870 censuses, and information of the number of paupers in almshouses from the 1880, 1890, 1904, 1910 and 1923 censuses of almshouses. The cross-sectional census comparisons are problematic in different ways. The state totals from 1850 through 1870 do not match well with data for New York, where detailed evidence by county is available (Kiesling and Margo, 1997). Meanwhile, the almshouses from 1880 to 1923 account for only part of the income maintenance programs, missing the people living in their own homes who received 'outdoor' relief.

The public spending numbers also miss the resources provided by private charities, which were extensive. In the 1870s and 1880s, for example, leaders of the Charitable Organization Societies (COS) orchestrated the abolition of public outdoor relief programs in major cities in an attempt to improve the efficiency of the provision of relief, as well as provide more moral guidance for the poor to aid to achieve the self-reliance that would move them out of poverty. The move led to a large increase in private charitable donations, and the poor shifted from public to private relief rolls, but the change had relatively little impact on efficiency. In comparisons to earlier periods, the poor stayed on the rolls roughly the same length of time, the same share (33% to 40%) left the rolls for higher earnings, very few if any achieved higher occupations under COS management, and the ratios of expenditures per person on indoor and outdoor relief to the earnings of common labour share have stayed remarkably constant nationwide at around 25% to 30% for most of US history.[3] Even as local and state governments regained more control of relief around the turn of the century, private charitable donations still played a large role. Recent research by Livingston (2010, unpublished data) on private and public funding of relief from 1900 to 1930 shows that private charities were prevalent and provided a broad range of services. Private charitable payments for income maintenance were roughly about double the payments made from public funds in Massachusetts between 1900 and 1930. Local spending was also double state spending, with a majority of spending going towards outdoor relief.[4]

As the USA entered the Progressive Era of the late 19th and earlier 20th century, state governments began playing an increasing role in income maintenance programs for the poor and disabled. In the 1910s a large number of states adopted workers' compensation and mothers' pension programs, as seen in Table 1. Workers' compensation provided payments to the families of workers injured or killed in all accidents arising out of or in the course of employment. Mothers' pensions in most states provided benefits to widows with children. By 1919 about one-third of the states explicitly provided benefits for mothers with children who were divorced or separated from their husband, two explicitly provided benefits for single mothers and seven more established the law for mothers of dependent children without referring to marital status (Moehling, 2007, pp. 120–121). In the late 1920s a handful of states passed laws creating county options to provide need-based old-age assistance (OAA) to the elderly to allow them to live on their own rather than in almshouses. In the early 1930s the states began raising the stakes and requiring local governments to provide OAA payments and in many cases providing state funding. In the meantime, many states were also providing payments to the blind to allow them to live on their own.

The drastic problems with unemployment led to a series of responses by governments at all levels. Some state and local governments expanded building programs to provide more jobs for workers, but their efforts were limited by declining tax revenues and the sharp rise in the unemployed. In 1933, Franklin Roosevelt described unemployment as a nationwide problem, and the federal government established the first of a series of emergency relief programs designed

Table 1. The Presence of State Social Welfare Programs in the USA in the Early 1900s.

State	Workers' compensation		Mothers' pension		OAA	AB	UI
	Year law permanently enacted	Year added some coverage of occupational disease	Year enacted if before 1935 when Federal Act passed	Year switched to ADC	Year enacted if before 1935 when Federal Act passed	Making cash payments as of 1 August 1935	Year of first payments to unemployed
Alabama	1919	1951	1931	1936	–	No	1938
Alaska	1915	1945	1917	1945	1915	No	1939
Arizona	1913	1943	1917	1936	1933	No	1938
Arkansas	1939	1940	1917	1936	–	Yes	1939
California	1911	1915	1913	1936	1929	Yes	1938
Colorado	1915	1945	1912	1936	1927	Yes	1939
Connecticut	1913	1930	1919	1941	–	Yes	1938
Delaware	1917	1937	1917	1936	1931	No	1939
Florida	1935	1945	1919	1938	–	No	1939
Georgia	1920	1945	–	1937	–	No	1939
Hawaii	1915	1930	1919	1937	1933	No	1939
Idaho	1917	1939	1913	1936	1931	Yes	1938
Illinois	1911	1930	1911	1941	–	Yes	1939
Indiana	1915	1937	1919	1936	1933	Yes	1938
Iowa	1913	1947	1913	1943	1934	Yes	1938
Kansas	1911	1953	1915	1937	–	Yes	1939
Kentucky	1916	1936	1928	1942	1926	Yes	1939
Louisiana	1914	1953	1920	1936	–	Yes	1938
Maine	1915	1945	1917	1936	1933	Yes	1938
Maryland	1912	1939	1916	1936	1927	Yes	1938
Massachusetts	1911	1930	1913	1936	1930	No	1938

Michigan	1912	1937	1913	1936	1933	No	1938
Minnesota	1913	1921	1913	1937	1929	Yes	1938
Mississippi	1948	1962	1928	1941	–	No	1938
Missouri	1926	1931	1917	1937	–	Yes	1939
Montana	1915	1953	1915	1937	1923	No	1939
Nebraska	1913	1935	1913	1936	1933	Yes	1939
Nevada	1913	1947	1913	1955	1925	Yes	1939
New Hampshire	1911	1947	1913	1936	1931	Yes	1938
New Jersey	1911	1929	1913	1936	1931	Yes	1939
New Mexico	1917	1945	1931	1936	–	No	1938
New York	1913	1920	1915	1937	1930	Yes	1938
North Carolina	1929	1935	1923	1937	–	No	1938
North Dakota	1919	1925	1915	1937	1933	No	1939
Ohio	1911	1929	1913	1936	1933	Yes	1939
Oklahoma	1915	1953	1915	1936	–	Yes	1938
Oregon	1913	1943	1913	1937	1933	Yes	1938
Pennsylvania	1915	1937	1913	1936	1934	Yes	1938
Rhode Island	1912	1936	1923	1937	–	No	1938
South Carolina	1935	1949	–	1937	–	No	1938
South Dakota	1917	1947	1913	1940	–	No	1939
Tennessee	1919	1947	1915	1937	–	No	1938
Texas	1913	1947	1917	1941	–	No	1938
Utah	1917	1941	1913	1936	1929	Yes	1938
Vermont	1915	1951	1917	1936	–	No	1938
Virginia	1918	1944	1918	1938	–	No	1938
Washington	1911	1937	1913	1936	1933	Yes	1939

Table 1. *Continued.*

State	Workers' compensation: Year law permanently enacted	Workers' compensation: Year added some coverage of occupational disease	Mothers' pension: Year enacted if before 1935 when Federal Act passed	Mothers' pension: Year switched to ADC	OAA: Year enacted if before 1935 when Federal Act passed	AB: Making cash payments as of 1 August 1935	UI: Year of first payments to unemployed
West Virginia	1913	1935	1915	1936	1931	No	1938
Wisconsin	1911	1929	1913	1936	1925	Yes	1936
Wyoming	1915	1966	1915	1936	1929	Yes	1939

ADC, aid to dependent children; AB, aid to the blind; UI, unemployment insurance.

Sources: See Fishback and Thomasson (2006, p. 2-709). Workers' Compensation Laws: see Fishback and Kantor (2000) for date of initial enactment. See Balkan (1998, p. 64) and Allen (2004, pp. 170–1) for the dates in which occupational diseases were covered. The date of initial enactment of the workers' compensation law listed above is the date at which a permanent law was enacted. New York passed a compulsory law in 1910 and an elective law in 1910, but the compulsory law was declared unconstitutional, and the elective law saw little use. New York passed a compulsory law in 1913 after passing a constitutional amendment. The Kentucky law of 1914 was declared unconstitutional and was replaced by a law in 1916. The Missouri General Assembly passed a workers' compensation law in 1919, but it failed to receive enough votes in a referendum in 1920. Another law passed in 1921 was defeated in a referendum in 1922 and an initiative on the ballot was again defeated in 1924. Missouri voters finally approved a workers' compensation law in a 1926 referendum on a 1925 legislative act (see Kantor and Fishback, 1995). Maryland (1902) and Montana (1909) passed earlier laws specific to miners that were declared unconstitutional.

Mothers' pension laws: For laws enacted prior to 1920, see Thompson (1919, pp. 7–11) and for laws enacted after 1920 see Skocpol (1992, p. 457). In the states of Missouri (1911), California (pre-1913), Wisconsin (1912), Michigan (1911) and Oklahoma (1908) there were state provisions that provided funds similar to mothers' pensions in indirect ways. Some of the provisions were limited to specific cities and others were indirect means of providing funds to dependent children. Arizona in a 1914 referendum passed a mothers' pension and old-age pension system that hinged on the abolishment of the almshouses in the state, but it was found unconstitutional (Thompson, 1919, pp. 7–9). More detail on the specifics of mothers' pension laws as of 1934 are available in Stevens (1970, pp. 28–29) and Committee on Economic Security (1937, pp. 233–249). Carolyn Moehling provided information on the year in which the state switched to an ADC program that was eligible for matching grants under the Social Security Act.

Old-age pensions: See Stevens (1970, pp. 20–24) and Committee on Economic Security (1937, pp. 160–171). Arizona set up an old-age pension subject to the elimination of almshouses in a referendum in 1915, but the pension was declared unconstitutional. Pennsylvania passed an old-age pension law in 1923 that was declared unconstitutional in 1924. Nevada also passed an act in 1923 that was replaced by the 1925 act listed above. Information contained there also offers more detailed descriptions of the laws.

AB: See 'Public Provision for Pensions for the Blind in 1934', *Monthly Labor Review* 41 (3) (1935), pp. 584–601; reprinted in Stevens (1970, pp. 29–31).

Year of First Payment of UI Benefits to the Unemployed: Balkan (1998, p. 75).

to provide aid to the unemployed and the destitute. The first was the Federal Emergency Relief Administration (FERA), which gave grants to the states to make direct relief payments to families in need and to provide relief with a work requirement for the able-bodied. For four months in the winter of 1933–1934, the Civil Works Administration (CWA) hired up to 4 million workers for public projects. Many of the people working on the CWA were shifted to FERA work relief projects in March 1934 when the CWA was phased out. Throughout the New Deal, the Civilian Conservation Corps provided an opportunity for young men aged 16 to 24 from poor families to work on federal conservation projects often located in other states. They worked roughly 40 hours per week in semi-military troops and were given room and board plus a dollar per day, of which the lion's share was paid to their parents.

Despite the emergency programs in place, estimated national unemployment rates were still over 20% in 1935; the figure is 14.2% if people on work relief are considered employed (Darby, 1976, p. 8). Frances Townsend and others led movements calling for programs to offer payments to the elderly as long as they spent the money quickly. State and local governments were overwhelmed by the combination of declining state revenues and the large numbers of poor seeking aid, and they faced constitutional restrictions on the issuance of debt to run deficits on current spending. Even had they sought to issue debt for public capital investment, they faced high real interest rates and investors who demanded risk premiums due to scepticism about the states' ability to repay the debt.

The Roosevelt administration and Congress negotiated a realignment of the income maintenance programs (Wallis *et al.*, 2006). The Roosevelt administration gained increased control of the short-run emergency work relief programs for the able-bodied by replacing the FERA programs with the Works Progress Administration (WPA) and some smaller programs, all of which ended in the early 1940s when World War II made them redundant. The federal government returned responsibility for the 'unemployable' poor to the state and local governments. Many people today describe the WPA as a jobs program, but the WPA did not create jobs at the time the way other federal agencies did. On the Public Works Administration (PWA), Public Roads Administration (PRA) and Public Buildings Administration (PBA) projects, the government hired contractors who then hired workers full-time at regular pay rates. The WPA, like the FERA before it, was a relief program with a work requirement. They paid enough for basic necessities, but opportunities to work were limited and the average hourly earnings on these programs were typically half the average hourly earnings on PWA, PBA and PRA programs. In some southern agricultural areas, however, the WPA hourly earnings were comparable to or even higher than local earnings (Howard, 1943; Neumann *et al.*, 2010).

The long-run programs were established in the Social Security Act of 1935. The Old Age Survivors' Insurance (OASI) program, what everybody calls Social Security today, established a national old-age pension plan for workers with taxes collected by the federal government, which then paid out benefits to people who had contributed to the plan. The federal government began collecting the taxes in 1938 and made the first payments to the elderly in 1940. Unemployment insurance (UI) programs were federal/state programs in which employers paid into reserve funds that paid benefits to unemployed workers. The states had leeway to set their own benefits structure and the federal government provided funds for administering the program (Baicker *et al.*, 1998). Although the federal government had off-loaded responsibility for direct relief on to state and local governments, it provided matching grants to the states to provide aid to dependent children (ADC), OAA and aid to the blind (AB). Over the next few years, some states quickly passed enabling legislation that established their own benefit levels and met the basic federal administrative guidelines, whereas others delayed several years (see Table 1). Nearly all states had passed the enabling legislation for UI by 1937. The payments of unemployment benefits were delayed until 1938 and 1939 (see Table 1) because each state had to build up a reserve fund for 2 years before the unemployed could receive benefits.

Unlike most developed countries, the USA has resisted the creation of a universal health insurance plan. In the late 1910s a number of states considered adopting sickness insurance laws that would offer state run programs to provide partial wage replacement for workers when they were ill. Such funds had been established in many European countries and were associated with lower adult and infant mortality rates.[5] The state run programs would have replaced many of the private funds operated by fraternal societies, unions and employers during the period. Murray (2007) finds that the support among the general public for the funds was relatively weak, as many people with sickness insurance were satisfied with their coverage, and some without coverage thought the taxes would be too high for the benefits received. The reform-minded American Association of Labor Legislation was not as effective at bringing together the coalition that contributed to the passage of workers' compensation laws. Employers who had supported workers' compensation because they feared increasing accident payments under negligence liability were not as concerned with sickness insurance because there were no legal doctrines requiring them to pay benefits for illness. Unions and employers with sickness funds did not push hard for the law because it would have reduced their competitive advantage in attracting workers. Meanwhile, the American Medical Association actively opposed the legislation in most states.[6]

The absence of sickness insurance did not prevent state and local governments from contributing public funds for hospitals and hospital care. The per capita government cost payments by state and city governments for specific cities in Figure 1 range from \$2 to \$46 year 1990 dollars with a mean of \$10.79 in 1923 and from \$2 to \$62 in 1930 with a mean of \$13.87. In addition, almshouses often provided some degree of medical care to the poor (Stoian and Fishback, 2010). During the Great Depression the Farm Security Administration (FSA) provided care from doctors and nurses in many underserved agricultural areas (Grey, 1989). Under the auspices of the 1950 amendments to the Social Security Act, the ADC, OAA and AB programs began making direct payments to medical providers who treated recipients. State and local governments continued providing medical services to the people receiving general assistance payments. These programs were eventually

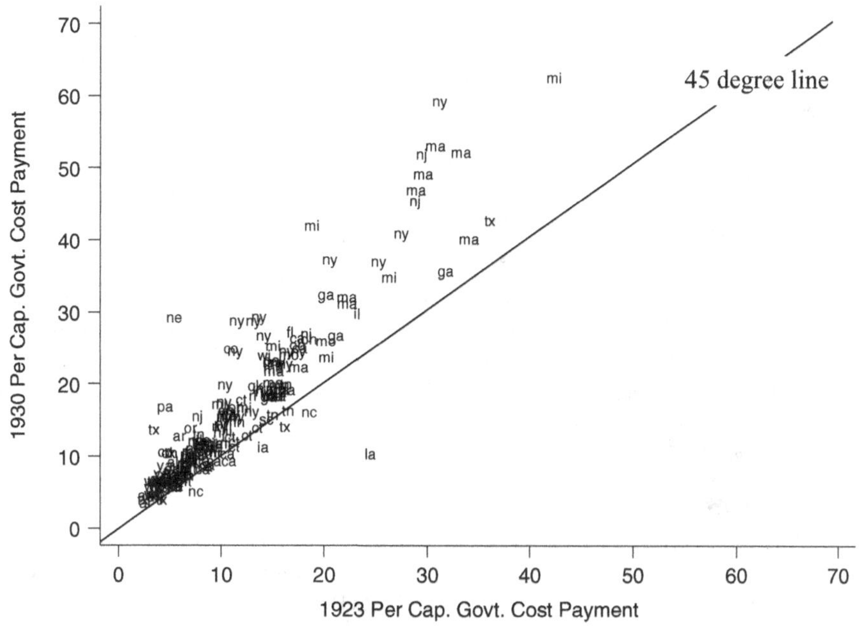

Figure 1. Per Capita Government Cost Payments on Hospitals by Cities and States in USA, 1923 and 1930 (state abbreviations).

Sources: Estimates for US cities are the sum of per capita spending on hospitals in the city plus per capita spending on hospitals for the state in 1923 and 1930 from the US Bureau of the Census's *Financial Statistics of Cities* and *Financial Statistics of States* for 1923 and 1930 (US Bureau of the Census, 1925c). The 1923 and 1930 values for the US cities were adjusted to 1990 dollars using the consumer price index (CPI) comparisons at Officer and Williamson's (2009) *MeasuringWorth* website. We did not include spending on hospitals listed as transfers from state government to other governments to avoid double counting if such state spending might have been used to fund city spending. County government spending is missing.

phased out after the introduction of Medicare for the elderly and Medicaid for the poor in the mid-1960s (Fishback and Thomasson, 2006, p. 2-795).

2. Geographic Variation and Its Persistence over Time

In the patchwork of American programs benefits have varied dramatically across geographic locations, just as they did in the per capita hospital government cost payments in Figure 1. The variation is present both before and after the federal government became heavily involved in social welfare spending in the 1930s. The per capita city and government cost payments on poverty and unemployment relief in 1923 in Figure 2 vary from lows of less than $1 in 1990 dollars in several southern cities to a high near $29 for several Massachusetts cities and a mean of

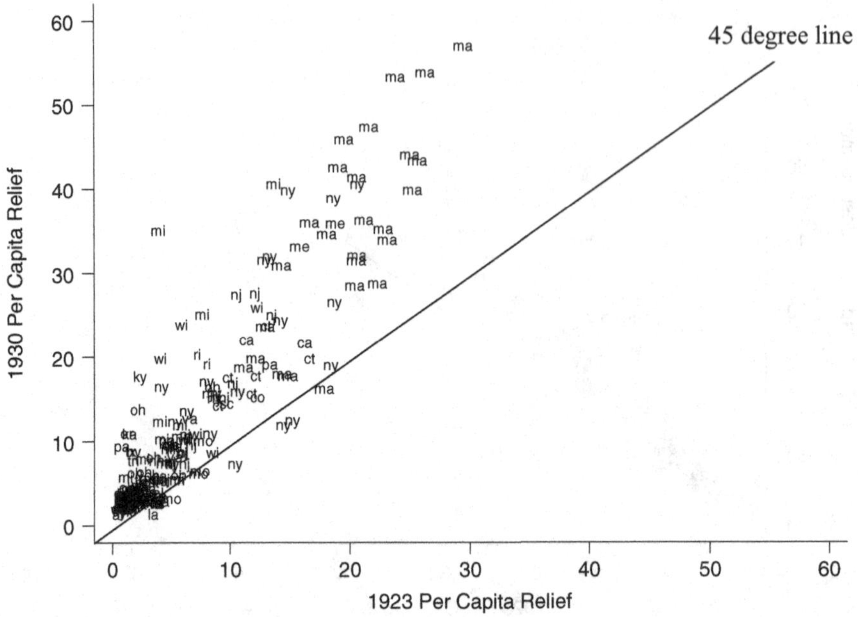

Figure 2. Rough Estimates of Per Capita Government Cost Payments on Poverty and Unemployment Relief in 1923 and 1930 by State and City Governments in 244 US Cities in 1990 Dollars.

Sources: Estimates for US cities are the sum of per capita spending in the city plus per capita spending for the state in 1923 and 1930 from the US Bureau of the Census's *Financial Statistics of Cities* and *Financial Statistics of States* for 1923 and 1930 (US Bureau of the Census, 1925c, 1925s, 1932c, 1932s). The 1923 and 1930 values for the US cities were adjusted to 1990 dollars using the CPI comparisons at Officer and Williamson's (2009) *MeasuringWorth* website. The per capita city spending includes governmental cost payments by the city government on outdoor poor relief, poor institutions, care of children, other charities and mothers' pensions. The state per capita spending includes governmental cost payments for outdoor poor relief, state poor institutions, care of children in state institutions, care of blind, deaf and mute in state institutions, other charities in state institutions, relief to mothers and relief to all others. We did not include spending on poor institutions all other, care of children all other, care of blind, deaf and mute all other, and other charities all other to avoid double counting if such state spending might have been used to fund city spending. Inclusion of this spending changes the positions in the figure only slightly. County government spending is missing.

$6.26. By 1930, the spending in Figure 2 had increased in response to the first full year of the Great Depression to a higher average of $10.76 and the range between the low southern cities and the high Massachusetts cities had broadened such that benefits ranged between $0.71 to $56.43. The figure shows that this rise occurred

Table 2. Elasticities from Regressions of the Natural Log of Per Capita Relief Spending in City (1967 dollars) in Year *t* on the Natural Log of Per Capita Relief Spending in 1923 and Change in Log State Manufacturing Employment from 1923 to Year *t*.

	ln(per capita poor relief) fsc	
	1929	1931
Natural log of per capita poor relief in city in 1923	0.9306	0.948
	22.98	*16.62*
Change in natural log of state manufacturing employment from 1923 to year	−1.482	−2.52
	−2.31	*−2.53*
Constant	0.2644	0.3705
	4.5	*1.16*
R-squared	0.817	0.68
Number of observations	167	147

t-statistics below each coefficient in italics.
Sources: Manufacturing employment from US Bureau of the Census (Manufacturing Censuses), 1929 and 1931; city per capita poor relief from US Bureau of the Census *Financial Statistics of Cities* (1925c, 1932a).

in nearly every city, because all of the points are clustered to the upper left of the 45 degree line that shows where the values in 1923 and 1930 are equal.

Over the course of the 1920s there was a clear sense of persistence in per capita government cost payments, as shown by the strong positive relationship between 1923 and 1930 spending in Figure 2. The spending per capita across cities around 1930 was influenced not only by the prior spending per capita in 1923 but also changes in employment. Table 2 shows regressions run on the natural log of per capita city government spending on care of the poor and veterans in 1930 as a function of the same measure as of 1923 and the change in the natural log of state manufacturing employment between 1923 and 1929 (or 1931). The coefficients can be read as elasticities. The strong path dependence is still there after controlling for changes in employment. Cities with per capita relief spending 1% higher in 1923, holding other things constant, tended to have per capita spending in 1929 and in 1931 that was 0.93% and 0.94% higher, respectively. Increases in per capita welfare spending were strongly associated with decreases in the natural log of employment. The negative elasticity implies that a 1% reduction in the change in the log of employment was associated with an increase in per capita relief spending of 1.48% in 1929 and 2.52% in 1931.

Unemployment rates reached nearly 25% in 1933, when Franklin Roosevelt took office and started the New Deal relief programs. Federal government involvement led to sizeable shifts in the per capita spending for relief of the poor and the unemployed. Figure 3 documents the dramatic rise in relief spending from all government and private sources between 1931 and 1939 as every point lies well above and to the left of the 45 degree line that shows the points where the values

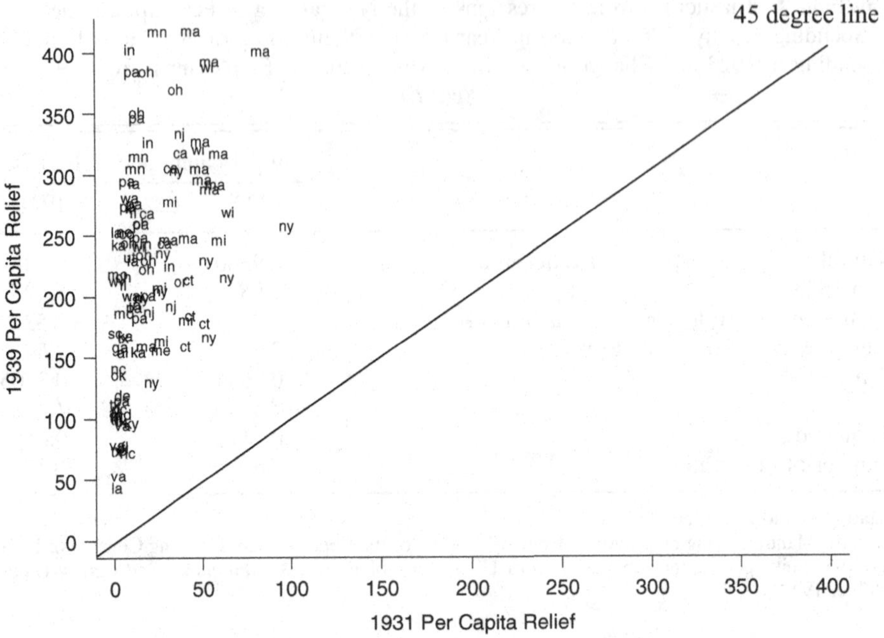

Figure 3. Per Capita Government Direct and Work Relief Spending in 114 US Cities in 1931 and 1939 in 1990 Dollars.

Source and Notes: Data are from Baird (1942). They are adjusted to 1990 dollars using the 1967 CPI from US Bureau of the Census 1975, series E-135, p. 211, and then multiplying by 3.91, which is the CPI conversion factor for 1967 dollars to 1990 dollars from Officer and Williamson's (2009) *MeasuringWorth* website. Per capita relief spending includes spending from federal, state and local sources. It includes direct relief payments, work relief payments and public assistance through OAA, AB and ADC (mothers' pensions).

in 1931 and 1939 are equal. The rise in spending is not necessarily due to a rise in unemployment. These years were chosen because the national unemployment rates in the 2 years were similar at 16.3% in 1931 and 14.8% (including work relief workers as unemployed) in 1940. The federal government did not become heavily involved in relief efforts until 1933; therefore, the changes wrought by the federal government involvement in relief are more obvious in comparisons of these 2 years. Boston, Massachusetts, and Rochester, New York, led the rankings in 1931 at over \$82 per head (1990 dollars). By 1939 the median expenditure per capita was \$221 in 1990 dollars and spending in Brocton, Massachusetts, was leading the country at over \$400 (1990 dollars) per capita on relief.

The introduction of federal spending in the 1930s had two effects on the geographic distribution of resources. The first was a reduction in the dispersion across cities. The coefficient of variation (the standard deviation divided by the

Table 3. Elasticities from Regressions of the Natural Log of Per Capita Relief Spending in City (1990 dollars) in 1939 on the Natural Log of Per Capita Relief Spending in 1931 and Change in Log State Manufacturing Employment from 1931 to 1939.

	Elasticity *t*-statistic
Per capita public relief in 1931 in 1990 dollars	0.17 *6.14*
Change in natural log of state manufacturing employment, 1939–1931	−1.11 *−4.60*
Constant	4.89 *47.26*

Sources: Manufacturing employment from US Bureau of the Census (Manufacturing Censuses), 1929 and 1931; city per capita poor relief in nominal terms from Baird (1942). They are adjusted to 1990 dollars using the 1967 CPI from U.S. Bureau of the Census 1975, series E-135, p. 211 and then multiplying by 3.91, which is the CPI conversion factor for 1967 dollars to 1990 dollars from Officer and Williamson's (2009) *MeasuringWorth* website.

mean) for the 115 cities fell from 0.95 in 1931 before federal involvement to 0.4 by 1939. Second, the persistence in the geographic rankings across the decade was much weaker across the 1930s than across the 1920s. The raw correlation is 0.58 in Figure 3 for the 1931/1939 comparison, compared with 0.89 in Figure 2 for the 1923/1930 comparison. The relationship between 1931 and 1939 per capita spending levels is even weaker after we control for the state of the economy in the cities in 1931 and 1939. The elasticity from the regression in Table 3 shows that a city with 1% higher relief spending per capita in 1931 on average had relief spending per capita that was only 0.17% higher in 1939. Meanwhile, the per capita spending was strongly influenced by changes in the labor market. The estimated elasticity of −1.11 implies that a 1% reduction in the change in the log of state manufacturing employment was associated with a 1.11% increase in per capita relief spending.

The states still retained a great deal of control over benefit levels after the Social Security Act transformed the role of the federal government in social welfare programs. Workers' compensation programs have always been state programs, although federal pressures, discussed below, led to some convergence of benefits in the 1970s. States retained control of basic benefit levels in UI and the categorical assistance programs through a shift that broadened ADC to become Aid to Families with Dependent Children (AFDC) in the 1960s and tightened requirements under Temporary Aid to Needy Families (TANF) in the 1990s. Supplemental Security Income (SSI) took over control of need-based payments to the elderly and the blind in the 1970s.

The legacy of the Social Security Act's reliance on state decisions about benefits is a relatively large variation across the country in each program to this day. The measure of expected workers' compensation benefits as a percentage of annual income for a worker earning the national average weekly wage in Figures 4(a) and 4(b) shows a large range spanning from 0.26 to 0.70 in 1940 that expanded to span 0.20 to 0.77 in 1970. The range then narrowed to span 0.36 to 0.84 in 2000. Similarly, the maximum monthly payments under the various incarnations of mothers' pensions, ADC, AFDC and TANF, measured in 1967 dollars had ranges that spanned $66 to $221 for four-person families under ADC in 1940, $48 to $282 for three-person families under AFDC in 1970 and $31 to $179 under TANF in 2000. In discussions of the geographic variation of benefits in these programs we focus on the statutory benefits for workers' compensation and UI and the monthly maximums offered for need-based programs like ADC, OAA and AB. The need-based programs base the payments on the household's current resources and supplement them up to a monthly maximum. In essence, the monthly maximum can be seen as a target base income that they are trying to reach. The maximum has fallen for ADC and OAA since the 1960s, as the Food Stamp program has eliminated the need to supplement the food budget.

Another legacy of the decision to rely on the states has been a relatively strong persistence of the state rankings of maximum benefits in each program within the same decade over the period from 1970 to 2000. Table 4 shows the cross-state correlations for benefits for different pairs of census years. The second diagonal from top left to lower right, i.e. the one below the first diagonal composed entirely of ones, shows the correlations between the end-points of the same decade. As the diagonal moves downwards to the right, the span between the years being compared increases.

The second diagonal for different programs shows relatively weak correlations between 1940 and 1950 of 0.1069 for UI and of 0.407 for the aid to families. The correlations then strengthen over time in comparisons of 1950 to 1960, 1960 to 1970, 1980 to 1990 and 1990 to 2000. This is likely a result of experimentation by the states in setting their benefits. When the states established the original benefits for UI and ADC in the late 1930s, states tend to be clumped into distinct groups that chose the same benefit levels. In Figure 5(a), for example, there were clusters of states that paid ADC maximums in 1940 of $66, $101, $125, $137 and $185 in 1967 dollars. Clusters for UI weekly maximums in 1940 are found at $36, $38 and $43 in 1967 dollars in Figure 6(a). Over time the states refined their choices and there was much less clustering in Figures 5(b) and 6(b). As a result, the correlations between 1940 and 1950 benefits across states was only 0.1069 for UI and 0.34 for AFDC. The correlations for 1950 and 1960 rose to 0.42 for UI and 0.76 for ADC. By the latter part of the 20th century the correlations for UI reached as high as 0.8037 for 1990 and 2000 and 0.93 for the same years for ADC. Workers' compensation did not go through the same experimentation process in the 1940s and 1950s because most laws were passed in the 1910s. Thus, the correlations between 1940 and 1950 were near or above 0.7 in all comparisons except 1970 and 1980.

It is worth noting that the relative rankings are not set in stone for the long run. As the time span increases, comparisons of the correlations as you read down the same column show that the correlations weaken significantly. Thus the correlations

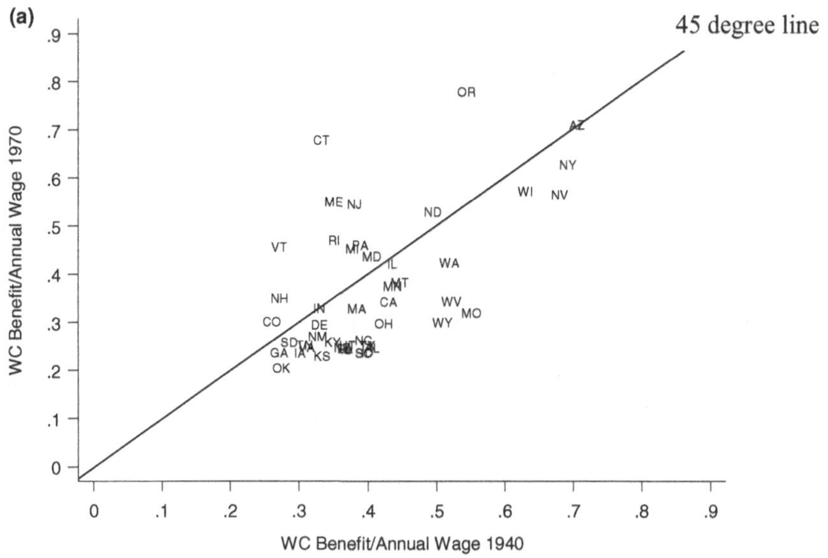

Figure 4. Ratio of Expected Workers' Compensation Benefits to Annual Manufacturing Earnings for Typical Worker Paid National Average Manufacturing Wage with Three Dependents by State (a) 1940 and 1970, (b) 1970 and 2000.

Source: See Allen (2004, 2009). The average expected benefit as a share of annual manufacturing earnings shows the typical workers' compensation payments for different types of injuries weighted by the probability of the accident in 1940 divided by a measure of the national average wage. The ratio here is for a worker with the national average weekly earnings. State workers' compensation benefits are calculated based on the workers' average earnings, the extent of the injury and waiting periods. Payouts for different types of injuries turn out to vary in ways across states that do not lead to especially high correlations across types of accidents. As a result, Allen (2004, 2009) and Fishback and Kantor (2000) developed a comprehensive expected benefits measure for workers' compensation based on the discounted present value at the time of the accident of the typical stream of workers' compensation benefits for four types of accidents: temporary total disability that lasts 5 weeks, a permanent partial disability of the loss of a hand (adjusted downwards because most permanent partial disabilities are less severe), permanent total disability and death. The discount rate for the present value is assumed to be 5%, which has been a typical discount rate chosen when states paid out lump sums. The 'typical' worker was assumed to be a married man with a wife and two children ages 8 and 10, and he was earning the national average in the year. The present values of the payout are then weighted by the probability of each type of accident in 1940. This expected benefit is then reported as a percentage of the annual earnings someone would receive earning the national weekly wage for the year. The goal in the measure is to show how the expected benefits as a share of the wage change across time and place based on the parameters in the law. Had we allowed the accident rates used to weight the payments for each type of injury to vary across years, the expected benefit ratio would have trended downwards because accident rates trended downwards over the course of the century.

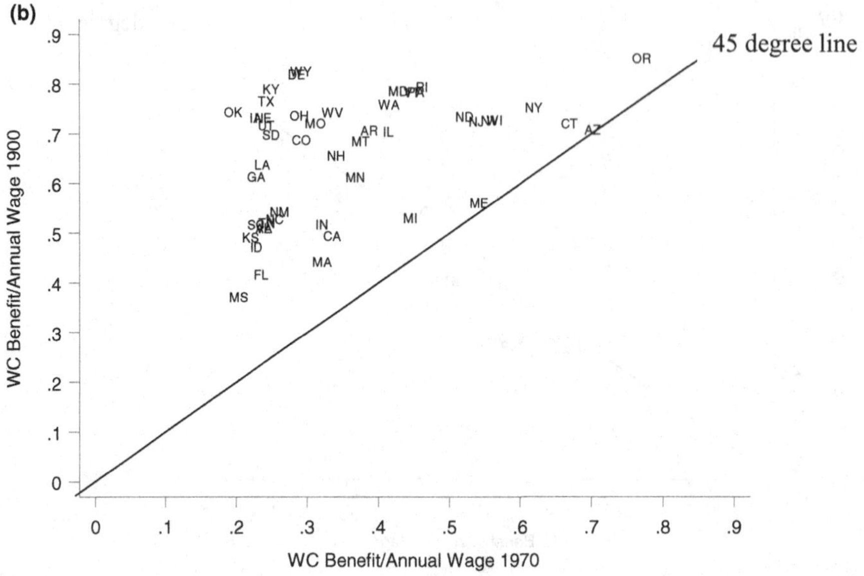

Figure 4. *Continued.*

for workers' compensation benefits fall from 0.92 for 1930 and 1940 to 0.78 for 1930 and 1950 to 0.68 for 1930 and 1960, to 0.58 for 1930 and 1970 and below 0.3 for 1930 and later years.

Differences in the target groups of the income maintenance programs lead to relatively weak correlations between UI and ADC and between workers' compensation and ADC in Table 5. UI and workers' compensation target people who are typically employed, whereas ADC and SSI tend to target people without employment or at the very low end of the employment scale. The correlations between workers' compensation and UI within the same year in 1940 and 1950 were nearly zero before they strengthened to rise above 0.4 after 1970. Correlations between workers' compensation and ADC within the same year rise from a low of 0.0867 in 1940 to peak around 0.55 in 1960 and then weaken a great deal to 0.275 in 2000. The correlations between UI and ADC within the same year are weak at 0.12.82 in 1940 and 0.047 in 1950, they peak at 0.56 in 1960 and then fall to 0.36 by 2000. The correlations within the same year of SSI with workers' compensation and UI in 1990 and 2000 are also relatively weak. The strongest correlations are found between the need-based programs of ADC and SSI in 1990 and 2000.

3. The Political Economy of the Variation in Benefits

Both mothers' pensions and workers' compensation were adopted in the majority of the states in a relatively short period of time during the heyday of the Progressive Era in the 1910s. Efforts to aid the 'worthy' poor who were struck by misfortune

Table 4. Cross-state Correlations of Maximum Benefits from Income Maintenance Programs Between Different Years.

	Maximum weekly unemployment payments in 1967 dollars						
	1940	1950	1960	1970	1980	1990	2000
1940	1						
1950	0.1069	1					
1960	0.3534	0.4201	1				
1970	0.0462	0.4291	0.534	1			
1980	0.078	0.375	0.2474	0.4323	1		
1990	−0.022	0.448	0.2485	0.5169	0.6552	1	
2000	−0.1714	0.501	0.2898	0.4383	0.5141	0.8037	1

	Workers' compensation expected benefits							
	1930	1940	1950	1960	1970	1980	1990	2000
1930	1							
1940	0.9203	1						
1950	0.7834	0.7658	1					
1960	0.6761	0.6551	0.913	1				
1970	0.5833	0.598	0.7968	0.8552	1			
1980	0.2724	0.2903	0.3632	0.4235	0.5045	1		
1990	0.2758	0.3118	0.3876	0.4044	0.4683	0.8441	1	
2000	0.2624	0.2824	0.4046	0.3926	0.426	0.624	0.6868	1

	Mothers' pension (1919)/ADC (1940–1960)/AFDC (1970–1990)/TANF (2000)							
	1919	1940	1950	1960	1970	1980	1990	2000
1919	1							
1940	0.4074	1						
1950	0.3618	0.3416	1					
1960	0.1769	0.2935	0.7624	1				
1970	−0.0199	0.3382	0.4965	0.6963	1			
1980	0.1335	0.5034	0.3832	0.6425	0.9079	1		
1990	0.224	0.4773	0.2367	0.4802	0.8697	0.9383	1	
2000	0.206	0.4437	0.199	0.4551	0.8135	0.8849	0.9577	1

Sources: Workers' compensation expected benefits are from a data set created by Samuel Allen and described in Allen (2004, 2009). Weekly maximums for unemployment are Moehling from Moffitt, Green Book, Allen 2004, 2009. The 1919 figures for mother's pensions are from Moehling (2007). For states with no maximum we chose a value that exceeded the highest maximum in the rest of the states. In all cases states with no law were treated as missing values. The values for ADC in 1940 are the actual maximum paid by the state to a family of four from data used by Carolyn Moehling (2006, 2007). States that had not yet switched to ADC were treated as missing in 1940.

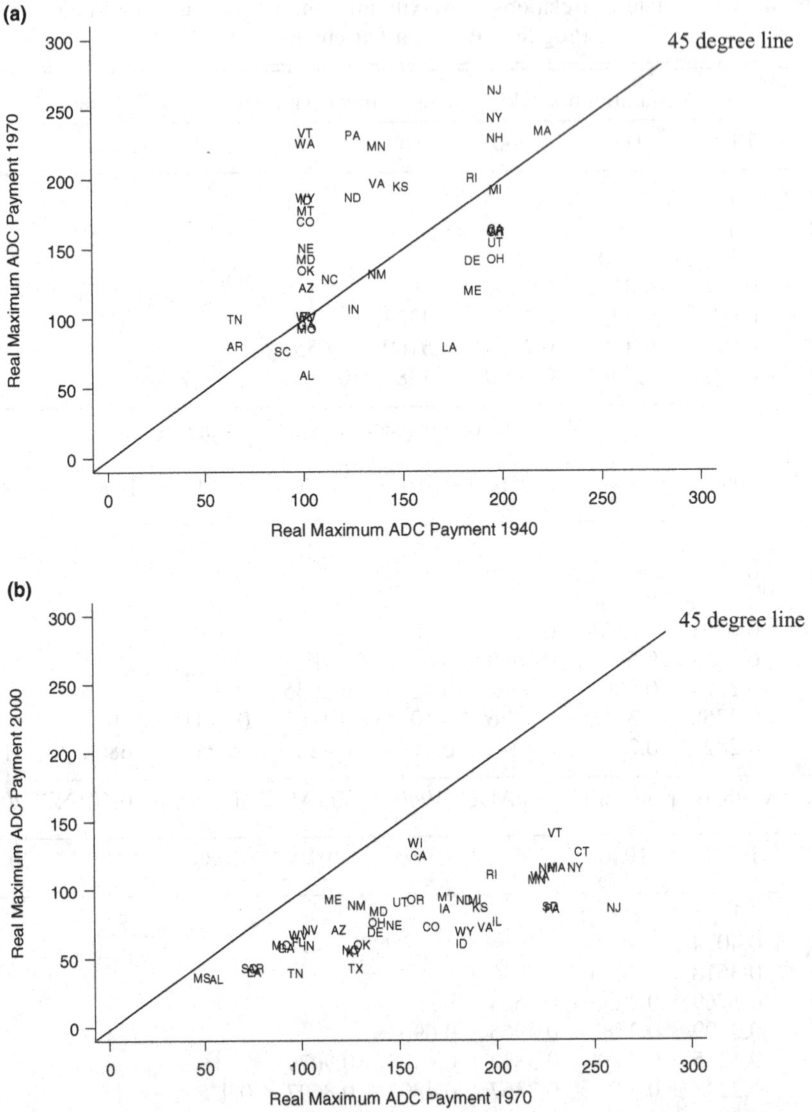

Figure 5. (a) ADC to Family of Three in 1970 and Maximum Payment to Family of Four in 1940 in 1967 Dollars. (b) ADC Maximum Payment to Family of Three in 1970 and ADC/TANF Maximum Payment in 2000 in 1967 Dollars.

Sources: The 1940 payments are from a data set provided by Moehling from her 2006 and 2007 papers. The 1970 and 2000 payments are from US House of Representatives, Ways and Means Committee (1990, 2000). The 1940 payments are the highest payments reported for ADC for families of four. In a number of cases the actual maximum exceeded the maximum listed in the state statute. A number of states had no maximums. The 1970 and 2000 payments are the maximums listed in the law.

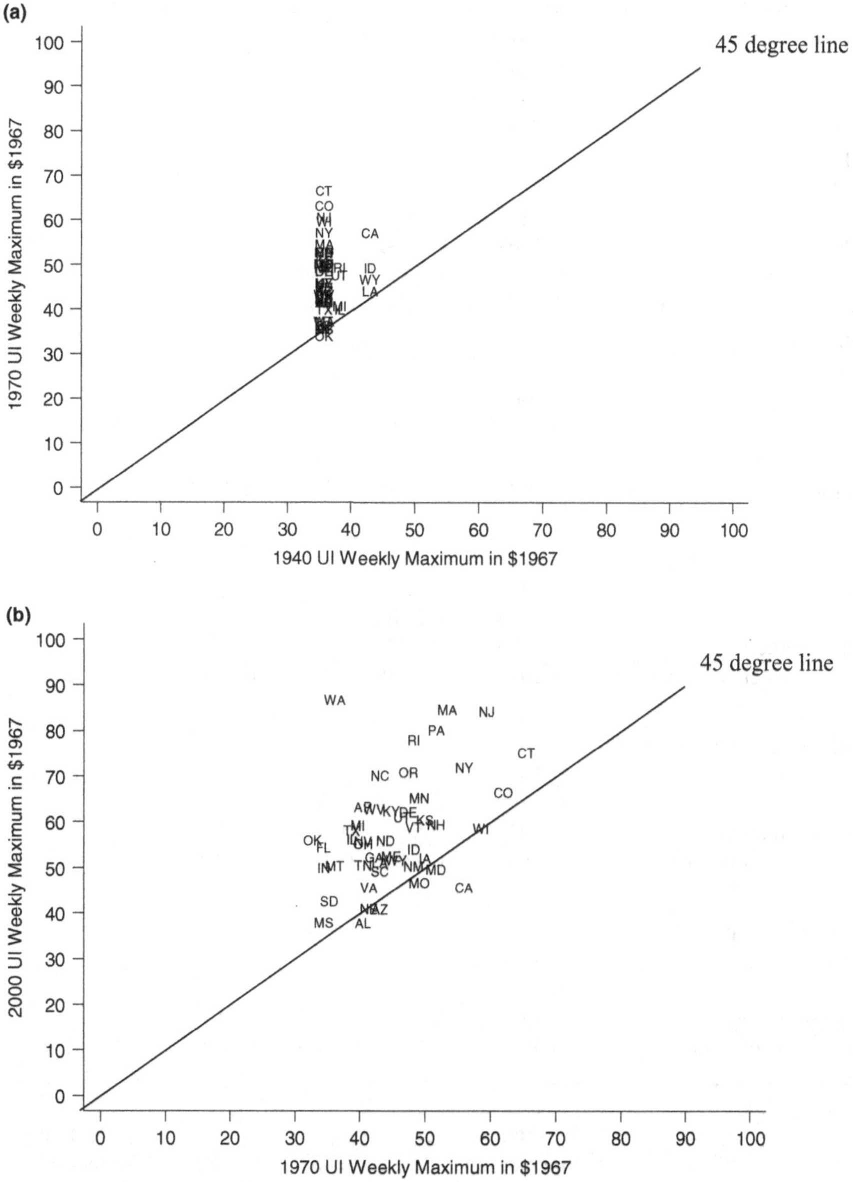

Figure 6. (a) Maximum Weekly Unemployment Benefits in 1940 and 1970 in 1967 Dollars. (b) Maximum Weekly Unemployment Benefits in 2000 and 1970 in 1967 Dollars.

Source: The data on unemployment weekly maximums can be found on the US Department of Labor: Employment and Training Administration's website: http://workforcesecurity.doleta.gov/unemploy/statelaws.asp#sigprouilaws

Table 5. Correlations Across States between Programs in Various Years.

	Workers' compensation	UI	ADC	Personal income	Average weekly earnings
1940					
Workers' compensation	1				
UI	0.0259	1			
ADC	0.0867	0.1282	1		
Personal income	0.1881	0.0871	0.5891	1	
Average weekly earnings	0.3692	0.1505	0.5623	0.7966	1
1950					
Workers' compensation	1				
UI	-0.0007	1			
ADC	0.2521	0.047	1		
Personal income	0.2305	0.1286	0.7052	1	
Average weekly earnings	0.3925	0.1888	0.7462	0.7331	1
1960					
Workers' compensation	1				
UI	0.2953	1			
ADC	0.5498	0.5682	1		
Personal income	0.4184	0.4233	0.6805	1	
Average weekly earnings	0.2026	0.3638	0.3701	0.2777	1
1970					
Workers' compensation	1				
UI	0.4044	1			
ADC	0.3636	0.4884	1		
Personal income	0.4924	0.569	0.6258	1	
Average weekly earnings	0.2881	0.1462	0.4145	0.6194	1
1980					
Workers' compensation	1				
UI	0.4376	1			
ADC	0.382	0.3345	1		
Personal income	0.4336	0.148	0.6173	1	
Average weekly earnings	0.3602	0.0979	0.3653	0.528	1

1990

	Workers' compensation	UI	SSI	ADC	Personal income
Workers' compensation	1				
UI	0.4187	1			
SSI	0.0816	0.2265	1		
ADC	0.2753	0.407	0.7096	1	
Personal income	0.3584	0.4883	0.5741	0.6883	1
Average weekly earnings	0.3688	0.3243	0.3575	0.4819	0.487

Table 5. *Continued.*

	Workers' compensation	UI	SSI	ADC	Personal income
2000					
Workers' compensation	1				
UI	0.3079	1			
SSI	0.0431	0.1672	1		
ADC	0.275	0.3572	0.691	1	
Personal income	0.1388	0.5258	0.4743	0.4838	1
Average weekly earnings	0.1619	0.3055	0.0872	0.1507	0.4147

Sources: See Table 4.

through no fault of their own drew backing from a diverse set of interest groups, ranging from major business and civic leaders to reform groups. Despite the broad-based support for the basic concepts, there was extensive debate about the specific features of the laws. The debate surrounding the benefit levels was particularly contentious.

3.1 *Mothers' Pensions and Aid to Dependent Children, 1919–1940*

In preliminary cross-sectional analyses of the factors determining the generosity of mothers' pensions in 1919, 1929 and 1940, Moehling (2006) found that states where women's clubs endorsed mothers' pension legislation earlier tended to choose less generous pensions. The negative relationship indicates the conflicts in the objectives of pension advocates. The early leaders of the mothers' pension movement wanted to provide relief to the 'deserving' poor, but they feared the creation of a permanent pauper class, a common fear throughout the progressive era that is echoed in many debates today. They did not want to raise benefits high enough to encourage desertion or divorce by spouses. Nor did they want to attract migration to the state to take advantage of higher benefits. The generosity of benefits was also lower in states with more blacks and higher in areas where women were a larger share of the labor force.

3.2 *Workers' Compensation*

Even though significant numbers of employers, workers and insurers anticipated gains from workers' compensation legislation, there were still intense debates over benefits and other features of the law.[7] In some cases, as in Missouri, the political maneuvering led to delays in adoption of the law. Fishback and Kantor (1998, 2000) performed an analysis of a panel of workers' compensation benefits between 1911 and 1930 to try to examine the factors influencing the levels of benefits chosen. They found that prior to 1930, employers in high-risk industries generally succeeded in keeping benefits low. On the other hand, states with more unionized manufacturing industries served as a countervailing force to push benefits higher. Once officials were in place to administer workers' compensation laws they also pressed for higher workers' compensation benefits. Finally, states in which the legislature shifted parties in both houses also tended to raise workers' compensation benefits as part of their new reforms when they took office.

In the original debates over workers' compensation, reformers and workers' advocates often accepted compromises on the initial benefits in hopes of putting some law in place and then seeking to raise the benefits in the future. Benefit levels therefore have continued to be a source of contention to the present day. A key determinant of the actual benefit levels paid is the weekly maximum benefit payment, which was originally set as a specific amount in nominal dollars. The law might state that the worker was eligible to receive as much as two-thirds of their normal weekly earnings, but a low maximum weekly payment could cut that percentage sharply. In fact, Allen's (2004, 2009) analysis of benefits and wages shows that the weekly maximum was binding for more than 90% of workers in various dangerous jobs across several decades of census surveys.

As wages rose with inflation, a very common experience throughout the century, legislatures had to adjust the weekly maximums for benefits to keep pace with nominal wage increases. The legislatures, many which met only every 2 years, often raised the weekly maximums after inflation eroded the benefits as a share of income. This led to the annual fluctuations in the national average expected benefit as a percentage of annual manufacturing wages, holding accident rates constant, seen in Figure 7. The national average disguises much larger fluctuations within the states. The legislative delays also meant that workers' compensation benefits as a share of manufacturing earnings stayed below its 1930s level until the early 1970s. In the plots of workers' compensation benefits as a share of annual income in 1940 and 1970 in Figure 4(a), the bulk of the states rest at points below and to the right of the 45 degree line of equality between the 2 years. The relative benefit levels show that most state legislatures allowed inflation to erode expected benefits in ways that caused the benefits relative to wage to be lower in 1970 than they were in 1940.

Allen (2009) shows that there was a substantial change in the situation in the 1970s. The federal government sponsored a National Commission on Workers' Compensation Laws in 1972 to assess the adequacy of state-mandated benefits. The National Commission called for several major reforms in state workers' compensation laws, including a large increase in benefit levels. Further, it added teeth to these recommendations by recommending that the federal government take control of workers' compensation if the states did not adopt substantial reforms. Indeed, a congressional bill was proposed that would have reopened the claims procedure in states with 'inadequate' benefits and required payment of the benefit shortfall in those cases.

One of the Commission's key recommendations was that the states move away from their practice of setting nominal maximum levels for weekly benefits every few years to indexing the benefits so that they adjusted to changes in the weekly wage rates in the states. Prior to 1972, only a handful of states had begun indexing

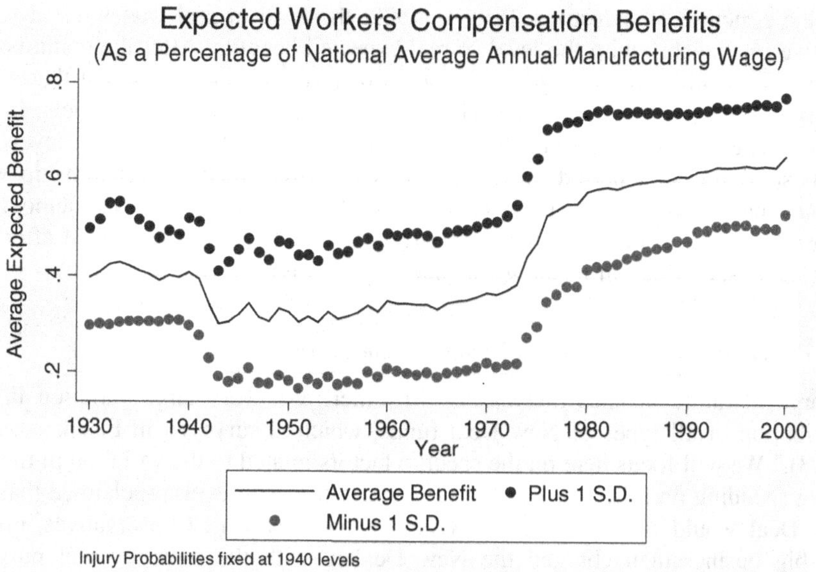

Figure 7.
Source: Allen (2009).

Source: The data on unemployment weekly maximums can be found on the US Department of Labor: Employment and Training Administration's website: http://workforcesecurity.doleta.gov/unemploy/statelaws.asp#sigprouilaws

their benefits. After the National Commission report, the vast majority of states made the shift. As a result, the expected benefits as a share of annual earnings holding accident rates constant in Figure 7 rises sharply in the 1970s and then displays a slightly rising trend thereafter. Similarly, the plots of expected benefits in each state in 1970 and 2000 show that the workers' compensation benefits area all clustered to the upper left of the 45 degree line in Figure 4(b). Allen performed a hazard analysis of the timing of the shift and found that states tended to adopt the indexing earlier if they already had high benefits, and had state senates dominated by Democrats. Southern states were slower to adopt the procedure. In contrast to the Fishback and Kantor studies prior to 1930, neither union representation nor the administrative structure of workers' compensation appeared to matter much.

The shift in procedure for benefit adjustments also led to a sharp change in the impact of various factors on the level of benefits. Allen set up a panel data set with annual information for the states for each year from 1940 through 2000 on the real level of benefits as a function of interest group activity, and political measures with interaction terms that allowed estimation of the change in the effect of the measures after 1972. The analysis controls for year and state fixed effects and the structure of industries. Prior to 1972, the level of real wages had a weak positive relationship with the level of real expected benefits. After the commission report, the relationship strengthened a great deal; the elasticity implied that a 1% rise in real wages was associated with a 0.565% rise in real benefit levels. In the pre-1972 period, more unionization was associated with higher benefit levels. In the post-commission period the shift to indexing weakened the relationship with annual changes in unionization. In a similar fashion, the effects of Democratic leadership in the state legislature was strong before 1972 and weakened after the Democrats succeeded in pushing for indexing of wages.

3.3 *The Distribution of New Deal Funds in the 1930s*

A large literature debates the reasons why there was very large variation in the distribution of all types of New Deal funds, which is surveyed in Fishback *et al.* (2003).[8] We will focus here on the specific factors related to the variation in the per capita spending on relief. In a famous Fireside Chat, Roosevelt proclaimed that the New Deal would promote 'Relief, Recovery and Reform'. Conservatives, critics and big businessmen charged the New Dealers with the more cynical purpose of using government programs to build patronage and to 'buy' voters to ensure the continuation of the Democrat's hegemony over the federal government. Many modern programs have explicit formulas that determine the distribution of federal spending through matching grants and specific counts. The inner workings of the emergency New Deal programs are more difficult to fathom. Explicit formulas for matching funds written into the FERA legislation were largely deemed unworkable after the first three months. Senate testimony from FERA administrators on the distribution of funds offers a long list of factors that were considered but little guidance on the weights each factor was given. Similarly, the WPA matching requirements were routinely ignored and the shares of funds provided by state and local governments varied widely.

Nearly all of the statistical analyses of the distribution of relief spending and emergency jobs have estimated regressions using cross-sections of counties, cities, or states. All find that the relief programs distributed funds to areas with at least one or more of the following: higher unemployment earlier in the 1930s, more of a decline in income and lower long-term incomes. They also find, however, that there is evidence of political maneuvering in a variety of sophisticated forms.[9] Various studies have shown that more monies were distributed in areas with higher voter turnout, more swing voting and loyal voters (Wright, 1974; Couch and Shugart, 1998; Fleck, 1999c, 2001a; Fishback *et al.*, 2003; Stromberg, 2004). Fleck (2001a) fine tuned the analysis to show that loyal voters mattered more in states loyal to the Democrats and swing voters mattered more in states where swing voting was more common. Stromberg (2004) showed that the Roosevelt administration spent more money where there were more radios, which gave them an advantage in gaining credit for the monies. More recently, Neumann *et al.* (2010) have used a panel of monthly evidence to examine the extent to which the Roosevelt administration used the timing of relief spending to influence elections. There was a clear pattern in the raw data showing increased spending near election dates, particularly in 1936 and 1938. The WPA defended the timing by arguing that these were periods of high unemployment (Howard, 1943). After controlling for changes in employment and nationwide shocks, the panel study finds that there were rises in spending in the months immediately before the November elections and a decline in spending in December.

3.4 *Family Aid Programs and Unemployment Insurance, 1940–2000*

To supplement the work by Sam Allen on the factors influencing workers' compensation benefits from 1930 through 1940, we have done some preliminary analyses on the relationships between the benefit maximums for the family aid programs and UI and political parties and incomes across states for the years 1940, 1950, 1960, 1970, 1980, 1990 and 2000. The estimating equation takes the following form:

$$B_{st} = \beta_0 + \beta_1 Y_{st} + \beta_2 P_{st} + \Delta + \theta + \Delta * \text{time} + \varepsilon_{st}$$

where B_{st} is the natural log of the maximum benefit in 1967 dollars in year t and state i. Y_{st} is the natural log of average income in 1967 dollars over the decade (average for 1931 through 1940 for 1940, 1941 through 1950 for 1950, etc.). P_{st} is a vector of averages across the decade of political measures, including the average of the percentage voting for the Democratic presidential candidate, the average percentage voting for other presidential candidates aside from Democrats and Republicans, the share of years in which the state simultaneously had a Democratic governor and the percentage Democrat exceeded the percentage Republican in both houses of the state legislature, the Democratic state dominance measure interacted with a southern dummy, the share of years in which the state simultaneously had a Republican governor and the percentage Republican exceeded the percentage Democrat in both houses of the state legislature and the share of years in which both legislatures shifted party dominance during the decade. The Δ is a vector of state dummies that control for features of the states that do not vary over time, and θ is a vector of year dummies to control for nationwide shocks to the political economy. The vector Δ is also interacted with a time counter (1900 $=$ 0) to control for state-specific time trends. The error term ε_{st} captures factors that are not measured in the analysis. Results are shown in Table 6 with and without the state and year fixed effects and the state specific time trends to show how the inferences change when these are not included.

The relationships between benefits and income change sharply as we add more controls to the analysis. When the state and year fixed effects and the state-specific time trends are not included, there is a strong positive relationship between personal income in the state and the maximum UI weekly benefit. The statistically significant coefficient implies that a 1% rise in state per capita income is associated with a 0.336% rise in the maximum UI benefit. Once state effects are included to control for long-term features of the state and nationwide changes associated with the

Table 6. Regressions of the Natural Log of Benefit Levels in Census Years on Decade-long Averages of Income and Political Variables with and without Fixed Effects and Time Trends.

	Expected workers' compensation benefit			Maximum weekly UI benefit			Maximum ADC benefit base		
Decade averages									
Percent voting Democrat for president	0.004	0.011	0.010	0.004	0.003	0.000	0.014	0.000	−0.012
	2.14	*7.09*	*4.82*	*3.51*	*2.03*	*−0.1*	*4.28*	*0.03*	*−2.36*
Percentage voting for a presidential candidate outside the major parties	0.002	0.007	0.003	0.002	0.002	−0.002	−0.001	0.000	−0.012
	0.97	*3.2*	*1.2*	*1.02*	*1.17*	*−0.87*	*−0.37*	*−0.1*	*−1.56*
Democrats control governor and both houses of state legislatures	0.081	0.072	0.032	0.014	0.055	0.008	0.104	−0.040	−0.083
	1.07	*1.26*	*0.56*	*0.32*	*1.35*	*0.18*	*0.94*	*−0.62*	*−1.37*
Democrats control governor and both houses of state legislatures in south	−0.254	−0.229	−0.106	−0.060	−0.070	−0.007	−0.764	0.092	0.175
	−3.7	*−2.51*	*−1.04*	*−1.46*	*−1*	*−0.07*	*−5.76*	*0.86*	*1.83*
Republican control of governor and both houses of state legislature	−0.243	0.037	−0.066	−0.063	0.029	0.009	0.160	−0.030	−0.033
	−3.5	*0.6*	*−1.08*	*−1.34*	*0.57*	*0.16*	*1.48*	*−0.45*	*−0.57*
Years in which both houses of state legislature shift	−0.025	0.087	−0.037	0.368	0.192	0.271	1.124	−0.146	0.175
	−0.09	*0.48*	*−0.16*	*2.14*	*1.26*	*1.54*	*2.17*	*−0.53*	*0.77*
Natural log of per capita state personal income in 1967 dollars	0.777	0.186	−0.429	0.336	−0.040	0.023	−0.604	0.001	0.144
	23.91	*1.68*	*−2.02*	*13.29*	*−0.47*	*0.2*	*−5.54*	*0*	*0.43*
Year fixed effects	No	Yes	Yes	No	Yes	Yes	No	Yes	Yes
State fixed effects	No	Yes	Yes	No	Yes	Yes	No	Yes	Yes
State time trends	No	No	Yes	No	No	Yes	No	No	Yes

Notes and Sources: Dependent variables are in natural logs and come from sources in Table 4. Decade-long averages of state per capita income were calculated with data collected by Allen (2009).

years, the effect becomes statistically insignificant and slightly negative, and the effect gets smaller still when the state-specific time trends are added.

Meanwhile, the relationship between ADC benefits and average personal income is negative in the absence of the state and year fixed effects and trends. Once we control for all three, the relationship changes markedly. The new point estimate suggests that a 1% rise in state per capita personal income is associated with a family maximum benefit that is 0.144% higher, although the relationship is not statistically significant. In the case of the dependent children benefits, it is particularly important to add the year fixed effects to control for changes in the definition of the measure being used.

The effect of political parties tends to be strong without the extra controls. Both types of benefits tended to be higher in states that tended to vote for Democrats for president and when there were more shifts in party dominance in the state legislature in the prior decade. In addition, the dependent children benefits were lower in states that voted for someone besides major party candidates in presidential elections and in southern states where Democrats dominated all parts of state government. The benefits were higher in areas where Republicans succeeded in capturing control of all aspects of state government. However, these effects are much weaker and statistically insignificant as we add the state and year fixed effects and then the state-specific time trends.

There is some debate among social scientists about the use of state and year fixed effects and state-specific time trends. Some claim that the extra controls are correlated with components of the remaining variables in the analysis. For example, if a state is fundamentally Democratic, the coefficient of the state fixed effect may also be picking up the role of Democrats in the state. Thus the coefficient of the Democratic variable when the state fixed effect is included is just capturing deviations from the long term fundamental Democratic nature of the state. On the other hand, there may be other time-invariant factors that are not measured in the model being estimated that influence the benefit levels and happen to be correlated with the Democrats. If so, the coefficient of the Democrat variable in an equation that eliminates the fixed effects and time trends is going to be biased in ways that will cause mis-measurement of the relationship in which we are interested.

We can get a sense of which states are most generous after controlling for income and political party by examining the coefficients of the fixed effects. For UI benefits, the states in the top 10 include Connecticut, Minnesota, Pennsylvania, New York, New Jersey, Wisconsin, Massachusetts, Colorado, Delaware and Kansas. The states in the bottom 10 include Mississippi, Indiana, Alabama, South Dakota, Arizona, South Carolina, Florida, Missouri, Tennessee and Georgia. For dependent child benefits the top 10 include Connecticut, New Hampshire, Wisconsin, California, New York, Minnesota, Vermont, Massachusetts, Utah and Washington and the bottom 10 are Mississippi, Alabama, South Carolina, Arkansas, Tennessee, Texas, Louisiana, Georgia, Florida and Kentucky.

4. The Impact of Poverty Programs on Socio-economic Outcomes Before 1950

There is a growing cliometric literature on the impact of social insurance and poverty programs on various measures of socio-economic welfare in the USA between 1900 and 1950. The stated primary goal of each program was to provide resources to people who have experienced either a drop in income or are permanently stuck in a low income situation. It seems obvious that receiving poverty and social insurance payments would make the person better off in the short run. Absent fraudulent activity, the recipient's income is higher during a period where their income is low. Some of the policy analyses therefore focus on how the programs influenced non-income measures for a class of people, such as mortality rates, family formation, crime rates and other factors. Others show how the programs influence the incentives for other decision makers in the rest of the economy. For example, an increase in public spending on poverty relief might lead to reductions in private charitable giving or might lead to downward adjustments in wages in the labour market because potential recipients are better protected by the public policy against bad times. Such changes, whether unintended or recognized in advance by policy makers, tend to offset the benefits of the public program to the recipients of the benefits.

4.1 *Procedures Used to Estimate Relationships*

The studies summarized in Table 7 tend to follow a similar set of procedures. The policies all varied across state and sometimes counties, so researchers have collected information on key features of the policies for each location. In most cases the researchers have put together panel data sets in which there is both variation across locations in any one year and variation across time within locations in the outcome measure and the policy measure. The number of years in the panels ranges from 2 to more than 10 years. Most of the studies use state or county averages in a particular year as the unit of observation. Given that the policies typically varied by state and time, use of averages for the outcome variables may not lead to severe aggregation bias. A small number of studies have access to information on individuals, but they do not have information on the same individual for more than 1 year and so the cross-sections are pooled into 'pseudo-panels'.

All the studies seek to identify the impact of the policy on the outcome in multivariate analysis that includes other factors that influence the outcome. Over the past 20 years, economic historians have paid increasing attention to elimination of 'endogeneity bias', which might arise when the policy measure is correlated with the error term in the regression equation to be estimated. This type of bias can occur if key variables that are correlated with both the outcome and the policy are not included in the analysis. This 'omitted variable bias' in the coefficient is a multiplicative function of the correlation between the left-out variable and the outcome variable and the correlation between the left-out variable and the policy measure. If both correlations have the same sign, the omitted variable bias will be

Table 7. Results of Cliometric Studies of Impact of Social Welfare Programs during the Period 1900 to 1950.

Program	Citation	Effect	Data	Method
Workers' compensation, 1907–1923	Fishback and Kantor (1995)	Wages: Higher workers' compensation expected benefits associated with lower wages for non-union workers but not union workers	Panel: Annual state averages for occupations 1907–1923	Controls plus state, year and occupation fixed effects with proxy measure of workers' compensation benefits to control for endogeneity
Workers' compensation, 1930s	Balkan (1998)	Wage rates: Workers' compensation was associated with lower wages	Unbalanced panel of hourly earnings for 72 industries in 48 states for years 1933, 1935, 1937 and 1939	Correlates and state and year fixed effects. Lagged proxy of workers' compensation benefit
Workers' compensation, 1917–1919	Fishback and Kantor (1995)	Savings: Higher workers' compensation expected benefits associated with reduced savings	Cross-section of individual working class families, 1917–1919	Control for income, family structure, age, accident risk. Measure of expected benefit used workers' actual wage
UI, 1930s	Balkan (1998)	Wages: Introduction of UI in late 1930s had little impact on wages	Unbalanced panel of hourly earnings for 72 industries in 48 states for years 1933, 1935, 1937 and 1939	Correlates and state and year fixed effects. Lagged measure of UI maximum paid for maximum duration

Table 7. *Continued.*

Program	Citation	Effect	Data	Method
Workers' compensation, 1903–1930	Fishback (1987)	Accident rates: Introduction of workers' compensation laws associated with higher fatal accident rates in the coal industry	Panel: Annual state averages for coal industry, 1903–1930	Controls for mine inspections, coal mining activity, technology, unions, mine size
Workers' compensation, 1900–1940	Chelius (1977)	Accident rates: Introduction of workers' compensation law associated with fall in nonfatal machinery accident rates per member of labor force	Panel: 26 states from 1900 to 1940	State fixed effects plus controls for state inspections
Workers' compensation, 1900–1940	Buffum (1992)	Accident rates: Introduction of workers' compensation associated with lower nonfatal machinery accident rates	Panel: 26 states from 1900 to 1940	Controls for factory inspection spending and various measures of structures of industry
Workers' compensation, 1900–1940	Buffum (1992)	Accident rates: Fatal industrial accidents per 100,000 workers rise in workers' compensation states	Panel: 8 states from 1900 to 1940	Controls for factory inspection spending and various measures of structures of industry
Workers' compensation, 1900–1930	Buffum (1992)	Accident rates: Fatal accident rate in bituminous coal mining higher in workers' compensation states	Panel of 24 coal mining states, 1900–1930	State effects and variety of controls

Mothers' pensions (precursor of ADC), 1910–1920	Moehling (2007)	Family structure: More generous mothers' pensions associated with increases in divorces and separations. States that extended eligibility to mothers other than widows experienced increases in births to single mothers	Pooled individual data of different people from 1910 and 1920 census from 48 states	Equivalent of state and year fixed effects with controls for many correlates
ADC, 1940–1970	Moehling (2007)	Family structure: ADC benefits not associated with more single motherhood for blacks in years 1940–1970 or for whites 1940–1960. Positive elasticity of 0.23 to 0.37 for whites in 1970	Individual cross-sections from 1940, 1950, 1960 and 1970 from census	Controls for individual characteristics and state-level economic factors
OAA, 1940 and 1950	Costa (1999)	Family structure: Elderly women more likely to live on own	Pooled cross-sections of different individuals from census, 1940 and 1950	Controls for individual characteristics, state and region fixed or random effects, differencing between eligible and noneligible populations

Table 7. *Continued.*

Program	Citation	Effect	Data	Method
OAA, 1940 and 1950	Friedberg (1999)	Labor force participation: Higher OAA benefits lowered labor force participation among the elderly	Pooled cross-sections of different individuals from census, 1940 and 1950	Probit with controls for individual characteristics and state economic conditions with state and year fixed effects. Additional regressions to show no effect for people not eligible for program
OAA, 1930–1950	Parsons (1991)	Labor force participation: OAA benefits account for about half of the decline in the elderly work force between 1930 and 1950	Panel of state averages, 1930, 1940 and 1950	Pooled regressions with controls and with random effects
OAA, 1934–1955	Balaan Cohen (2009)	Death rates of elderly: OAA reduced several types of mortality after 1940 but not before	Panel: Annual averages for 48 states, 1934–1955; 1937–1955; 1940–1955	State and year fixed effects and state-specific time trends with instrument for OAA variable, plus regression to show no effects for people not eligible for program

OAA, 1930–1938	Stoian and Fishback (2010)	Death rates of elderly: OAA did not reduce elderly death rates	Panel: Annual averages for 75 cities, 1930–1940	Difference between eligible and non-eligible age groups with city and year fixed effects and instrument for OAA variable
Local public aid to poor, 1923–1932	Fox (2009, unpublished)	Infant and child death rates: About \$781,000 (in 2007 dollars) of poverty relief associated with reduction of one infant death in fixed effects estimates. Effect reduced by city-specific time trends. No effect on children of other ages	Panel: Annual averages for 67 cities, 1923–1932	Controls for city characteristics, city and year fixed effects, city-specific time trends
New Deal relief spending, 1929–1940	Fishback *et al.* (2007)	Death and birth rates: About \$2 million (in 2000 dollars) in additional relief spending associated with reduction of one infant death, half a homicide, one suicide, 2.4 deaths from infectious disease, one death from diarrhea. A one standard deviation increase in relief spending associated with 0.82 standard deviation rise in general fertility rate	Panel: Annual averages for 114 cities, 1929–1940	Controls for city characteristics, city and year fixed effects, instruments

Table 7. *Continued.*

Program	Citation	Effect	Data	Method
New Deal relief spending, 1930–1940	Johnson *et al.* (forthcoming)	Crime rates: 10% rise in work relief spending associated with 1.5% reduction in property crime rate. Smaller effect of direct relief spending	Panel: Annual averages for 81 large cities, 1930–1940	Controls for city characteristics, city and year fixed effects, city-specific time trends and instruments
New Deal emergency relief employment, 1937, 1940	Fleck (1999b)	Private employment: Increase of one emergency relief job associated with an increase in measured unemployed but little effect on private employment	Separate cross-sections of county averages in 1937 and again in 1940	Large number of correlates and instrument for relief jobs
New Deal FERA employment, 1935	Wallis and Benjamin (1981)	Private employment: Little or no effect of FERA cases per capita spending on private monthly wages. Little effect of FERA average benefits on FERA caseloads	Cross-section of 52 cities in fiscal year, 1934–1935	In wage equation correlates for aggregated demand and prior wages. In case equation correlates and instruments for FERA benefit levels
New Deal relief spending, 1932–1940	Neumann *et al.* (2010)	Private employment: Positive effect of relief spending on private employment prior to 1936. Negative effect of relief spending on private employment after 1936	Panel of monthly averages from January 1933 through December 1939 for 44 major cities	Panel VAR with differencing and controls for serial correlation. No endogeneity if there is a one-month or more lag in effects of each variable on other variables

Relief spending, 1930s	Matthews and Benjamin (1992)	Private employment: An additional New Deal relief job crowded out about one-third of a private job in 1933 and about nine-tenths of a private job in 1939	Panel of annual state averages, 1932 through 1939	Pooled regressions with controls and instruments
New Deal relief and public works spending, 1933–1939	Fishback *et al.* (2005)	Retail sales: Dollar increase of public works and relief spending per capita associated with rise in retail sales per capita of roughly 40 cents	Cross-section of growth rates for US counties, 1929–1939, 1929–1935, 1933–1939	Large number of correlates and instrument for public works and relief
New Deal relief and public works spending, 1933–1939	Fishback *et al.* (2006)	Net migration: Increase in public works and relief spending leads to increase in net migration	Cross-section of county averages during 1930s	Large number of correlates and instrument for public works and relief
New Deal relief and public works spending, 1933–1939	Sorensen *et al.* (2009, unpublished)	Internal migration: Public works and relief spending led to 15% more internal migration within the USA	Cross-section of 460 state economic areas, 1935–1940	Several correlates and instrument for public works and relief in a structural choice model
New Deal relief spending	Hungerman and Gruber (2007)	Private charitable spending: An additional dollar of New Deal spending reduced church charitable spending by about 3 cents. This reduced total church spending by 29% of the maximum it could have reduced it	Panel of annual state averages, 1933 through 1939	State and year fixed effects, region-specific time trends, instruments

positive. If the two correlations have different signs, the omitted variable bias will be negative.

Endogeneity bias might also arise if there is a feedback relationship such that the outcome variable itself influences the decision makers when they design the policy measure. For example, in a study of the impact of a program on average incomes, there are likely to be situations where decreases in average incomes lead to adoption of a more generous poverty policy. This feedback will cause the estimates of the impact of the poverty program to be less positive than the true causal relationship between the program and income.

To deal with the omitted variable problem, all of the studies adopt some form of the following estimating equation. In this case the estimation is performed on a panel with each observation as an average from state s in year t.

$$O_{st} = \beta_0 + \beta_1 \text{POLICY}_{st} + \beta_2 X_{st} + \Delta + \theta + \Delta * \text{time} + \varepsilon_{st}$$

where O_{st} is the outcome measure in year t and state s, POLICY_{st} is a measure of the policy and X_{st} is a vector of a set of factors that vary across states and time that influence the outcome measure. To control for factors in each state that do not vary across time within a state but do vary across states, a vector Δ of state fixed effects is included. Such factors might include the fundamental legal environment, the climate and other factors. A vector θ of year effects can be included to control for factors that hit all states in the same year but vary across years, such as wars, monetary policy, and the introduction of new nationwide knowledge. Another vector of state-specific time trends ($\Delta * time$) can be used to control for trends within each state that vary across states. The error term (ε_{st}) is the sum of all of the unmeasured factors.

The coefficient β_1 is an estimate of the relationship between a change in policy and a change in the outcome. In statistics there is no way to ascribe true causation to this estimate of the relationship because statistics can only get at correlation. If the POLICY_{st} measure is not correlated with the error ε_{st}, then β_1 is often considered an unbiased measure of the relationship. Economists also use the term 'causal' in this situation.

In seeking to control for omitted variable bias, some of the earlier studies only included the vector X_{st} of variables that varied across time and place. Worries that there are many factors that have gone unmeasured have led economists to increasingly use the state and year fixed effects and state-specific time trends to reduce the potential problems with omitted variable bias. These extra controls have the advantage of controlling for all sorts of factors that had gone unmeasured, but that were correlated with both the outcome and policy variables. On the other hand, researchers do not necessarily know which factors are being controlled by the fixed effects and some researchers are worried that the fixed effects and state time trends are picking up some aspects of the policy and causing the β_1 estimate to understate the policy effects, as we discussed in the previous section.

To some extent, the fixed effects and state time trends control for the feedback form of endogeneity. Researchers have also explored using instrumental variable (IV) analysis in which they seek a variable that is correlated to a strong degree with the policy measure but is uncorrelated with the error term ε_{st}. It should be emphasized that this is composed of the unobservables after controlling for all of the other factors in the equation. Most of the studies that have used the IV approach used a two-stage least squares approach in which a first-stage equation of the following form is estimated.

$$\text{POLICY}_{st} = \alpha_0 + \alpha_1 \text{Instrument}_{st} + \alpha_2 X_{st} + \Delta_1 + \theta_1 + \Delta_1 * \text{time} + u_{st}$$

Note that the equation includes all of the factors in the right hand side of the earlier equation along with the IV. Then a prediction of the POLICY variable is substituted in the final stage outcome equation.

$$O_{st} = \gamma_0 + \gamma_1 \text{Predicted POLICY}_{st} + \gamma_2 X_{st} + \Delta_2 + \theta_2 + \Delta\theta_2 * \text{time} + \varepsilon_{st}$$

This technique is designed to capture the impact of the portion of the actual policy measure that is correlated with the instrument, and thus not correlated with the error term in the final equation. There are potentially a number of instruments that might be used and there is no guarantee that the results will always be the same for each instrument.

Most of the studies in Table 7 show comparisons of the results with estimates of the raw relationship between the policy and the outcome in the absence of any controls, as well as estimates with the various controls included. In many cases, the inclusion of the controls reduces the absolute value of the coefficient, suggesting that omitted variable bias is a problem when just looking at raw correlations or graphs of the relationship between the outcome and policy variable. In a number of cases, but not all, the use of IV estimation leads to stronger relationships between the policy measure and the outcome that was disguised in the coefficient estimates performed without IVs.

4.2 *Workers' Compensation Studies*

The studies of workers' compensation, the first of the major social insurance programs summarized in Table 7, show that the switch to workers' compensation laws served to raise the average amounts of post-accident compensation received by workers when they were injured. The changes in liability rules and in the size of benefits were associated with reductions in non-union hourly earnings in dangerous industries like coal mining and lumber. Unionized workers were more effective at staving off these reductions and thus gained more from the legislation. The initial introduction of social insurance, however, did not always influence wages. When UI programs began paying benefits in the late 1930s, there is no sign that hourly earnings adjusted downwards (Balkan, 1998).

The impact of workers' compensation on accident rates was more complex and largely determined by the relative costs of preventing accidents for workers and employers. Because workers' compensation insurance premiums were experience rated, higher post-accident benefits gave employers more incentive to prevent accidents while allowing workers to be less careful.[10] Panel data studies by several scholars show that workers' compensation laws were associated with higher accident rates in coal mining, where the costs to employers of preventing accidents were high enough that they chose to pay higher premiums rather than incur the very high costs of doing more to prevent accidents in each miner's workplace deep in the mine. In manufacturing, where employers had much more control over the conditions in the workplace, some studies show a reduction in accident rates when workers' compensation was introduced.

4.3 *Mothers' Pensions and Aid to Dependent Children*

When mothers' pensions were introduced in many states, the opponents feared that the provision of benefits to female-headed households might lead to higher divorce or separation rates. The compromise solution in a number of the states was to limit payments to widowed mothers. Carolyn Moehling has assessed the impact of mothers' pension and ADC laws on family formation using individual level data from the census during several years. Her results suggest that divorce rates and separation rates were higher in states with more generous mothers' pension programs by 1920. She does not find the same kinds of effects for the years 1940, 1950 and 1960 after the Social Security Act established the federal matching programs for the state ADC programs that replaced mothers' pensions in the late 1930s. She does find a relatively strong positive relationship between family break-ups and ADC benefits for white women in 1970.

4.4 *Old-age Assistance*

The original state OAA laws declared that one goal was to provide enough benefits to the elderly to live on their own. Dora Costa (1999) has found that higher benefits under the federal matching grant version of OAA established under the Social Security framework after 1935 allowed more women to live on their own. Friedberg (1999) and Parsons (1991) show that OAA allowed a significant number of elderly to stay out of the labour force.

OAA did not serve to reduced mortality rates of the elderly after controls for other factors are included. Even though raw correlations suggest that the introduction of OAA was associated with lower death rates among the elderly between 1930 and 1938, Stoian and Fishback (2010) find that death rates fell as much or more in the same states for other age groups not eligible for OAA. They suggest that OAA had little effect on death rates in the 1930s because it largely was substituting for benefits through almshouses and other programs that the elderly were receiving under the general poverty programs. Andreea Balan-Cohen (2010, unpublished data) finds that OAA is associated with lower death rates in the 1940s and 1950s in part because a broader range of the elderly received benefits. In addition, new technologies like penicillin in the early 1940s meant that relatively small increases in benefits in the 1940s and 1950s could be used to purchase much more effective treatments of some mortal illnesses that had not been treatable in the 1930s.

4.5 *Poverty Relief Programs*

On the other hand, poverty relief programs in the 1920s and 1930s were more successful at reducing death rates among the most vulnerable population in society, infants below the age of one. Jonathan Fox (2010, unpublished data) finds that an additional $780,000 (in 2007 dollars) of spending in cities on poverty relief before the New Deal was associated with the reduction of one infant death. Public health education programs were even more successful. Death rates for children older than one were not influenced nearly as much by these programs. The federal government began offering very large amounts of relief funds in 1933 that swamped the spending by state and local governments before. Fishback *et al.* (2007) find that about $2 million (in 2000 dollars) in additional relief spending associated with reduction of one infant death, half a homicide, one suicide, 2.4 deaths from infectious disease, one death from diarrhoea in large urban areas between 1929 and 1940. Greater relief spending also gave families enough income to allow them to return to more normal fertility rates.

Relief spending also contributed to reductions in property crime rates. Kantor *et al.* (forthcoming) examine crime rates in 81 cities during the 1930s. They find that work relief poverty programs, like the WPA, served to reduce property crime rates. A 10% increase in spending on work relief was associated with a 1.5% reduction in property crime. In most specifications the effect of relief payments without a work requirement was smaller in part because people on direct relief were not having their hours soaked up by a work requirement during the day. Relief spending was not as successful as private employment in reducing property crime. The estimates suggest that a 1% decline in employment in a city was associated with a 1% rise in property crime rates in the 1930s. The employment results are similar to findings in a study of the USA between 1979 and 1997 by Raphael and Winter-Ebmer (2001).

The federal government's spending on emergency relief programs like the FERA and the WPA during the 1930s led to complaints by some employers that they created disincentives for workers to accept private employment, and thus work relief jobs in particular might crowd out private employment. The debate in the 1930s mirrored the long standing discussions of the issue, which suggested that benefits for the unemployed provided an outside option that raised unemployed workers' reservation wage when seeking private employment. What was unusual in the 1930s was that the unemployment rate was so high, over 20% in several years, that there seemed to be plenty of unemployed workers to soak up before crowding out could occur.

A series of labour market studies cited in Table 7 offer conflicting pictures of the impact of relief programs on private employment in the 1930s. Studies of cross-sectional data using IV estimation by Fleck (1999b) for county data in 1937 and 1940 and by John Wallis and Daniel Benjamin (1981) using city data in 1934/1935 suggest that areas with higher relief employment did not experience a reduction in private employment.

On the other hand, studies using panel data sets, which allow the research to take advantage of variation both across geographic areas and over time, find some degree of crowding out that varies across time. In the early years of the decade when unemployment was at its peak above 20%, Matthews and Benjamin (1992) find that the addition of one work relief job reduced private employment by about one-third of a job, whereas Neumann *et al.* (2010) find a slight positive effect of relief spending on private employment. After 1935, when unemployment rates fell below 20%, both studies find that an additional work relief job was associated with a reduction of up to nine-tenths of a private job.

The relief jobs may have helped workers in ways that, oddly enough, caused the official measures of unemployment to rise. High unemployment rates often discourage workers from seeking work. These discouraged workers are not considered unemployed under standard definitions of unemployment, which require that someone be actively seeking work to be defined as unemployed. Meanwhile, during the 1930s relief workers were treated as unemployed in the official statistics. As a result, when a relief job in the 1930s became available and was filled by a discouraged worker, the number of unemployed in the official statistics rose by one. Hence we see the odd effect that the creation of an additional relief job could make the official unemployment statistics look worse during the 1930s.

The impact of public works and relief programs extended well beyond the labour market. An added dollar of public works and relief spending in a US county was associated with an increase in retail sales of roughly 40 cents (Fishback *et al.*, 2005). Given typical ratios of retail sales to income, this suggests that incomes in the county grew roughly 85 cents at the mean when a dollar was added to public works and relief spending. Counties with greater public works and relief spending appeared to be more attractive to workers, as these counties experienced more in-migration during the 1930s (Fishback *et al.*, 2006; Sorensen *et al.*, 2008, unpublished data).

5. Summary

Social welfare programs in the USA have long been designed to serve as safety nets for people who hit hard times, which contrasts with the universal approach currently found in many other developed western nations. Even though the focus is more on the safety net, modern US public social welfare spending per capita spending rivals the spending in other western countries in comparisons based on purchasing power parity. Include private social welfare spending and the USA ranks among the highest in the world in total per capita social welfare spending.

The average for the USA disguises enormous variation in the extent of the programs across states within the USA. This variation arose in part because most public social welfare programs were the responsibility of local and state governments until the New Deal programs were introduced during the Great Depression. Even after the federal government became involved, many federal programs have left decisions about benefit levels and other features in the hands of the states, after setting some base rules and offering matching grants. Thus, benefit levels still vary substantially across states. For most types of programs, the cross-state correlations of benefit levels at the end-points of a decade are relatively high, although the strength of the correlation weakens as the interval between years compared rises. There were some periods when federal intervention or threats of intervention led to a re-ordering of benefit levels across states, including the New Deal's impact on per capita relief spending during the 1930s and the shifts in workers' compensation benefits seen in the 1970s. The patchwork nature of the safety net is illustrated best by the correlations of benefit levels for different programs in the same year. The correlations are relatively low suggesting that benefit generosity in one program has not been tightly matched by generosity in other programs within the same state. Analysis of the economic and political determinants of benefit levels suggests that both economic and political factors influenced the process, although their importance varies from program to program.

All of the programs are designed to provide resources to people in dire straits. It seems obvious that more resources makes the recipient better off in the short run; therefore, most of the cliometric studies of the benefit programs have focused on the indirect and/or unintended consequences of the programs. Wage reductions for non-union workers were associated with increases in workers' compensation benefits in the early years although not with the introduction of UI programs in the late 1930s. The introduction of workers' compensation had varied effects on accident rates that depended strongly on the costs to employers of preventing accidents. Mothers' pension programs contributed to an increase in separations and divorces when they were first introduced, but the matching-grant ADC programs that replaced mothers' pensions in the 1930s showed little relationship to breakups until after 1960. OAA programs had little impact on elderly death rates in the 1930s, in part because the elderly were being moved off of general welfare rolls. By the 1940s when penicillin was introduced, the programs contributed to reductions in death rates. The programs also allowed more elderly women to live on their own and reduced the labour supply of the elderly in 1940 and 1950. Studies of a range of effects of general relief and work relief programs in the 1920s and 1930s suggest that they contributed to reduced death rates for infants and for specific types of diseases, lowered crime rates, increased economic activity and stimulated in-migration into the counties with more spending.

Acknowledgements

The authors thank Shawn Kantor, Peter Lindert, Les Oxley, Carolyn Moehling, Robert Margo, Paul Rhode, David Ribar, Adrian Stoian, John Wallis and an anonymous referee for sharing data and their insights on the issues addressed in this chapter.

Notes

1. Fishback (2009) put together these comparisons from OECD statistics. For comparisons of many countries over long periods of time see Lindert (2004, vols 1 and 2).
2. See Moss (1996), Skocpol (1992), Costa (1998), Fishback and Thomasson (2006, vol. 2).

3. See Ziliak and Hannon (2006, pp. 698–699), Ziliak (1996, 2002) and Lebergott (1976, pp. 61–65).
4. Livingston's (2010, unpublished data) statements are based on data reported by Massachusetts State Board of Charity from 1900 through 1919 and the Massachusetts Department of Public Welfare for the years 1920 through 1930.
5. See Winegarden and Murray (1998) and Bowlbis (forthcoming).
6. See Murray (2007) and Thomasson (2002).
7. Fishback and Kantor (2000) showed that the political economy of the original adoption of workers' compensation was the result of groups of employers and insurance companies joining with groups of reformers and workers to pass the laws. The employers anticipated a reduction in uncertainty about their accident liability payments associated with the negligence laws and changing court decisions. Employers also ending up passing along a significant portion of the costs of the new workers' compensation benefits through compensating wage reductions for non-union workers. Despite the wage offsets, many non-union workers still benefited from the new law because they were better insured against accident risk. They typically received payments for nearly all accidents and the average payouts overall tended to be higher than negligence liability. The insurance companies also benefited from selling a great deal more workers' compensation insurance than they had sold previously of the combined package of employers' liability insurance and worker's accident insurance, although they benefited less when the state created a competitive insurer or lost out in the seven states that created a monopoly state insurer. The issue of state-provided insurance raised the hackles of insurers and those fearful of government replacement of general business. Fishback and Kantor (2000) found state insurance schemes were adopted in the states where unions and progressive reformers had more strength.
8. See Couch and Shugart (1998), Wallis (1984, 1987, 1998, 2001), Wright (1974), Reading (1973), Anderson and Tollison (1991), Fleck (1994, 1999a, b, c, 2001a,b 2008), Stromberg (2004), Arrington (1970), Reading (1973), Mason (2003). For discussions of corruption, see Fishback *et al.* (2006).
9. See Fleck (1999a, b) shows that greater voter turnout, swing voting and loyal voters all mattered to the distribution of FERA spending and WPA work relief jobs (Fishback *et al.*, 2003).
10. Programs are experience-rated if they charge higher premiums to firms in which accident rates are higher.

References

Abrams, B.A. and Schmitz, M.D. (1984) The crowding-out effect of governmental transfers on private charitable contributions: cross-section evidence. *National Tax Journal* 37(4): 563–568.

Allen, S. (2004) The economics and politics of workers' compensation, 1930–2000. PhD dissertation, University of Arizona.

Allen, S. (2009) State variation in workers' compensation insurance: the political economy of benefits, 1930–2000. Working Paper, Virginia Military Institute.

Anderson, G. and Tollison, R. (1991) Congressional influence and patterns of New Deal spending, 1933–1939. *Journal of Law and Economics* 34: 161–175.

Arrington, L. (1970) Western agriculture and the New Deal. *Agricultural History* 44: 337–353.

Baicker, K., Goldin, C. and Katz, L. (1998) A distinctive system: origins and impact of U.S. unemployment compensation. In M. Bordo, C. Goldin and E.N. White (eds), *Defining Moment: The Great Depression and the American Economy in the Twentieth Century*. Chicago, IL: University of Chicago Press.

Baird, E. (1942) *Public and Private Aid in 116 Urban Areas: 1929–1938 With Supplement for 1939 and 1940*. Federal Security Agency, Bureau of Public Assistance, Public Assistance Report No. 3. Washington, DC: Government Printing Office.

Balan-Cohen, A. (2008) The effect on elderly mortality: evidence from the old age assistance programs in the United States. Unpublished Working Paper, Tufts University.

Balkan, S. (1998) Social insurance programs and compensating wage differentials in the United States. PhD Dissertation, University of Arizona.

Bowlbis, J. (forthcoming) The decline in infant death rates, 1878–1913: the role of early sickness insurance programs. *Journal of Economic History*.

Buffum, D. (1992) Workmen's compensation: passage and impact. PhD dissertation, University of Pennsylvania, PA.

Chelius, J.R. (1977) *Workplace Safety and Health: The Role of Workers' Compensation*. Washington, DC: American Enterprise Institute.

Costa, D.L. (1998) *The Evolution of Retirement: An American Economic History, 1880–1990*. Chicago, IL: University of Chicago Press.

Costa, D.L. (1999) A house of her own: old age assistance and the living arrangements of older nonmarried women. *Journal of Public Economics* 72: 39–59.

Couch, J. and Shugart, W. (1998) *The Political Economy of the New Deal*. New York: Edward Elgar.

Darby, M.R. (1976) Three and a half million U.S. employees have been mislaid: or, an explanation of unemployment, 1934–1941. *Journal of Political Economy* 84: 1–16.

Fishback, P. (1987) Liability rules and accident prevention in the workplace: empirical evidence from the early twentieth century. *Journal of Legal Studies* 16: 305–328.

Fishback, P. (2009) Social expenditures in the United States and the Nordic countries: 1900–2003. Paper presented at the International Economic History Association Congress in Utrecht, The Netherlands, August.

Fishback, P. and Kantor, S. (1995) Did workers pay for the passage of workers' compensation laws? *Quarterly Journal of Economics* 110: 713–742.

Fishback, P. and Kantor, S. (1998) The adoption of workers' compensation in the United States, 1900–1930. *Journal of Law and Economics* 41: 305–341.

Fishback, P. and Kantor, S. (2000) *Prelude to the Welfare State: The Origins of Workers' Compensation*. Chicago, IL: University of Chicago Press.

Fishback, P. and Thomasson, M. (2006) Social welfare: 1929 to the present. In S. Carter, S.S. Gartner, M. Haines, A. Olmstead, R. Sutch and G. Wright (eds), *Historical Statistics of the United States: Millennial Edition*, Vol. 2. New York: Cambridge University Press.

Fishback, P., Kantor, S. and Wallis, J. (2003) Can the New Deal's three R's be rehabilitated? A program-by-program, county-by-county analysis. *Explorations in Economic History* (October): 278–307.

Fishback, P., Horrace, W. and Kantor, S. (2005) The impact of New Deal expenditures on local economic activity: an examination of retail sales, 1929–1939. *Journal of Economic History* 65: 36–71.

Fishback, P., Horrace, W. and Kantor, S. (2006) Do federal programs affect internal migration? The impact of New Deal expenditures on mobility during the Great Depression. *Explorations in Economic History*.

Fishback, P., Haines, M. and Kantor, S. (2007) Births, deaths, and New Deal relief during the Great Depression. *Review of Economics and Statistics* 89 (February): 1–14.

Fleck, R. (1994) Essays on the political economy of the New Deal. PhD dissertation, Stanford University, Stanford, CA.

Fleck, R. (1999a) Electoral incentives, public policy, and the New Deal realignment. *Southern Economic Journal* 63(January): 377–404.

Fleck, R. (1999b) The marginal effect of New Deal relief work on county-level unemployment statistics. *Journal of Economic History* 59(September): 659–687.

Fleck, R. (1999c) The value of the vote: a model and test of the effects of turnout on distributive policy. *Economic Inquiry* 37(October): 609–623.

Fleck, R. (2001a) Inter-party competition, intra-party competition, and distributive policy: a model and test using New Deal data. *Public Choice* 108(July): 77–100.

Fleck, R. (2001b) Population, land, economic conditions, and the allocation of New Deal spending. *Explorations in Economic History* 38(April): 296–304.

Fleck, R. (2002) Democratic opposition to the Fair Labor Standards Act of 1938. *Journal of Economic History* 62(March): 25–54.

Fleck, R. (2008) Voter influence and big policy change: the positive political economy of the New Deal. *Journal of Political Economy* 116: 1–37.

Friedberg, L. (1999) The effect of old age assistance on retirement. *Journal of Public Economics* 71: 213–232.

Grey, M. (1989) Poverty, politics, and health: the Farm Security Administration Medical Care Program, 1935–1945. *Journal of the History of Medicine and Allied Sciences* 44: 320–350.

Gruber, J. and Hungerman, D. (2007) Faith-based charity and crowd-out during the Great Depression. *Journal of Public Economics* 91: 1043–1069.

Hannon, J.U. (1984a) Poverty and the antebellum Northeast: the view from New York State's poor relief rolls. *Journal of Economic History* 44: 1007–1032.

Hannon, J. (1984b) The generosity of antebellum poor relief. *Journal of Economic History* 44(3): 810–821.

Hannon, J. (1985) Poor relief policy in antebellum New York State: the rise and decline of the poorhouse. *Explorations in Economic History* 22(3): 233–256.

Howard, D. (1943) *The WPA and Federal Relief Policy*. New York: Russell Sage Foundation.

Johnson, R., Fishback, P. and Kantor, S. (forthcoming) Striking at the roots of crime: the impact of social welfare spending on crime during the great depression. *Journal of Law and Economics*.

Kiesling, L. and Margo, R. (1997) Explaining the rise in antebellum pauperism: 1850–1860. *Quarterly Review of Economics and Finance* 37: 405–418.

Lebergott, S. (1976) *The American Economy: Income, Wealth, and Want*. Princeton, NJ: Princeton University Press.

Lindert, P. (2004) *Growing Public: Social Spending and Economic Growth Since the Eighteenth Century*. Cambridge: Cambridge University Press.

Mason, J. (2003) Fundamentals, panics and bank distress during the Depression. *American Economic Review* 95: 1615–1647.

Massachusetts Department of Public Welfare (1920–1930) *Annual Report of the Department of Public Welfare*. Boston: Wright & Potter Printing Co.

Matthews, K. and Benjamin, D. (1992) *U.S. and U.K. Unemployment Between the Wars: A Doleful Story*. London: Institute of Economic Affairs.

Moehling, C. (2006) Mothers' pension legislation and the cross-state variation in welfare generosity. Unpublished Working Paper, Yale University, August.

Moehling, C. (2007) The American welfare system and family structure: an historical perspective. *Journal of Human Resources* 42: 117–155.

Moss, D. (1996) *Socializing Security: Progressive-era Economists and the Origins of American Social Policy*. Cambridge, MA: Harvard University Press.

Murray, J. (2007) *Origins of American Health Insurance: A History of Industrial Sickness Funds*. New Haven, CT: Yale University Press.

Neumann, T., Fishback, P. and Kantor, S. (2010) The dynamics of relief spending and the private urban labor market during the New Deal. *Journal of Economic History* 70 (March): 195–220.

Officer, L.H. and Williamson, S.H. (2009) Purchasing power of money in the United States from 1774 to 2008. *MeasuringWorth*. URL: http://www.measuringworth.com/ppowerus/.

Parsons, D.O. (1991) Male retirement behavior in the United States, 1930–1950. *Journal of Economic History* 51: 657–674.

Raphael, S. and Winter-Ebmer, R. (2001) Identifying the effect of unemployment on crime. *Journal of Law and Economics* 64(April): 259–283.

Reading, D.C. (1973) New Deal activity and the States, 1933 to 1939. *Journal of Economic History* 33(December): 792–810.

Skocpol, T. (1992) *Protecting Soldiers and Mothers: The Political Origins of Social Policy in the United States*. Cambridge, MA: Belknap Press of Harvard University Press.

Social Security Administration. *Social Security Bulletin: Annual Statistical Supplement* (SSBASS), various years.

Stoian, A. and Fishback, P. (2010) Welfare spending and mortality rates for the elderly before the Social Security era. *Explorations in Economic History* 47: 1–27.

Stromberg, D. (2004) Radio's impact on public spending. *Quarterly Journal of Economics* 119 (February): 189–221.

Thomasson, M. (2002) From sickness to health: the twentieth century development of U.S. health insurance. *Explorations in Economic History* 39: 233–253.

Thompson, L. (1919) Laws relating to 'mothers' pensions' in the United States, Canada, Denmark, and New Zealand. *U. S. Department of Labor, Childrens' Bureau Publication No. 63, Legal Series No. 4*. Washington, DC: Government Printing Office.

US Bureau of the Census (1923) *Birth, Stillbirth, and Infant Mortality Statistics, 1921: Seventh Annual Report*. Washington, DC: Government Printing Office.

US Bureau of the Census (1925a) *Biennial Census of Manufactures, 1923*. Washington, DC: Government Printing Office.

US Bureau of the Census (1925b) *Financial Statistics of Cities Having a Population over 30,000, 1923*. Washington, DC: Government Printing Office.

US Bureau of the Census (1925c) *Financial Statistics of States, 1922*. Washington, DC: Government Printing Office.

US Bureau of the Census (1931a) *Financial Statistics of Cities Having a Population over 30,000, 1929*. Washington, DC: Government Printing Office.

US Bureau of the Census (1931b) *Financial Statistics of States, 1929*. Washington, DC: Government Printing Office.

US Bureau of the Census (1932a) *Financial Statistics of Cities Having a Population over 30,000, 1929*. Washington, DC: Government Printing Office.

US Bureau of the Census (1932b) *Financial Statistics of States, 1930*. Washington, DC: Government Printing Office.

US Bureau of the Census (1933a) *Fifteenth Census of the United States, Manufactures: 1929*, Vol. III. Washington, DC: Government Printing Office.

US Bureau of the Census (1934) *Biennial Census of Manufactures, 1931*. Washington, DC: Government Printing Office.

US Bureau of the Census (1943) *Sixteenth Census of the United States, Manufactures: 1939*, Vol. III. Washington, DC: Government Printing Office.

US Bureau of the Census (2007) Income, poverty, and health insurance coverage in the United States: 2006. *Current Population Reports, P60–233*. Washington, DC: Government Printing Office.

US Children's Bureau (1930) *Eighteenth Annual Report of the Children's Bureau.* Washington, DC: Government Printing Office.

US Committee on Economic Security (1937) *Social Security in America; the Factual Background of the Social Security Act as Summarized from Staff Reports to the Committee on Economic Security*. Washington, DC: Government Printing Office.

Wallis, J.J. (1984) The birth of the old federalism: financing the New Deal, 1932–1940. *Journal of Economic History* 44(March): 139–159.

Wallis, J.J. (1987) Employment, politics, and economic recovery during the Great Depression. *Review of Economics and Statistics* 69(August): 516–520.

Wallis, J.J. (1998) The political economy of New Deal spending revisited, again: with and without Nevada. *Explorations in Economic History* 35(April): 140–170.

Wallis, J.J. (2001) The political economy of New Deal spending, yet again: a reply to Fleck. *Explorations in Economic History* 38(April): 305–314.

Wallis, J.J. and Benjamin, D.K. (1981) Public relief and private employment in the Great Depression. *Journal of Economic History* 41(March): 97–102.

Wallis, J.J. and Oates, W. (1998) The impact of the New Deal on American federalism. In M. Bordo, C. Goldin and E. White (eds), *The Defining Moment: The Great Depression and the American Economy in the 20th Century* (pp. 155–180). Chicago, IL: University of Chicago Press.

Wallis, J.J., Fishback, P. and Kantor, S. (2006) Politics, relief, and reform: Roosevelt's efforts to control corruption and political manipulation during the New Deal. In C. Goldin and E. Glaeser (eds), *Corruption and Reform: Lessons from America's Economic History* (pp. 343–372). Chicago, IL: University of Chicago Press.

Winegarden, C.R. and Murray, J.E. (1998) The contributions of early health-insurance programs to mortality declines in pre-World War I Europe: evidence from fixed-effects models. *Explorations in Economic History* 35(4): 431–446.

Wright, G. (1974) The political economy of new deal spending: an econometric analysis. *Review of Economics and Statistics* 56(February): 30–38.

Ziliak, S. (1996) The end of welfare and the contradiction of compassion. *Independent Review* 1: 55–73.

Ziliak, S. (2002) Some tendencies of social welfare and the problem of interpretation. *Cato Journal* 21(Winter): 499–513.

Ziliak, S. and Hannon, J. (2006) Public assistance: colonial times to the 1920s. In S. Carter, S.S. Gartner, M. Haines, A. Olmstead, R. Sutch and G. Wright (eds), *Historical Statistics of the United States: Millennial Edition*, Vol. 2 (pp. 2-693–2-702 and 2-720–2-733). New York: Cambridge University Press.

6

THE CLIOMETRICS OF INTERNATIONAL MIGRATION: A SURVEY

Timothy J. Hatton

1. Introduction

This survey provides an overview of the quantitative historical literature on international migration that has developed over the last 30 years or so. I focus on those contributions that are classified as 'cliometric' in the sense that they use explicit theoretical models and/or use econometric methods, or are to some degree quantitative. This historical literature has flourished side by side with a burgeoning literature on contemporary migration issues. As I will show, the historical literature has borrowed from, and has often been stimulated by, the work of economists concerned with current policy issues. But the traffic is not all one way.

I concentrate on six key themes that that have been the subject of both historical and contemporary analysis. The first is to account for the trends and fluctuations in established migration streams. This was the focus of much of the early quantitative literature that followed from debates over the links between migration and business cycles, but which has not featured quite so prominently in the analysis of economists. The key issues there are whether push or pull forces dominate in migration and what other variables matter. The second theme asks who migrated and why. Why does the propensity to migrate differ across countries, regions, towns and villages and how does it vary between individuals? This literature seeks not only to understand what motivates migrants but also the forces that initiate migration streams, and what mechanisms cause them to persist.

Although the first two themes concentrate on the causes of migration, the next two focus on the results of migration, particularly in the receiving countries. The third theme is immigrant assimilation. This has been one of the most fiercely debated issues among economists and it is the one where economic historians have borrowed most from the contemporary literature. The fourth theme is the effects of migration on the economy at large and in particular on the wages and living standards of those in the receiving country with whom migrants compete. Did mass migration foster wage convergence between sending and receiving countries? And how did it affect income distributions and skill premia? These too are highly

Economics and History, First Edition. David Greasley and Les Oxley

contentious issues in the literature on recent migrations and no less so in the historical context.

The last two themes are areas where the cliometric literature is still relatively thin but which have attracted growing interest in recent years. The fifth theme is the political economy of immigration policy. This literature seeks to understand the forces that led to the adoption increasingly restrictive immigration policies in the half century after 1890. Can this be interpreted as a backlash to growing immigration pressures? And if so, what political-economy mechanisms were at work? The final theme is the study of international migration outside the traditional focus of European migration to the New World. As has often been noted, migration from and within Asia was even larger than emigration from Europe. Although there is a rich historical literature that documents and discusses Asian migration, until recently, it has not featured widely in cliometric research.

As with any survey article, much has to be omitted. I focus chiefly on migration from Europe to the New World, from the mid-19th century to the middle of the 20th century, which is where the bulk of the cliometric literature has concentrated. As a result I ignore the lively, but somewhat independent literature on the slave trade and I omit the significant literature on migration under indentured servitude before the mid-19th century. I concentrate largely on intercontinental migration, leaving aside the literature on rural–urban, inter-regional and cross-border migration, a literature so rich and extensive as to deserve separate treatment.

2. Push and Pull

The earliest cliometric analyses focused on whether fluctuations in international migration streams were driven chiefly by 'push' factors operating at home or 'pull' effects from abroad. It originated in the debate between Jerome (1926) who argued that the timing of US immigration before 1914 was dominated by the American business cycle and Thomas (1941) who, in the context of Swedish migration, stressed the effect of home country factors. The literature that followed was facilitated by the monumental work of Ferenczi and Willcox (1929), which provided a rich time series database on emigration from Europe and immigration to the New World from the middle of the 19th century to the 1920s. The literature that subsequently developed in the 1960s and 1970s was critically reviewed as part of an excellent series of articles by Gould (1979).

The typical study in this genre specified a regression for the aggregate migration flow (or rate) from a source country to a destination country as a function of business cycle indicators (such as industrial output gaps or unemployment rates) at home and abroad and some measure of wage rates or incomes at home and abroad. These models are often estimated with lags to capture adjustment dynamics and sometimes also include a measure of the stock of previous migrants. In his critique of the earlier literature Gould pointed out that, where both home and foreign business cycle indicators are included, the latter typically dominate in terms of size and significance of the coefficients. He also noted that indicators of wage or incomes often fail to achieve significance in the presence of business cycle indicators and typically fail to support the view that the incentive to migrate is positively related to incomes abroad and negatively to incomes at home. He concluded that 'By and large, reaction to this literature is one of some disappointment, for not only has it failed to generate important new insights . . . it has had only limited success in confirming or denying old interpretations' (Gould, 1979, p. 668).

An important shortcoming in the studies reviewed by Gould is that they lack a coherent economic model of the emigration decision, which makes the results difficult to interpret. It is hard to believe that the decision to emigrate depends only cyclical conditions at the destination or, for that matter, exclusively on conditions at home (except perhaps in the case of war or famine). Similarly, emigration decisions must have been based on some comparison, however approximate, between wage rates or expected incomes at home and abroad, especially in the long run. Accordingly, Hatton (1995) developed a model of the migration decision using a simple microeconomic framework in which potential migrants base their decision on the comparison of future expected incomes at home and abroad. Following Todaro (1969) expected income at a given location depends on the probability of employment and the wage rate. Because migrants are risk averse and because greater uncertainty attaches to the employment probabilities than to the wage rates, the former takes a larger 'weight' in the migration function. Dynamics are accounted for by an adaptive expectations process and the model also includes the migrant stock to represent the so-called friends and relatives effect.[1]

This model provides a benchmark for evaluating the relationship among the coefficients attached to different variables in an econometric model of emigration. Estimates on annual time series for gross emigration from the UK between 1870 and 1913 broadly support these priors. Specifically they show that wage rates *and* employment rates, both at home *and* abroad all matter, with the coefficients on the employment rates exceeding those on wage rates. Although short run fluctuations are largely driven by employment or activity rates (which typically are not trended), long run trends are determined by relative wage rates and the trend in the migrant stock, which is itself determined by previous emigration. Applying the same model to emigration from Ireland, Hatton and Williamson (1998, p. 83) found that the 17% fall in the (foreign to home) wage ratio between 1876–1880 and 1909–1913 accounted for a decline of 4 per 1000 in the emigration rate. Over the same period the fall in the ratio of the migrant stock to home population contributed a similar amount to the fall in the emigration rate.

When it has been included in time series models, the migrant stock almost always proves to be very powerful. This is often interpreted as evidence of migrant networks generating strong persistence through chain migration. But as the migrant stock is essentially the cumulative flow it is sometimes difficult to distinguish network effects from the equation dynamics. In particular, if it is more recent immigrants that matter, then lags of the dependent variable may be picking up these effects. One important mechanism is the flow of remittances, a significant part of which took the form of pre-paid tickets and other assistance to new migrants.

Magee and Thompson (2006a) provide new estimates of the flow of remittances to the UK from 1875 to 1913, which amounted to 3.4% of the value of exports in the latter year. Magee and Thompson (2006b) study the determinants of the flow of money orders, which they find to depend on the migrant stock and income in the migrant-receiving country. This would be consistent with the idea that the effect of these variables on the flow of new migrants works partly through remittances.

A number of studies have identified other variables that determine trends and variations in time series migration rates. One important variable is the age structure of the population. Because the potential gains from migration are greater at younger ages demographic structure should matter independently of other variables in the model.[2] Quigley (1972) found that demographic forces mattered for emigration from Sweden as did Larsen (1982) for Denmark. Using the rate of natural increase 25 years earlier as a proxy for the size of the birth cohort, Hatton and Williamson (1998, p. 72) find similar results for three Scandinavian countries. They estimate that between 1895 and 1905 lagged natural increase raised the emigration rate by 1 per 1000 in Sweden, by 1.3 per 1000 in Norway and by 0.3 per 1000 in Denmark. However, these effects were weaker for countries such as Spain and Italy (Hatton and Williamson, 1998, p. 113; Sánchez-Alonso, 2000b, p. 747). Interestingly, Greenwood (2007) finds that a higher *current* birth rate tends to reduce emigration of those at parenting age, probably reflecting the higher cost of family emigration. Overall, these studies offer some support for the hypothesis that demographic structure was an important determinant of emigration.

Any sensible economic model of migration must take account of the costs as well as the benefits. The costs of migration have been absent from most studies, because of the lack of suitable time series data. Yet there is reason to think they are important, and a full accounting of the costs would include not only the costs of an ocean passage, but also the overland costs at each end of the journey, and the living costs (or forgone income) while in transit. The cost of passage fell after 1850 with the transition from sail to steam, a decline that occurred later on the longer routes.[3] And effective prices fell rather more steeply because of shorter passage times and better quality on-board accommodation (Keeling, 1999a; Sánchez-Alonso, 2007), not to mention overland travel. On the routes to North America there were sharp swings in passage prices associated with the effectiveness of shipping cartels (Keeling, 1999b). Deltas *et al.* (2008) estimate the effects of cartels on quarterly data for the volume of migration on different shipping routes to the USA and Canada between 1899 and 1911. Periods when cartels were in operation were associated with lower emigration, implying a price elasticity of about −0.7.

Policy related variables also influenced the costs of migration, either directly or indirectly. Some receiving countries such as Australia and Brazil directly encouraged immigration by providing assisted passages to selected groups of migrants. The programme of assisted passages in Australia substantially reduced the costs for UK migrants in 1911–1913, and Pope (1981) found that this accounted for much of the surge in immigration in those years. For emigrants from Spain, the depreciation of the Peseta after 1892 sharply increased the costs of migration, which were denominated in gold currencies. Sánchez-Alonso (2000a) finds that the exchange rate had a negative effect on emigration from Spain, such that emigration would have been as much as 40% higher between 1892 and 1905 in the absence of the depreciation. By contrast, tariff protection increased emigration by more than 20%. On a more speculative level, Khoudor Castéras (2008) argues that, for Germany, the rise of social insurance and the fall in working hours contributed to the decline in the emigration rate from the 1880s.

Overall the push–pull model of international migration has worked pretty well on a variety of time series for different migration streams.[4] But one issue that remains is why migration flows were so volatile. Emigration rates often increased or fell by a quarter or even a half in a year or two, only to recover again a few years later. In the time series models much of the volatility is explained by the cyclical employment variables and the equation dynamics. But this is itself a puzzle. Given that migration decisions were based on comparing future expected lifetime earning profiles, one might expect that short run changes, quickly reversed, would have little effect. One reason for the surprising short run volatility is the option value of waiting. Although it might be worth emigrating today even though unemployment was high in the destination, it would be better still to wait a year or two if conditions were expected to improve. Although it is tempting to think that emigrants timed their moves in order to maximize the life cycle benefits overall, we have little direct evidence for this.[5]

3. Source Countries, Regions and Localities

A greater challenge is to explain the differences in the levels and the trends in emigration rates across countries. There was certainly a wide variety of emigration rates from European countries in the late 19th century. The highest overall was Ireland where the annual gross emigration rate averaged 12 per 1000 of the population between 1850 and 1913. Countries such as Sweden and Norway had rates approaching 5 per 1000 between 1870 and 1913; the rates for Germany and Belgium were under 2 per 1000, whereas that for France was less than 1 per 1000. Furthermore the long run trends in emigration differed widely: the Irish emigration rate declined from the 1860s and the German and Norwegian rates declined from the 1880s. But at almost the same time the Italian and Spanish emigration rates began a steep ascent which was halted only by the outbreak of War, and a similar pattern is observed for a number of Eastern European countries.

One important stylized fact is that during the onset of modern economic growth in Europe, national emigration rates often rose, steeply at first from very low levels, rising more gently to a peak, and then gradually falling. This evolution, often seen as a multistage process, has sometimes been called the 'mobility transition' (Zelinsky, 1971). Though not universal, such patterns have been identified in studies of aggregate emigration rates from a number of countries (Akerman, 1976, p. 25; Hatton and Williamson, 1998, p. 47). In his pioneering study of European emigration rates, Easterlin (1961) stressed the effects of population growth spilling over into emigration. On the other hand Tomaske (1971) found little effect for source country per capita income on cross-country emigration rates. Thus income or real wage differences alone can explain little of the cross-country variation in emigration rates – their effects can only be observed in the presence of other variables. But the early studies of emigration across countries and over time were constrained by lack of suitable data. The development of internationally comparable data such as Williamson's (1995) database on real wages in Europe and the New World gave a fillip to further research.

Hatton and Williamson (1998) studied decade-average emigration rates from 12 European countries between 1860 and 1913 using a limited set of explanatory variables. In this analysis the real wage ratio (source to destination) has the expected negative effect. A 10% increase in the wage ratio reduced emigration in the long run by 1.27 per 1000 per annum – a substantial effect that is broadly consistent with the results from annual time series. But the share of the labour force in agriculture had only a weak negative effect – suggesting that, on balance, agricultural populations were less mobile than urban/industrial populations.[6] The effect of lagged natural increase strongly supports Easterlin's view that the demographic transition drove emigration. This estimate suggests that half of excess births spilled over into emigration – a very large effect indeed and one deserving further investigation.

It has often been observed that emigration gathered momentum first in the richer countries of Europe and, as it spread to the countries of Southern and Eastern Europe, it often coincided with a quickening in the pace of development. It has been argued that those with the greatest incentive to migrate were initially too poor to afford the costs of long-distance migration but economic development served to ease this 'poverty trap'. Using annual time series, Faini and Venturini (1994) find for Italy, and Sánchez-Alonso (2000b) finds for Spain, that the rise in emigration after 1880 was positively influenced by per capita income at home. For Italy, the gradual increase in the migrant stock also helped to ease the poverty trap as previous migrants helped to finance the passage of subsequent cohorts of migrants (Moretti, 1999). The evidence suggests that, the higher was the migrant stock, the less binding was the poverty trap (Hatton and Williamson, 2005, p. 65). In Ireland, the large migrant stock inherited from the Famine era meant that the poverty trap was much less binding from mid-century than it was for countries with fewer past emigrants. In contrast to Italy, the Irish emigration rate fell as conditions at home improved because the declining incentive to emigrate dominated the growing capacity to emigrate.

The wide diversity of regional emigration rates within any given country and their apparent convergence over time presents a similar puzzle. Gould (1980b) argued that this was due to a process of information diffusion, often originating from ports or trade routes, but as information is not directly measurable, this is rather hard to test formally. Baines (1994, p. 532) has argued that convergence was not universal among regional emigration rates in different European countries. Clearly, in some countries where emigration was relatively well established, the information diffusion hypothesis would have less force. Thus, across the 32 Irish counties, the coefficient of variation in emigration rates rose from 0.31 in 1881 to 0.71 in 1901, falling back to 0.41 in 1911. By contrast in Italy and Spain there was strong convergence. Although greater literacy might have been expected to foster the flow of information, evidence for Italian provinces and for Irish counties indicates that emigration rates were not positively associated with literacy (Hatton and Williamson, 1998, chapters 5 and 6). But, looking across Spanish provinces in 1888 and 1911, Sánchez-Alonso (2000b) finds that the *growth* in literacy had positive effects on the emigration rate.

Studies of emigration across regions find that the degree of urbanization has mixed effects (e.g. Lowell, 1987, pp. 48–52, 217–218). Although urban populations were typically more mobile, they also enjoyed higher incomes than did rural dwellers. Key factors in rural areas include local demographic growth, which is almost always positive, and the patterns of landholding, which seems to have had different effects in different countries. For Norway and Sweden, Lowell (1987, pp. 212–216, 221) found that emigration was negatively related to local wage rates, but also positively related to the number of landless labourers and the share of land occupied by large estates. For Ireland, Hatton and Williamson (1998, chapter 5) found that the prevalence of smallholdings had a negative effect on emigration whereas measures of poverty had positive effects. Thus attachment to small parcels of land kept the Irish at home, but in Italy emigration increased with the incidence of owner occupation and sharecropping. The differing effects of variables reflecting small holding are puzzling. A partial explanation might be that in countries like Italy, with high rates of return migration, emigration was often undertaken with the objective of acquiring land on returning home.

It is difficult to advance much further without getting down to the local level, and in series of important papers Wegge (1998, 1999, 2002) studied emigration from the Hesse-Cassel region of Germany between 1832 and 1857. Although those with resources such as land, which could be sold or mortgaged, would not face liquidity constraints they also had less incentive to move; by contrast unskilled labourers were more often constrained. As a result the highest emigration rates were among artisans – those with transferrable skills and enough resources to emigrate (Wegge, 2002).[7] Consistent with this, village level data indicates that higher wages and greater scarcity of land led to higher emigration. It also provides strong evidence that network effects were powerful; current emigration rates were strongly related to past emigration from the same village and from the surrounding county. In addition, those emigrants that could be identified as networked carried less cash with them (Wegge, 1998). This further supports the idea that network effects helped to unlock the poverty trap. Another interesting finding is that emigration was higher from villages where the custom was for one son to inherit rather than for the previous generation's assets (particularly land) to be evenly divided among the male siblings (Wegge, 1999).

There are three interrelated issues that remain under-explored in cliometric work on the causes of international migration. One is the role of politics and oppression. Some migrants left Europe for reasons of religious or political persecution – a parallel with today's asylum seekers. Perhaps the most prominent example is the persecution of Jews that is often associated with the steep rise in emigration from the Russian empire after 1880. In her study of annual time series Boustan (2007) finds that the key events of 1891, 1903 and 1905–1906 had substantial effects on emigration in the short run but that most of the upward trend in emigration was due to the standard economic variables.[8] The political climate in host countries (such as the ebb and flow of nativist sentiment in the USA) may also, at times, have had some influence (Cohn, 2000). Bertocchi and Strozzi (2008) examine the effects of host country political variables across 14 countries in Europe and the New World. They find that immigration was positively related to political participation (democracy and suffrage) and also to rights for immigrants (access to citizenship, land and education). Nevertheless the dominant forces were the usual economic and demographic variables.

A second issue is the choice of destination. Migrants from a given country went to a relatively narrow range of destinations. Although the USA was the main destination for most migrants from Europe, large numbers of British and Irish went to the British dominions and a large share of Southern Europeans went to South American countries. It is often suggested that colonial ties, common language and cultural affinity meant that different destinations were poor substitutes (Taylor, 1994), a feature that was reinforced by the friends and relatives effect. Yet there were potential substitutes among the English speaking countries and within South America. As Green *et al.* (2002) show, British migrants moved between Canada and the USA, to where their skills were best rewarded. Interestingly migrants from northern Italy (more often skilled and urban) went to South America, those from the Italian South (more often unskilled and rural) went increasingly to the USA. This apparent paradox may be explained by the fact that unskilled labour commanded higher wages in the USA (and language was less of an impediment for unskilled employment), whereas the more skilled northern Italians moved easily into business and trade in Argentina (see Baily, 1983; Klein, 1983).

However, attempts to identify substitution between destinations in migration equations have not been very successful. Analysing the destinations of emigrants across 69 Italian provinces, Hatton and Williamson (1998, p. 119) found that the choice between Latin America and the USA was driven mainly by the share and type of agricultural employment and by the destination choice of past emigrants. In a recent paper, Balderas and Greenwood (2010) analyse times series for emigration from 12 source countries to three destinations: Argentina, Brazil and the USA. Like other studies they find relative wages and the migrant stock mattered, with mixed results for economic activity. Using instrumental variables they examine the effect of migration to one destination on migration to other destinations in order to measure the substitution effect. But they find little evidence of substitution between Argentina and Brazil or between either of these and the USA.

A third issue is return migration. As Gould (1980a, p. 50) remarked: 'If the immigrants came, as so many models assert, because of higher wages and better job opportunities in the USA than in Europe, why did so many go back? As obvious a question as this has been totally ignored by the majority of econometric studies on Pre world War One migration.' Gould's question is still as apposite now as it was 30 years ago. Some migrants moved with the seasons;[9] others timed their stay according to essentially the same variables that drove outward migration. Over time, return migration increased as transport costs fell and as the share of Southern and Eastern Europeans rose. A key indicator of the intention to return is the rising share of males in the outward flow (Gould, 1980a, p. 60; Hatton and Williamson, 2005, p. 80). Although there has been some analysis of the impact of return migrants (e.g. Cinel, 1991), the data are somewhat limited and the question of why return migration varied so much across different source countries (and across localities) remains under-researched.

4. Migrants in the Labour Market

There has been a vigorous debate in the economics literature about how well or badly immigrants assimilate after arrival in the host country, and the main focus has been on earnings. On arrival, immigrants have earnings significantly lower than the native-born but the gap narrows as they acquire host country skills and experience. In his pioneering study of US immigrants in 1970 Chiswick (1978) found that male immigrant earnings converged on those of the native-born, and even overtook them after 10–15 years of US experience. But others such as Borjas (1985, 1994) argued that cross-sectional estimates overestimate the true assimilation effect if the 'quality' of cohorts declined over time.

This is illustrated in Figure 1. The solid lines represent the 'true' age–earning profiles for different cohorts of immigrants and the native-born. Here the most recent arrivals, cohort 3, have the lowest earnings profile and the earliest arrivals, cohort 1, have the highest profile. At a given point in time, the most recent cohort is observed at age A3 whereas the oldest cohort is observed around age A1. The dotted line shows what the estimated age earning profile for immigrants might look like when estimated from a single cross-section. The cross-sectional estimate generates a (somewhat misleading) steeper upward slope as the earlier cohorts have both higher labour market quality and longer experience in the host country. Because a cross-section cannot distinguish between host country experience effects and cohort effects, it tends to overestimate the assimilation effect for any given cohort. Analysing wage data from different US censuses Borjas (1992) found that cohort quality declined by about 20% between those who arrived in 1955–1960 those who arrived in 1975–1980.

There is a striking parallel between the debates over US immigrant assimilation in the 30 years after 1970 and in the 30 years after 1880. Some late 19th century observers argued that the waves of 'new immigrants' arriving from Southern and Eastern Europe assimilated less well and had lower labour market quality than those who came earlier from Northwestern Europe. This view was expressed by the US Immigration Commission (the Dillingham Commission), which reported in 1911 after deliberating this issue for four years. In the recommendations of the (majority) report it was argued that 'while the American people, as in the past, welcome the oppressed of other lands, care should be taken that immigration be such, both in quality and quantity as not to make too difficult the process of assimilation'

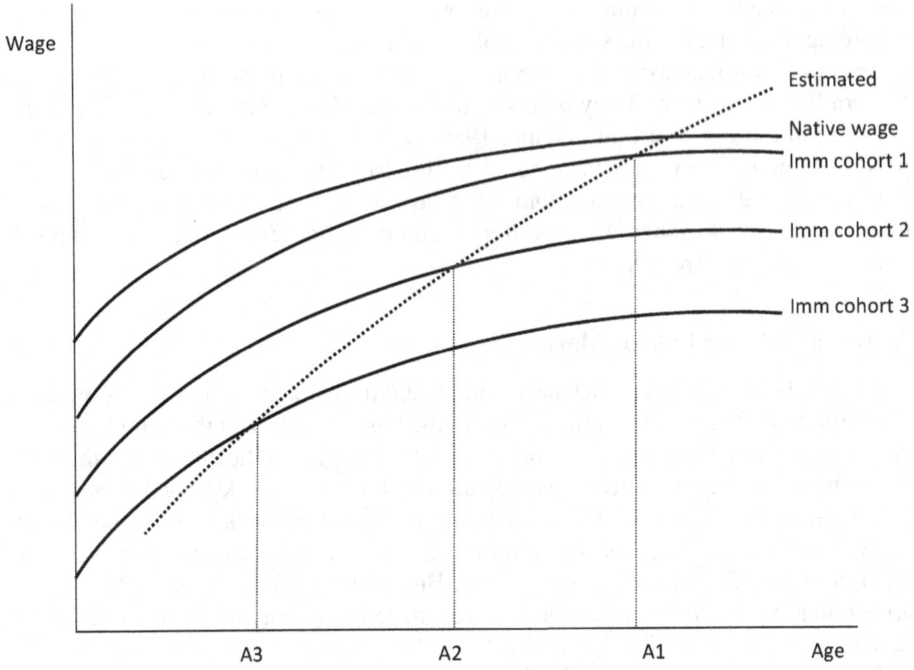

Figure 1. Immigrant and Native Age–Earning Profiles.

(Vol. 1, p. 45). Similarly in a widely circulated book, Jenks and Lauck argued of the new immigrants that 'their general as well as their industrial progress and assimilation are retarded by segregation in colonies and communities where they have very little contact with American life and small opportunity to acquire the English language' (1926, p. 78).

In the light of Figure 1 one might expect that cross-sectional estimates of earnings function for natives and immigrants would give an (over) optimistic picture of immigrant assimilation. But several studies that exploit microdata collected by state labour bureaus, have come to the opposite conclusion. For workers in Michigan's copper mines and in agricultural implements and ironworking industries around 1890, Hannon (1982a, b) found that immigrant wage profiles were relatively flat, with at best very little convergence on the earnings of the native-born. Eichengreen and Gemery (1986) obtained similar results for workers in Iowa in 1884–1885 and concluded that assimilation was slow, especially for those who acquired their skills prior to emigration. And in his study of earnings profiles in Michigan and California, Hanes (1996) found that immigrant earnings growth was well below that of natives up to the age of about 40. However, these findings seem to be the result of using a quadratic age–earnings function. Using a more flexible functional form on the same data Hatton (1997) finds that immigrant earnings gradually converge on those of the native-born.[10]

Surveys from around 1890 contain relatively few new immigrants, making it difficult to measure their assimilation. Using grouped data on wages in 1909 reported by the Dillingham Commission, Blau (1980) found that male immigrants from Northwest Europe earned 12.2% less than natives on arrival but caught up after 11.4 years whereas those from Southern and Eastern Europe started with a 17.8% disadvantage but caught up after 16.6 years. Using the same data source, this more optimistic picture is confirmed by Chiswick (1992) and Hatton (2000). Allowing for individual source-country effects, the latter finds that immigrant wages converged on those of the native-born by about 1% per year over the 20 years since migration. After 20 years, those from Northwest Europe earned 4.7% more than the native-born whereas those from Southern and Eastern Europe earned 2.9% less. As a result of the change in the source-country composition, immigrant quality (based on earnings) declined by about 5% between 1873 and 1913 compared with around 25% between 1935–1940 and 1975–1980 (Hatton, 2000). Thus the shift in source composition before the First World War had much less effect on the labour market performance of immigrants than has been the case post the Second World War.

Evidence from the census produces a similar account for a wider range of occupations. Minns (2000) found that immigrant cohorts tracked across the US censuses of 1900 and 1910 experienced the same level of upgrading as in the cross-section. But particularly notable was the rate of movement up the occupational ladder from blue collar to white collar, especially among the new immigrants. This paints a rather more optimistic picture than do studies that concentrate only on blue collar occupations, and hence ignore a key part of upward mobility. But there are differences by nationality and by host country. Thus Green and MacKinnon (2001) find slower assimilation for British immigrants observed in the 1901 Canadian census than for Jews or non-whites. Clearly, occupational mobility was a key element in the immigrants' assimilation process, and nowhere more so than among Russian Jews in the USA (Chiswick, 1991). For Jews, upward movement into self-employment and small business was an important route and it seems to have operated more strongly for those who migrated to New York than for those who migrated to London (Godley, 2001). Evidence for Canada indicates that Jews were much more likely to become self-employed than non-Jewish immigrants (Minns and Rizov, 2005).

It is often argued that upward mobility is partly a result of positive self-selection. It is widely believed that, on average, immigrants were healthier, more energetic and enterprising and had more human capital than the populations from which they were drawn. Certainly they had more education than non-emigrants, particularly the Southern Europeans (Sánchez-Alonso, 2007, pp. 414–416).[11] But other characteristics such as ability are much harder to measure.[12] Mokyr and Ferrie (1994) suggest that immigrants supplied a disproportionate number of entrepreneurs and businessmen in the USA. One piece of circumstantial evidence comes from the labour market performance of second-generation immigrants. Their outcomes were better than for first-generation immigrants, and the evidence from wage surveys and from the census suggests that they often outperformed the native-born (Hatton, 1997; Minns, 2000). An interpretation of this is that second-generation immigrants inherited some of the characteristics of their positively selected parents but suffered less of the disadvantage faced by first-generation immigrants.

Ferrie (1999) examined upward mobility among antebellum immigrants by matching individual-level data recorded in ships passenger lists and in the censuses of 1850 and 1860. He found that there was some downward occupational mobility on arrival, but this was followed by steep upward mobility, particularly for the young and literate British and German immigrants. Ferrie (1999) also studied the links between the occupational and geographic mobility of immigrants. More than two thirds of immigrants arriving in 1840–1950 moved county in the subsequent decade and these moves were associated with both upward and downward occupational mobility. Relative to non-movers, labourers who moved location increased their wealth – the more so the further they moved. The high rates of mobility observed among immigrants raises the further question of what determined their initial location.

A number of studies have analysed the intended destination of immigrants on arrival in the USA at the turn of the 20th century (Dunlevy and Gemery, 1977; Dunlevy, 1980, 1983; Dunlevy and Saba, 1992). Regression analysis indicates that immigrants migrated towards states on the eastern seaboard (close to New York), towards those with relatively high incomes and towards those with high population densities. But the most important single influence is the location of previous immigrants from the same source country. The evidence indicates that geographic dispersion increased somewhat with onward moves (Dunlevy, 1980), but that immigrants avoided the US South (Dunlevy, 1983). A study of the intended destinations of Canadian immigrants in 1912 found, in addition, that they selected destinations and sectors that made best use of their skills (Green and Green, 1993). Although migrants often moved to opportunity, there were nevertheless distinct regional and local concentrations, typically in urban areas and gateway cities and often differing by ethnicity.

As immigrants chose specific locations, this raises the question of whether they crowded out or displaced the native-born population. Hatton and Williamson (1998, p. 168) found that foreign born in-migration to the Northeast States in 1880–1910 led to out-migration of the native-born. Furthermore the effect is large: for every 100 foreign born in-migrants to a state, native out-migration increased by 40. Thus the westward movement of the native-born was not just the pull of opportunity in the West but partly an immigrant-induced push from the East. When the immigration to the Northeast slowed dramatically in the 1920s this process slowed down. Collins (1997) finds that it also quickened the movement of blacks from the South to the Northern states. One implication of findings like these is that, even though immigrants were highly concentrated, their effects on the labour market percolated throughout the economy.

5. The Impact of Migration

One of the most contentious issues in the immigration debate has been what the economy-wide effects of immigration are and one reason it has been so contentious

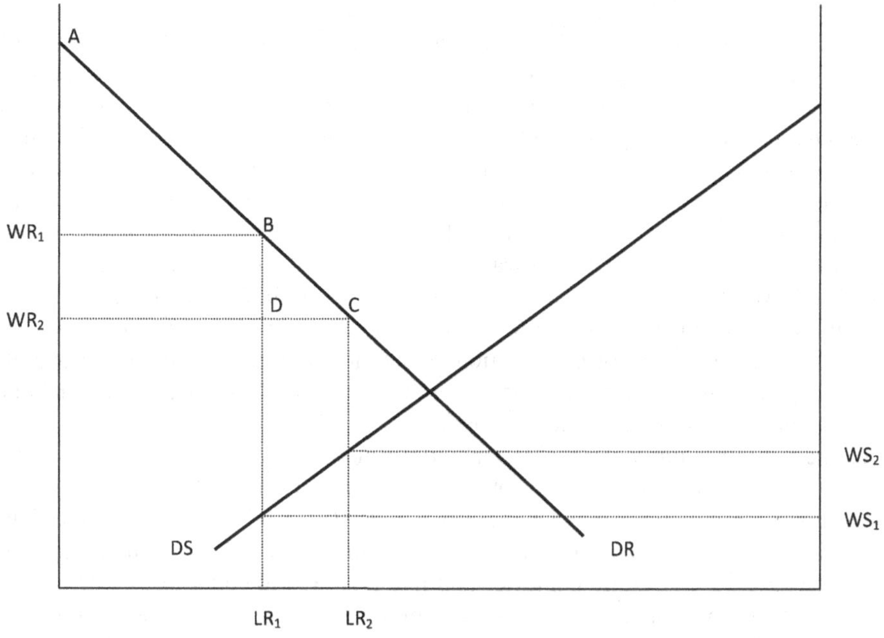

Figure 2. The Economic Effects of Migration.

is because of the link with policy. The issues that have been debated in the historical literature can best be illustrated in with a textbook diagram (Figure 2). Here there are two countries (R and S) with combined labour force measured as the width of the box. The receiving country's labour demand curve, DR, slopes down from the left and the sending country's labour demand, DS, curve slopes down from the right. The initial allocation of labour in the receiving country is LR_1 and its wage, WR_1, exceeds that of the sending country, WS_1. Migration from S to R increases the labour force in country R to LR_2, so that the wage falls to WR_2; in country S the labour force shrinks and the wage increases to WS_2.

The research questions that stem from this are as follows. First, did immigration depress real wages in the New World and increase them in the Old World, and if so, by how much? Second, how far did migration lead to convergence of wage rates between the New and Old Worlds? Third, are there other forces associated with migration – or with pre-1914 globalization more generally – that shifted labour demand curves such that they either offset or reinforced the partial equilibrium effects depicted in Figure 1? And finally, how far did immigration affect the distribution of income in the New and Old Worlds? This is illustrated in the diagram by recognizing that the income of other (fixed) factors of production in country R is measured in the initial situation as the area of the triangle A, B, WR_1, which after the migration becomes A, C, WR_2.

What was the impact of mass migration on real wage rates and on wage convergence between sending and receiving countries before 1914? Several different approaches have been employed. Using regression analysis on annual time series for Australia for 1860–1913, Pope and Withers (1994) found little evidence of a negative effect of immigration on wages. However, they used the immigrant *flow* to explain the wage *level*, whereas theory suggests immigrant *flows* should explain wage *change*. A similar point applies to their finding that the immigrant flow had no effect on the unemployment rate (Pope and Withers, 1993). Other studies have correlated immigration with changes in wages across locations within a country (the so-called spatial correlations approach). Ljungberg (1997) finds that emigration explained about half of the rise in wages across Swedish counties between in 1870 and 1910. And Goldin (1994) found a negative relationship between wage growth and immigration across US cities between 1890 and 1923. Although this approach captures the *local* effects of immigration it may not be a good guide to the overall national effects if (as suggested above) there is significant interregional labour mobility in response to migration inflows.

In their multi-country study, Taylor and Williamson (1997) first calculate the cumulative effect of migration on total labour supply from 1870 to 1910 in order to estimate the counterfactual labour force in 1910 in the absence of migration. They then use labour demand elasticities to estimate the effects of migration on real wages for 12 Old World countries and five New World countries.[13] The effects are roughly proportional to the scale of immigration so that in the absence of mass migration after 1870 real wages in 1910 would have been higher by 27% in Argentina, by 17% in Australia and by 9% in the USA; conversely real wages would have been lower by 24% in Ireland, by 22% in Italy but by only 5% in Great Britain and 2% in Germany. Overall the real wage ratio between the New and Old Worlds fell by 11%, whereas under the no-migration counterfactual it would have increased by 10% (Taylor and Williamson, 1997, p. 41). Thus, international migration more than accounts for the observed wage convergence between 1870 and 1910.

These assessments can be enriched by using computable general equilibrium (CGE) models to allow for a variety of economy-wide adjustments, although usually for only one country at a time. For Sweden, Karlstrom (1985) estimated that emigration up to 1890 raised the real wage by 9%, whereas for Norway Riis and Thonstad (1989) estimated that emigration up to 1910 raised income per capita by 6%. O'Rourke and Williamson (1995) found that emigration served to raise urban wages in Sweden by 12.3% above what they would have been in its absence. Boyer *et al.* (1994) find that, in the absence of emigration after 1851, Irish real wages would have been lower by between 19% and 34%. For Argentina, Taylor (1997) finds that real wages would have been 25% higher by 1914 in the absence of immigration from 1870. O'Rourke *et al.* (1994) estimated that in the absence of emigration urban real wages would have been higher in 1910 by as much as 34% in the USA and lower by 12% in Britain. In terms of broad magnitudes, most of these figures are consistent with those estimated using the much cruder method of applying labour demand elasticities to counterfactual labour force estimates, but two points are worthy of note.

The first is that the CGE models allow a rich array of adjustments. Thus in the absence of emigration, labour-intensive sectors would have shrunk less in the

Old World and would have expanded less in the New World. In countries like Ireland and Sweden the share of agriculture would have declined more slowly, especially the most labour-intensive sectors. And because these are open economy models, adjustments also come through international trade. To the extent that factor intensities become more similar, migration tends to be a substitute for trade, and so trade grows less rapidly than it would have in the absence of migration. On the other hand falling transport costs stimulated trade, which served to magnify the real wage effects of differing labour intensities. The latter effect tended to cause divergence rather than convergence in real wages.

The second is that the size of the wage effects depends critically on the assumption that is made about capital mobility. The results quoted above are based on the assumption that the capital stock in the end year in the counterfactual is the same as the observed level. The models show that, in the absence of the mass migrations, rates of return on capital would have been much lower in the New World and much higher in the Old World. It seems likely that much of the capital that flowed from the Old World to the New was effectively chasing the higher returns brought about by migration-induced labour force growth. If those returns were effectively arbitraged by the international capital market, then in the absence of migration, capital would have retreated to Europe and rates of return would not have diverged. Thus with perfectly mobile capital, the wage effects of migration are much smaller. To give one illustration: in the absence of emigration since 1870 the British wage in 1910 would have been 6.6% lower with capital mobility compared with 12.2% lower with no capital mobility (O'Rourke *et al.*, 1994, p. 209).[14] This has important implications for wage convergence in the Atlantic economy. Taylor and Williamson (1997) estimate that whereas migration explains 125% of the observed wage convergence in the absence of capital adjustment, it explains 'only' 70% when capital is perfectly mobile.

That there are *any* wage effects under capital mobility reflects the fact that there are other fixed factors, most importantly land. As its relative scarcity increased, land prices and rental rates tended to increase in the New World relative to those the Old World (O'Rourke and Williamson, 1999, p. 179). And as land scarcity increased relative to labour in the New World the wage–rental ratios fell although they tended to increase in the Old World. Because the average landowner was richer than the average labourer these trends contributed to increasing inequality in the New World and decreasing inequality in the Old World. It is important to stress, however, that the focus is on distribution rather than on income per capita or overall efficiency. This is illustrated by Figure 2, where capital (which we could think of here as land) is assumed immobile. Considering the initial population only, the overall 'immigration surplus' is the area of the triangle BCD, which is typically small. By contrast, the transfer from wage earners to land owners is the rectangle, WR_1, B, D, WR_2, which is much larger.[15]

As O'Rourke and Williamson (1999) show, the magnitude of these effects differed between countries, according to scale of migration, the structure of the economy and the reaction to globalization. Thus the rise in the wage–rental ratio was more muted in the European countries that resorted to agricultural protection

(France, Germany, Spain) than in those that maintained free trade. This has led to a lively debate on the distributional effects of globalization before 1914. A number of studies have sought to refine the original findings sometimes by revising the data series. Bohlin and Larsson (2007) find that the wage–rental ratio in Sweden increased more slowly than previously thought, which they argue is due to Sweden's turn to protectionism from 1888. Others stress regional diversity within the New World. Emery *et al.* (2007) find that the wage–rental ratio fell strongly from 1880 in land-abundant Western Canada but not in the East. This convergence within Canada was reversed in the period of de-globalization from 1914. For the Australian colonies Shanahan and Wilson (2007) find that whereas New South Wales, Victoria and Queensland exhibited declining wage–rental ratios, South Australia bucked the trend until the 1880s due to differing colonial land policies.

In the debate on inequality and globalization since the 1970s most of the focus has been on trends in the wage distribution. If skilled and unskilled workers are imperfect substitutes then unskilled immigration should widen the wage distribution.[16] Were the effects of migration on wage–rental ratios and wage–income ratios before 1914 also reflected in the distribution of wages? The evidence suggests that immigration before 1914 increased the share of unskilled labour in the USA and Canada where the wage distribution widened and reduced it for Britain, where the wage distribution narrowed. For other countries (both sending and receiving) the impact of migration on the skill mix and hence on the wage distribution is less clear. In his counterfactual analysis Anderson (2001) finds that the wage effects were generally in the expected direction but that they correlate poorly with the actual *ex post* changes in wage inequality. Clearly other factors were at work. Using regression analysis Betrán and Pons (2004) find that net migration increased the skill premium for the USA but narrowed it for France, the UK, Spain and Italy. But this effect is only observed in the presence of a range of other variables that represent skill-biased technical change, capital intensity, structural change and a range of variables reflecting labour market institutions. These results are qualitatively similar to those obtained from a CGE analysis of the trend in the skill premium for UK economy from 1880 to 1913 (Betrán *et al.*, 2010).

6. Immigration Policy

As emigration to the New World ascended to ever greater heights in the two decades before the First World War pressures for restricting immigration mounted – nowhere more so than in the USA, which eventually imposed a literacy test in 1917 followed by the first immigration quota in 1921. Some observers have seen this as a policy backlash in response to the rise in immigration itself (Williamson, 1998); thus mass migration sowed the seeds of its own destruction. But what were the mechanisms involved? As Foreman-Peck (1992, p. 360) puts it: 'The two key questions of any political economy of international migration are: (1) who gains and who loses from migration? And (2) who is in a position to do something about it? The answer to the first question identifies a demand for policies and that to the second reveals a policy supply.'

The answer to the first question is discussed in the previous section and is illustrated in Figure 1. Those who competed most directly with immigrants, such as low-skilled blue collar workers, had the most to lose and are likely to complain the most loudly. The answer to the second question depends on who has the vote and what particular interest they would vote for. As the franchise widened it typically percolated down the hierarchy of class and income diluting the political weight of landowners and capitalists and giving a stronger voice to urban unskilled labour. As Engerman and Sokoloff (2005) show, voting rates at the turn of the century were about a third for adults in North America and but less than 10% in South America where the *Latifundia* retained its grip on power. Immigration restrictions came earlier in the USA than in the (comparably democratic) land-abundant dominions partly due to their membership of the British Empire. In labour-abundant Europe, labour's interest was to encourage emigration and hence the wider the franchise the less emigration was discouraged (Foreman-Peck, 1992, pp. 366–367).

So what underlies public attitudes towards immigration? Two candidates stand out. The first is that, as Figure 1 illustrates, those who compete most directly with immigrants have the most to lose and are likely to complain the most loudly. Low-skilled workers in blue collar occupations, who were gaining the franchise and joining unions, would be the natural constituency to support restrictive immigration policy. The alternative is the cultural hypothesis: that the growing numbers of Southern and Eastern Europeans were seen as challenging existing cultural norms and therefore as less acceptable.[17] As the Southern and Eastern Europeans whose numbers were increasing steeply tended also to be less skilled and less educated, these hypotheses are (almost) observationally equivalent. Both the literacy test of 1917 and the Quota Acts of 1921 and 1924 deliberately discriminated against these 'new immigrants'.[18]

Following the literature on immigration opinion for more recent times,[19] Richardson (2005) provides an interesting test of these hypotheses using data on opinion towards immigration collected by the Kansas State Labor Bureau in 1895–1897. He finds that the overwhelming majority of workers in this blue collar sample wanted immigration to be restricted or to be suppressed altogether. Union members were more strongly opposed to immigration than non-unionists and those with incomes in the middle of the range were more opposed than the poorest. Although increasing immigration in a locality leads to stronger opposition to immigration, the source-country composition of those immigrants matters much less. Hence the results favour the labour market competition hypothesis over the ethnic differences hypothesis. There is also evidence that opinion was more negative in years when unemployment was high. This is consistent with much of the qualitative literature that links the ebb and flow of anti-immigrant sentiment with business cycle conditions.[20]

How did anti-immigrant sentiment get translated into restrictive immigration policy? In a highly influential paper Goldin (1994) examines voting patterns in the US Congress. Beginning in 1897 a series of bills incorporating a literacy test failed to pass into law until, in 1917, the House of Representatives and the Senate both overrode Presidents Wilson's veto.[21] Labour market effects seem to have been an important factor. Analysing the vote for an override in the House in 1915 Goldin found that representatives were more likely to vote for restriction the more rapid the growth of the foreign-born population and slower the growth of wages rates in their district during the preceding years. But the higher the district's immigrant density (the level, not the change) the less likely was a vote for restriction. This is consistent with evidence that first- and second-generation immigrants were less anti-immigration that the native-born (Richardson, 2005, p. 16).

Although the run up to restriction in the USA has gained most of the attention there has also been a search for more general patterns. In other New World countries the door remained ajar for longer, but there is evidence that in Canada, Australia and New Zealand policy was also tightening. That meant reducing or eliminating inducements to immigrants, and as in the USA, eventually imposing tests (such as the dictation test of the white Australia policy) that screened out migrants from less-favoured sources. Timmer and Williamson (1998) developed an index of immigration policy in five New World countries from 1870 up to 1930. Using these data they found that for Argentina, Brazil, Canada and the USA tougher policies were associated with declining unskilled relative wages. In Argentina and Australia with relatively homogenous immigration streams the rising share of foreign born also led to increasing restriction. In Canada and the USA where immigrant origins were more diverse it was the rise in immigration from low-wage countries, differing in ethnicity and religion from earlier immigrants, that helped to close the door.

Although immigration policies typically get tighter in recessions (Shughart *et al.*, 1986), recessions seem to have more decisive effects when they are preceded by a gradual accumulation of forces that shift opinion against immigration.[22] This may help explain the imposition of the emergency quota in the USA, as the unemployment rate increased from 5.2% in 1920 to 11.7% in 1921. Although the USA led in the early 1920s, the door slammed shut in other New World countries during the Great Depression.[23] But two other factors may also have been important. The first is that the interwar period saw a dramatic decline in international capital flows. So the effect of capital mobility in muting the wage effects of immigration would have been smaller than before 1914 and thus we might suppose that workers would have been more opposed to immigration than in the era when capital chased labour (Hatton and Williamson, 2008). Second, the continuing expansion of the franchise gave greater voice to those at the bottom of the income distribution (Hatton and Williamson, 2007).

Not surprisingly international migration was dramatically lower in the interwar period compared with the decades before 1914. Some of this was clearly the result of policy. Thus Pope (1981) found that lower immigration to Australia after 1920 could be accounted for by the reduction in subsidies and the tightening of eligibility. Taylor (1994) found shifts in the migration equations for both Australia and Argentina and Gemery (1994) found that the push–pull model no longer explained immigration to the USA. In the USA where the quotas bore heavily on the 'new immigrant' countries, the fall was the most dramatic of all. However, immigration declined even for source countries for which the quotas were not binding. During the Great Depression immigration fell even further as policy tightened more and as migrants were deterred by the high rates of unemployment in the New World. It possible also that the declining young adult cohorts and expanding welfare states caused Europeans to stay at home, but such hypotheses await more formal investigation.

The deglobalization of the interwar period reversed many of the trends that had been underway since the middle of the 19th century. What migration there was shifted back from 'new' to 'old' sources; immigrant 'quality' increased, and the skill premium in the USA declined as low-skilled immigration plummeted (Hatton and Williamson, 2005, pp. 193–195). And although the skill premium also declined in European countries the decline was less dramatic than in the USA and Canada (Anderson, 2001, p. 94; Betrán and Pons, 2004, p. 39). More generally, wage convergence ceased and wage–rental ratio stopped rising in the New World and falling in the Old World. One implication is that the conditions that gave rise to the immigration backlash were gradually reversed. These conditions ultimately provided the backdrop to the easing of immigration policies in the post-war period (Hatton and Williamson, 2005, chapter 10). In the USA where the (long delayed) policy backlash was sharpest the resumption took longer than in other New World countries where the backlash was less intense.

7. International Migration in the Third World

The preceding sections focus exclusively on emigration from Europe to the New World, within what might be called the greater Atlantic economy. This has received the vast bulk of the attention in cliometric work on migration. Yet as McKeown (2004) points out, it accounts for only a third to 40% of long-distance international migration in the era up to 1940.[24] Most notable were the 50 million or more migrants from labour-abundant India and South China to labour-scarce regions such as Burma, Ceylon, parts of Southeast Asia and the Pacific Islands as well as more distant locations on the coast of Africa, South America and the Caribbean. They were largely shut out of the greater Atlantic economy, first by the costs of migration and, from the 1880s, by anti-Asian immigration policies. The bulk of intercontinental migrants from Asia travelled as indentured labourers (reflecting the high costs of migration), until this too was curtailed by policy. Hence the largest numbers moved to the primary product exporters within Asia. Not surprisingly, migration within Asia has received growing attention, although the cliometric literature is still relatively small.

Were these migrations driven by the same forces that were observed in the Atlantic migrations? Huff and Caggiano (2007) focus on emigrants moving from India and South China to work on plantations in Burma, Thailand and Malaya. Using the standard push–pull model outlined above, they find evidence that relative wages were important, just as for transatlantic migration, but that proxies for labour demand are generally insignificant. This possibly reflects that migrants were contracted to specific sectors rather than responding to economy-wide labour market conditions. Except in one case the migrant stock was found to exert a powerful influence, something that Huff and Caggiano (2007, p. 49) attribute to the spread of information about opportunities for migration.[25] Just as in Europe, the regional origins of migrants were very unevenly distributed, with notably high rates of emigration from Madras in India and Fukien and Kwangtung in China. Although high-emigration localities were often on or near the coast, we lack detailed studies of the other factors involved. One interesting study of migration from different Japanese prefectures to the Northwest USA stresses the importance of information flows set in train by pioneer migrants (Murayama, 1991). It seems likely that information flows were (even) more important in the context of Asian emigration that they were in Europe.

In Asia the volume of migration was often large relative to the receiving country population but small relative to that of the source country. Taken together, Burma, Thailand and Malaya received 15 million immigrants between 1881 and 1939, a figure in excess of their combined population in 1881. However, about four fifths returned, typically after a stay of 3 to 5 years (Huff and Caggiano, 2007, pp. 38–39). Given the vast populations of India and China, some observers have followed W.A. Lewis in characterizing them as highly elastic sources of labour. As a result, the wage in the Southeast Asian destinations should be pinned down by labour market conditions in India and China. Using cointegration and error correction models, Huff and Caggiano (2007, 2008) find that Indian wages in Burma and Malaya and Chinese wages in Thailand and Malaya were strongly related to the wage in the respective source countries, with little trend in the wage gap and little evidence of reverse causality.[26] Thus the long run supply of labour to these booming Asian economies seems to have been more elastic than was the supply of European labour to the New World.

Longer-distance migrations to the plantation enclaves of the Caribbean, the Pacific and Africa were much smaller in magnitude and were conducted through contract or indenture (more so for Indians than Chinese). One reason is that the costs were much higher. Relative to the home wage, the cost of passage for these Indian and Chinese migrants were of the order of 10 times those facing Europeans migrating to the New World (Hatton and Williamson, 2005, p. 140). The key element in migration under indentured servitude in the middle of the 19th century was the length of the contract (Northrup, 1995, pp. 115–116). The further the distance, the longer it took to recoup the costs of passage and recruitment, and hence the longer was the contract. But if the cost were high relative to the home wage so were the rewards. Wage ratios between destination and source in the range of five to nine for intercontinental migration were two to three times those for migration to Southeast Asia and were vastly higher than they were around the greater Atlantic economy (Hatton and Williamson, 2005, p. 137).

The fall in transport costs and the export-led boom that characterized Southeast Asia pervaded much of the resource-abundant periphery.[27] That raises two questions. First, did it also lead to convergence in real wages and in factor price ratios? And second, how important a part did migration play? Huff and Caggiano (2007) find some evidence of real wage convergence within Asia. However, Williamson (2002) has developed a real wage database for a wider range of countries of the periphery, which shows the opposite: real wage divergence (Hatton and Williamson, 2005, p. 146). On the other hand there is evidence of convergence in the wage–rental ratios from 1870 to 1940, which is largely accounted for by the trends in land rents. Regression evidence indicates that wage–rental ratios were driven chiefly by trends in the terms of trade, as Heckscher–Ohlin trade theory would predict (Williamson, 2002, p. 78). Thus 'either the terms of trade shocks were simply too big and favoured the land- and resource-abundant regions, or the net migrations were too small or both' (Hatton and Williamson, 2005, p. 146).

Was there a policy backlash comparable with that in the Atlantic economy? Migration under indentured servitude, which had partially filled the labour supply gap left by the abolition of slavery, came under fire from the middle of the 19th century. On the fringes of the Atlantic economy, where there was potential competition with workers of European origin, it was fiercely opposed and severely restricted. But it survived longer in island economies like those of the West Indies, Mauritius, Reunion and Fiji, until the Indian trade was finally abolished by Britain in 1916 and in India itself a few years later. But by that time it has been in decline for two or three decades mainly because the deteriorating terms of trade reduced the demand for migrant labour (Hatton and Williamson, 2005, p. 150). Closer to home, a dramatic tightening of policy took place in Southeast Asia in the 1930s as export markets collapsed. For example, Thailand introduced a literacy test and costly residence permits in 1932. And in Malaya, where unemployment fell disproportionately on immigrants, the government embarked on a massive policy of subsidized repatriation (Huff, 2001). Thus although there are parallels with the Atlantic economy in the timing of restriction, it does not seem to have been driven by quite the same long run forces.

8. Conclusion

The cliometrics of international migration has been a vibrant research area for the last three decades. And while it has borrowed extensively from the parallel literature in economics it has examined a range of experience that has placed some of the issues studied by economists in sharper relief would otherwise be possible. For example, it offers the opportunity to assess the determinants of migration largely free of restrictive immigration policies and it offers a valuable testing ground for the political economy of immigration policy. But the cliometric literature is patchy; the debate is most lively, and the literature is densest, where the available data are richest. For that reason, if not for others, the bulk of research has focused on the rise and fall of mass migration in the greater Atlantic economy, and especially on immigration to the USA. Countries in regions such as Latin America and Eastern Europe have received rather less attention. But one of the triumphs of recent research is to provide an integrated, multi-country view of the causes and effects of mass migration in the Atlantic economy as a whole. By contrast migration in Asia and elsewhere in the periphery has remained underdeveloped, notwithstanding the efforts of a number of pioneering scholars. No doubt we shall see more on that topic in the future.

Acknowledgements

I am grateful for useful comments from Blanca Sánchez-Alonso and Chris Minns as well as an anonymous referee.

Notes

1. The model is derived from a logarithmic utility function and assumes that future expected values of the wage and of employment probabilities are related with geometric lags to past values in an adaptive process. This gives the following model for migration (see Hatton and Williamson, 1998, pp. 61–63 for the full derivation):

$$M_t = (1-\lambda)\beta \ln(w_f/w_h)t + (1-\lambda)\beta^{3/2}\ln(e_f)t - (1-\lambda)\beta\gamma^{3/2}\ln(e_h)t$$
$$+ (1-\lambda)\beta\varepsilon_0 + (1-\lambda)\beta\varepsilon_1 MST_t + (1-\lambda)\beta\varepsilon_2 t + \lambda M_{t-1}$$

   where M is the emigration rate, w denotes wage rates and e employment rates abroad (f) and at home (h). The terms in the lower line of the equation (with parameters ε) are the costs of migration as reflected by the migrant stock (*MST*) and a time trend for falling transport costs. The last term is the lagged dependent variable arising from the adaptive expectations process with parameter λ. In the upper line of the equation, the fraction 3/2 reflects the greater weight given to the employment terms as a result of employment uncertainty (arising from the concavity of the utility function). The coefficient γ allows for lower uncertainty to attach to home employment compared with abroad. Thus it could range between 1 (equal uncertainty with abroad) and 2/3 (no uncertainty). Further dynamics are added to the estimating equation to reflect the option value of waiting – see Hatton (1995).
2. To illustrate, let the wage difference (destination minus source country) per year of working life be a constant D. If the age range of potential working-age migrants, a, runs from 20 to 65, and the discount rate is r, then the present value of the gains will be

$$PV(a) = \frac{D}{r}[1-(1+r)^{-(46-a)}]$$

   which is a decreasing function of a.
3. Sánchez-Alonso (2007) shows that fares from the UK to the USA fell from the 1850s, whereas those from Spain to Argentina, Brazil and Cuba declined from the 1870s. McDonald and Shlomowitz (1991) find no downward trend in the contract price of passages to Australia between 1847 and 1885.
4. For example, Taylor (1994) finds that similar results emerge for migration to Argentina (largely from Italy and Spain) as for migration to Australia (from the UK).
5. For example, Deltas *et al.* (2008) found little evidence of inter-temporal substitution in response to shifts in the cost of migration.
6. Looking at panel data for the same 12 countries Greenwood (2007) finds that the larger the manufacturing and agricultural shares in total employment the younger were the emigrants and the more they responded to job opportunities.

7. Summarizing occupational data for ships lists Cohn (2009, chapter 5) confirms this pattern for German immigrants but finds that the English, and especially the Irish, were rather less skilled than the populations from which they were drawn. The evidence also suggests that from around 1830 the skills of immigrants to the USA declined as migration costs fell and mass migration accelerated.
8. These events are the expulsion of Jews from Moscow in 1891, the Kishinev massacre of 1903 and the pogroms that followed the riots of 1905.
9. Those from Southern Europe were known as *golondrinas* (swallows).
10. The typical age–earning profile slopes steeply upwards from the age of about 16 to 25 and then follows a much flatter curve. In these data sets the native-born are relatively young and so the quadratic function picks up the steep rise at the younger ages. By contrast, immigrants are typically older and so the quadratic estimated for them is much flatter. From the estimated profiles it thus appears that the earnings of natives grow faster up to about age 40, and then decline faster at higher ages.
11. Even more striking is the positive educational selection of immigrants from Mexico to the USA in 1910 and 1940; despite this, Mexican immigrants still had much less education than the US born (Feliciano, 2001).
12. There is some suggestion that male immigrants from Southern Italy to the USA were taller than average, but women were shorter (Danubio *et al.*, 2004).
13. In these calculations the labour demand elasticities are based on the assumption that aggregate production functions are of Cobb–Douglas form (i.e. where the elasticity of factor substitution is -1). It is worth stressing that in this and most of the other studies noted below the effect of immigration wages in sending or receiving countries is based on the assumption that labour demand curves are downward sloping, and so the migration effect is not tested directly.
14. For other countries the results for 1870–1910 (capital immobile versus capital mobile) are: USA, 34.0, 9.2 (O'Rourke *et al.*, 1994, p. 209); Argentina, 27.0, 25.0 (Taylor, 1997, p. 121); and Ireland (from 1850), −19, −6 (Boyer *et al.*, 1994, p. 235).
15. To give an illustration, for the immigration to the USA up to 1990, Borjas (1995, p. 8) calculated the loss to native-born workers would be 1.9% of GDP and the gain to native capital 2.0% of GDP, so that the immigration surplus is just 0.1% of GDP. But the overall surplus could be larger for skilled migration in a model that distinguishes between skilled and unskilled workers and where capital and skills are complements.
16. In fact there are two issues: (a) substitutability between skill (or education) groups and (b) substitutability between immigrants and non-immigrants within skill groups. The latter point is reflected in the recent debate following Borjas (2003). For US manufacturing in 1890, Foreman-Peck (1992) found evidence of less than perfect substitutability between immigrants and non-immigrants, some of which may reflect differences in skills.
17. Just as the Irish had been regarded in the two decades after the Famine.
18. The Emergency Quota Act (also known as the Johnson Quota Act) limited annual immigration from each national origin to 3% of the stock in the 1910 census. The Immigration Act of 1924 (the Johnson-Reed Act) limited the number of migrants to 2% of the number in the 1890 census (effective 1929). Asians remained excluded. For the background to legislation in this period see Daniels (2004, chapter 2).
19. See for example Mayda (2006), O'Rourke and Sinnott (2005) and Dustmann and Preston (2007).

20. It may also explain the imposition of the emergency quota in 1921, as the unemployment rate increased from 5.2% in 1920 to 11.7% in 1921. An alternative hypothesis is that with rapid growth in education in Southern and Eastern Europe the literacy test was proving less effective than anticipated (Goldin, 1994, p. 226).
21. The Dillingham Commission had previously recommended using a literacy test to restrict immigration.
22. A good example from a later era is the sudden abandonment of guestworker programmes (*arbeitstopp*) in Germany and other European countries at the time of the first oil price shock in 1973–1974.
23. In Canada, the mildly restrictive Immigration Acts of 1906, 1910 and 1923 were followed much tougher regulation in 1930 and 1931, when Orders in Council banned all new immigration except for British and Americans with sufficient capital or assured employment. In Australia, the White Australia Policy was introduced in 1901 and tightened in 1924 and 1928 and then in 1930 a £50 immigration fee was introduced. In New Zealand, government assistance to immigration was abandoned in 1930 and the Department of Immigration was closed in 1931. In newly created South Africa, the immigration laws of 1902 and 1906 (framed along similar lines to those of Australia) were followed in 1930 by national origins quota based on the American model. See Daniels (1995).
24. Two caveats are appropriate here. One is that a far larger proportion of Third World transoceanic migration was temporary or short-term. The other is that a significant share of McKeown's total for Asia is migration within the same country or landmass – notably the migrations (mainly of Chinese and Russians) to Manchuria and Siberia.
25. Interestingly they find that the migrant stock is not significant for Indian migration to Burma, the majority of whom were recruited by a *kangany* (head man, or gang leader).
26. Nevertheless the absolute real wages in the destination were two to three times those at the source. Huff and Caggiano (2008, pp. 305–306) attribute some of this to the costs of migration and relocation, but the largest component was due to the 'universal stipulation' among migrants to accumulate savings and to send back remittances.
27. In addition to Southeast Asia (Burma, Java, Malaya, the Philippines, Thailand and the Straits settlements), it embraced South Asia (Assam, the Punjab and Ceylon), tropical and semitropical Latin America (the Caribbean, the Brazilian northeast, British and French Guyana, and coastal Peru), North Africa, East Africa and the Indian ocean (Egypt, Kenya, Mauritius, Natal and Reunion).

References

Akerman, S. (1976) Theories and methods of migration research. In H. Rundblom and H. Norman (eds), *From Sweden to America: A History of the Migration*. Minneapolis, MN: University of Minnesota Press.

Anderson, E. (2001) Globalisation and wage inequalities, 1870–1970. *European Review of Economic History* 5: 91–118.

Baily, S.L. (1983) Italian immigrants in Buenos Aires and New York. *American Historical Review* 88: 281–305.

Baines, D. (1994) European emigration, 1815–1930: looking at the emigration decision again. *Economic History Review* 47: 525–544.

Balderas, J.U. and Greenwood, M.J. (2010) From Europe to the Americas: a comparative panel-data analysis of migration to Argentina, Brazil and the United States, 1870–1910. *Journal of Population Economics* 23: 1310–1318.
Bertocchi, G. and Strozzi, C. (2008) International migration and the role of institutions. *Public Choice* 137: 81–102.
Betrán, C. and Pons, M.A. (2004) Skilled and unskilled wage differentials and economic integration, 1870–1930. *European Review of Economic History* 8: 29–60.
Betrán, C., Ferri, J. and Pons, M.A. (2010) Explaining UK wage inequality in the past globalisation period, 1880–1913. *Cliometrica* 4: 19–50.
Blau, F.D. (1980) Immigration and labor earnings in early twentieth century America. *Research in Population Economics* 2: 21–41.
Bohlin, J. and Larsson, S. (2007) The Swedish wage–rental ratio and its determinants, 1877–1926. *Australian Economic History Review* 47: 49–72.
Borjas, G.J. (1985) Assimilation, changes in cohort quality and the earnings of immigrants. *Journal of Labor Economics* 3: 463–489.
Borjas, G.J. (1992) National origins and the skills of immigrants in the postwar period. In G.J. Borjas and R.B. Freeman (eds), *Immigration and the Workforce: Economics Consequences for the United States and Source Areas*. Chicago, IL: University of Chicago Press.
Borjas, G.J. (1994) The economics of immigration. *Journal of Economic Literature* 32: 1667–1717.
Borjas, G.J. (1995) The economic benefits from immigration. *Journal of Economic Perspectives* 9: 3–32.
Borjas, G.J. (2003) The labor demand curve *is* downward sloping: reexamining the impact of immigration on the labor market. *Quarterly Journal of Economics* 118: 1335–1374.
Boustan, L.P. (2007) Were Jews political refugees or economic migrants? Assessing the persecution theory of Jewish emigration, 1881–1914. In T.J. Hatton, K.H. O'Rourke and A.M. Taylor (eds), *The New Comparative Economic History: Essays in Honor of Jeffrey G. Williamson*. Cambridge, MA: MIT Press.
Boyer, G.R., Hatton, T.J. and O'Rourke, K. (1994) The impact of migration on real wages in Ireland, 1850–1914. In T.J. Hatton and J.G. Williamson (eds), *Migration and the International Labor Market, 1850–1939*. London: Routledge.
Chiswick, B.R. (1978) The effect of Americanization on the earnings of foreign-born men. *Journal of Political Economy* 86: 897–921.
Chiswick, B.R. (1991) Jewish immigrant skill and occupational attainment at the turn of the century. *Explorations in Economic History* 28: 64–86.
Chiswick, B.R. (1992) Jewish immigrant skill wages in America in 1909: an analysis of the Dillingham Commission data. *Explorations in Economic History* 29: 274–289.
Cinel, D. (1991) *The National Integration of Italian Return Migration, 1870–1929*. Cambridge: Cambridge University Press.
Cohn, R.L. (2000) Nativism and the end of the mass migration of the 1840s and 1950s. *Journal of Economic History* 60: 361–383.
Cohn, R.L. (2009) *Mass Migration under Sail: European Antebellum Immigration to the United States*. New York: Cambridge University Press.
Collins, W. (1997) When the tide turned: immigration and the delay of the great migration. *Journal of Economic History* 57: 607–632.
Daniels, R. (1995) The growth of restrictive immigration policy in the colonies of settlement. In R. Cohen (ed.), *The Cambridge Survey of World Migration*. Cambridge: Cambridge University Press.
Daniels, R (2004) *Guarding the Golden Door: American Immigration Policy and Immigrants since 1882*. New York: Hill and Wang.
Danubio, M.E., Amicone, E. and Vargui, R. (2004) Height and BMI of Italian immigrants to the USA, 1908–1970. *Economics and Human Biology* 3: 33–43.

Deltas, G., Sicotte, R. and Tomczak, P. (2008) Passenger shipping cartels and their effect on transatlantic migration. *Review of Economics and Statistics* 90: 119–133.

Dunlevy, J.A. (1980) Nineteenth century immigration to the United States: intended versus lifetime settlement patterns. *Economic Development and Cultural Change* 29: 77–90.

Dunlevy, J.A. (1983) Regional preferences and migrant settlement: on the avoidance of the south by nineteenth century immigrants. *Research in Economic History* 8: 217–251.

Dunlevy, J.A. and Gemery, H.A. (1977) The role of migrant stock and lagged migration in the settlement patterns of nineteenth century immigrants. *Review of Economics and Statistics* 59: 137–144.

Dunlevy, J.A. and Saba, R.P. (1992) The role of nationality-specific characteristics on the settlement patterns of late nineteenth century immigrants. *Explorations in Economic History* 29: 228–249.

Dustmann, C. and Preston, I. (2007) Racial and economic factors in attitudes to immigration. *B.E. Journal of Economic Analysis and Policy* 7(Advances), Article 62, pp. 1–39.

Easterlin, R. (1961) Influences in European overseas migration before World War I. *Economic Development and Cultural Change* 9: 33–51.

Eichengreen, B.J. and Gemery, H.A. (1986) The earnings of skilled and unskilled immigrants at the end of the nineteenth century. *Journal of Economic History* 46: 822–834.

Emery, J.C.H., Inwood, K. and Thille, H. (2007) Heckscher–Ohlin in Canada: new estimates of regional wages and land prices. *Australian Economic History Review* 47: 22–48.

Engerman, S.L. and Sokoloff, K.L. (2005) The evolution of suffrage institutions in the New World. *Journal of Economic History* 65: 891–921.

Faini, R. and Venturini, A. (1994) Italian emigration in the pre-war period. In T.J. Hatton and J.G. Williamson (eds), *Migration and the International Labor Market, 1850–1939*. London: Routledge.

Feliciano, Z.M. (2001) The skill and economic performance of Mexican immigrants from 1910 to 1990. *Explorations in Economic History* 38: 386–409.

Ferenczi, I. and Willcox, W.F. (1929) *International Migrations*, Vol 1. New York: National Bureau of Economic Research.

Ferrie, J.P. (1999) *Yankeys Now: Immigrants in the Antebellum United States*. New York: Oxford University Press.

Foreman-Peck, J. (1992) A political economy of international migration, 1815–1914. *Manchester School* 60: 359–376.

Gemery, H.A. (1994) Immigrants and emigrants: international migration and the U.S. labor market in the Great Depression. In T.J. Hatton and J.G. Williamson (eds), *Migration and the International Labor Market, 1850–1939*. London: Routledge.

Godley, A. (2001) *Jewish Immigrant Entrepreneurship in New York and London, 1880–1914*. London: Palgrave Macmillan.

Goldin, C.D. (1994) The political economy of immigration restriction in the United States. In C. Goldin and G. Libecap (eds), *The Regulated Economy: A Historical Approach to Political Economy*. Chicago, IL: University of Chicago Press.

Gould, J.D. (1979) European inter-continental emigration: patterns and causes. *Journal of European Economic History* 8: 593–679.

Gould, J.D. (1980a) European inter-continental emigration. The road home: return migration from the USA. *Journal of European Economic History* 9: 41–112.

Gould, J.D. (1980b) European inter-continental emigration: the role of 'diffusion' and 'feedback'. *Journal of European Economic History* 9: 267–315.

Green, A.G. and Green, D.A. (1993) Balanced growth and the geographical distribution of European immigrant arrivals to Canada, 1900–1912. *Explorations in Economic History* 9: 41–112.

Green, A.G. and MacKinnon, M. (2001) The slow assimilation of British immigrants in Canada: evidence from Montreal and Toronto, 1901. *Explorations in Economic History* 38: 315–338.

Green, A.G., MacKinnon, M. and Minns, C. (2002) Dominion or republic? Migrants to North America from the United Kingdom, 1870–1910. *Economic History Review* 55: 666–696.

Greenwood, M.J. (2007) Modeling the age and age composition of late 19th century U.S. immigrants from Europe. *Explorations in Economic History* 44: 255–269.

Hanes, C. (1996) Immigrants' relative rate of wage growth in the late nineteenth century. *Explorations in Economic History* 33: 35–64.

Hannon, J.U. (1982a) Ethnic discrimination in a nineteenth century mining district: Michigan copper mines, 1888. *Explorations in Economic History* 19: 28–50.

Hannon, J.U. (1982b) City size and ethnic discrimination: Michigan agricultural implements and ironworking industries, 1890. *Journal of Economic History* 42: 825–845.

Hatton, T.J. (1995) A model of U.K. emigration, 1870–1913. *Review of Economics and Statistics* 77: 407–415.

Hatton, T.J. (1997) The immigrant assimilation puzzle in late nineteenth century America. *Journal of Economic History* 57: 34–62.

Hatton, T.J. (2000) How much did immigrant 'quality' decline in late nineteenth century America? *Journal of Population Economics* 13: 509–525.

Hatton, T.J. and Williamson, J.G. (1998) *The Age of Mass Migration: Causes and Economic Impact*. New York: Oxford University Press.

Hatton, T.J. and Williamson, J.G. (2005) *Global Migration and the World Economy: Two Centuries of Policy and Performance*. Cambridge, MA: MIT Press.

Hatton, T.J. and Williamson, J.G. (2007) A dual policy paradox: why have trade and immigration policies always differed in labor scarce economies? In T.J. Hatton, K.H. O'Rourke and A.M. Taylor (eds), *The New Comparative Economic History: Essays in Honor of Jeffrey G. Williamson*. Cambridge, MA: MIT Press.

Hatton, T.J. and Williamson, J.G. (2008) What determines immigration's impact? Comparing two global centuries. *World Development* 36: 345–361.

Huff, W.G. (2001) Entitlements, destitution and emigration in the 1930s Singapore Great Depression. *Economic History Review* 54: 290–323.

Huff, G. and Caggiano, G. (2007) Globalization, immigration and Lewisian elastic labor in pre-World War II Southeast Asia. *Journal of Economic History* 67: 33–68.

Huff, G. and Caggiano, G. (2008) Globalization and labor market integration in late nineteenth- and early twentieth-century Asia. *Research in Economic History* 25: 285–347.

Jenks, J.W. and Lauck, W.J. (1926) *The Immigration Problem*, 6th edn. New York: Huebsch.

Jerome, H. (1926) *Migration and Business Cycles*. New York: National Bureau of Economic Research.

Karlstrom, U. (1985) *Economic Growth and Migration during the Industrialization of Sweden*. Stockholm: Stockholm School of Economics.

Keeling, D. (1999a) The transport revolution and trans-Atlantic migration, 1850–1914. *Research in Economic History* 19: 39–74.

Keeling, D. (1999b) Trans-Atlantic shipping cartels and migration between Europe and America, 1880–1914. *Business and Economic History* 17: 195–213.

Khoudor Castéras, D. (2008) Welfare state and labor mobility: the impact of Bismark's social legislation on German emigration before World War I. *Journal of Economic History* 68: 211–243.

Klein, H.S. (1983) The integration of Italian immigrants in to the United States and Argentina: a comparative analysis. *American Historical Review* 88: 306–329.

Larsen, U.M. (1982) A quantitative study of emigration from Denmark to the United States, 1870–1913. *Scandinavian Economic History Review* 30: 101–128.
Ljungberg, J. (1997) The impact of the great emigration on the Swedish economy. *Scandinavian Economic History Review* 44: 159–189.
Lowell, B.L. (1987) *Scandinavian Exodus: Demography and Social Development of 19th Century Rural Communities*. Boulder, CO: Westview Press.
Magee, G. and Thompson, A.S. (2006a) 'Lines of credit, debts of obligation': migrant remittances to Britain, c. 1875–1913. *Economic History Review* 59: 539–577.
Magee, G. and Thompson, A.S. (2006b) The global and local: explaining migrant remittance flows in the English speaking world, 1880–1914. *Journal of Economic History* 66: 177–202.
Mayda, A.M. (2006) Who is against immigration? A cross country investigation of individual attitudes towards immigrants. *Review of Economics and Statistics* 88: 510–530.
McDonald, J. and Shlomowitz, R. (1991) Passenger fares on sailing vessels to Australia in the nineteenth century. *Explorations in Economic History* 28: 192–208.
McKeown, A. (2004) Global migration, 1846–1940. *Journal of World History* 15: 155–189.
Minns, C. (2000) Income, cohort effects and occupational mobility: a new look at immigration to the United States at the turn of the 20th century. *Explorations in Economic History* 37: 326–350.
Minns, C. and Rizov, M. (2005) The spirit of capitalism? Ethnicity, religion and self-employment in early 20th century Canada. *Explorations in Economic History* 42: 259–281.
Mokyr, J. and Ferrie, J.P. (1994) Emigration and entrepreneurship in the nineteenth century U.S. In H. Giersch (ed.), *Aspects of International Migration*. Berlin: Springer.
Moretti, E. (1999) Migrations and social networks: Italy 1889–1913. *International Migration Review* 33: 640–657.
Murayama, Y. (1991) Information and emigrant inter-prefectural differences in Japanese emigration to the Pacific Northwest, 1880–1915. *Journal of Economic History* 51: 125–147.
Northrup, D. (1995) *Indentured Labor in the Age of Imperialism, 1834–1922*. Cambridge: Cambridge University Press.
O'Rourke, K.H. and Sinnott, R. (2005) The determinants of individual attitudes towards immigration. *European Journal of Political Economy* 22: 838–861.
O'Rourke, K.H. and Williamson, J.G. (1995) Open economy forces and late 19th century Swedish catch-up: a quantitative accounting. *Scandinavian Economic History Review* 43: 171–203.
O'Rourke, K.H. and Williamson, J.G. (1999) *Globalization and History: The Evolution of the Nineteenth Century Atlantic Economy*. Cambridge, MA: MIT Press.
O'Rourke, K., Williamson, J.G. and Hatton, T.J. (1994) Mass migration, commodity market integration and real wage convergence. In T.J. Hatton and J.G. Williamson (eds), *Migration and the International Labor Market, 1850–1939*. London: Routledge.
Pope, D.H. (1981) Modelling the peopling of Australia, 1900–1930. *Australian Economic Papers* 20: 258–282.
Pope, D.H. and Withers, G. (1993) Do migrants rob jobs from locals? Lessons from Australian history. *Journal of Economic History* 53: 719–742.
Pope, D.H. and Withers, G. (1994) Wage effects of immigration in late nineteenth century Australia. In T.J. Hatton and J.G. Williamson (eds), *Migration and the International Labor Market, 1850–1939*. London: Routledge.
Quigley, J.M. (1972) An economic model of Swedish emigration. *Quarterly Journal of Economics* 86: 111–126.
Richardson, G. (2005) The origins of anti-immigrant sentiments: evidence from the heartland in the age of mass migration. *B.E. Press, Topics in Economic Analysis and Policy* 5, Article 16, pp. 1–48.

Riis, C. and Thonstad, T. (1989) A counterfactual study of economic impacts of Norwegian emigration and capital imports. In I. Gordon and A.P. Thirlwall (eds), *European Factor Mobility: Trends and Consequences*. London: Macmillan.

Sánchez-Alonso, B. (2000a) European emigration in the late nineteenth century: the paradoxical case of Spain. *Economic History Review* 53: 309–330.

Sánchez-Alonso, B. (2000b) Those who left and those who stayed behind: explaining emigration from the regions of Spain, 1880–1914. *Journal of Economic History* 60: 730–755.

Sánchez-Alonso, B. (2007) The other Europeans: immigration into Latin America (1870–1914). *Revista de Historia Economica/Journal of Iberian and Latin American Economic History* 25: 395–426.

Shanahan, M.P. and Wilson, J.K. (2007) Measuring inequality trends in colonial Australia using factor price ratios: the importance of boundaries. *Australian Economic History Review* 47: 6–21.

Shughart, W., Tollinson, R. and Kimenyi, M. (1986) The political economy of immigration restrictions. *Yale Journal on Regulation* 51: 79–97.

Taylor, A.M. (1994) Mass migration to distant southern shores: Argentina and Australia. In T.J. Hatton and J.G. Williamson (eds), *Migration and the International Labor Market, 1850–1939*. London: Routledge.

Taylor, A.M. (1997) Peopling the Pampa: on the impact of mass migration to the River Plate, 1870–1914. *Explorations in Economic History* 34: 100–132.

Taylor, A.M. and Williamson, J.G. (1997) Convergence in the age of mass migration. *European Review of Economic History* 1: 27–63.

Thomas, D.S. (1941) *Social and Economic Consequences of Swedish Population Movements*. New York: Macmillan.

Timmer, A.S. and Williamson, J.G. (1998) Immigration policy prior to the 1930s: labor markets, policy interactions, and globalization backlash. *Population and Development Review* 24: 739–771.

Todaro, M.P. (1969) A model of labor migration and urban unemployment in less developed countries. *American Economic Review* 59: 138–148.

Tomaske, J.A. (1971) The determinants of intercountry differences in European emigration, 1881–1900. *Journal of Economic History* 31: 840–853.

US Immigration Commission (1911) *Reports*, 61st Congress, 3rd Session. Washington, DC: Government Printing Office.

Wegge, S.A. (1998) Chain migration and information networks: evidence from nineteenth-century Hesse-Cassel. *Journal of Economic History* 58: 957–986.

Wegge, S.A. (1999) To part or not to part: emigration and inheritance institutions in nineteenth century Hesse-Cassel. *Explorations in Economic History* 26: 30–55.

Wegge, S.A. (2002) Occupational self-selection of European emigrants: evidence from nineteenth century Hesse-Cassel. *European Review of Economic History* 6: 365–394.

Williamson, J.G. (1995) The evolution of global labor markets since 1830: background evidence and hypotheses. *Explorations in Economic History* 32: 141–196.

Williamson, J.G. (1998) Globalization, labor markets and policy backlash in the past. *Journal of Economic Perspectives* 12: 51–72.

Williamson, J.G. (2002) Land, labor and globalization in the third world, 1870–1940. *Journal of Economic History* 62: 55–85.

Zelinsky, W. (1971) The hypothesis of the mobility transition. *Geographical Review* 61, 219–249.

7

CLIOMETRICS AND TIME SERIES ECONOMETRICS: SOME THEORY AND APPLICATIONS

David Greasley and Les Oxley

1. Introduction

The power of a popular test is irrelevant. A test that is never used has zero power (McAleer, 1994, 2005)

The publications of Granger and Newbold (1974), Dickey and Fuller (1979, 1981), Nelson and Plosser (1982), Engle and Granger (1987) and Johansen (1988, 1995) have changed the way we think about and undertake time series econometrics. Although discussion of trends and their importance in economic time series can be traced to Yule (1926) and Kendall (1954), until the 1970s and 1980s the field remained mostly a curiosity. Statistical research focused on the isolation of trends from cycles in a world (implicitly) assumed to be generating stationary data. This was the world that quantitative economic historians occupied and where some remain. However, the message of Granger and Newbold (1974) were simple, yet powerful:

> In our opinion the econometrician can no longer ignore the time series properties of the variables with which he is concerned – except at his peril. The fact that many economic 'levels' are near random walks or integrated processes means that considerable care has to be taken in specifying one's equations.

The seminal time series papers and the research agendas they created have particular relevance for quantitative economic history. Perhaps in more than any other area of applied economics, time series cliometrics utilizes long time spans of data which will often have the characteristics of non-stationarity in levels and/or which might experience structural change, persistence, large 'shocks', large outliers, conditional heteroskedasticity and potentially switching time series properties. The traditional cliometrics topics relating, for example, to 'trends', 'cycles' and 'path dependency' have been both challenged and given new and different meanings as a consequence of the ways we now typically analyse, estimate and test time series data.

Economics and History, First Edition. David Greasley and Les Oxley

Whether or not macroeconomic time series exhibit 'unit roots' still remains a hotly debated issue, see for example, Darne (2009), and research continues to seek out, if not the 'truth', at least the 'data-generating process'. However, whatever the outcome, current cliometrics research involving time series data has been fundamentally changed by the recent developments in time series econometrics.

The purpose of this chapter is to both inform those who may be unfamiliar with the changes in econometric methods that have ensued as a consequence of this econometric revolution of the nature and effects of these changes and also to provide some examples of how these new approaches have been (and might be) used to address some traditional and new areas of cliometrics. The intention is not to provide a full presentation of all the technical properties of each and every test and estimation method, but rather to motivate the need for and use of such tests (and methods) and refer the reader to software where such tests and methods can be applied. Most of the tests and methods discussed below can be easily and robustly implemented via packages such as EViews 7 (2009); STATA 9, 10 or 11 (STATA 9, 10, 11); STAMP and RATS (2010). The excellent user manuals that accompany these packages are also a comprehensive source of technical detail which, on occasion, we will also refer to in this chapter. Exceptions to these intentions relate to sections where we highlight new and emerging areas where, as one might expect, implementation in the packaged software tend to lag the theoretical developments.

The chapter will start by outlining the nature of what we believe are the more important changes in method and interpretation that have occurred as a consequence of the new time series developments (non-stationarity and unit root testing; measures of persistence; cointegration; Granger causality). Examples drawn from the cliometrics literature will complement the more technical aspects of the discussion. Finally some new and emerging areas of time series econometrics will be discussed in relation to their potential applications to cliometrics research including long memory models and applications of graphical methods.

In a single chapter it is impossible to cover all areas of relevance to cliometrics research with time series data. As a consequence, the following areas are excluded or given little emphasis, or simply enter by way of a specific example; spectral-based methods; Bayesian-based methods; non-parametric and semi-parametric approaches.

Prior to the new developments in time series methods, the 'meat and drink' of time series quantitative economic history was the detection and measurement of (deterministic) 'trends' (if only to then subsequently remove them), their potential shifting location based upon tests for 'structural breaks' and the decomposition of data into trends, cycles and possibly deviations from 'long-run trend'. The new econometrics considers stochastic trends versus deterministic trends; nonlinear trends; common trends (and common cycles, see Vahid and Engle, 1993); detrending and trend extraction (Harvey, 1989; Harvey and Jaeger, 1993; Hodrick and Prescott, 1997). Phillips (2005) provides an excellent overview of the challenges faced by the notion of trends, arguing that we have 'only scratched the surface' when it comes to understanding what trends are, how to model them and the consequences of getting that modelling wrong.

The chapter comprises the following sections. In Section 2, we consider the notion and the importance of spurious regression as a precursor to Section 3 which introduces a range of statistical issues relating to ideas of and tests for non-stationarity, cointegration, Granger causality, persistence and structural time series modelling. Section 4 comprises a range of empirical applications which utilize the estimation methods and tests discussed in Section 3. Section 4.1 contains a brief overview of the time series papers and topics published in the two main cliometrics journals, *Explorations in Economic History* (2000–2009) and *Cliometrica* (2007–2009). Sections 4.2–4.5 present applications of such topics as; when did the British Industrial Revolution begin and what were its causes; development blocks and New Zealand economic development, testing for convergence in real GDP per capita; and new results interpreting English real wages data 1264–1913. Section 5 introduces new developments/applications with potential for cliometrics including the mildly explosive process of Phillips and Yu (2009); graphical modelling and implications for causality testing; and long memory estimation. Section 6 offers some final thoughts and Section 7 concludes.

2. Prologue: Spurious Regression

Granger and Newbold (1974) state that:

> It is common to see reported... time series regression equations with apparently high degree of fit as measured by R^2, but with very low reported Durbin Watson statistics. We find this strange given that almost every econometrics textbook warns of the dangers of autocorrelated errors. ...The most extreme example we encountered was an $R^2 = 0.99$ and $d = 0.093$.... There are three main consequences of autocorrelated errors:
>
> 1. Estimates are inefficient
> 2. Forecasts based upon the regression are sub-optimal
> 3. The usual significance tests on the coefficients are invalid.

They then concentrate on point 3 and the ‘discovery’ of spurious relationships – the ‘nonsense correlations’ between a pair of independent $I(1)$ processes reported in Yule (1926). In what was an empirically based paper, they show that with non-stationary series, a high R^2 should not, on the basis of traditional tests, be regarded as evidence of a significant relationship between autocorrelated series. In a practical sense, whenever DW $< R^2$ alarm bells should sound as the classical properties of the error term have been violated with empirically, a highly persistent error equated with highly persistent dependent and independent variables. These highly persistent variables will typically have the property, in levels, of non-stationary series.

Phillips (1986, 1998) provide a theoretical foundation to the empirical examples of Granger and Newbold (1974). Consider a regression of:

$$X_t = \alpha + \beta Y_t + \varepsilon_t \tag{1}$$

where X and Y are independent random walks and ε_t is a zero mean Gaussian white noise process. Under these conditions Phillips shows that the ordinary least squares (OLS) estimates of the model of equation (1) have no interpretable t-statistics for α and β, as the distributions of these statistics diverge as the sample size increases. The estimate of β converges to some random variable whose value changes from sample to sample and the Durbin–Watson statistics for the equation tends to zero.

Rather worryingly, it is not just random walks that can cause spurious regression-type results. Granger *et al.* (2001) consider a variety of independent stationary (but highly persistent) processes and produced some 'worrying' results. For example, if the two processes were AR1, one with a coefficient of 0.5 and the other a coefficient >0.75, then 20–26% of the regressions would spuriously suggest a relationship.

3. Some Statistical Issues

3.1 *Overview*

It has now become standard practice in time series econometrics to use univariate tests to consider the existence of a unit root as a pre-test prior to subsequent estimation or inference. Such a practice is seen as consistent with the guidelines of Granger and Newbold (1974) on the dangers of 'spurious regression' and the need to consider only 'balanced' relationships. Here 'balance' relates to a situation where a relationship to be estimated/tested includes only variables with the same (or lower) orders of integration. Order of integration relates to the numbers of times a series needs to be differenced to produce the property of stationarity. For example, a stationary series is said to be 'integrated of order 0', denoted $I(0)$ as it needs to be differenced 'zero times' to become stationary (as it already is stationary). 'Integrated of order 1' means the series is rendered stationary by differencing 1 times (first differenced); $I(2)$ differenced twice (difference of the difference), etc. The idea of 'balance' is that any attempt to explain (say) an $I(1)$ variable by a series of $I(0)$ would be theoretically impossible (although due to the low power of some of the empirical tests we might produce evidence of such an occurrence – perhaps the source of some assumed 'puzzling results' in econometrics see the *Epilogue* Section 6 below). To be a balanced relationship, the 'order of integration' of the variables in a relationship to be estimated must be of equal orders of integration. In an 'all variables are stationary world' this is ensured by definition, but in a world where some variables are non-stationary in levels, some in differences, some stationary as linear combinations (cointegrated), etc., careful thought and modelling is required.

Below we will provide a very brief overview of unit root tests and developments, including the effects of 'structural breaks' and in Section 4 we consider how the unit root testing approach can be applied to cliometrics research.

3.2 *Plain Vanilla Unit Root Tests*

At the centre of some of the practical implications of the difference between stationary and non-stationary processes is the *persistence* of shocks, i.e. transitory or permanent. One of the simplest ways to model and subsequently *infer* persistence is to investigate the properties of univariate series, in particular, whether they are *trend stationary* (TS) or *difference stationary* (DS). The class of model most commonly used to describe temporary, i.e. non-persistent, deviations about a trend is:

$$y_t = a + bt + u_t \tag{2}$$

where y_t is typically the natural logarithm of the variable of interest, t describes the trend and u_t is a stationary invertible autoregressive moving average (ARMA) process. This process is stationary in levels or TS.

The simplest class of model which captures permanent, i.e. persistent fluctuations is the random walk:

$$y_t = \rho y_{t-1} + e_t \tag{3}$$

The random walk is non-stationary in levels, but stationary when differenced, i.e. DS where in this case $\rho = 1$.

It has become common practice to discriminate between DS and TS processes and hence *infer* persistence or otherwise by using the Dickey–Fuller unit root tests see Dickey and Fuller (1981). The usual form of the test treats DS as the null hypothesis and involves estimation of a regression like equation (4) below which presents the test in its 'augmented' form. Transforming (3) above, now the dependent variable is expressed as a first difference and $\alpha = (\rho - 1)$, giving a null hypothesis (unit root) of Ho: $\alpha = 0$; H_1: $\alpha < 0$,

$$\Delta y_t = \alpha y_{t-1} + \sum_{i=1}^{p} \varphi_i \Delta y_{t-i} + \upsilon_t \tag{4}$$

where υ_t is assumed to be serially uncorrelated. The original, (un)augmented, Dickey–Fuller test simply sets all the lags of the dependent variable equal to zero. Assuming drift adds an intercept, μ, to equation (4) above:

$$\Delta y_t = \mu + \alpha y_{t-1} + \sum_{i=1}^{p} \varphi_i \Delta y_{t-i} + \upsilon_t \tag{4'}$$

and the possibility of a deterministic trend gives:

$$\Delta y_t = \mu + \alpha y_{t-1} + \gamma t + \sum_{i=1}^{p} \varphi_i \Delta y_{t-i} + \upsilon_t \tag{4''}$$

In all cases, however, the hypothesis of interest remains the DS null, $H_0: \alpha = 0$.

As is now well known, under the null hypothesis the usual t-ratios are distributed as Dickey and Fuller τ (1981) rather than Student's t. This is the approach pioneered by Nelson and Plosser (1982) and followed on numerous occasions (see Gaffeo *et al.* (2005) for an excellent, up to date review).

3.2.1 *The Dickey–Fuller Test with Generalized Least Squares Detrending, (ADF-GLS)*

There have been many developments in unit root testing since Dickey and Fuller, including a range of Bayesian-based methods we are not going to consider here. Instead we will present some recent developments in testing for a unit root where, in particular, these new tests can be found in, for example, EViews, STATA and RATS.

Elliott *et al.* (1996) use a modification of the ADF tests where the data are detrended so that explanatory variables are removed from the data prior to running the test regression. This ADF-GLS test is based upon the following regression:

$$\Delta y_t^{\tau} = \alpha y_{t-1} + \sum_{i=1}^{k} \varphi_i \Delta y_{t-i}^{\tau} + u_t \tag{5}$$

where u_t is assumed *iid* $N(0, \sigma^2)$ and Δy_t^{τ} is the locally detrended process. Under the null hypothesis, H_0: $\alpha = 0$, the ADF-GLS τ is the t-ratio on α with rejection inferred if it is significantly less than zero when compared with the response surface estimates in Cheung and Lai (1995).

3.2.2 *The Phillips–Perron (PP) Test*

The size distortions in the original DF test due to serial correlation in the error term was the reason for the adoption of lagged dependent variables in its 'augmented' form of the DF test, the ADF. This augmented form of the DF remains the most common unit root test used in practice.

Phillips and Perron (1988) take a different approach to the potential effects of serial correlation – they use semi-parametric estimation of the long-run effects of the short run dynamics. In particular, consider the auxiliary regression:

$$\Delta y_t = \mu + \alpha y_{t-1} + \gamma_t + \eta_t \tag{6}$$

where $\eta_t = \phi(L)\varepsilon_t$, $\varepsilon_t \sim$ *iid* $N(0, 1)$. If we define the residuals from the OLS regression of y_t on a constant and t, the Phillips and Perron test statistic can be defined as:

$$Z_t = \hat{\sigma}_{\xi}\hat{\omega}^{-1}t_{\alpha} - \hat{\lambda}\left[\hat{\omega}\left(T^{-2}\sum_{t=2}^{\hat{T}} D_{t-1}^2\right)^{1/2}\right]^{-1}$$

where ω^2 and λ are nuisance parameters consistently estimated by applying the Newey and West (1987) estimator. Under the null hypothesis of a unit root, Z_t converges in the limit to the Dickey–Fuller distribution, although they may differ in finite samples. Empirically, however, Schwert (1989) showed that Z_t is biased towards rejection of the null if the error term is an MA(p) process with negative first-order serial correlation. This is something to be considered in empirical applications.

3.2.3 *The Kwiatkowski, Phillips, Schmidt and Shin (KPSS) Test*

In contrast to the tests considered above, these authors assume that the null hypothesis of the univariate process is stationarity. The test is based on modelling the series as the sum of one stationary and one non-stationary component and testing the null hypothesis that the variance of the non-stationary component is zero. The TS null is rejected when the KPSS statistic is larger than the approximate critical values tabulated in Kwiatkowski *et al.* (1992). Given the null of stationarity, this test is often uses as part of a 'battery' of tests to consider the robustness of other (non-stationary null) test results.

3.2.4 *Ng and Perron Tests*

Ng and Perron (2001) develop four test statistics based upon the Dickey–Fuller GLS approach with detrended data. In particular, they consider two variants of Phillips and Perron (1988), the Bhargava (1986) R_1 statistic and the Elliott, Rothemberg and Stock, Point Optimal statistic. For further details and implementation, see for example, EViews 7.

3.3 *Unit Roots with Exogenous or Endogenous Change*

Perron (1989) demonstrated how structural breaks in a series can lead to biased unit root test results (in favour of DS). He uses the idea of exogenously determined breaks informed by prior knowledge. Such exogenous assumptions have effects on the timing and properties of the critical values that are used to compare with the test results. Zivot and Andrews (1992) allow for endogenously determined breaks chosen on the basis of particular statistical criteria in an economically atheoretical way. Their critical values are likewise affected by the testing methods and in the original form the number of breaks permitted is limited.

Ignoring the presence of breaks, when they actually occur can lead to spurious non-rejection of the null hypothesis of a unit root. The main differences in the testing procedures proposed by Perron (1989), and subsequently Zivot and Andrews (1992), over the original Dickey–Fuller approach, involves the addition of various dummy variables to equation (4) to capture changes in the intercept and/or time trend and the use of recursive estimation methods, i.e.

$$y_t = \mu + \rho y_{t-1} + \beta t + \gamma DT + \theta DU + \sum_{i=1}^{p} \varphi_i \Delta y_{t-i} + u_t \tag{7}$$

where DU $=$ 1 if $t >$ TB, 0 otherwise and DT $= t$ if $t >$ TB and 0 otherwise and TB refers to the time of the break.

In the original Perron formulation, the variables DU and DT were included to capture the possibility of 'crashes' (DU) trend changes (DT) and joint crashes and trend changes (DU and DT). In the empirical section below we consider the possibility of 'jumps' where the coefficient attached to DU could be positive rather than negative as in the case of a 'crash'. Likewise a joint 'jump' and trend change (denoted j&t), would involve the inclusion of both DU and DT in the equation. Tests of the null hypothesis of DS still involve $H_0 : \rho = 1, \beta = 0$ although critical values are now given in Perron (1989) for exogenous breaks or Zivot and Andrews (1992) for endogenously located breaks.

The original motivation for the Perron (1989) approach and modifications by Zivot and Andrews (1992) was in response to the lack of power to reject the null of a unit root in the presence of structural change. However, Perron and Zivot and Andrews are only one-break models. If the data-generating process involves more than one break as might be expected in the very long time series often used in cliometrics, we are left with the same problem the original approach was attempting to remove biased unit root test results (in favour of DS). Vogelsang (1997), presents results showing the loss of power that ensures when using a one-break model in a world of two breaks. Empirically, Ben-David and Papell (1998) present evidence of more than one break and Lumsdaine and Papell (1997), discussed below, consider a generalization of the endogenous break-point procedure of Zivot and Andrews (1992).

3.3.1 *Lumsdaine–Papell Test*

The Lumsdaine and Papell (1997) test extends the Zivot and Andrews test equation (7) above, by adding in additional dummy variables for intercept and slope changes as shown below:

$$y_t = \mu + \rho y_{t-1} + \beta t + \gamma DT_1 + \theta DU_2 + \gamma DT_2 + \theta DU_1 + \sum_{i=1}^{p} \varphi_i \Delta y_{t-i} + u_t \tag{8}$$

As in the single break tests of Zivot and Andrews, three types of models can be considered, but now there are more variations including two breaks in the intercept; two breaks in the slope, etc. Being a variation of a standard unit root test, the t-statistic on ρ is compared to the relevant critical value found in Lumsdaine and Papell (1997).

3.3.2 *Lee–Strazicich (2001, 2003) Tests*

Lee and Strazicich (2001, 2003) take a similar approach to Lumsdaine and Papell (1997), but their test statistic uses a minimum Lagrange multiplier, *LM,* test criteria. This approach is based upon the results from Schmidt and Phillips (1992) on the potential for unit root tests to report spurious rejections when the null includes a genuine structural break. The Lee and Strazicich *LM*-based test therefore starts with an assumption that the null hypothesis is a unit root with up to two breaks and as should be clear, the t-statistic to test the null arises via a *LM* principle based upon the score. The ability to permit (up to) two breaks in the null and two breaks in the level or slope of the alternative makes the approach particularly flexible and attractive. This test procedure was recently utilized by Greasley *et al.* (2010) to consider the empirics of long-run growth.

3.4 *Panel Unit Root Tests*

It is now well know that conventional univariate ADF unit root tests often tend to suffer from low power when applied to series of only moderate length. The idea of panel-based unit root testing is to pool the data across individual members of a panel to address this issue by making available considerably more information regarding the series under investigation. Panel unit root ADF techniques are intended to allow researchers to selectively pool information regarding common long-run relationships from across the panel while allowing the associated short-run dynamics and fixed effects to be heterogeneous across different members of the panel see Maddala and Wu (1999). We consider below three common forms of panel unit root tests, Levine *et al.* (2002, hereafter LLC), Im *et al.* (2003, hereafter IPS) and Hadri (2000).

LLC propose an ADF test with a panel setting that restricts parameters γ_i by assuming them identical across cross-sections as follows:

$$\Delta y_{it} = \alpha_i + \gamma_i y_{it-1} + \sum_{j=1}^{k} \alpha_j \Delta y_{it-j} + e_{it} \tag{9}$$

where $t = 1, 2, \ldots, T$ refers to the time periods and $i = 1, 2, \ldots, N$ refers the numbers in the panel. The null hypothesis of LLC test is $\gamma_i = \gamma = 0$ for all i indicating that the panel data are non-stationary while the alternative hypothesis is $\gamma_1 = \gamma_2 = \cdots = \gamma < 0$. This test is based on the statistics, $t_y = \hat{\gamma}/s.e.(\hat{\gamma})$.

It is clear that the null hypothesis of the LLC test is very restrictive and the test of IPS (2003) relaxes this assumption by allowing γ to vary across i under the alternative hypothesis. The null hypothesis of the IPS test is therefore that $\gamma_i = 0$ for all i, while the alternative hypothesis is $\gamma_i < 0$ for all i. The IPS test then uses the mean-group approach and obtains the average of t_y to compute the following statistic:

$$\tilde{Z} = \sqrt{N}(\bar{t} - E(\bar{t}))/\sqrt{\mathrm{var}(\bar{t})}$$

where $\bar{t} = (1/N)\sum_{i=1}^{N} t_{y_i} E(\bar{t})$ and $\mathrm{Var}(\bar{t})$ represents the mean and variance of each t_y, respectively. The statistic $\tilde{Z}$ converges to a *Normal* distribution, and we can compute the significance level in a simple way.

By contrast, Hadri (2000) argues that the null hypothesis should be reversed to be stationarity in order to produce a test with more power. His *LM* statistics is given by the follow expression:

$$LM = \frac{1}{N}\sum_{i=1}^{N}\left(\frac{T^{-2}\sum_{t=1}^{T}\sum_{j=1}^{t}\hat{\varepsilon}_{ij}}{\hat{\sigma}_{\varepsilon}^{2}}\right) \tag{10}$$

where $\hat{\sigma}_{\varepsilon}^{2}$ is the consistent Newey and West (1987) estimate of the long-run variance of disturbance terms (ε_{ij}).

Panel-based tests, which are now available via, for example, EViews 7 include; Levine *et al.* (2002), Breitung (2000), Im *et al.* (2003), Fisher-type tests using ADF and PP tests (Maddala and Wu, 1999; Choi, 2001) and Hadri (2000). A summary of some aspects of these tests is provided below. All use lags as corrections for autocorrelation, as with the ADF, and permit the option of fixed effects; individual effects and individual trends where relevant to the tests:

Levin *et al.* (2002); H_0: unit root; H_1: no unit root.
Breitung (2000); H_0: unit root; H_1: no unit root.
Im *et al.* (2003); H_0: unit root; H_1: Some cross-sections without a unit root.
Maddala and Wu, Fisher-ADF (1999); H_0: unit root; H_1: Some cross-sections without a unit root.
Maddala and Wu, Fisher-PP (1999); H_0: unit root; H_1: Some cross-sections without a unit root.
Hadri (2000); H_0: No unit root; H_1: unit root.

3.5 *Direct Measures of Persistence*

One of the possible outcomes of testing for whether a series is a DS versus TS processes is to infer that that shocks implied by the process will have either infinite or zero persistence, respectively. Campbell and Mankiw (1987) and Cochrane (1988), amongst others consider this as extreme and provide methods to measure the actual *persistence* of shocks, i.e. how much does a one-unit shock to output (say), affect forecasts into the future? Furthermore, Cochrane (1988) demonstrates how any DS process can be represented as the sum of a stationary and random walk component where the issue of persistence revolves around the *size of the random walk element*. In particular assume y is a linear DS process, i.e.

$$\Delta y_t = (1 - L)y_t = \mu + A(L)\varepsilon_t = \mu + \sum_{j=0}^{\infty} aj\varepsilon t - j \qquad (11)$$

Utilizing the Beveridge and Nelson (1981) decomposition, let

$$y_t = z_t + c_t \qquad (12)$$

where

$$z_t = \mu + z_{t-1} + \left(\sum_{j=0}^{\infty} aj\right)\varepsilon_j$$

$$-c_t = \left(\sum_{j=1}^{\infty} aj\right)\varepsilon_t + \left(\sum_{j=2}^{\infty} aj\right)\varepsilon_{t-1} + \left(\sum_{j=3}^{\infty} aj\right)\varepsilon_{t-2} + \cdots$$

Here z_t is to be considered the permanent and c_t, the temporary component of y_t. Long-term forecasts of y_t are unaffected by c_t, the temporary component.

Cochrane (1988) considers the innovation variance of the random walk component as a natural measure of the importance of the random walk element. He gives two equivalent formulations of this measure. The variance of the random walk element $\sigma^2_{\Delta z}$ is given by:

$$\sigma^2_{\Delta z} = \left(\sum_{j=0}^{\infty} aj\right)^2 \sigma^2_{\varepsilon} = |A(1)|^2\sigma^2_{\varepsilon}$$

Equivalently, $\sigma^2_{\Delta z}$ is equal to the spectral density of Δy_t at frequency zero, i.e.

$$\sigma^2_{\Delta z} = \left(\sum_{j=0}^{\infty} aj\right)^2 \sigma^2_{\varepsilon} = S_{\Delta y}\left(e^{-i0}\right)\sigma^2_{\varepsilon}$$

which can be estimated by the Bartlett estimator. However, as demonstrated by Cochrane (1988), the Bartlett estimator will be biased in small samples where the bias can be corrected by multiplying the estimates by $T/(T - k)$, where T is the effective sample size and k the window size. One of the main advantages of the $\sigma^2_{\Delta z}$ measure over parsimonious ARMA representations, is that it captures all the effects of a unit root on the behaviour of a series in a finite sample. Notice that tests of TS in this framework involve a test of $\sigma^2_{\Delta z} = 0$. However, further note that the size of the random walk element is a continuous choice where series can be more fruitfully categorized by the size of $\sigma^2_{\Delta z}$ or the *persistence* of y.

However, the persistence measure is derived assuming an underlying linear model, (without discontinuities). If y_t were a pure random walk, the variance of the kth difference would grow linearly with k. If it were TS, however, the variance of the kth difference approaches a constant. Non-linearities in the underlying series would invalidate this relationship and the relevance of the Cochrane-type persistence measure.

In circumstances when breaks in the series might be expected the following approach can be adopted; firstly check the order of integration of the data using standard or extended versions of the Augmented Dickey–Fuller test. If the series is TS without breaks measure the degree of persistence using the methods discussed above, however, if it is TS with breaks use the timing of the breaks, as a first approximation, to distinguish between persistence measure periods. If it is DS after testing for breaks, present persistence measures for the full and, where necessary sub-samples. Check the sensitivity of the results to specific sample periods and investigate the existence of significant non-linear elements, (see below Section 4.2 and Greasley and Oxley (1997d, 1998a, 1999) for examples).

3.6 *Cointegration*

In their classic paper, Engle and Granger (1987) show that a linear combination of two or more $I(1)$ series may be stationary, or $I(0)$. In this case, the series are said to be *cointegrated*. The linear combination, if it exists, defines a cointegrating equation with the resulting cointegrating vector of weights characterizing the long-run relationship between the variables. Stated more formally:

> The components of the vector $x_t = (x_{1t}, x_{2t}, x_{3t}, \ldots x_{nt})'$ are said to be cointegrated of order d, b and denoted $x_t \sim CI(d, b)$ if the following two

conditions hold: i) All elements of x_t are integrated of order d and ii) there exists a vector (the cointegrating vector) $\beta = (\beta_1, \beta_2, \beta_3, \ldots \beta_n)$ such that the linear combination $\beta x_t = \beta_1 x_{1t} + \beta_2 x_{2t} + \beta_3 x_{3t} + \cdots \beta_n x_{nt}$ is integrated of a lower order $(d - b)$ where $b > 0$.

3.6.1 *Single Equation Engle–Granger (1987) 2 Step Methods (Residual-Based Tests)*

This original form of testing for cointegration is effectively a test of the time series properties of the residuals in an (OLS) regression of the levels of the variables where the null hypothesis is of no-cointegration (no significant linear combination).

Consider the following:

$$y_t = \beta_0 + \beta_1 x_t + e_t \tag{13}$$

where x and y are variables of interest; the β are coefficients to be estimated and e_t a random disturbance term. If x and y are non-stationary $I(1)$, they have no tendency to revert to the mean, long-run level. However, if x and y are cointegrated, that is a linear combination of x and y are stationary, or $I(0)$, then we can think of the relationship above as exhibiting a long-run equilibrium.

The nature of the residual-based cointegraion tests is that we can rewrite equation (13) above as:

$$e_t = y_t - \beta_0 - \beta_1 x_t \tag{14}$$

and if this linear combination of integrated variables is cointegrated, then e_t must be $I(0)$ or stationary (this is another example of the 'balance' property discussed above). Engle–Granger *two-step methods*, therefore involve OLS regressions of equations like equation (13) above (*step one*) followed by a test of the order of integration of the error term from that equation (e_t) as *step two*. Because the residual is derived from the step-one process it has the property of a generated regressor (see Pagan, 1984; Oxley and McAleer, 1993) and the critical values of the ADF test need to account for this property. Software packages like EViews take account of this automatically, otherwise incorrect inference could result. Variations of the *residual-based* approach include Phillips and Ouliaris (1990) residual-based tests, Hansen (1992) and Park (1992).

If cointegration exists, and it should be stressed that not all integrated variables are cointegrated, see Granger (1986), not only is OLS an appropriate method to use it also has the property of *superconsistency* such that OLS estimates converge to the true value at the rate n compared to the usual rate $\sqrt{n}$ where n is the sample size.

If we consider a special case of equation (14) above where $e_t = 0$, then effectively the relationship estimated would be in long-run equilibrium. However, typically $e_t \neq 0$ and the term represents the *equilibrium error* often referred to as the *error-correction term*. Note, that this is captured as the second stage of the cointegration testing procedure. The error-correction term plays an important role in the *error (or equilibrium) correction models* (*ECM*) which involves estimation of the short-run dynamics consistent with the long-run equilibrium captured by the cointegrating relationship. If cointegration exists between the $I(1)$, integrated variables, the error-correction term (e_t) must be $I(0)$. To be a valid ECM model of the short-run dynamics, therefore all the other variables in an ECM must be stationary. As the long-run model involves $I(1)$ in levels variables, the ECM will typically include variables in first differences for example:

$$\Delta y_t = \alpha + \beta_1 \Delta x_t + \beta_2 \Delta x_{t-1} + \beta_3 \Delta z_{t-2} + \beta_4 e_{t-1} + \zeta_t \tag{15}$$

where equation (15) may have been derived as part of a *General-to-Specific* search process yielding a relationship with an error term ζ_t with appropriate properties. Note e_t enters with a lag and an expectation that $\beta_4 < 0$. As e_{t-1} has been derived from the long-run cointegrating model, it effectively links the long-run and short run aspects of the relationship. For discussions on alternative ways of constructing and interpreting the ECM see Muscatelli and Hurn (1992).

3.6.2 *Johansen Maximum Likelihood Estimation-Based Cointegration Methods*

As can be seen from the discussion above, Engle–Granger type methods for establishing the existence (or otherwise) of cointegration are simple, based upon an OLS regression of current valued variables, and powerful, having the property of superconsistency should cointegration be established. However, the EG methods have a number of shortcomings. The first is that the normalization can matter. Normalization here effectively means 'which variable is on the left hand side'. Consider our relationship described by equation (13) above.

As written we have chosen to assume y is the variable explained by x. If x and y were $I(1)$, but cointegrated, it should not matter whether we estimate $y = f(x)$ or $x = f(y)$ as the test for cointegration is based upon the e_t. This is the case asymptotically, but not necessarily in small samples. If we extend the relationship to include other variables the potential problem is expanded. Furthermore, the EG approach can only identify (up to) one cointegrating relationship. This is not a problem in the bivariate case, but again once we go beyond two variables the potential to identify more than one significant cointegrating relationship is possible. Whether this means there are more than one 'economic' equilibrium is a mute point and requires careful consideration of the 'economic sense' of the linear combination(s) identified by the testing procedure.

In contrast to Engle–Granger type methods, the Johansen (1988, 1995) approach utilizes a multivariate model where the sensitivity to normalization problem outlined above, disappears. At this stage it is also worth stressing that cointegration identifies linear combinations of variables integrated of a lower order. If we have *two* variables this implies at most, *one* (unique) cointegrating relationship; if we have *three* variables at most *two* cointegrating relationships; *four* variables at most *three* cointegrating relationships; k variables at most $k - 1$ cointegrating relationships, etc. If we establish via testing, k *significant* cointegrating relationships from k variables then it says *any* linear combination of the k variables is stationary which implies all the k variables are in fact stationary in levels (not non-stationary as thought or suggested by univariate pre-tests)! Of course, it should be stressed again that there may be no significant cointegrating relationships at all and in this case there is no tendency for the variables in the model to move together over time as the equilibrium interpretation of the mathematical notion of cointegration would imply.

The Johansen approach utilizes this rank property as the basis for its tests of the existence of cointegration, in particular consider a multivariate version of the ADF equation:

$$x_t = A_1 x_{t-1} + A_2 x_{t-2} + A_3 x_{t-3} + \cdots A_p x_{t-p} + \upsilon_t \tag{16}$$

Defining this in vector form so that $x_t = (x_{1t}, x_{2t}, x_{3t}, \ldots x_{nt})'$ we can rewrite it as

$$\Delta x_t = \pi x_{t-1} + \sum_{i=1}^{p-1} \pi_i \Delta x_{t-i} + \upsilon_t \tag{17}$$

where $\pi = -(1 - \sum_{i=1}^{p} A_i)$ and $\pi_i = -\sum_{j=i+1}^{p} A_j$.

Here we can now see how the rank of π is crucial in determining the number of cointegating relationships and the issue of potential neglected stationarity. If the rank of $\pi = 0$ then no significant cointegrating relationship exists. If the rank of $\pi = n$, then any linear combination is stationary. If the rank $= 1$, a single cointegrating relationship exists and πx_{t-1} represents the error correction term, whereas if the rank of $\pi > 0$, $<n$, then multiple cointegrating relationships exist.

Testing for the number of significant cointegrating relationships using the Johansen approach involves checking the significance of the characteristic roots of π. Using the property that the rank of a matrix is equal to the number of characteristic roots that differ from zero, Johansen proposes two tests for cointegration; one based upon the trace and one on the maximum eigenvalue. In particular, if we denote the ordered n characteristic roots of the matrix π are denoted $\lambda_1 > \lambda_2 > \lambda_3 > \ldots \lambda_n$ the trace test is defined as:

$$\lambda_{\text{trace}}(r) = -T \sum_{i=r+1}^{n} \ln(1 - \hat{\lambda}_i) \tag{18}$$

and the maximum eigenvalue as:

$$\lambda_{\max}(r, r+1) = -T(\ln(1 - \hat{\lambda}_{r+1}) \tag{19}$$

The null hypotheses of the two differ in that the *trace* tests whether the number of distinct eigenvalues is $\leq r$; whereas the maximum eigenvalue tests the null of r cointegrating relationships against $r + 1$. In a practical setting, one may find that the trace test results may find 'more evidence' of a (or several) significant cointegrating relationships than the maximum eigenvalue test. Therefore in analysing and assessing empirical research, one should be careful to consider which test(s) have been reported and whether (if both trace and eigenvalue are reported) they support or contradict.

3.6.3 *Panel-Based Cointegration Methods*

Pedroni (1999, 2004) develops a number of *panel-based tests* for cointegration. Pedroni (1999) allows for cross-sectional interdependence with different individual effects. If the panel data follow an $I(1)$ process, the Pedroni (1999, 2004) panel cointegration model can be applied to ascertain whether a cointegration relationship exists. Pedroni (1999) suggests the following time series panel expression:

$$y_{it} = \alpha_i + \gamma_i t + X_{it}\beta_{it} + e_{it} \tag{20}$$

where y_{it} and X_{it} are the observable variables with dimension of $(N * T) \times 1$ and $(N * T) \times m$, respectively. He develops the asymptotic and finite-sample properties of the test statistics to examine the null hypothesis of *non-cointegration* in a panel. The tests allow for heterogeneity among individual members of the panel, including heterogeneity in both the long-run cointegration vectors and in their dynamics.

Pedroni develops two types of *residual-based* tests. For his first type, four tests are distributed as standard Normal asymptotically and are based on pooling the residuals of the regression for the within-group. The four tests in this class are: the panel υ-statistic; the panel ρ-statistic; the panel PP-statistic (or t-statistic, non-parametric) and the panel ADF-statistic (or t-statistic, parametric). For the group of second type tests, three are also distributed as standard Normal asymptotically, but are based on pooling the residuals for the between group. The three tests in this class are: the group ρ-statistic; the group PP-statistic (or t-statistic, non-parametric) and the group ADF-statistic (or t-statistic, parametric). Pedroni (1999) presents the following heterogeneous panel cointegration statistics:

$$\text{Panel } \upsilon\text{-statistic}: \quad Z_{\hat{\upsilon}} = \left(\sum_{i=1}^{N} \sum_{t=1}^{T} \hat{L}_{11i}^{-2} \hat{e}_{it-1}^{2} \right) \tag{21}$$

$$\text{Panel } \rho\text{-statistic}: \quad Z_{\hat{\rho}} = \left(\sum_{i=1}^{N} \sum_{t=1}^{T} \hat{L}_{11i}^{-2} \hat{e}_{it-1}^{2} \right)^{-1} \sum_{i=1}^{N} \sum_{t=1}^{T} \hat{L}_{11i}^{-2} (\hat{e}_{it-1} \Delta \hat{e}_{it} - \hat{\lambda}_i) \tag{22}$$

$$\text{Panel } t\text{-statistic (non-parametric)}: Z_t = \left(\hat{\sigma}^2 \sum_{i=1}^{N} \sum_{t=1}^{T} \hat{L}_{11i}^{-2} \hat{e}_{it-1}^{2} \right)^{-1/2} \times \sum_{i=1}^{N} \sum_{t=1}^{T} \hat{L}_{11i}^{-2} (\hat{e}_{it-1} \Delta \hat{e}_{it} - \hat{\lambda}_i) \tag{23}$$

$$\text{Panel } t\text{-statistic (parametric)}: \quad Z_t^{*} = \left(\hat{s}^{*2} \sum_{i=1}^{N} \sum_{t=1}^{T} \hat{L}_{11i}^{-2} \hat{e}_{it-1}^{*2} \right)^{-1/2} \sum_{i=1}^{N} \sum_{t=1}^{T} \hat{L}_{11i}^{-2} \hat{e}_{it-1}^{*} \Delta \hat{e}_{it}^{*} \tag{24}$$

And the following heterogeneous group-mean panel cointegration statistics:

$$\text{Group } \rho\text{-statistic}: \quad \tilde{Z}_{\hat{\rho}} = \sum_{i=1}^{N} \left(\sum_{t=1}^{T} \hat{e}_{it-1}^2 \right)^{-1} \sum_{t=1}^{T} (\hat{e}_{it-1} \Delta \hat{e}_{it} - \hat{\lambda}_i) \tag{25}$$

$$\text{Group } t\text{-statistic (non-parametric)}: \quad \tilde{Z}_t = \sum_{i=1}^{N} \left(\hat{\sigma}_i^2 \sum_{t=1}^{T} \hat{e}_{it-1}^2 \right)^{-1/2} \sum_{t=1}^{T} (\hat{e}_{it-1} \Delta \hat{e}_{it} - \hat{\lambda}_i) \tag{26}$$

$$\text{Group } t\text{-statistic (parametric)}: \quad \tilde{Z}_t^* = \sum_{i=1}^{N} \left(\sum_{t=1}^{T} \hat{s}_i^2 \hat{e}_{it-1}^{*2} \right)^{-1/2} \sum_{t=1}^{T} (\hat{e}_{it-1}^* \Delta \hat{e}_{it}^*) \tag{27}$$

where $\hat{e}_{it}$ is the estimated residual from equation (20) above and $\hat{L}_{11i}^{-2}$ is the estimated long-run covariance matrix for $\hat{e}_{it}$. Similarly, $\hat{\sigma}_i^2$ and $\hat{s}_i^2$ ($\hat{s}_i^{*2}$) are, respectively, the long-run and contemporaneous variances for individual i. The other terms are defined in Pedroni (1999) with the appropriate lag length determined by the Newey–West method. All seven tests are distributed as standard Normal asymptotically. This requires standardization based on the moments of the underlying Brownian motion function. The panel υ-statistic is a one-sided test where large positive values reject the null of no cointegration. The remaining statistics diverge to negative infinitely, which means that large negative values imply rejection of the null. The critical values are also tabulated in Pedroni (1999).

The statistics above are based on estimators that simply average the individually estimated coefficients for each member, and each of these tests is able to accommodate individual specific short-run dynamics, individual specific fixed effects and deterministic trends, as well as individual specific slope coefficients (Pedroni, 2004). The number of observations available is greatly increased in a panel framework when testing the stationarity of the residual series in a levels regression and this can substantially increases the power of the cointegration tests see, Rapach and Wohar (2004).

3.7 *Granger-Type Causality*

3.7.1 *Conventional Granger-Type Tests*

Many tests of causality have been derived and implemented, including Granger (1969, 1988), Sims (1972) and Geweke *et al.* (1983). We are not going to debate here whether Granger causality tests 'causality', but note that Granger-type causality tests are tests of temporal ordering. Granger showed via his *Representation Theorem* that a bivariate cointegrated system must have causal ordering in at least one direction. These inherent links between Granger causality and cointegration have been exploited to formulate the current suite of tests for causality used in time series econometrics. The tests are all based upon the estimation of autoregressive or vector autoregressive (VAR), models involving (say), the variables X and Y, together with significance tests for subsets of the variables.

Although it is quite common to test for the direction of causality, the conclusions drawn in some studies are fragile for two important reasons. Firstly, the choice of lag lengths in the autoregressive or VAR models is often ad hoc, see for example, Jung and Marshall (1985), Chow (1987) and Hsiao (1987), although the length of lag chosen will critically affect results. Secondly, in the absence of evidence on cointegration, 'spurious' causality may be identified.

Engle and Granger (1987), show that if two series are individually $I(1)$, and cointegrated, a causal relationship must exist in at least one direction. Furthermore, the Granger representation theorem demonstrates how to model cointegrated $I(1)$ series in the form of a VAR model. In particular, the VAR can be constructed either in terms of the levels of the data, the $I(1)$ variables; or in terms of their first differences, the $I(0)$ variables, with the addition of an error-correction term (ECM) to capture the short-run dynamics. If the data are $I(1)$, but not cointegrated, causality tests cannot validly be derived unless the data are transformed to induce stationarity which will typically involve tests of hypotheses relating to the growth or first difference of variables (if they are defined in logarithms), and not their levels. To summarize, causality tests can be constructed in three ways, two of which require the presence of cointegration. The three different approaches are defined below.

The *first stage* in testing for causality involves testing for the order of integration. Conditional on the outcome of such tests, the *second stage* involves investigating bivariate cointegration utilizing the Johansen maximum likelihood approach. If bivariate cointegration exists then either unidirectional or bidirectional Granger causality must also exist, although in finite samples there is no guarantee that the tests will identify it. On the basis of the bivariate cointegration results, a multivariate model of cointegration may then be investigated to examine interaction effects, taking the error term from this cointegrating regression as a measure of the ECM term to capture the short run dynamics of the model. The *third stage* (or second if bivariate cointegration is rejected), involves constructing standard Granger-type causality tests, augmented where appropriate with a lagged error-correction term, see Giles *et al.* (1993).

The *three-stage procedure* leads to *three* alternative approaches for testing causality. In the case of cointegrated data, Granger causality tests may use the $I(1)$ data because of the superconsistency properties of estimation. With two variables X and Y:

$$X = \alpha + \sum_{i=1}^{m} \beta i X_{t-i} + \sum_{j=1}^{n} \gamma_j Y_{t-j} + u_t \tag{28}$$

$$Y = a + \sum_{i=1}^{q} bi Y_{t-i} \sum_{j=1}^{r} cj X_{t-j} + v_t \tag{29}$$

where u_t and v_t are zero-mean, serially uncorrelated, random disturbances and the lag lengths m, n, q and r are assigned on the basis of minimizing some form of Information Criteria.

Secondly Granger causality tests with cointegrated variables may utilize the $I(0)$ data, including an error-correction mechanism term, i.e.

$$\Delta X = \alpha + \sum_{i=1}^{m} \beta i \Delta X_{t-i} + \sum_{j=1}^{n} \gamma j \Delta Y_{t-j} + \delta ECM_{t-1} + u_t \qquad (28')$$

$$\Delta Y = a + \sum_{i=1}^{q} bi \Delta Y_{t-i} + \sum_{j=1}^{r} cj \Delta X_{t-j} + dECM_{t-1} + v_t \qquad (29')$$

where the error-correction term, derived from the cointegrating relationship, is denoted ECM.

Thirdly if the data are $I(1)$, but not cointegrated valid Granger-type tests require transformations to induce stationarity. In this case the tests deploy formulations like equations (28′) and (29′) above, but *without* the ECM term, i.e. equations (28″) and (29″) below.

$$\Delta X = \alpha + \sum_{i=1}^{m} \beta i \Delta X_{t-i} + \sum_{j=1}^{n} \gamma j \Delta Y_{t-j} + u_t \qquad (28'')$$

$$\Delta Y = a + \sum_{i=1}^{q} bi \Delta Y_{t-i} + \sum_{j=1}^{r} cj \Delta X_{t-j} + v_t \qquad (29'')$$

Granger causality tests based upon equations (28) and (29) involve the following:

Y Granger causes (GC), X if, $H_0 : \gamma_1 = \gamma_2 = \gamma_3 = \cdots = \gamma_n = 0$ is rejected against the alternative $H_1 :=$ at least one $\gamma_j \neq 0$, $j = 1, \ldots, n$.

X GC Y if, $H_0 : c_1 = c_2 = c_3 = \cdots = c_r = 0$ is rejected against the alternative $H_1 :=$ at least one $c_j \neq 0$, $j = 1, \ldots, r$.

For equations (28′) and (29′) Granger causality tests involve the following:

ΔY GC, ΔX if, $H_0 : \gamma_1 = \gamma_2 = \gamma_3 = \cdots = \gamma_n = 0$ is rejected against the alternative, $H_1 :=$ at least one $\gamma_j \neq 0$, $j = 1, \ldots, n$, *or* $\delta \neq 0$, (see Granger, 1986).

ΔX GC ΔY if, $H_0 : c_1 = c_2 = c_3 = \cdots = c_r = 0$ is rejected against the alternative $H_1 :=$ at least one $c_j \neq 0$, $j = 1, \ldots, r$, *or* $d \neq 0$, (see Granger, 1986).

Notice in this case however, with the possibility of causality being inferred from the significance of d or δ alone that the causal nexus is altered, i.e. causality runs from the past *level* to the current rate of *change* without any lagged change effects.

For *non-cointegrated* data (X and Y, $I(1)$), Granger causality tests involve tests based upon equations (28″) and (29″), in particular:

ΔY GC, ΔX if, $H_0 : \gamma_1 = \gamma_2 = \gamma_3 = \cdots = \gamma_n = 0$ is rejected against the alternative, $H_1 :=$ at least one $\gamma_j \neq 0$, $j = 1, \ldots, n$.

ΔX GC ΔY if, $H_0 : c_1 = c_2 = c_3 = \cdots = c_r = 0$ is rejected against the alternative $H_1 :=$ at least one $c_j \neq 0$, $j = 1, \ldots, r$.

Given the inclusion of lagged dependent variables in equations (28) and (29), (28′) and (29′) and (28″) and (29″), tests of the hypotheses utilizing OLS results require the modified Wald statistics, nF_1 and rF_2, distributed (asymptotically) as χ^2 with n and r degrees of freedom, where F_1 and F_2 are the 'normal' F statistics of the joint significance of the γ's and c's, respectively. Furthermore, in the case of equations (28) and (29) we invoke the results of Lutkepohl and Leimers (1992) and Toda and Phillips (1991), which show that in bivariate non-stationary cointegrated models the Wald test will have the usual asymptotic χ^2 distribution.

In addition to the Wald test of zero restrictions, and 't'-tests on d and δ where appropriate, the final prediction error (FPE) can be used as an additional *indication* of causality, i.e. if FPE(m^*, n^*) < FPE(m^*), it implies *Y Granger causes X* (or ΔY GC ΔX, where appropriate), likewise for r^* and q^*, see Giles *et al.* (1993) for more details. All three criteria are used in the empirical section of the paper.

3.7.2 *Toda and Phillips (1991) – Type Tests*

Under conditions of cointegration, the ECM-based tests discussed above involve some form of two-step process, i.e. test for cointegration and retain the residuals as the ECM term and utilize this variable in the second stage either as a direct test of causality following Granger (1986) and Engle and Granger (1987), or as part of the modelling strategy when testing the significance of the VAR terms.

In Toda and Phillips (1991), – henceforth TP – the authors consider a different, single-stage estimation, but (potentially), sequential testing, framework as well as a critical review of previous tests.

Consider the n-vector time series y_t generated by the kth order VAR:

$$y_t = J(L)y_{t-1} + u_t \qquad t = -k+1, \ldots, T \tag{30}$$

where L is the lag operator defined as, $J(L) = \sum_{i=1}^{k} J_i L^{i-1}$ and u_t an n-dimensional random vector. Making sufficient assumptions to ensure that y_t is cointegrated, CI(1,1) with r cointegrating vectors ($r \geq 1$), see TP for details, rewrite equation (30) in the equivalent ECM form:

$$\Delta y_t = J^*(L)\Delta y_{t-1} + \Gamma A' y_{t-1} + u_t \tag{31}$$

where $J^*(L)$ is defined analogous to the expression above.

Following Sims *et al.* (1990), consider a test of whether the last $n3$ elements of y_t cause the first $n1$ elements of the vector, where y_t is partitioned as:

$$y_t = \begin{pmatrix} y_{1t} \\ y_{2t} \\ y_{3t} \end{pmatrix} \begin{matrix} n_1 \\ n_2 \\ n_3 \end{matrix} \tag{32}$$

(1) *Levels VAR*

The null hypothesis of non-causality based upon equation (32) would be:

$$H : J_{1,13} = \cdots = J_{k,13} = 0 \tag{33}$$

and $J_{13} = \sum_{i=1}^{k} J_{i,13}L^{i-1}$ is the $n1 \times n3$ upper-right submatrix of $J(L)$. Denoting A_3 as the last $n3$ rows of the matrix of cointegrating vectors A, if rank$(A_3) = n3$, then via TP, Corollary 1, under the null hypothesis from equation (33):

$$F \xrightarrow{d} \chi^2_{n1n3k}$$

However, the rank condition on the sub-matrix (A_3), based upon OLS estimates, suffers from simultaneous equation bias, such that there is no valid statistical basis for determining whether the required sufficient condition applies. When the condition fails, the limit distribution is more complex than that shown above and involves a mixture of a χ^2 and a non-standard distribution and generally involves nuisance parameters.

(2) *Johansen-type ECMs*

Based now upon equation (34), the null hypothesis of non-causality becomes:

$$H^* : J^*_{1,13} = \cdots = J^*_{k-1,13} = 0 \quad \text{and} \quad \Gamma_1 A'_3 = 0 \tag{34}$$

and $J_{13} = \sum_{i=1}^{k} J_{i,13}L^{i-1}$ is the $n1 \times n3$ upper-right submatrix of $J^*(L)$, and Γ_1 are the first $n1$ rows of the loading coefficient matrix Γ. If rank $\Gamma_1 = n1$ *or* rank$(A_3) = n3$, then under the null hypothesis (34)

$$F^* \xrightarrow{d} \chi^2_{n1n3k}$$

Again, if neither of these conditions are satisfied, causality tests based upon χ^2 will not in general be valid. However, unlike the case above, tests of such conditions are relatively easy to construct and constitute the *sequential testing strategy* of TP.

Consider for the moment either $n1 = 1$ or $n3 = 1$, (or $n1 = 1$ and $n3 = 1$), such that Γ_1 is a scalar denoted γ_1 as is A_3 denoted α_3, then define the following null hypotheses:

$$H^* : J^*_{1,13} = \cdots = J^*_{k-1,13} = 0 \,\text{and}\, \gamma_1\alpha'_3 = 0$$

$$H^*_{\uparrow} : J^*_{1,13} = \cdots = J^*_{k-1,13} = 0$$

$$H^*_1 : \gamma_1 = 0$$

$$H^*_3 : \alpha_3 = 0$$

$$H^*_{13} : \gamma_1\alpha'_3 = 0$$

The TP *sequential testing strategy* involves :

$$(P1)\ \text{Test}\ H_1^*: \begin{cases} \text{If } H_1^* \text{ is rejected test } H^* \\ \text{Otherwise test } H_\uparrow^* \end{cases}$$

$$(P2)\ \text{Test}\ H_3^*: \begin{cases} \text{If } H_3^* \text{ is rejected test } H^* \\ \text{Otherwise test } H_\uparrow^* \end{cases}$$

and when $n_1 = n_3 = 1$:

$$(P3)\ \text{Test}\ H_\uparrow^* \begin{cases} \text{If } H_\uparrow^* \text{ is rejected, reject the null hypothesis of noncausality} \\ \text{Otherwise, test } H_1^* \text{ and } H_3^* \begin{cases} \text{If both } H_1^* \text{ and } H_3^* \text{ are rejected test } H_{13}^* \text{ if } \hat{r} > 1 \text{ or reject the null if } \hat{r} = 1 \\ \text{Otherwise, accept the null of noncausality} \end{cases} \end{cases}$$

(where $\hat{r}$ is an estimate of r).

Having established this *theoretical hierarchy of testing*, based upon their Monte Carlo results, TP make the following observations/recommendations:

(1) *(P1) generally performs better than (P2) and should be preferred over (P2)*
(2) *When n1 = n3 = 1, (P1) and (P2) are less vulnerable to size distortions than (P3) which should be avoided*
(3) *None of the sequential procedures (or conventional tests), performed well for sample sizes below 100, at least with systems of three or more variables*
(4) *The sequential tests outperform the conventional VAR tests which suffer considerable size distortions where tests are not valid asymptotically* χ^2.

Furthermore, consideration of their Monte Carlo results reveals that for many cases considered, 'our testing procedures do not have much power unless the lag length k is specified correctly. This is not surprising because if $k > 1$ the coefficients of the lagged differences of y_3 are all zero'. For other cases, 'If we choose 22% critical values for those sub tests (H_1^*, H_3^*), then we would have approximately 5% significance level for the overall causality test... but of course we cannot do so without allowing large upward size distortions in other cases...' – TP. More generally, under many plausible cases it seems that the sequential procedures involve the potential to introduce large size distortions for relatively small deviations from assumed theoretical values, i.e. lag length, coefficient values and properties of the error term.

3.7.3 *Toda and Yamamoto (1995)*

The Toda and Yamamoto (1995) method can also be utilized to ascertain the direction of causality and involves using the levels of the variables irrespective of their order of integration. The test involves adding additional lags based upon the potential order of integration, i.e. one additional lag if one assumes the data are $I(1)$, two if $I(2)$, etc. It has the advantage that it can be used when the order of integration is ambiguous or uncertain; however, the cost is in terms of efficiency.

3.8 *The Structural Time Model (STM) approach of Harvey (1989)*

In a series of papers, Andrew Harvey has argued that *structural time series models* provide the most useful framework within which to consider 'stylized facts' about time series data. Nested within the general models he proposed, one can consider tests of TS v DS; the Hodrick and Prescott (1997) filter (and many other more general filters); etc. In a particularly useful paper in this respect, Harvey and Jaeger (1993) examine some of the consequences of the 'mechanical detrending methods of Hodrick and Prescott' and show that their uncritical use can lead to potentially spurious cycle detection. Instead of H-P, they propose the structural time series approach.

Below we will present the basics of the approach – those interested could usefully consult Harvey (1989).

3.8.1 *The Trend Plus Cycle Model*

Consider the following representation:

$$y_t = \mu_t + \psi_t + \varepsilon_t, \quad t = 1, \ldots T \tag{35}$$

where y_t is the series of interest; μ_t is the trend; ψ_t is the cycle and ε_t is the irregular component. The local linear trend model is defined as:

$$\mu_t = \mu_{t-1} + \beta_{t-1} + \eta_t \quad \eta_t \sim NID(0, \sigma_\eta^2) \tag{36}$$

$$\beta_t = \beta_{t-1} + \zeta_t \quad \zeta_t \sim NID(0, \sigma_\zeta^2) \tag{37}$$

where β_t is the slope and independence is assumed between the white noise errors ζ_t and η_t.

The stochastic cycle is modelled as:

$$\begin{aligned} \psi_t &= \rho \cos \lambda_c \psi_{t-1} + \rho \sin \lambda_c \psi_{t-1}^* + \kappa_t \\ \psi_t^* &= -\rho \sin \lambda_c \psi_{t-1} + \rho \cos \lambda_c \psi_{t-1}^* + \kappa_t^* \end{aligned} \tag{38}$$

where ρ represents the damping factor, $0 \leq \rho \leq 1$, and λ_c is the frequency of the cycle in radians and κ_t and κ_t^* are both $NID(0, \sigma_\kappa^2)$. The disturbances in all three equations are treated as independent and the irregular component is also assumed to be $NID(0, \sigma_\varepsilon^2)$. Estimation of the hyperparameters, $(\sigma_\eta^2, \sigma_\zeta^2, \sigma_\kappa^2, \sigma_\varepsilon^2, \rho, \lambda_c)$ can be undertaken by maximum likelihood methods and separate estimates of the trend, cycle(s) and irregular components obtained. STAMP (Structural Time Series Analysis Modeller and Predictor) 8.3 is a powerful, flexible and very user friendly, Windows 'drop-down' menu-based software package written specifically for estimation and prediction of such models and methods.

This structural time series modelling approach is also very flexible as it nests within its general structure a range of special cases. For example:

(1) The trend is a *random walk with drift and the cycle is an autoregressive component AR2* with the irregular either white noise or zero. In this case the level is 'stochastic' and the slope 'fixed'.
(2) The model is assumed to be a *local linear trend*. Here the level is 'stochastic' as is the slope. A stationary trigonometric cycle is included as is an irregular.
(3) Assume a *smooth trend* with level 'fixed' and slope 'stochastic'. The cycle may be a generalized version of the simple case considered above as in Harvey and Trimbur (2003).

Consider some useful properties of, for example, the *local level* model:

$$\begin{aligned} y_t &= \mu_t + \varepsilon_t, \quad \varepsilon_t \sim NID(0, \sigma_\varepsilon^2), \quad t = 1, \ldots T \\ \mu_t &= \mu_{t-1} + \eta_t, \quad \eta_t \sim NID(0, \sigma_\eta^2) \end{aligned} \tag{39}$$

Maximum likelihood estimates of σ_η^2 and σ_ε^2 and their relative variance $\sigma_\eta^2/\sigma_\varepsilon^2$ allow the calculation of, for example, the 'signal to noise' ratio. STAMP can also create an H-P filter, for example, assume a *local linear trend* (see equation (38) above) with the level 'fixed' the slope 'stochastic' and include an irregular component. Fix $\sigma_\eta = 0$, $\sigma_\xi = 0.000625 = 1/1600 = \lambda^{-1}$ will create the classic Hodrick–Prescott filter calibrated for quarterly (US) data.

4. Empirical Applications

4.1 *Overview*

The use of modern time series-based methods in cliometrics research is growing. Tables 1 and 2 below collate and summarize the methods used in empirical, time series based papers published in the two main cliometrics journals, *Explorations in Economic History* (2000–2009) and *Cliometrica* (2007–2009). The creation of *Cliometrica* itself is testimony to the growing number of quantitative economic history papers being written. Furthermore, it is clear from the tables, that there are a growing number of papers using modern time series methods in cliometrics more generally.

The most common methods applied in the papers identified are simple unit root tests, typically of a Dickey–Fuller or Augmented Dickey–Fuller form. Cointegration, mainly Johansen-based and Granger causality are also commonly undertaken methods. Simple VAR (see Sims, 1980) methods are also used by several authors. Testing for structural breaks; Kalman filter estimation; auto regressive distributed lag (see Pesaran *et al.*, 2001); generalized auto regressive conditional heteroskedasticity (GARCH) (see Bollerslev, 1986); TAR (threshold autoregression) and STAR (smooth transition autoregressive) (see Tong, 1990; Terasvirta, 1998);

Table 1. Papers using Time Series Methods: *Explorations in Economic History*, 2000–2009.

Year	Author(s)	Title	Methods
2000	Greasley and Oxley	British industrialization, 1815–1860: a disaggregate time series perspective	Unit root tests/ Kalman filter/ Stochastic trends
2000	Weidenmier	The market for confederate cotton bonds	VAR/unit roots/ Granger causality
2000	Lew	The diffusion of tractors on the Canadian prairies: the threshold model and the problem of uncertainty	Unit roots
2000	Keay	Scapegoats or responsive entrepreneurs: Canadian manufacturers, 1907–1990	Unit roots/trends
2000	Baten and Murray	Heights of men and women in 19th-century Bavaria: economic, nutritional and disease influences	Unit root tests
2000	Yousef	The political economy of interwar Egyptian cotton policy	Autoregressive distributed lag/unit roots
2001	Fratianni and Spinelli	Fiscal dominance and money growth in Italy: the long record	Unit root/Granger/ VAR
2001	Greasley *et al.*	Income uncertainty and consumer spending during the Great Depression	GARCH
2001	Allen and Keay	The first great whale extinction: the end of the bowhead whale in the Eastern Arctic	AR/Structural break/ trends
2002	Temin	Price behaviour in Ancient Babylon	Random walk
2002	Waldenstrom	Taxing emerging stock markets: a beneficial policy? Evidence from the Stockholm Stock Exchange, 1907–1939	ADF/ Johansen-cointegration
2002	Goodwin *et al.*	Mechanical refrigeration and the integration of perishable commodity markets	Unit root tests/Engle–Granger regression/cointegration
2002	della Paolera and Taylor	Internal versus external convertability and emerging market crises: lessons from Argentine history	Unit Root tests/VAR
2003	Antras and Voth	Factor prices and productivity growth during the British Industrial Revolution	ARMA/Crafts and Harley

Table 1. *Continued.*

Year	Author(s)	Title	Methods
2003	Tattara	Paper money but a gold debt: Italy on the gold standard	Cointegration/unit root/Johansen
2003	Toniolo *et al.*	Monetary Union, institutions and financial market integration: Italy, 1862–1905	ARMA/Kalman Filter/Structural break
2003	Grant	Globalization versus de-coupling: German emigration and the evolution of the Atlantic labour market 1870–1913	Cointegration/unit root tests
2004	Greasley and Oxley	Globalization and real wages in New Zealand 1873–1913	Unit root tests/ Cointegration/ADF
2004	Crafts and Mills	Was 19th-century British growth steam-powered?: the climacteric revisited	AR(2)/Johansen/ cointegrating vectors
2004	Grubb	The circulating medium of exchange in colonial Pennsylvania, 1729–1775: new estimates of monetary composition, performance and economic growth	AR(2)/Dickey–Fuller Tests
2004	Keay and Redish	The micro-economic effects of financial market structure: evidence from 20th-century North American steel firms	Structural break/ AR(3)
2005	Rousseau and Sylla	Emerging financial markets and early US growth	Granger causality/ VAR-Sims/Dickey–Fuller/ Johansen
2005	Klug *et al.*	How could everyone have been so wrong? Forecasting the Great Depression with the railroads	ARIMA
2005	Officer	The quantity theory in New England, 1703–1749: new data to analyse an old question	AR(1)/Dickey–Fuller Test
2005	Lazaretou	The drachma, foreign creditors and the international monetary system: tales of a currency during the 19th and the early 20th centuries	ARCH(1)/ARCH(2)
2005	Temin and Voth	Credit rationing and crowding out during the Industrial Revolution: evidence from Hoare's Bank, 1702–1862	AR(1)/VAR

Table 1. *Continued.*

Year	Author(s)	Title	Methods
2005	Sanz-Villarroya	The convergence process of Argentina with Australia and Canada: 1875–2000	Structural break/ AR(1)
2005	Hickson *et al.*	*Much ado about nothing*: the limitation of liability and the market for 19th-century Irish bank stock	Structural break/ ARIMA/AR(1)
2006	Van Nieuwerburgh *et al.*	Stock market development and economic growth in Belgium	Cointegration/ Johansen/Granger causality/ Dickey–Fuller
2006	Burhop	Did banks cause the German industrialization?	Causality/Engle and Granger/Toda and Yamamoto
2006	Ogren	Free or central banking? Liquidity and financial deepening in Sweden, 1834–1913	VAR
2006	Sabate *et al.*	Does fiscal policy influence monetary policy? The case of Spain, 1874–1935	VAR Model/Granger Causality
2006	Jacks	What drove 19th-century commodity market integration?	AR/random walk
2006	Mattesini and Quintieri	Does a reduction in the length of the working week reduce unemployment? Some evidence from the Italian economy during the Great Depression	Time series/ heteroskedasticity
2006	Kling	The long-term impact of mergers and the emergence of a merger wave in pre–World War I Germany	VAR
2007	Crafts *et al.*	Total factor productivity growth on Britain's railways, 1852–1912: a reappraisal of the evidence	Random effects/ stochastic cost frontier model
2007	Ciccarelli and Fenoaltea	Business fluctuations in Italy, 1861–1913: the new evidence	Cycle/random walk/ Kalman filter
2007	Herranz-Locan	Infrastructure investment and Spanish economic growth, 1850–1935	VAR/Cointegration/ Granger Causality/Dickey–Fuller

Table 1. *Continued.*

Year	Author(s)	Title	Methods
2007	Landon-Lane and Rockoff	The origin and diffusion of shocks to regional interest rates in the USA, 1880–2002	VAR/time series/Unit root/Dickey–Fuller
2007	Eichengreen and Hataseb	Can a rapidly growing export-oriented economy exit smoothly from a currency peg? Lessons from Japan's high-growth era	Dickey–Fuller
2007	Bodenhorn	Usury ceilings and bank lending behaviour: Evidence from 19th-century New York	Unit root/AR/ARMA
2007	Streb *et al.*	Knowledge spill-over from new to old industries: The case of German synthetic dyes and textiles (1878–1913)	VAR/VECM/Unit root tests/Johansen/ Granger causality
2007	Solomou and Shimazaki	Japanese episodic long swings in economic growth	Kalman filter/ Stochastic shifts/ Johansen cointegration/unit root tests
2007	Federico	Market integration and market efficiency: the case of 19th-century Italy	TAR/unit root/MA
2007	Jacks	Populists versus theorists: futures markets and the volatility of prices	GARCH/time series
2008	Craig and Holt	Mechanical refrigeration, seasonality and the hog–corn cycle in the USA: 1870–1940	TV-STAR/random walk/Dickey–Fuller/unit root/TVAR
2008	Siklos	The Fed's reaction to the stock market during the Great Depression: fact or artefact?	VAR/GARCH/ structural VAR/ impulse response
2008	Diebolt and Parent	Bimetallism: the 'rules of the game'	VAR and Granger causality
2009	Rousseau	Share liquidity, participation and growth of the Boston market for industrial equities, 1854–1897	VAR and Granger causality/Unit roots
2009	Klovland	New evidence on the fluctuations in ocean freight rates in the 1850s	Cointegration/ Johansen/ Dickey–Fuller

Table 1. *Continued.*

Year	Author(s)	Title	Methods
2009	Grossman and Imai	Japan's return to gold: turning points in the value of the yen during the 1920s	Non-stationary process/random walk/structural breaks
2009	Esteves *et al.*	Market Integration in the Golden Periphery. The Lisbon/London Exchange, 1854–1891	Random walk/ stationary/AR1
2009	Sarferaz and Uebele	Tracking down the business cycle: a dynamic factor model for Germany 1820–1913	Hodrick–Prescott filter/AR

are less commonly used methods reflecting the particular applications under investigation. Overall, however, it is clear that many in the cliometrics group have adopted appropriate methods to consider the time series questions they have chosen to consider, however, it is also clear from reading some applications by other authors, that more people need to consider their data, methods used and hence conclusions more carefully. This is not unique to cliometrics, but we will not take this point further here.

4.2 *When Did the Industrial Revolution Begin? Some Results Utilizing Unit Root Tests, Structural Breaks and Direct Measures of Persistence*

In a series of papers we used time series methods to identify the timing and potential causes of the British Industrial revolution see, Greasley and Oxley (1994a, 1994b, 1996b, 1997c, 1997e, 1997f, 1998a, 1998b, 2000). In this section, we will present some of these results to demonstrate how time series methods were used to consider such questions and also present some new results based upon the tests of Leybourne *et al.* (2007).

The data used in this series of papers relate to an extended version of Crafts and Harleys (1992) 'best guess' estimates of the index of British Industrial Production, extended from 1913 to 1992. In a series of papers, we consider structural breaks in the series utilizing both the Dickey and Fuller (1981) approach and the extensions of Perron (1989) and Zivot and Andrews (1992). On the basis of the results repeated below as Table 3, we identify an alternating TS/DS/TS characterization of the data for the period 1700–1913 and present a case for dating the British Industrial Revolution as 1780–1851, see Greasley and Oxley (1994a, 1994b, 1996b, 1997c, 1997f). Furthermore, Greasley and Oxley (1996a, 1997b) use Perron (1989) and Zivot and Andrews (1992) methods to identify crashes and breaks in the post 1913 data coinciding with World War I; the post (WW1) decline; a 1973 trend

Table 2. Papers using Time Series Methods: *Cliometrica*, 2007–2009.

Year	Author(s)	Title	Methods
2007	Neilson	UK money demand 1873–2001: a long-run time series analysis and event study	VAR/Johansen/ stochastic trends
2008	Mills	Exploring historical economic relationships: two and a half centuries of British interest rates and inflation	GARCH/EGARCH/ non-stationary series/Dickey–Fuller/AR(2)
2008	Ricciuti	The quest for a fiscal rule: Italy, 1861–1998	Non-stationary/ Engle–Granger/ autoregressive model/Dickey–Fuller
2009	Prados de la Escosura and Sanz-Villarroya	Contract enforcement, capital accumulation and Argentina's long-run decline	Hodrick–Prescott/ Granger Causality/ augmented Dickey–Fuller test
2009	Weisdorf and Sharp	From preventive to permissive checks: the changing nature of the Malthusian relationship between nuptiality and the price of provisions in the 19th century	VAR/CVAR/structural break
2009	Ljunberg and Nilsson	Human capital and economic growth: Sweden 1870–2000	Granger causality/ Toda and Yamamoto/VAR/ ADF
2009	Franck and Krausz	Institutional changes, wars and stock market risk in an emerging economy: evidence from the Israeli stock exchange, 1945–1960	VAR/Regression/ Break
2009	Mills	Modelling trends and cycles in economic time series: historical perspective and future developments	ARIMA/Cycles/ Kalman Filter/HP filter
2009	Baubeau and Cazelles	French economic cycles: a wavelet analysis of French retrospective GNP series	Cycles/Time series/ non-stationary

break and a 1979 crash, see Table 4 below. This leads to an alternating TS/DS/TS characterization for the whole sample period 1700–1992.

Furthermore, on the basis of ADF test results we concluded that the period 1700–1992 comprises several distinct epochs of industrial growth, in particular:

Table 3. Testing for Unit Roots: Levels Data.

	1700–1913	1700–1780	1780–1851	1851–1913
ADF(2)	−1.13	−3.66*	−1.16	−4.55*
LM(SC)	0.20	2.51	0.84	0.81

ADF(2) denotes 2 augmentations; LM(SC) is a Lagrange multiplier test of first-order serial correlation; *Denotes significant at the 5% level based upon MacKinnon (1991). Results not presented here indicate that for the periods 1700–1913 and 1780–1851, the data are $I(1)$ and not $I(2)$.

Table 4. Perron-Type Unit Root Tests – 1922–1992.

Year	Crash	Trend	Crash and trend
1929	−2.362	−2.084	−2.046
1939	−2.758	−2.550	−2.600
1945	−3.191	−2.672	−2.741
1973	−2.948	−4.827*	−4.809*
1979	−4.362*	−4.419*	−4.718*

*denotes significant at the 0.05 level using Perron (1989) critical values.

1700–1780; 1781–1851; 1852–1913; 1922–1973 and *1973–1992.* The defined periods are supported by the rich economic historiography and by the statistical results.

However, as discussed above, the characterization of the time series properties of a series as *either* DS *or* TS is an extreme one. In contrast, the results presented as Table 5 consider the Cochrane measure of persistence over a number of periods, including Greasley–Oxley epochs. This is crucial as Cochrane (1988) demonstrates that measures of persistence constructed for periods (segments) of differing growth rates, will tend to bias the results in favour of finding *too much persistence.*

If we consider the results presented as Table 5, and limit discussion initially to the column 'Chatfield' which gives the Chatfield (1989) $2\sqrt{T}$ criteria for the choice of window width (where T is the effective sample size), a number of features emerge. Firstly, the periods identified by Greasley and Oxley (1994a, 1994b) have markedly different measures of persistence which lend support to the results based upon ADF tests. As can be seen, the persistence measures for Greasley–Oxley epochs (pre-WW1) are, respectively, 0.132, (1700–1780), 0.607, (1781–1851) and 0.449 (1851–1913) showing that the Industrial Revolution exhibited a marked difference in persistence from the earlier and later periods.

Turning to the preferred Cochrane window width of 30, the results are even more pronounced with measures of 0.098, 0.912 and 0.653 for the respective periods.

Using the full sample period 1700–1992 and assuming no breaks in the series implies a high degree of persistence, i.e. 0.712 for the Chatfield rule, or 0.659

Table 5. Cochrane (1988) Measure of Persistence.

	$k = 5$	$k = 10$	$k = 15$	$k = 20$	$k = 30$	Chatfield	k
1701–1992	0.521	0.469	0.465	0.544	0.659	0.712	34
	(0.077)	(0.096)	(0.116)	(0.153)	(0.218)	(0.248)	
1701–1780	0.340	0.265	0.164	0.135	0.098	0.132	18
	(0.092)	(0.094)	(0.066)	(0.058)	(0.043)	(0.056)	
1781–1851	0.389	0.464	0.577	0.704	0.912	0.607	16
	(0.111)	(0.173)	(0.241)	(0.310)	(0.396)	(0.258)	
1852–1913	0.832	0.538	0.497	0.558	0.653	0.449	16
	(0.251)	(0.209)	(0.214)	(0.248)	(0.270)	(0.195)	
1852–1992	0.807	0.558	0.532	0.622	0.559	0.549	24
	(0.169)	(0.159)	(0.179)	(0.232)	(0.234)	(0.217)	
1922–1992	1.225	0.975	0.980	1.223	1.377	1.058	16
	(0.349)	(0.362)	(0.411)	(0.543)	(0.597)	(0.449)	
1922–1973	1.209	0.789	0.593	0.774	0.716	0.531	14
	(0.391)	(0.195)	(0.172)	(0.343)	(0.265)	(0.233)	
1974–1992	0.918	0.504	0.817	a	a	0.660	8
	(0.362)	(0.192)	(0.172)			(0.279)	

k denotes the window size for the Bartlett estimator; figures in parentheses are asymptotic standard errors; a denotes not calculated. All figures are corrected for small sample bias following Cochrane (1988).

for $k = 30$, reflecting the bias raised by Cochrane (1988) in favour of excessive persistence (or in favour of DS). A similar problem arises if the 20th century is treated as a single epoch. In particular, the results for 1922–1992 imply a degree of persistence close to 1 i.e. 1.058 for $k = 14$ or 1.377 for $k = 30$. However, if the Greasley–Oxley epochs are considered, the pattern of persistence presented as Figure 1 (derived from Table 5), emerges.

For either $k = 30$ or the Chatfield rule, persistence rises during the Industrial Revolution from the very low levels of pre-industrial Britain. It then declines pre-WW1, recovering only slowly to (or approaches, based upon $k = 30$) its Industrial Revolution level. However, some caution needs be expressed about the period 1974–1992 given the small sample size. The results based on $k = 30$ or $k =$ Chatfield are qualitatively the same, however, because of the quantitative differences the interpretation differs in important ways. In particular based upon $k = 30$, the Industrial Revolution represents a historical high point in terms of persistence. Twentieth century persistence levels are moderately high and higher than the mid-late 19th century, but lower than the period 1780–1851. This result is not as clear-cut based upon $k =$ Chatfield, although it depends crucially upon the small sample results of the period 1974–1992. On these bases, the Industrial Revolution period identified by Greasley and Oxley represents a unique period of high persistence.

Notice, however, that using a low value window, $k = 5$, which is similar to a low-order ARMA measure, such as Campbell and Mankiw (1987), suggests a

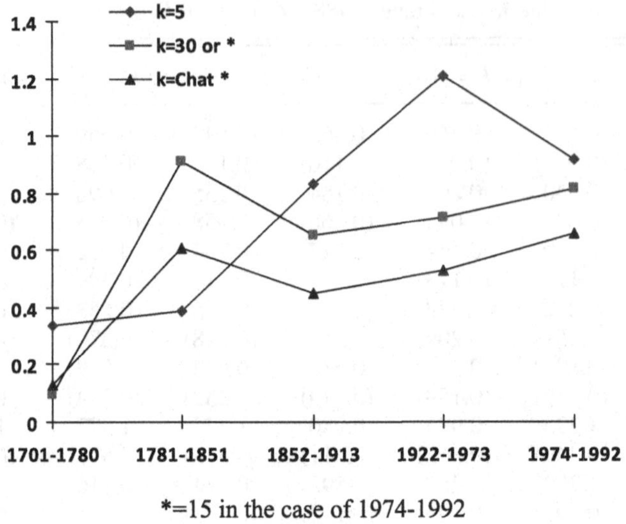

Figure 1. Measures of Persistence Over Various Epochs.

much different picture, see Table 5 and Figure 1. Here, the Industrial Revolution seems unremarkable and the tendency for persistence to rise to very high levels into the 20th century seems to emerge. Treating the period 1922–1992 as a valid era would exaggerate the position even further. The $k = 5$ results help explain why some other measures exaggerate the degree of persistence experienced during the 20th century. This coupled with the treatment of the post WW1 period as a single era explain why some results, i.e. Mills (1991) and Capie and Mills (1991) find in favour of a switch from TS to DS at this juncture. However, on statistical grounds, see Cochrane (1988), we would suggest that results based upon low valued k are in fact spurious.

Apart from providing a measure of persistence, interpretation of the normalized spectral density function gives a measure of the proportion of total variance of the process accounted for by cycles of various lengths, $l = 2\pi/\omega$ where ω is the frequency, see Priestley (1981).

Table 6, above, presents estimates of the cycle lengths contributing most to the explanation of the variance of industrial production based upon the Chatfield rule for choosing window width.

For the period up to 1913 it can be seen how pre- and post-industrial production cyclical elements differ. Short cycles (around 2–3 years), or a low cyclical element to the data, explain most of the variance in output pre-1780. Whereas post 1851 cycles of around 10 years, or a high cyclical element to the series, explain most of the variance in production. The cyclical nature of the Industrial Revolution period is similar to the pre-revolution period – in both cases the data suggest an economy not best classified as cyclical. However, as discussed below, for different reasons. These measures are qualitatively similar (though with a somewhat different interpretation

Table 6. Cycle Lengths, $l = 2\pi/\omega$.

Years	k	Cycle
1701–1780	18	2
1781–1851	16	3
1852–1913	16	10
1922–1973	14	15
1974–1992	9	9

k = Chatfield window width.

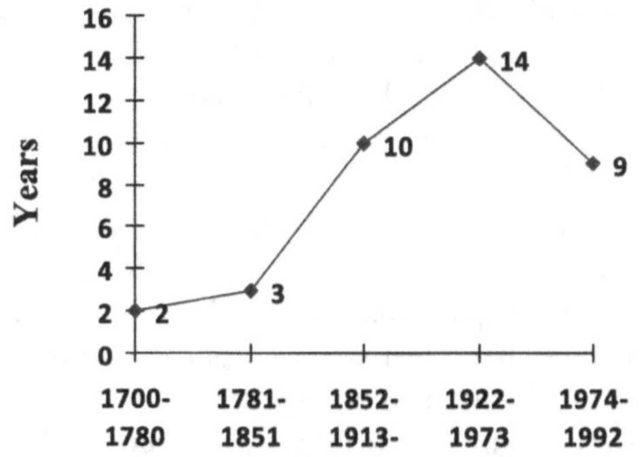

Figure 2. Implied Cycle Lengths.

given the methods of analysis) to those presented by Crafts *et al.* (1989) where they consider the periods pre-1783, with cycles of around 4 years, and post 1815, with cycles of around 7 years. Plots of the spectrum also indicate the following phenomena. For the periods 1701–1780, 1781–1852, the spectrum tends to rise continuously from low to high frequencies indicating the contribution of short cycles in explaining the variance of output. However, the shape of the spectrum reverses post 1852, including the 20th century, indicating the contribution of longer cycles. Taking the post 1922 period as a whole suggests that cycles of 14–15 years contribute most to the explanation of output variance. These conform closely to the results of Leung (1992). However, as with the persistence measure, treating the 20th century as a single epoch can be misleading. Taking the Greasley–Oxley epochs produces the following description, presented as Figure 2 below, of the cycle lengths which contribute most the explanation of the variance of industrial production.

The amount of variance explained by longer cycles (or a more cyclical characteristic to the data), increases after the Industrial Revolution. However, cycle length appears to decline as persistence appears to increase. It does seem however, that there is strong quantitative and historical evidence in favour of distinct periods of growth, as argued by Greasley and Oxley.

Table 7. Leybourne *et al.* (2007) *M*-Tests.

Sample period	1700–1992	1700–1853	1913–1992
M statistic	−4.813*	−6.252*	−5.605*
I(0) start – end	1853–1913	1775–1816	1949–1973

* denotes significant at the 5% level.

4.2.1 *When Did the Industrial Revolution Begin: Revisited. The Multiple Persistence Change Model of Leybourne et al. (2007)*

In the approach presented above, it is relatively easy to identify a change in persistence stemming from a shift from a TS process to one that is DS. However, it is less simple to identify a process whose time series properties appear to alternate, TS–DS–TS, etc., as the properties of the data in the apparent DS section would tend to dominate the TS sections. Leybourne *et al.* (2007), consider testing for multiple changes in persistence model, in particular, they propose a test for the presence of multiple regime shifts and how to consistently estimate the associated change-point fractions. They partition yt, $t = 1, 2, \ldots, T$, into its separate $I(0)$ and $I(1)$ regimes and show that a test statistic appropriate for this purpose is based on a doubly recursive application of a unit root statistic where they employ the local GLS detrended ADF unit root testing methodology of Elliott *et al.* (1996) – discussed above – used for detecting a single change in persistence. For further details of the test see Leybourne *et al.* (2007).

Utilizing the same data as above on the log British industrial production for the period 1700–1992, the Leybourne, Kim and Taylor *M*-test (with a maximum of four lags) implies that the series were:

(1) $I(1)$ from 1700–1775; $I(0)$ from 1775–1816; $I(1)$ from 1816–1853; $I(0)$ from 1853–1913; $I(1)$ from 1913–1949; $I(0)$ from 1949–1973; $I(1)$ from 1973–1992.

The detailed test results are provided in Table 7 below.

Although the subsamples are slightly different to those proposed by Greasley and Oxley (1996b), the notion of alternating time series properties of the data are supported as is the macro-based timing of the Industrial Revolution.

4.3 *Testing for Causality*

4.3.1 *What Caused the British Industrial Revolution: Disaggregate Data?*

In Section 3.7 above, we presented a number of approaches to testing for Granger-type causality and stressed the need to consider the order of integration of the variables under consideration as this will crucially affect the validity of the inferences drawn.

Table 8. Unit Root Tests 1815–1860 (Augmented Dickey–Fuller Statistics+).

	ADF(1)	Trend (% p.a.)
A. Minerals		
1. Coal	−0.597	
2. Copper ore	−3.005	
B. Metals		
1. Pig iron and steel	−1.061	
2. Iron and steel products, machines and tools	−1.248	
3. Copper	−1.491	
4. Tin	−3.180	
C. Textiles		
1. Cotton yarn	−0.603	
2. Cotton cloth	−0.831	
3. Woollen and worsted yarn	−3.984*	1.77
4. Woollen and worsted cloth	−5.117*	1.40
5. Silk thread	−4.552*	2.95
6. Silk goods	−5.299*	3.61
7. Linen yarn	−4.203*	1.50
8. Linen goods	−4.265*	0.60
9. Hemp products	−3.385*	1.61
D. Food, drink and tobacco		
1. Wheaten flour	−5.847*	0.80
2. Bread and cakes	−5.706*	0.96
3. Sugar	−1.538	
4. Beer	−2.577	
5. Malt	−2.471	
6. Spirits	−1.715	
7. Tobacco	−0.881	
E. Miscellaneous		
1. Shipbuilding	−2.617	
2. Paper	−0.281	
3. Leather	−3.843*	1.60
4. Leather goods	−3.937*	1.60

+ All the results are for ADF(1).
*Denotes significant at the 5% level according to MacKinnon (1991) critical values.

In this section we will present some results taken from Greasley and Oxley (2000) where we consider the question which sectors ‘caused’ the British Industrial Revolution by utilizing measures of disaggregated British industrial production, 1815–1851.

Causality in the context of these data and this question concern the linkages among the industries whose output defined early British industrialization. Of particular interest are those industries which are also ascribed in the historiography with key roles in leading industrialization. Specifically we consider the importance

Table 9. Johansen Cointegration Test Results for 12 $I(1)$ Series 1815–1860.

H_0	H_1	Maximal eigenvalue	Trace
$r = 0$	$r = 1$	171.7*	683.0*
$r \leq 1$	$r = 2$	113.3*	511.2*
$r \leq 2$	$r = 3$	91.60*	397.9*
$r \leq 3$	$r = 4$	85.67*	306.2*
$r \leq 4$	$r = 5$	64.51*	220.6*
$r \leq 5$	$r = 6$	44.60	156.1*
$r \leq 6$	$r = 7$	37.95	111.4*
$r \leq 7$	$r = 8$	26.89	73.54
$r \leq 8$	$r = 9$	20.78	46.64
$r \leq 9$	$r = 10$	14.36	25.86
$r \leq 10$	$r = 11$	8.18	11.49
$r \leq 11$	$r = 12$	3.31	3.31

*Denotes rejects the null at the 5% level.

Table 10. Johansen Cointegration Test Results Mining and Metals Group, 1815–1860.

H_0	H_1	Maximal eigenvalue	Trace
$r = 0$	$r = 1$	85.81*	254.6*
$r \leq 1$	$r = 2$	72.47*	168.7*
$r \leq 2$	$r = 3$	42.21*	96.32*
$r \leq 3$	$r = 4$	25.68*	54.11*
$r \leq 4$	$r = 5$	20.74*	28.42*
$r \leq 5$	$r = 6$	7.68	7.68

The group comprises $I(1)$ variables: coal, copper, copper ore, iron-steel goods, pig iron and tin; $I(0)$ variables: none. $r =$ the number of cointegrating vectors where VAR lag length is 3, and *Denotes rejects the null at the 5% level.

of cotton, see Rostow (1963), utilizing the data for cotton cloth; iron and steel goods, see Hirschman (1958); coal, see Wrigley (1988), and elements of the food processing sector, see Horrell *et al.* (1994), paying particular attention to beer and sugar. We show below that each of these industries have non-stationary output data for the period 1815–1860, and were part of wider groupings of industries which shared stochastic common trends. Any causal links among the industries with non-stationary data may be long-term, since their output movements have permanent effects. At issue is whether or not particular industries within the cotton, mining and metals, or the food and drink groups played leading roles within their sector, or had causal linkages which spilled across the common trend groupings.

Table 8 below presents unit root tests of the individual series from which those series identified as $I(1)$ and $I(0)$ can be identified. Given that total industrial production is deemed to be a unit root process over this period, if we are interested

Table 11. Johansen Cointegration Test Results Textiles Group, 1815–1860.

H_0	H_1	Maximal eigenvalue	Trace
$r = 0$	$r = 1$	21.95*	27.73*
$r \leq 1$	$r = 2$	5.78	5.78

The Group comprises $I(1)$ variables: cotton pieces, cotton yarn. $I(0)$ variables: linen yarn, linens, silk products, silk thread, woollens, worsted, hemp products, leather and leather products. $r =$ the number of cointegrating vectors where VAR lag length is 2, *Denotes rejects the null at the 5% level.

Table 12. Johansen Cointegration Test Results Food, Drink and Tobacco Group, 1815–1860.

H_0	H_1	Maximal eigenvalue	Trace
$r = 0$	$r = 1$	102.2*	206.8*
$r \leq 1$	$r = 2$	49.56*	104.6*
$r \leq 2$	$r = 3$	34.64*	55.02*
$r \leq 3$	$r = 4$	19.41*	20.37*
$r \leq 4$	$r = 5$	0.96	0.96

The group comprises $I(1)$ variables: beer, malt, sugar, spirits and tobacco products. $I(0)$ variables: bread, wheaten flour. r = the number of cointegrating vectors where VAR lag length is 4, *Denotes rejects the null at the 5% level.

in ascertaining which series (variables) 'caused' this non-stationary outcome, we need to consider only those that are individually $I(1)$. As discussed in 3.7, the form of the causality testing depends crucially on the order of integration of the univariate series. Of the 15 series deemed $I(1)$, several combinations were used to consider robustness amongst the $I(1)$ series.

Table 9 below presents Johansen-based test results for cointegration using a 12 variable group which comprises the $I(1)$ variables: coal, copper, cotton yarn, cotton pieces, pig-iron, malt, paper, shipbuilding, spirits, sugar, tobacco products and beer. The discontinuity in the spirits data around 1823 would tend to promote an idiosyncratic trend for this industry, and thereby reduce by one the number of common trends. $r =$ the number of cointegrating vectors where the VAR lag length is chosen to 2 on the basis of information criteria tests.

Tables 10–12 present cointegration results for groupings of the $I(1)$ variables into sectors. The results from Table 9 identify seven significant cointegrating relationships and hence five stochastic trends; Table 10, five significant cointegrating relationships and one stochastic trend; Table 11, one significant cointegrating relationships and one stochastic trend and Table 12, four significant cointegrating relationships and one stochastic trend.

The results of tests for bivariate causality between cotton pieces, iron and steel goods, coal, beer, sugar and the other industries with non-stationary output series are shown in Table 13 below, using the Toda and Yamamoto (1995) method:

Table 13. Toda and Yamamoto-Type Tests of Causality, $I(1)$ Variables 1815–1860.

Variable 1	Variable 2	*p*-value 1 does not cause 2	*p*-value 2 does not cause 1
Coal	Copper	0.253	0.626
	Copper ore	0.342	0.662
	Cotton pieces	0.429	0.003*
	Cotton yarn	0.340	0.008*
	Sugar	0.765	0.049*
	Malt	0.256	0.336
	Spirits	0.338	0.966
	Tobacco products	0.597	0.004*
	Iron and steel	0.738	0.011*
	Tin	0.672	0.994
	Pig iron	0.614	0.091**
	Paper	0.122	0.000*
	Shipbuilding	0.012*	0.230
	Beer	0.265	0.367
Cotton pieces	Copper	0.236	0.601
	Copper ore	0.508	0.487
	Cotton yarn	0.001*	0.003*
	Sugar	0.030*	0.252
	Malt	0.256	0.185
	Spirits	0.355	0.275
	Tobacco products	0.245	0.690
	Iron and steel	0.002*	0.003*
	Tin	0.657	0.811
	Pig iron	0.001*	0.001*
	Paper	0.000*	0.117
	Shipbuilding	0.064**	0.822
Sugar	Copper	0.681	0.536
	Copper ore	0.032*	0.198
	Cotton yarn	0.351	0.021*
	Malt	0.865	0.991
	Spirits	0.934	0.414
	Tobacco products	0.670	0.869
	Iron and steel	0.170	0.156
	Tin	0.415	0.944
	Pig iron	0.159	0.225
	Paper	0.004*	0.164
	Shipbuilding	0.932	0.291
Iron and steel	Copper	0.149	0.207
	Copper ore	0.524	0.192
	Malt	0.046*	0.922
	Spirits	0.463	0.922
	Tobacco products	0.785	0.933

Table 13. *Continued.*

Variable 1	Variable 2	p-value 1 does not cause 2	p-value 2 does not cause 1
	Tin	0.927	0.794
	Pig iron	0.493	0.385
	Paper	0.404	0.334
	Shipbuilding	0.368	0.057**
Beer	Copper	0.536	0.353
	Copper ore	0.171	0.903
	Malt	0.349	0.091**
	Spirits	0.205	0.226
	Tobacco products	0.898	0.519
	Tin	0.405	0.632
	Pig iron	0.785	0.374
	Paper	0.335	0.213
	Shipbuilding	0.170	0.293
	Cotton piece	0.260	0.467
	Cotton yarn	0.316	0.467
	Iron and steel	0.588	0.482
	Sugar	0.187	0.036*
	Malt	0.349	0.091**

p-value denotes the probability of a causal relationship.*Denotes reject non-causality null in favour of causality at the 5% level.**Denotes reject non-causality null in favour of causality at the 10% level.

On the basis of the causality tests, the industries with the most pervasive links to other industries are coal and cotton. Clearly, coal appears to be a follower, with its output determined by previous output levels of cotton yarn, cotton cloth, sugar, tobacco, iron and steel goods, pig iron and paper. Only shipbuilding appears to have been led by coal, a finding which possibly reflects the importance of coal to the British coastal trade, especially between Newcastle and London, in the first half of the 19th century. A widening industrial demand for coal as a fuel and power source in the 1815–1860 period from the metals, foods and textiles sectors, was the key to coal's expansion. Cotton pieces, to the contrary, played a leading role in industrialization by stimulating coal, sugar, iron and steel goods, pig iron, paper, shipbuilding and cotton yarn, though the latter is partly an artefact of data construction. The two industries with idiosyncratic stochastic output trends, paper and shipbuilding, were both led by the cotton industry. To some extent the cotton results highlight the separateness of the foods sectors, with a causal link found only in the case of sugar.

Iron and steel goods, identified by the input–output studies of Chenery and Watanabe (1958), and Hirschman (1958) as the industry with the widest transactions linkages, had fewer causal links than cotton in the 1815 to 1860 period. Iron and steel goods were led by shipbuilding, and had no significant links with paper, though like cotton pieces it led one foods industry, in its case, malt and coal. However, the results do not provide a simple basis for favouring cotton pieces over iron goods as the key to early industrialization, as the results indicate bidirectional causality between the two industries. Thus, the cotton, mining and metals sector appears jointly dominated by cotton and iron, while coal appears as a follower, and no causal links emerge for tin, copper, or copper ore.

The causal links surrounding the foods sector appear less widespread. Beer, malt, spirits, sugar and tobacco form the key foods grouping with a single stochastic common trend. Of these, beer is awarded the largest weight at 2.6% in Hoffmann's industrial production index (excluding building) for 1831–1860. Beer does not lead any other industry according to the causality tests, but follows both malt and sugar. In the foods sector, sugar has the widest causal links leading coal, paper and copper ore, but following cotton. Generally the results play-down the importance of the linkages surrounding the foods sector, and its role in defining the profile of early British industrialization. In part this arises from the large bread and flour industries having TS output, which excludes both from shaping the swings in aggregate output and from having long-run causal links with the other foods industries, and with the cotton, mining and metals grouping. Sugar did lead, along with several other industries, the expansion of coal output, but had no causal links with iron goods and was led by cotton.

The causality test results help to refine further the interpretation of early industrialization, which emerged from the common trends perspective. In the case of the cotton, mining and metals grouping, cotton and iron are revealed as the leading industries, and coal as a follower. Outside the sector, cotton had the wider linkages, statistically causing paper and shipbuilding production. However, cotton cannot be regarded as the more important lever to industrialization in the 1815–1860 period as bidirectional causality between iron goods and cotton output lies at the heart of the cotton, mining and metals sector. The findings for the foods sector show fewer within sector causal links, though both malt and sugar led beer. Only sugar appears to have causal links reaching outside the foods sector, to paper, coal and copper ore. Together, the common trends and causality results point to cotton, iron goods and possibly sugar, as the key industries promoting swings in British industrialization to 1860.

4.3.2 *What Caused the British Industrial Revolution: Aggregate Level Data?*

In Section 4.3.1 above, and Greasley and Oxley (2000), we consider testing for the causes of the Industrial Revolution using Hoffmann's (1955) disaggregate industrial production data. However, debate also revolves around the possible macro-level causes. In Greasley and Oxley (1997e, 1998a), we utilize time series methods to identify the causes for the extended period 1780–1851. Several candidates for causality exist in the literature including:

(i) *Export-led growth (ELG)*: export growth *causes* growth in output. This view is supported by, for example, O'Brien and Engerman (1991) and Hatton and Lyons (1983), and was tested utilizing data on industrial production and exports.

(ii) *Technological factors:* developments in technology *cause* a change in the productive process and/or efficiency of production leading to a discernible change in the pattern of output growth. This view is supported by Tsoulouhas (1992), and was tested utilizing data on the number of patents registered and processes stemming from such patents, as measured by Sullivan (1989).

(iii) *Population growth:* here growth in the population influences output by both providing a growing pool of workers and also a growing source of domestic demand. Supporters of this view include Komlos (1990) and Simon (1994).

(iv) *Domestic factors (general):* other domestic factors including, for example, wages and the change in domestic demand, are seen as contributing to a *domestically determined* revolution. Clearly population growth could be included in this category, although it is generally assigned a separate potential route of influence. Supporters of the domestically determined growth include Deane and Cole (1969) and McCloskey (1994). Such authors' views are often contrasted with supporters of the ELG hypothesis, and (i) and (iv) could be regarded as two of the main competing explanations of the Industrial Revolution. In testing iv) data on real wages taken from Crafts and Mills (1994) are utilized to test whether real wage levels, or rates of growth, caused industrial production or vice versa.

(v) *Subsidiary hypotheses – imports cause exports:* Deane and Cole (1969), posit that imports lead exports in the 18th century as British trade shifts from Europe to the W. Indies and North America. Colonial economies, however, had limited spending power and as such needed to export to Britain if they were to buy imports from Britain. If this hypothesis were true and were coupled with the ELG hypothesis, the data may suggest that imports *cause* output growth.

(vi) *Other possible candidate hypotheses:* given the current level of interest in endogenous growth models see Rebelo (1991), it may seem natural to test for the effects of, for example, human capital on growth. However, for the period of interest, 1780–1851, the absence of annual data precludes formal investigation of the roles played by investment in education and even physical capital in the Industrial Revolution.

As such there are five feasible testable hypotheses, (i)–(v) above. The first stage of the causality testing procedure investigates the order of integration of the data. The results of the tests (not presented here, but can be found in Greasley and Oxley (1997e, 1998a), where definitions of the variables used can also be found) on the log levels of, total industrial production; real wages; exports; imports; patents; processes and population show in all cases that the null hypothesis of non-stationarity is not rejected. Results for tests of bivariate and multivariate cointegration (also not presented here but can be found in Greasley and Oxley (1997e, 1998a) between industrial production and the other variables of interest, namely, real wages; exports; imports; patents; processes and population identify a single significant bivariate cointegrating relationship between industrial production and the variable of interest in all cases, but imports. Utilizing these results a multivariate Johansen approach was adopted including all variables except imports and one significant cointegrating vectors was identified. A test of the restriction that the coefficient on population equals unity was not rejected implying that a proportionate relationship between the level of population and the level of industrial production cannot be rejected. The results, therefore, demonstrate the existence of both bivariate and multivariate cointegration between the variables of interest. The only candidate variable for which cointegration was not identified was imports. This constrains tests of causality to the $I(0)$ representation of the import data, i.e. in this case, first difference or growth rates, and does not rule-out the identification of a spurious relationship. The potential for cointegration between exports and imports was discussed in Greasley and Oxley (1997e, 1998a) and is not considered further here, nor are the standard Granger-type causality tests except to summarize the results of such methods being the overall assessment is of unidirectional causality from processes to output or that *technological change caused changes in industrial production–the Industrial Revolution.*

4.3.3 *Development Blocks, Innovation and Causality in New Zealand 1861–1939*

The concept of a 'development block', where innovations in leading industries promote complementary activities, has been utilized widely to understand economic development see Dahmen (1988) and Rostow (1963). Early work, including that of Hirschman (1958) and Chenery and Watanabe (1958) measured input–output transactions to identify leading industries, highlighting the strategic importance of the linkages from iron and steel industries. In Greasley and Oxley (2010a) we gauge which, if any, New Zealand industry or groups of industries led her economic development.

A variety of approaches have been used to identify development blocks. Horrell *et al.* (1994) constructed an input–output table for 1841 to gauge the leading industries of the British Industrial Revolution, but the input–output method offers only a static perspective. Moser and Nicholas (2004) used historical patent citations to assess to the impact of electricity as a general purpose technology.

Enflo *et al.* (2008) also consider how *development blocks* formed around electricity by using a combination of cointegration and causality analysis. They define a development block as consisting of a number of sectors that share a common long-run trend (i.e. are cointegrated) and linked to each other by mutually reinforcing Granger causality, where the latter ensures short term complementarities among industries. The method of using modern time series methods to identify leading industries was earlier used by Greasley and Oxley (2000) to gauge the leading sector groups of the British Industrial Revolution.

In Greasley and Oxley (2010a) we firstly investigated the existence of common long-run trends among the conventional industry sectors; pastoral, agriculture, manufacturing, minerals and a miscellaneous group. The unit root tests showed New Zealand's economic development was driven by 18 industries with the non-stationary output trends. At issue is how many of these trends were common to more than one industry, pointing to the existence of development blocks. If trends were common to groups of industries then the possible sources of growth are simplified, as the effects of output innovations, including those from new technology will spill across industries. The cointegration tests showed (see Greasley and Oxley, 2010a, Table 3) that a small number of stochastic common trends drove output in most sector groups. Both the pastoral and agricultural sectors have two stochastic common trends, and the manufacturing sector only one. A cointegrating relationship was not observed for the mineral sector, and gold and kauri gum have individual output trends.

These findings show a small number of industry groups were central to the long-run development of New Zealand economy to 1939, with, for example, the 8 manufacturing industries forming a unified group. Interestingly though the pastoral sector did not form a singular development block. The existence of two common trends in the pastoral sector shows the dairy and the meat industries were not simply connected by the opportunities of refrigeration, but that different forces shaped their output. Possibly the dichotomy stems from much of the frozen meat trade originating in the South Island corporate enterprises, whereas North Island cooperatives dominated dairying. Dairying expansion also required the clearing and cultivation of wetter, forested North Island land and different technologies, most especially that connected to cream separation. In the case of agriculture the existence of two stochastic trends probably relates to differences between the output drivers of potatoes and the two grain crops (wheat and oats).

The existence of development blocks also requires short term complementarities between industries, and these are evaluated using tests of Granger causality. Additionally the list of possible leading industries will be made clearer by considering the direction of causal relationships between the industries. For example, sectors or development blocks which shared common trends may have been led by one particular industry. Of special interest is whether or not the impact of any industry spanned beyond its sector group to lead other sectors and overall commodity output.

The causal links between the 18 industries with non-stationary output are shown in Table 14, above. Generally, manufacturing, the pastoral industries and construction have the most causal links. However, construction and most manufacturing industries were followers, while pastoral industries' output often led the output of other industries. Thus beer has 15 causal links, including that with total commodity output, but in 10 cases beer followed, and in one other the causality was bidirectional. Similarly wool cloth has 15 causal links, with 13 of these as a follower or bidirectional. Construction has 13 causal links, but was unambiguously led by output in other industries. Several other manufacturing industries, including saw mills and doors, and foundry and engineering have multiple causal links, but principally these show bidirectional causality within manufacturing or a follower relationship with the pastoral sector. Within manufacturing, printing and publishing is the industry with the most leading causal links. Printing and publishing accounted for around 23% of (non-pastoral) manufacturing from 1915, becoming the largest

Table 14. Summary of Granger Causality Tests (Number of Causal Links).

	Leading	Following	Bidirectional
Pastoral Industries			
Meat	8	0	3
Cheese	6	1	3
Butter	8	1	1
Manufacturing industries			
Wool cloth	2	8	5
Beer	4	10	1
Grain milling	5	2	1
Biscuits	4	4	1
Saw mills and doors	3	7	2
Foundry and engineering	3	7	2
Printing and publishing	7	1	2
Shoes and boots	4	4	2
Agriculture			
Wheat	0	2	0
Oats	3	5	1
Potatoes	0	3	0
Mining and other industries			
Gold	2	0	4
Gas	4	3	2
Construction	0	11	2

element of the sector by 1935. The results show printing and publishing had bidirectional causality with all commodity output and wool cloth, and led beer, saw mills and doors, foundry and engineering, shoes and boots, potatoes, kauri gum and construction.

In the mining sector, gold was of principal importance and still contributed around 7% of commodity output in 1905. Gold had bidirectional causal links with all commodity output and the pastoral sector, and led beer output. The pastoral sector dominates the leading causal links with other industries. Meat and butter are the only industries which led all commodity output. Meat led the output of nine industries, and had bidirectional causality with two others. Interestingly though, no evidence was found of causality between the meat and dairy industries. In addition to all commodity output butter also led seven industries, and cheese led the output of six industries, including butter.

The pastoral sector dominated economic development in New Zealand, but the meat and dairy sectors each had individual driving forces, and formed separate development blocks. Gold was important, at least until the early years of the 20th century, and made a contribution to stimulating pastoral and all commodity output. The manufacturing sector (other than the manufacture of pastoral goods) did form a unified block which shared a single stochastic common trend, but most linkages of the sector, with one exception, were bidirectional or following. The exception is printing and publishing, which comprised a sizeable element of New Zealand manufacturing, and led four other manufacturing industries as well as potatoes, kauri gum and construction. A small number of key industries, specifically, meat, cheese, butter, gold and printing and publishing, shaped the directions of New Zealand's economic development.

4.4 *Time Series Based Test for Convergence*

The economic underpinnings of the 'convergence hypothesis', the view that poorer countries, in terms of GDP per capita, tend to grow faster than richer countries and as a result, economies should 'converge' in terms of per capita income, arises naturally within the standard or augmented Solow neoclassical growth model. Here differences in initial endowments are seen to have no long-term effects on economic growth with deficient countries able to catch-up to the leaders who suffer from diminishing returns. In contrast, Rebelo-type models of economic growth imply leadership can be maintained with non-convergence the likely outcome. As such, not only are tests of convergence interesting in their own right, but they emerge as one natural testable implication of alternative models of growth. However, convergence is but one implication of such models and does not in itself represent a full test of the competing approaches. In order to test for convergence some form of clear definition and some appropriate form of time series data are required where, as we will see, the crucial feature to be exploited are the time series properties of the data.

Bernard and Durlauf (1995) utilize the Dickey–Fuller unit root testing procedure and cointegration as time series based tests of convergence. Here convergence implies output innovations in one economy should be transmitted internationally. The absence of transmission implies that per capita output differences between countries contains a unit root, since output shocks generating relative GDP movement infinitely persist causing economic divergence – an implication of the endogenous growth models of Rebelo.

Bernard and Durlauf (1995) define two types of convergence and two types of 'common trend'

Definition 2.1. Convergence in output.

Countries i and j converge if the long-term forecasts of output in both (countries) are equal at a fixed time t:

$$\lim_{k\to\infty} E(y_{i,t+k} - y_{j,t+k}|I_t) = 0 \qquad (40)$$

Definition 2.1′. Convergence in multivariate output.

Countries p = 1, ..., n converge if the long-term forecasts of output for all (countries) are equal at a fixed time t:

$$\lim_{k\to\infty} E(y_{i,t+k} - y_{p,t+k}|I_t) = 0 \quad \forall p \neq 1 \qquad (41)$$

Definition 2.2. Common trends in output.

Countries i and j contain a common trend if the long-term forecasts (of output) are proportional at a fixed time t:

$$\lim_{k\to\infty} E(y_{i,t+k} - \alpha y_{j,t+k}|I_t) = 0 \tag{42}$$

Definition 2.2′. Common trends in multivariate output.

Countries p = 1, ..., n contain a single common trend if the long-term forecasts of output for all (countries) are equal at a fixed time t.

Letting $\bar{y}_t = [y_{2t}, y_{3t}, \ldots y_{pt}]$ then

$$\lim_{k\to\infty} E(y_{1,t+k} - \alpha'_p \bar{y}_{t+k}|I_t) = 0 \tag{43}$$

In terms of estimation and testing of the various types of convergence and common trend models, the main factor to note is that convergence implies that long-run forecasts of, in the case of output convergence, output differences, tend to zero at $t \to \infty$. If y_i and y_j etc, are $I(1)$, which seems to be the empirical observation for most countries, it means that there is a natural way to test for convergence in the framework by invoking the properties and testing frameworks of unit roots and cointegration we have discussed earlier. In terms of Definition 2.1, *i* and *j* converge if their outputs are cointegrated with a restriction on the coefficients in cointegrating vector being $[1, -1]$. Alternatively in this bivariate case we can consider a simple unit root test on the differences in output. Note that if y_i and y_j are TS, then we can re-think of the definitions requiring that the time trends for each of *i* and *j* must be the same.

If the countries do not satisfy the strict requirement of convergence they may still be subject to the same permanent shocks. These are the cases relevant to Bernard and Durlauf's Definitions 2.2 and 2.2′. Testability in these cases can also invoke cointegration, but in this case the requirements are not as strong – now the restrictions on the coefficients in cointegrating vector are $[1, -\alpha]$.

We can also consider slight variations on the Bernard and Durlauf (1995) definitions which can be illustrated via the concepts of *catching-up* and *long-run convergence.*

Definition: ***Catching-up:*** *consider two countries i and j, and denote their per capita real output as y_i and y_j. Catching-up implies the absence of a unit root in their difference ($y_i - y_j$).*

This concept of convergence relates to economies *out of long-run equilibrium* over a *fixed interval of time*, but assumes that they are sufficiently similar to make tests (and rejections), of the hypothesis non-trivial. In this case *catching-up* relates to the tendency for the difference in per capita output to narrow over time. Hence non-stationarity in ($y_i - y_j$) must violate the proposition although the occurrence of a non-zero time trend, a deterministic trend, in the process in itself, would not.

Definition: ***Long-run convergence:*** *consider two countries i and j, and denote their per capita real output as y_i and y_j. Long-run convergence implies the absence of a* *unit root in their difference ($y_i - y_j$) or a time trend in the deterministic process, i.e. the absence of both a stochastic and deterministic trend.*

Catching-up differs from long-run convergence in that the latter relates to some particular period T equated with long-run steady-state equilibrium. In this case the existence of a time trend in the non-stationary ($y_i - y_j$) would imply a narrowing of the (per capita output) gap or simply that the countries though *catching-up* had *not yet* converged. Conversely, the absence of a time trend in the stationary series implies that catching-up has been completed.

Clearly long-run convergence and catching-up are related in that both imply stationary ($y_i - y_j$). However, long-run convergence relates only to (similar) economies in long-run equilibrium and therefore represents a much stronger version of the convergence hypothesis.

As defined above, tests of catching-up and long-run convergence hinge, therefore, on the time series properties of ($y_i - y_j$). The natural route for such tests involves Dickey–Fuller type tests based on the bivariate difference in per capita output between pairs of countries, i and j, i.e.

$$y_{it} - y_{jt} = \mu + \alpha(y_{i,t-1} - y_{j,t-1}) + \beta t + \sum_{\kappa=1}^{\nu} \delta\Delta(y_{i,t-k} - y_{j,t-k}) + \varepsilon_t \quad (44)$$

where y indicates the logarithm of per capita output. If the difference between the output series contains a unit root, $\alpha = 1$, output per capita in the two economies will diverge. The absence of a unit root, $\alpha < 1$, indicates either catching-up, if $\beta \neq 0$, or long-run convergence if $\beta = 0$.

The main reservation surrounding the robustness of unit root tests in general, and therefore their application to tests of convergence in particular, concerns the possibility that structural discontinuities in the series may lead to erroneous acceptance of the unit root hypothesis.

Time series based tests of convergence, with and without breaks, were presented in Greasley and Oxley (1995, 1997a, 1998c) and a summary of some of those results are presented next.

4.4.1 *Some Results on Convergence: Australia and Britain*

Here we present pairwise tests for long-run (steady state) convergence, and catching-up between Britain, Australia and the USA for the period 1870–1992 using the unit root approach. On the basis of the results in Table 15 below, based on equation (43), neither version of the convergence hypothesis receives support, since a unit root cannot be rejected in the cross-country differences in GDP per capita.

However the likelihood of structural discontinuities in the Australian (and the British) growth record, for example, that associated with the crash of 1891, suggests their impact on the convergence process warrants investigation.

However, the failure of the time series approach to identify convergence may stem from discontinuities in the process generating the data and can be assessed by

Table 15. Unit Root Tests UK–Australia, USA–Australia and UK–USA, GDP Per Capita (Without Discontinuities).

Countries	Sample	ADF	LM(SC)
UK–Australia	1870–1992	*−3.250*	0.792
USA–Australia +	1870–1992	*−2.301*	0.047
UK–USA +	1870–1992	*−3.160*	0.994

*Denotes significant at the 5% level based upon MacKinnon (1991), ADF denotes ADF(4) except those marked + which relate to ADF(2). # *p*-value on included time trend = 0.627.

Table 16. Unit Root Tests – Differences in GDP Per Capita Zivot and Andrews Approach.

Country	*k*	Year	Crash	Trend	Crash and trend
UK–Australia	4	1870–1992	−5.418*	−4.192	−5.440*
			[1891]	[1899]	[1891]
USA–Australia	2	1870–1992	−4.085	−4.483*	−4.585
			[1891]	[1943–44]	[1941]
UK–USA	3	1870–1992	−4.303	−4.828	−5.342
			[1966]	[1950]	[1941]

k is the degree of augmentation *Denotes significant at the 5% level based upon Zivot and Andrews (1992), [] denotes the year of the maximum absolute value of the ADF.

applying, for example, the Zivot and Andrews' search procedure to the comparative series. The results in Table 16 below report the maximum absolute ADF statistics obtained by searching over the period 1870–1992 for crash, trend and joint crash and trend changes in a naturally extended version of equation (44).

All three pairwise results reject the existence of a unit root in some variant of the model and are supportive of some form of the convergence hypothesis. The UK–Australia results support long-run convergence, with the 1891 crash marking a discontinuity in the process.

The UK–Australia results do contain a significant joint crash and trend change discontinuity in 1891, but the absence of a significant individual trend break and the closeness of the crash and joint crash and trend break ADF statistics point to the dominance of the 1891 crash. Alternatively, both the USA–Australia and UK–USA results contain significant trend discontinuities, and hence favour the weaker, *catching-up* version of the convergence hypothesis. Catch-up towards the USA's GDP per capita appears to date from 1950 for the UK and the years of World War II for Australia.

The results therefore show how the omission of significant discontinuities can lead to incorrect inferences being drawn regarding convergence and importantly the possible causes of economic growth. In particular, in the UK–Australia case where long-run convergence is inferred, support for the Solow growth model emerges. Catching-up in the UK–USA and USA–Australia case is supportive of the augmented Solow model, while no case supports one important implication of the Rebelo model, i.e. long-term non-convergence. However, as stated earlier such implications do not constitute full tests of the growth models.

4.4.2 *Alternative Time Series Based Tests of Convergence: St. Aubyn (1999)*

St. Aubyn (1999), defines convergence as follows:

Two series, $y_i - y_j$, converge if:

$$(y_i - y_j) \rightarrow p\varepsilon_t \text{ as } t \rightarrow \infty \tag{45}$$

where $\rightarrow p$, means converges in probability and ε_t is a random variable where:

$$E(\varepsilon_t) = D_{XY} \tag{46}$$

$$\text{var}(\varepsilon_t) = \sigma < 0 \tag{47}$$

Via equations (45)–(47), convergence implies that the difference between the two series converges in probability to a third series which is stationary, with constant mean D_{XY} and a constant variance σ. St. Aubyn (1999), relates these characteristics to previous notions of economic convergence, i.e.;

(1) *Point wise convergence* $\rightarrow$ $\text{var}(\varepsilon_t) = 0$,
(2) *Unconditional convergence* $\rightarrow$ $D_{XY} = 0$ and
(3) *Conditional convergence* $\rightarrow$ $D_{XY} \neq 0$.

The results presented as Tables 17–19, which use the St. Aubyn approach, are taken from Oxley and Greasley (1997b) where they are particularly interested in establishing whether some groups of countries converge (but not others) via the idea of 'Convergence Clubs'.

The results treat France as the leader, i.e. y_i in all instances where a 'European Club' is considered and likewise Sweden for the 'Nordic' group. For the full sample, 1900–1987, the null hypothesis of non-convergence is rejected in all cases with the weakest result being between France and Germany where rejection is at the 10% level only. On the basis of the full sample period results the concept of a European Convergence Club comprising France, Belgium, Germany, Italy, The Netherlands and the United Kingdom cannot be rejected and likewise a Nordic Club of Sweden, Denmark, Finland and Norway.

St. Aubyn (1999) finds in his study of convergence, where he treats the USA as the leader, that in all cases that pre- and post-World War II results differ. Tables 18 and 19 taken from Greasley and Oxley (1997b, g), present results for the sample sub-periods 1900–1938 and 1946–1987. The results from Table 18 lead to non-rejection of the non-convergence null for all cases. The results from Table 19, however, confirm, with somewhat more significant, results from the full sample conclusions, i.e. rejection of the non-convergence null in all cases for the European Club, but not non-rejection in the Nordic case.

Table 17. Tests of Convergence: St. Aubyn Test.

Countries	1900–1987
France–Austria	*−3.359**
France–Belgium	*−2.681**
France–Germany	*−2.297***
France–Italy	*−9.004**
France–Netherlands	*−6.277**
France–UK	*−6.082**
Sweden–Denmark	*−3.143**
Sweden–Finland	*−5.474**
Sweden–Norway	*−2.847**

*Denotes significant at the 5% and ** 10% level based upon St. Aubyn (1999).

Table 18. Tests of Convergence: St. Aubyn Test.

Countries	1900–1938
France–Austria	*0.200*
France–Belgium	*1.583*
France–Germany	*1.436*
France–Italy	*−0.154*
France–Netherlands	*0.107*
France–UK	*−0.025*
Sweden–Denmark	*1.339*
Sweden–Finland	*−0.217*
Sweden–Norway	*−0.601*

The sub-sample results seem to imply that, in the European case, convergence occurs most strongly post WWII. However, the full sample convergence implications for the Nordic Club are not supported by either sub-period. This could be due to small sample estimation problems.

4.5 *Application of STM Model to English Real Wages Data 1264–1913*

In Section 3.8 above, some benefits of utilizing the STM of Harvey (1989) were detailed. In the examples below we present some new results from applying these methods to the English (chiefly London) real wages data 1264–1913 using STAMP version 8.3. The real wages data are for building labour as discussed by Allen (2001). long-run real wages data have been utilized by Galor (2005) and by Crafts and Mills (2009) to consider the timing of the transition from the Malthusian era. The STM model provides an especially useful route to examining such issues

Table 19. Tests of Convergence: St. Aubyn Test.

Countries	1946–1987
France–Austria	*−10.24**
France–Belgium	*−4.336**
France–Germany	*−6.352**
France–Italy	*−2.651**
France–Netherlands	*−4.376**
France–UK	*−3.463**
Sweden–Denmark	*−0.119*
Sweden–Finland	*−1.142*
Sweden–Norway	*1.673*

*Denotes significant at the 5% level based upon St. Aubyn (1999).

by distinguishing between level and trend breaks and outliers in long-run time series.

In the STM model the 'one-off' outliers are captured by interventions (for a discussion of the types of intervention see Harvey and Koopman, 1992), where outliers could be simply data driven measurement errors or 'obvious' one year only effects; the level shifts will typically pick up longer periods of level changes (possibly associated disease, including the Black Death, famine or wars); whereas a detected trend change will likely need an explanation via technological changes. Of course, if the underlying model structure is mis-specified then the interventions are just trying to handle the model misspecification. Thus the model we 'choose' should correspond with historical evidence of structural changes that suggest any dates identified for breaks are 'understandable and acceptable', most especially for any level and trend changes.

Figure 3 above presents a plot of the data, presented in logs.

As discussed in Section 3.8 above there are alternative ways these data can be modelled within the STM approach. Some of the possible assumptions that can be made are shown and tested below, using the real wages data to illustrate. The key issues of the historiography concern the timing of the shift to higher trend real wages growth (associated either with the end of the Malthusian era, the Industrial Revolution or a post-Industrial Revolution demographic transition); and the existence or otherwise of a long period of constant real wages before any decisive shift to higher trend growth. Identifying trend breaks in the long-run real wages data are complicated by particular demographic or monetary events, notably the near century of population decline associated with the Black Death from 1347 which reduced Europe's population by around one-third (Persson, 2010), and the debasements and re-coinages of the 16th century (Outhwaite, 1969). Real wages rose as population fell with the Black Death, but discerning the post-plague real wages peak is further complicated by currency manipulations in the 1540s. English real wages show a peak around 1548. There were sharp spikes in London

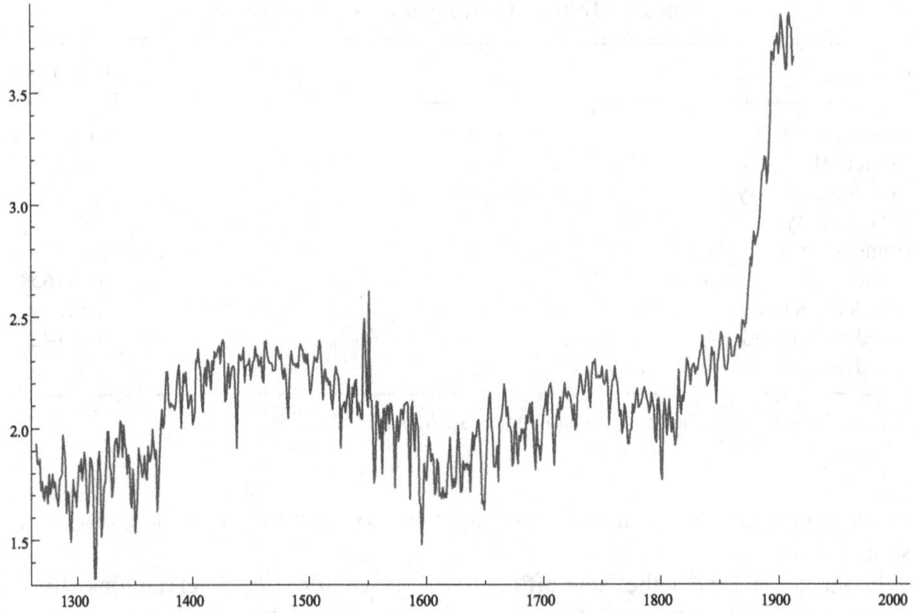

Figure 3. Log of English Building Labour Real Wages, 1264–1913.

real wages around that date probably connected to currency manipulations, and post Black Death wage growth in England may not have been sustained beyond 1500.

The ability of the STM model to reveal outliers as well as level and trend breaks offers the promise of disentangling the complex forces shaping long-run English real wages. Some of the possible modelling strategies are listed 1–7, and a range of implications are illustrated below in Sections 4.5.1–5.

(1) The trend is a random walk with fixed drift (level stochastic and slope fixed) plus irregular (white noise), illustrated below in 4.5.1 as Model 1 in Figure 4.
(2) As above (1) but with a cycle which is AR2, not illustrated.
(3) As above (2) but allowing for interventions to capture outliers. Therefore we have: the trend is a random walk with fixed drift (level stochastic and slope fixed) the cycle is AR2 plus irregular (white noise) + interventions (automatic), which are illustrated below in 4.5.2 as Model 2 in Figure 5.
(4) A local linear model: the level is stochastic; slope stochastic plus cycle plus irregular, not illustrated.
(5) As above (4) but allowing for interventions, illustrated below, using a 5 year cycle, in 4.5.3 as Model 3 in Figure 6, and 20-year cycle in 4.5.5 as Model 5 in Figure 8.
(6) As 4 above but fixed level; stochastic slope plus cycle plus irregular, not illustrated.

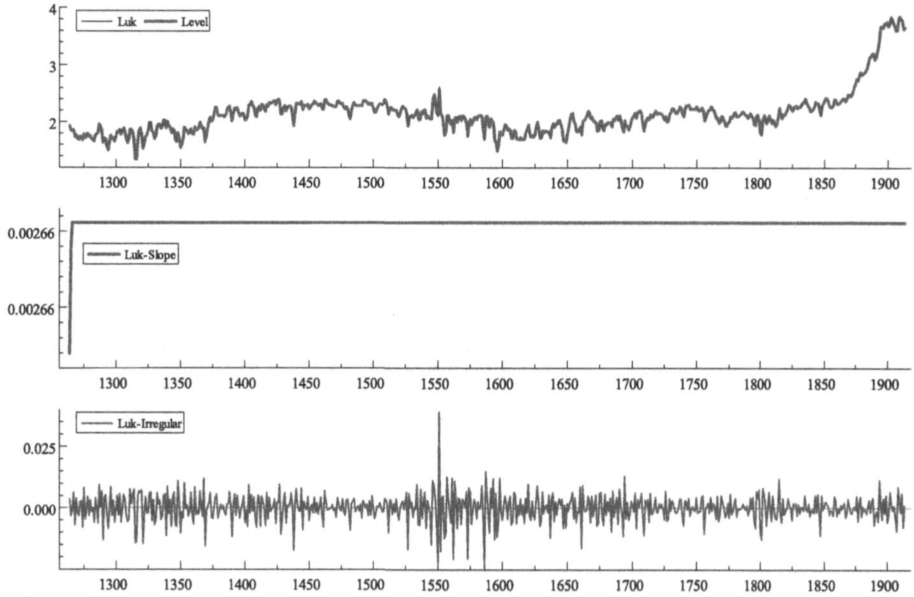

Figure 4. English Real Wages Model 1.

(7) As above (6) but allowing for interventions, illustrated in 4.5.4 using a 5 year cycle as Model 4 in Figure 7.

4.5.1 *Trend is a Random Walk with Fixed Drift*

This model, without interventions to capture outliers, fits the data very poorly; the Durbin–Watson statistic = 1.98 and $R^2 = 0.004$. The trend, shown in the middle segment of Figure 4 (the slope of the log of real wages) is constant by assumption; it would be clearly wrong to impose this formulation to represent the data.

4.5.2 *Trend is a Random Walk with Fixed Drift Plus Interventions*

This formulation adds the use of interventions to the previous model to capture outliers. In STAMP interventions can be user defined or automated. Automation involves the use of the standardized smoothed estimates of the disturbances referred to as the *auxiliary residuals*. The auxiliary residuals are smoothed estimates of the irregular and level disturbances. Graphs of these residuals, in conjunction with normality tests, are used for detecting data irregularities such as *outliers*, *level changes* and *slope changes*. Here an outlier is an unusually large value of the *irregular* disturbance at a point in time which can be handled via an impulse intervention variable which takes a value 1 at that point, 0 otherwise. In contrast a *structural break in the level* is captured by a shift up or down as a *step intervention*,

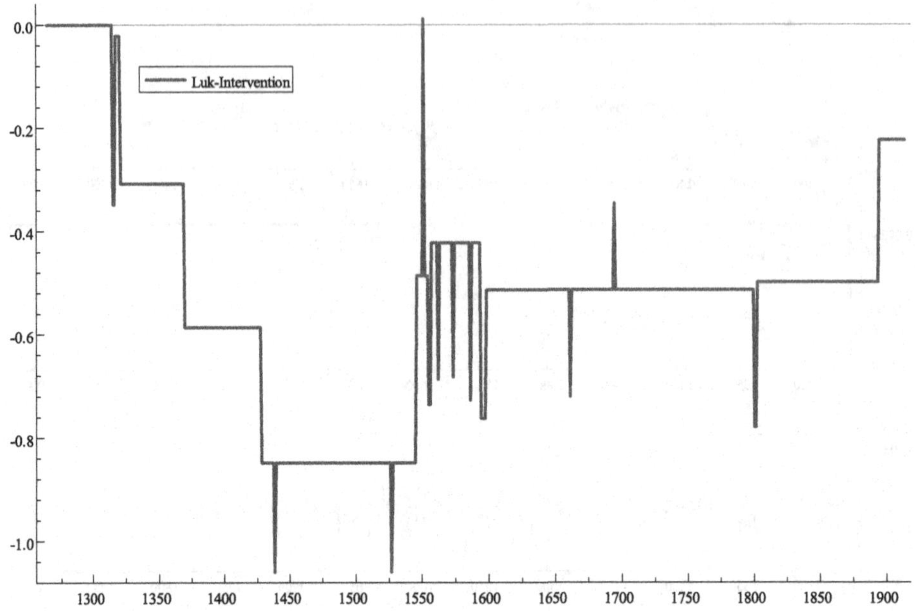

Figure 5. Timing and Location of Interventions Model 2.

Notes. The outlier and level interventions are: Outliers 1438, 1527, 1551, 1562, 1573, 1586, 1661 and 1694; Levels breaks 1315, 1317, 1321, 1369, 1428, 1546, 1555, 1557, 1594, 1598, 1800, 1802 and 1894.

0 before the event and 1 subsequently, and a structural break in the slope as a staircase intervention, 1, 2, 3,..., starting after the detected break.

Figure 5 above plots the timing of the interventions as selected automatically by STAMP. The adding of the outliers leads to considerable improvement in goodness of fit; now the Durbin–Watson statistic = 1.90 and $R^2 = 0.40$. It should be noted this model retains the assumption of a fixed trend, and the level and outlier interventions may reflect these types of interventions are attempting to fit the data when the underlying model choice is too constraining. The volume of level breaks shown by this model for the 16th century appears excessive, and casts doubt on whether or not outlier and levels interventions are appropriately identified.

4.5.3 *A Local Linear Model: The Level is Stochastic; Slope Stochastic, Plus 5 Year Cycle Plus Irregular Plus Interventions*

This model relaxes the assumption of a fixed slope, and shows a further improvement in specification; the Durbin–Watson statistic = 1.88; and $R^2 = 0.43$. Figure 6 above plots the timing of the interventions as selected automatically by STAMP. They include a single trend break at 1867, which suggests that Industrial Revolution technology's impact of real wages was long delayed, and interrupted by

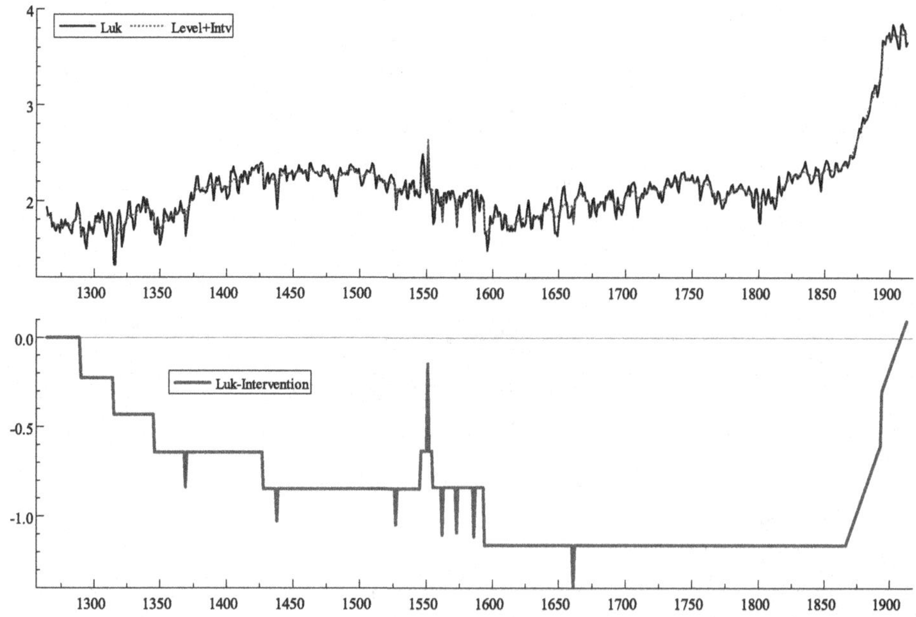

Figure 6. English Real Wages Model 3.

Notes. The interventions are: Outliers 1369, 1438, 1527, 1551, 1562, 1573, 1586 and 1661; Levels breaks 1290, 1315, 1346, 1428, 1546, 1555, 1594 and 1894; Slope breaks 1867.

a level shift around 1894. Overall the model shows fewer levels breaks than 4.5.2, and thus a representation of the long-run data the accords more closely with the historiography. Between 1594 and 1867 the model shows no structural breaks in real wages and a single outlier in 1661. The long stagnation of English real wages following the higher levels during the century of population collapse to 1450 shown by this variant of the SMT model provides a plausible interpretation of English real wages history.

4.5.4 *Fixed Level; Slope Stochastic, Plus 5 Year Cycle Plus Irregular Plus Interventions*

This variant retains the stochastic trend assumption, but adopts a fixed level representation. The model is shown inferior to that which incorporates a stochastic level, with Durbin–Watson statistic = 1.76; and R^2 = 0.40. However this representation also shows a long stagnation of real wages 1594–1868, see Figure 7 above.

4.5.5 *Stochastic Level; Stochastic Trend; 20 Year Cycle; Irregular Plus Interventions*

This variant replicates model 4.6.3 but adopts a 20-year cycle, which improves the goodness of fit, with Durbin–Watson statistic = 1.87; and R^2 = 0.52. The timing of

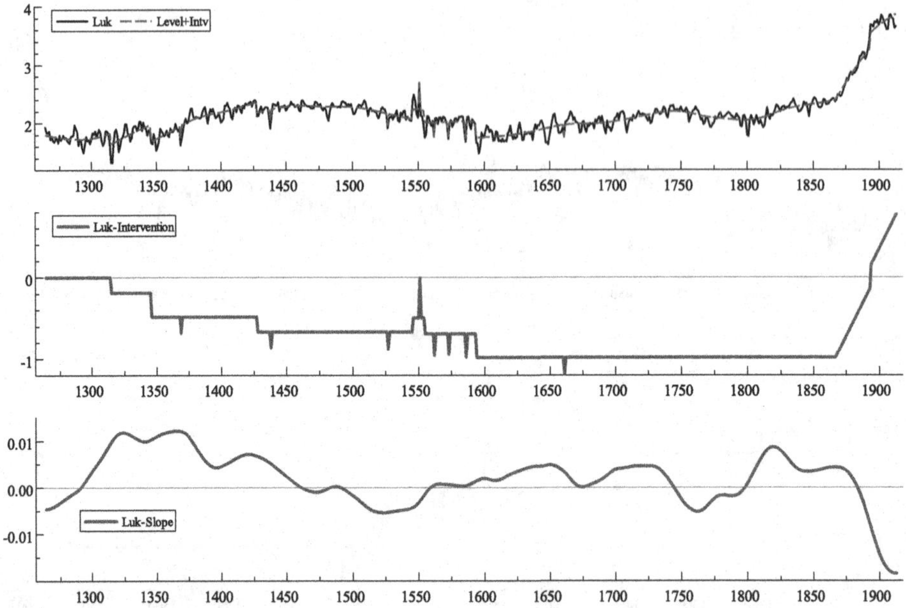

Figure 7. English Real Wages Model 4.

Notes. The interventions are: Outliers, 1369, 1438, 1527, 1551, 1562, 1573, 1586 and 1661; Levels breaks 1315, 1346, 1428, 1546, 1555, 1594 and 1894; Slope break 1868.

all interventions are the same as for model 4.6.3, including the single trend break in 1867, see Figure 8 above.

By using a sequence of SMT modelling strategies this section illustrates how English real wages 1264–1913 can be represented, by adopting varying assumptions surrounding trends, levels, irregular outliers and cycles. The interventions identified by STAMP shed light on real wages history, but also in the plausibility of the alternative models. The flexible models which allow both the level and slope to be stochastic, and include cyclical elements provide the best representations of the data. The results from these simple illustrations conflict with elements of the published literature. For example, the unified theory of Galor and Weil (2000) postulates a two break model where incomes per capita accelerate modestly around the Industrial Revolution of the late 18th century and more dramatically around the later 19th century demographic transition. The preferred results shown as Model 5, in contrast, show a long period of stagnant real wages 1594–1867. Moreover Crafts and Mills (2009) utilizing Clark's (2005) alternative real wages find a trend break around 1800 in conflict with the results from the SMT model which show a later break of 1867.

4.6 *Multiple Changes in Persistence and English Real Wages 1264–1913*

An alternative way to investigate long-run trends in English real wages is to consider if the series have alternating stochastic properties. In Section 4.3.1

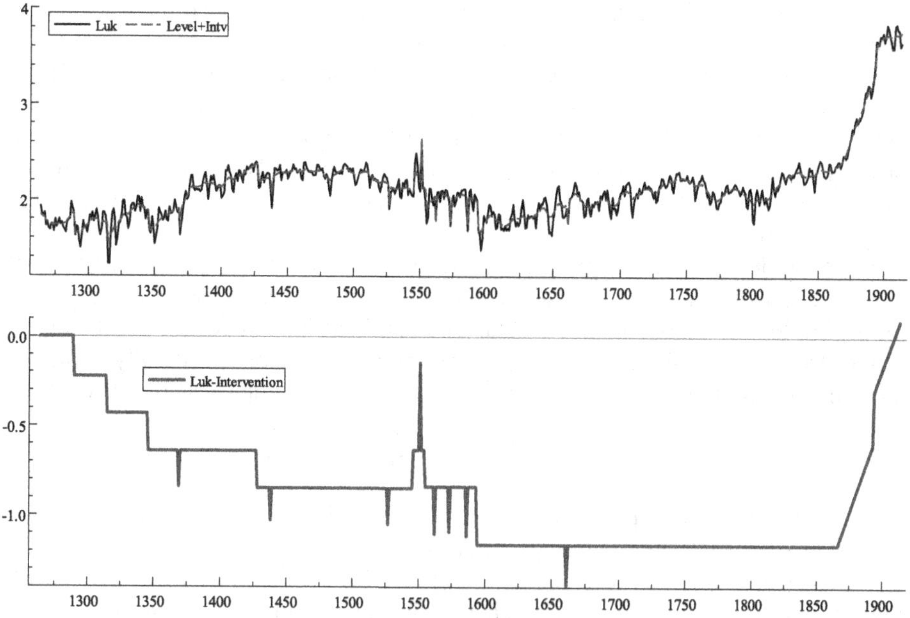

Figure 8. English Real Wages Model 5.

Notes. The interventions are: Outliers 1369, 1438, 1527, 1551, 1562, 1573, 1586 and 1661; Levels breaks 1290, 1315, 1346, 1428, 1546, 1555, 1594 and 1894; Slope breaks 1867.

above, we considered the test of Leybourne *et al.* (2007) applied to British industrial production data, 1700–1992. The same test applied to the real wages data considered in Section 4.6 suggests the following: $I(0)$ 1264–1858, with effectively a zero trend then $I(1)$ to 1913. The results, however, also suggest the potential for a short return to trend stationarity for the period 1881–1894, but the sample size is too small to confirm this categorically.

5. Some New Developments/Applications with Potential for Cliometrics

In Section 5, we introduce some new and emerging methods which we believe will be of importance to cliometrics research in the future. In particular we will discuss: the *mildly explosive processes* of Phillips and Yu (2009); *graphical Modelling*; and although not totally new to cliometrics, a discussion of *fractionally integrated processes* and their *long memory* interpretations.

5.1 *Mildly Explosive Processes – Phillips and Yu (2009)*

Phillips and Yu (2009) have developed a new econometric methodology to test if and when bubbles emerge and collapse and apply it in various stock markets, real estate markets, mortgage markets, commodity markets and the foreign exchange market over the period surrounding the subprime crisis.

The basis of their new approach is to consider *mildly explosive processes.* If we consider the typical DS versus TS testing procedures for a unit root, we restrict our attention to regions of 'no more than' a unit root process – an autoregressive process where $\rho \leq 1$. Phillips and Yu (2009) model 'mildly explosive' behaviour by an autoregressive process with a root ρ that exceeds unity, but still in the neighbourhood of unity.

The basic idea of their approach is to recursively calculate right-sided unit root tests of a standard form, for example, Dickey–Fuller-type, to assess evidence for mildly explosive behaviour in the data. The test is a right-sided test and therefore differs from the usual left-sided tests for stationarity. More specifically, consider the following autoregressive specification estimated by recursive least squares:

$$X_t = \mu + \delta X_{t-1} + \varepsilon_t, \quad \varepsilon_t \sim NID(0, \sigma^2) \tag{48}$$

The usual H_0: $\delta = 1$ applies, but unlike the left-sided tests which have relevance for a stationary alternative, Phillips and Yu (2009) have H_1: $\delta > 1$ which with $\delta = 1 + c/kn$, where $kn \to \infty$ and $kn/n \to 0$ allows for their 'mildly explosive' cases. Phillips and Yu (2009) argue that their tests have discriminatory power because,

> They are sensitive to the changes that occur when a process undergoes a change from a unit root to a mildly explosive root or vice versa. This sensitivity is much greater than in left-sided unit root tests against stationary alternatives . . . Although a unit root process can generate successive upward movements, these movements still have a random wandering quality unlike those of a stochastically explosive process where there is a distinct nonlinearity in movement and little bias in the estimation of the autoregressive coefficient.

We believe these new approaches to identifying growing bubbles and their collapse will make a significant impact on this aspect of time series applied econometrics and because of the nature of the data and the questions on financial cliometrics.

5.2 *Graphical Modelling and Implications for Causality Testing*

Graphical modelling is a relatively new statistical approach whose major development started in the 1970s. It is a very convenient interface to obtain and crucially present in a graphical way, pairwise relationships among random variables in a multivariate context. It has important links to causality and testing for causality and its manifest output makes it much easier to understand the linkages between variables of interest. Below, we will present some of the basis of the approach, some references to the technical details for those interested, some past applications and current developments. We believe the approach has enormous potential for cliometricans in the future, in particular, its ability to easily – graphically – present results on causality and exogeneity.

The initial step in the graphical modelling approach is the computation of the partial correlations among the variables in the multivariate system where this can be

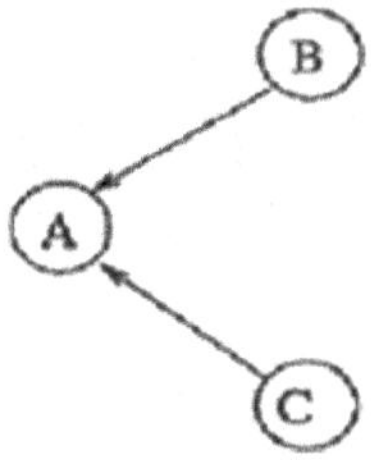

Figure 9. DAG.

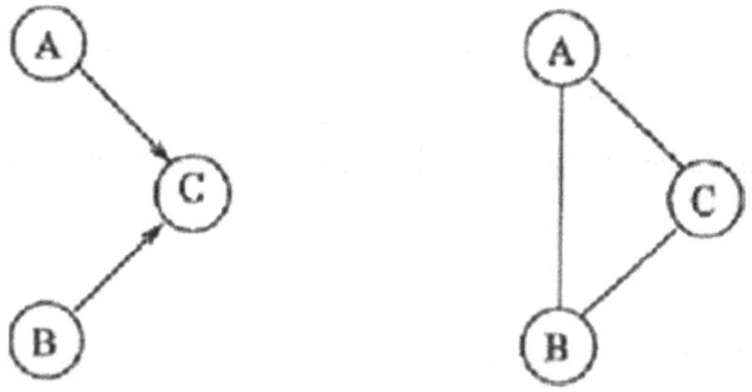

Figure 10. Moralization of a DAG.

achieved by inverting and rescaling the covariance matrix as suggested by Whittaker (1990). With these computations complete, we can then distinguish between significant and non-significant partial correlations using an opportune test. Finally we can present the results by a graph where the random variables are represented by *nodes* and a significant partial correlation between two random variables is indicated by a line that links them. The line in graph theory terminology is called and *edge*. If the variables in the graph are jointly distributed as a multivariate Gaussian distribution a significant partial correlation implies the presence of conditional dependence. For this reason the graph described by these conditions is called a *conditional independence graph* or CIG.

A more informative object is the *directed acyclic graph* or DAG. This is a directed graph where the arrows linking the nodes are where the joint distribution of the variables can be expressed as a sequence of marginal conditional distributions. For example, consider the graph in Figure 9 below.

Its joint density function can be defined as: $f(a, b, c) = f(a|b, c)f(b)f(c)$.

Although the DAG and the CIG represent a different definition of the joint probability, there is a correspondence between the two graphs which is embodied by the *moralization rule*. The rule means that we can obtain the CIG from the DAG by transforming the arrow into lines linking unlinked parents. Consider by way of example Figure 10 below.

A and B are called the *parents* of C. The moralization of the DAG on the left is obtained by transforming the existing arrows into edges and by adding an edge

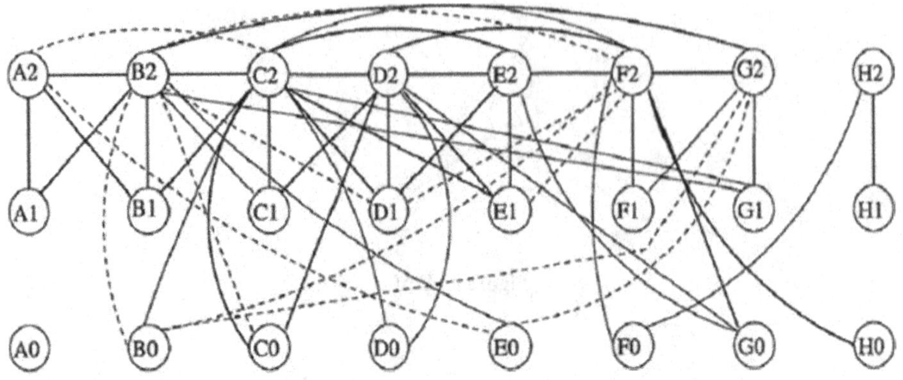

Figure 11. CIG (a Range of Quarterly NZ and Foreign Interest Rates, 1987–2001).

which links the parents. These edges are called *moral edges*.

Importantly, while the CIG represents the associations among the variables either in terms of conditional dependence or simply in terms of partial correlations, if the joint distribution is not Gaussian, the DAG has a natural interpretation in terms of *causality*. For those wishing to consider more in this area of graphs and causality we refer you to; Shafer (1996); Glymour and Cooper (1999); Lauritzen (2000); Pearl (2000) and Lauritzen and Richardson (2002).

The DAG is very attractive because of its causal interpretation, but all we can observe in practise is the CIG obtained by the sample partial correlation. Therefore, we need to perform the inverse to the moralization, the *demoralization*. While the transformation of a DAG to a CIG is unique, there are several DAGs which might give the same CIG. In this case we need to identify the moral links and remove them and to do that we need to use all the knowledge we have about the relationships among the random variables in the system.

In Oxley *et al.* (2009), we apply these methods to identifying an interest rate transmission mechanism for New Zealand and the sort of graphical interpretations, which in the paper are compared to more traditional Structural VAR models look like Figures 11 and 12 below, where the A's–H's relate to a range of increasing in maturity interest rates, both domestic and foreign (US).

5.3 *Fractional Integration and Long Memory*

In Section 3 above, we discussed the implications for the persistence of shocks in the DS and TS data generating worlds. In the former case, with a unit root, shocks to the $I(1)$ process would have infinite persistence – in the later mean $I(0)$ case with mean reversion, shocks have zero persistence.

However, what about cases where the order of integration is a fraction $d > 0$ and <1? In this case we have a case of *fractional integration,* or in the discrete case,

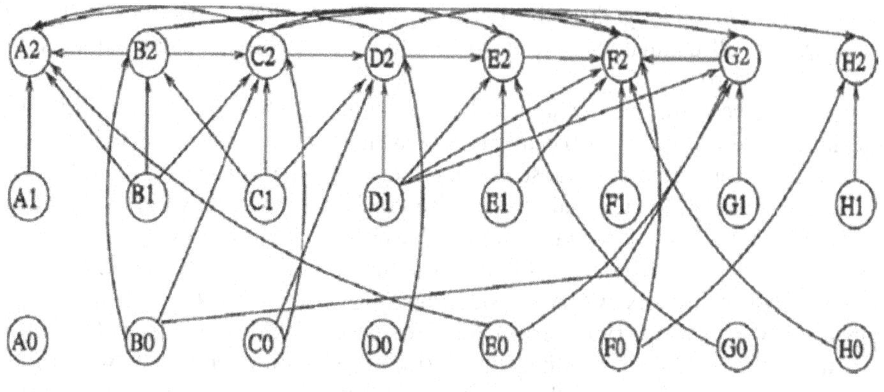

Figure 12. Chosen Model Representation.

ARFIMA (*autoregressive, fractionally integrated moving average*) and the degree of persistence will depend on the size of d. With $0 < d < 1$ we have processes that are typically described as having *long memory* or *long range dependence*. When $-1/2 < d < 0$ we describe the process as *anti-persistent*.

Some of the original work on such processes was undertaken by Hurst (1951) studying the Nile river, but in economics the processes were popularized by Granger and Joyeux (1980) with other major contributions by Robinson (1995, 2003), Beran (1992) and Hosking (1981). The importance of this class of processes derives from smoothly bridging the gap between short memory stationary processes and unit roots in an environment that maintains a greater degree of continuity (Robinson, 1994). For an up-to-date survey see Gils-Alana and Hualde (2009).

In economics and finance it appears common to see estimates of $d \cong 0.4$, implying significant long memory (but not infinite persistence) in the data considered. In economic history, Mishra *et al.* (2009) argue that long memory in economic growth occurs because of stochastic memory in population growth. They estimate d using the Kim and Phillips (2000) modified log-periodgram estimator of Geweke and Porter Hudak (1983) to 'provide evidence of fractionally integrated population growth with non-mean convergent shock dynamics . . . in 63 countries from 1950–2004'. Michelacci and Zalaroni (2000) also consider long memory issues, also in relation to economic growth. They present estimates of d based on the log-periodogram estimator of Geweke and Porter Hudak (1983) and conclude that there is evidence of long memory and present a case for fractional (beta) convergence extending the ideas of the Solow–Swan growth model.

Several potential issues arise when considering long memory models. The first is whether long memory processes make sense. In finance, Rea *et al.* (2008a) argue it makes little sense to consider long-memory or long range dependence in finance theories such as, option pricing models. In the case of economic growth or population, however, long range dependence may make sense. Secondly, however, long memory and structural change are 'observationally equivalent' such that either assumptions can equally describe the data see Rea *et al.* (2008a). Finally and crucially, 'not all estimators of d are born equal', especially in small samples see Rea *et al.* (2008b).

Of the twelve estimators examined by Rea *et al.* (2008b) the Whittle estimator and Haslett and Raftery (1989) estimators performed the best on simulated series. If we require an estimator to be close to unbiased across the full range of d values for which long memory occurs and have a 95% confidence interval width of less than 0.1 d units (that is 20% of the range for d values in which long memory is observed), then for series with fewer than 4000 data points Whittle and Haslett–Raftery are the only two estimators worth considering. For series with 4000 or more data points, the Peng *et al.* (1994) estimator gave acceptable performance. For series with more than 7000 data points the periodogram estimator was a worthwhile choice. For series with more than 8200 data points the wavelet became a viable estimator. The remaining seven estimators they considered did not give acceptable performance at any series lengths examined and are not recommended. If you wish to conclude that long memory processes exist, be sure that the estimator used is 'fit for purpose' as the typical sample sizes, even in long-run cliometric applications are very, very short compared to what is needed for efficient and unbiased estimation.

6. Epilogue

Keynes reminds us that 'Practical men, who believe themselves to be quite exempt from any intellectual influence, are usually the slaves of some defunct economist'. Keeping the slavishly following analogy, we wish to reiterate one quote and pass-on a message which represents a significant warning about delving into the world of time series econometrics and relying, slavishly, on the outcome of tests without recourse to history.

The quote is where we opened this chapter: '*The power of a popular test is irrelevant. A test that is never used has zero power*' (McAleer, 1994, 2005). Although David Hendry might say, 'test, test, test', not all tests are born equal and both type I and type II (or even type III, see Kennedy, 2002) errors pervade empirical work.

The message comes from the genius that was Sir Clive Granger. In Granger (unpublished) he considers a number of so called 'puzzles' in economics and in many cases links them to his famous notion of spurious regressions. However, he also discusses a case where he and a colleague considered the potential for *reintegration* and why relying on the results of statistical tests (especially those with known low power) can be extremely dangerous. To demonstrate the point consider Granger's example from that paper.

In the case of cointegration, the sum of two $I(1)$ series produces a linear combination that is $I(0)$. The complete opposite case would have $I(0) + I(0) = I(1)$. From a theoretical perspective this is impossible and Granger obviously knew this, however Granger and Jeon (unpublished) explored the case empirically. Assume that X_t is a zero mean white noise process with large variance and let $Y_t = Z_t + X_t$, where Z_t is a random walk with white noise inputs having a zero mean and small variance. In their empirical examples with 500 observations standard unit root tests concluded that X and Y were $I(0)$, but their sum (Z_t) was $I(1)$. The testing process, with standard tests, suggested it was possible to sum two $I(0)$'s and obtain an $I(1)$ series! The moral here: never state 'the test proves/demonstrates the data are $I(1)$ or $I(0)$ or I(anything)'. Likewise never forget some of the messages of Kennedy (2002), i.e. Rule #1: Use common sense and economic theory; Rule #3: Know the context; Rule #7: Understand the costs and benefits of data mining and Rule #9: Do not confuse statistical significance with meaningful magnitude.

7. Conclusions

Cliometrics has been with us for half a century and its original hallmarks were the links between economics and economic history see Greasley and Oxley (2010b). However, the use of econometric methods has become more common in quantitative economic history. Understanding modern time series methods and their application, therefore becomes much more important in cliometrics than perhaps ever in the past. The developments in time series econometrics, which started around 1974, have radically changed what cliometricians do, or should do. Granger and Newbold (1974), reminded us of the dangers of spurious regression; Dickey and Fuller (1979) began a research agenda on unit root testing which remains unresolved and provided tests which, although lacking power, are as popularly applied as ever. Engle and Granger (1987), gave us cointegration and the rest, as they say is history.

Acknowledgements

We wish to acknowledge the numerous, wide ranging and stimulating conversations on time series econometrics with the late Sir Clive Granger – his brilliance will be deeply missed. Section 4.1 benefited from the research assistance of Elizabeth Duston. The second author acknowledges financial support from the Marsden Fund.

References

Allen, R.C. (2001) The great divergence in European wages and prices from the middle ages to the First World War. *Explorations in Economic History* 38: 411–447.

Allen, R.C. and Keay, I. (2001) The first great whale extinction: the end of the bowhead whale in the Eastern Arctic. *Explorations in Economic History* 38: 448–477.

Antras, P. and Voth, H.-J. (2003) Factor prices and productivity growth during the British Industrial Revolution. *Explorations in Economic History* 40: 52–77.

Baten, J. and Murray, J.E. (2000) Heights of men and women in 19th-century Bavaria: economic, nutritional, and disease influences. *Explorations in Economic History* 37: 351–369.

Baubeau, P. and Cazelles, B. (2009) French economic cycles: a wavelet analysis of French retrospective GNP series. *Cliometrica* 3: 275–300.

Ben-David, D. and Papell, D. (1998) Slowdowns and meltdowns: postwar growth evidence from 74 Countries. *The Review of Economics and Statistics* 80: 561–571.

Beran, J. (1992) A goodness-of-fit test for time series with long range dependence. *Journal of the Royal Statistical Society B* 54: 749–760.

Bernard, A. and Durlauf, S. (1995) Convergence in international output. *Journal of Applied Econometrics* 10: 97–108.

Beveridge, S. and Nelson, C.R. (1981) A new approach to decomposition of economic time series into permanent and transitory components with particular attention to measurement of the business cycle. *Journal of Monetary Economics* 7: 151–174.

Bhargava, A. (1986) On the theory of testing for unit roots in observed time series. *Review of Economic Studies* 52: 369–384.

Bodenhorn, H. (2007) Usury ceilings and bank lending behavior: evidence from nineteenth century New York. *Explorations in Economic History* 44: 179–202.

Bollerslev, T. (1986) Generalised autoregressive conditional heteroskedasticity. *Journal of Econometrics* 31: 307–327.

Breitung, J. (2000) The local power of some unit root tests for panel data. In B.H. Baltagi (ed.), *Advances in Econometrics, Volume 15: nonstationary Panels, Panel Cointegration, and Dynamic Panels* (pp. 161–178). Amsterdam: JAY Press.

Burhop, C. (2006) Did banks cause the German industrialization? *Explorations in Economic History* 43: 39–63.

Campbell, J. and Mankiw, G. (1987) Are output fluctuations transitory? *The Quarterly Journal of Economics* 102: 857–880.

Capie, F. and Mills, T. (1991) Money and business output in the US and UK, 1870–193. *The Manchester School* 59: 38–56.

Chatfield, C. (1989) *The Analysis of Time Series*. London: Chapman Hall.

Chenery, H.B. and Watanabe, T. (1958) International comparisons of the structure of production. *Econometrica* 29: 487–521.

Cheung, Y.-W. and Lai, K.S. (1995) Lag order and critical values of the augmented Dickey-Fuller test. *Journal of Business & Economic Statistics* 13: 77–280.

Choi, I. (2001) Unit root tests for panel data. *Journal of International Money and Finance* 20: 249–272.

Chow, P.C.Y. (1987) Causality between export growth and industrial performance: evidence from the NIC'S. *Journal of Development Economics* 26: 55–63.

Ciccarelli, C. and Fenoaltea, F. (2007) Business fluctuations in Italy, 1861–1913: The new evidence. *Explorations in Economic History* 44: 432–451.

Clark, G., 2005. The condition of the working class in England, 1209 to 2004. *Journal of Political Economy* 113: 1307–1340.

Cochrane, J. (1988) How big id the random walk in GNP. *Journal of Political Economy* 96: 893–920.

Crafts, N.F.R. and Harley, C.K. (1992) Output growth and the British Industrial Revolution: a restatement of the Crafts-Harley view. *Economic History Review* 45: 703–730.

Crafts, N.F.R. and Mills, T.C. (1994) Trends in real wages in Britain, 1750–1913. *Explorations in Economic History* 31: 176–194.

Crafts, N. and Mills, T.C. (2004) Was 19th century British growth steam-powered? The climacteric revisited. *Explorations in Economic History* 41: 156–171.

Crafts, N.F.R. and Mills, T.C. (2009) From Malthus to Solow: how did the Malthusian economy really evolve. *Journal of Macroeconomics* 31: 68–93.

Crafts, N.C.R., Leybourne, S.J. and Mills, T.C. (1989) Trends and cycles in British industrial production 1700–1913. *Journal of the Royal Statistical Society* 152(1): 43–60.

Crafts, N., Mills, T.C. and Mulatu, A. (2007) Total factor productivity growth on Britain's railways, 1852–1912: A reappraisal of the evidence. *Explorations in Economic History* 44: 608–634.

Craig, L. and Holt, M. (2008) Mechanical refrigeration, seasonality, and the hog–corn cycle in the United States: 1870–1940. *Explorations in Economic History* 45: 30–50.

Dahmen, E. (1988) Development blocks in industrial economics. *The Scandinavian Economic History Review* 36: 3–14.

Darne, O. (2009) The uncertain unit root in real GNP: A re-examination. *Journal of Macroeconomics* 31: 153–166.

Deane, P. and Cole, W.A. (1969) *British Economic Growth, 1688–1959*. Cambridge: Cambridge University Press.

della Paolera, G. and Taylor, A.L. (2002) Internal versus external convertibility and emerging market crises: lessons from Argentine history. *Explorations in Economic History* 39: 357–389.

Dickey, D.A. and Fuller, W.A. (1979) Distribution of the estimators for autoregressive time series with a unit root. *Journal of the American Statistical Association* 74: 427–431.

Dickey, D.A. and Fuller, W.A. (1981) Likelihood ratio tests for autoregressive time series with a unit root. *Econometrica* 49(4): 1057–1072.

Diebolt, C. and Parent, A. (2008) Bimetallism: the "rules of the game". *Explorations in Economic History* 45: 288–302.

Eichengreen, B. and Hataseb, M. (2007) Can a rapidly growing export-oriented economy exit smoothly from a currency peg? Lessons from Japan's high-growth era. *Explorations in Economic History* 44: 501–521.

Elliott, G., Rothenburg, T. and Stock, J. (1996) Efficient tests of an autoregressive unit root. *Econometrica* 64: 813–836.

Enflo, K., Kander, A. and Schon, L. (2009) Identifying development blocks – a new methodology implemented on Swedish industry. *Journal of Evolutionary Economics* 18: 57–76.

Engle, R. and Granger, C.W.J. (1987) Co-integration and error correction: representation, estimation and testing. *Econometrica* 55: 251–276.

Esteves, R.P., Reis, J. and Ferramosca, F. (2009) Market integration in the golden periphery. The Lisbon/London exchange, 1854–1891. *Explorations in Economic History* 46: 324–345.

EViews 7. QMS: quantitative micro software. http://www.eviews.com/index.html. Last accessed 21 September 2010.

Federico, G. (2007) Market integration and market efficiency: the case of 19th century Italy. *Explorations in Economic History* 44: 293–316.

Franck, R. and Krausz, M. (2009) Institutional changes, wars and stock market risk in an emerging economy: evidence from the Israeli stock exchange, 1945–1960. *Cliometrica* 3: 141–164.

Fratianni, M. and Spinelli, F. (2001) Fiscal dominance and money growth in Italy: the long record. *Explorations in Economic History* 38: 252–272.

Gaffeo E., Gallegati, M. and Gallegati, M. (2005) Requiem for the unit root in per capita real GDP? Additional evidence from historical data. *Empirical Economics* 30: 37–63.

Galor, O. (2005) From Stagnation to Growth: unified Growth Theory. In P. Aghion and S.N. Durlauf (eds), *Handbook of Economic Growth* (Vol. 1A, pp. 171–285). Amsterdam: Elsevier.

Galor, O. and Weil, G. (2000) Population, technology, and growth: from Malthusian stagnation to the demographic transition and beyond. *American Economic Review* 90: 806–828.

Geweke, J and Porter-Hudak, S. (1983) The estimation and application of long memory time series models, *Journal of Time Series Analysis* 4: 221–38.

Geweke, J., Meese, R. and Dent, W. (1983) Comparing alternative tests of causality in temporal systems: analytic results and experimental evidence. *Journal of Econometrics* 21: 161–94.

Giles D.E.A., Giles, J.A. and McCann, E. (1993) Causality, unit roots and export-led growth: the New Zealand experience. *Journal of International Trade and Economic Development* 1: 195–218.

Gils-Alana, L and Hualde, J. (2009) Fractional integration and cointegration: an overview and empirical application. In T. Mills and K. Patterson (eds), *Palgrave Handbook of Econometrics* (Vol. 2). Basingstoke: Macmillan.
Glymour, C. and Cooper, G.F. (1999) *Computation, Causation and Discovery*. Cambridge: MIT Press.
Goodwin, B.K., Grennes, T. and Craig, L. (2002) Mechanical refrigeration and the integration of perishable commodity markets. *Explorations in Economic History* 39: 154–182.
Granger, C.W.J. (1969) Investigating causal relations by econometric models and cross spectral methods. *Econometrica* 37: 424–438.
Granger, C.W.J. (1986) Developments in the study of co-integrated economic variables. *Oxford Bulletin of Economics and Statistics* 48: 213–228.
Granger, C.W.J. (1988) Some recent developments in a concept: causality. *Journal of Econometrics* 39: 199–211.
Granger, C.W.J. and Joyeux, R. (1980) An introduction to long-range time series models and fractional differencing. *Journal of Time Series Analysis* 1: 15–30.
Granger, C.W.J. and Newbold, P. (1974) Spurious regression in econometrics. *Journal of Econometrics* 2: 111–120.
Granger, C.W.J. Hyung, N. and Yeon, Y. (2001) Spurious regression with stationary series. *Applied Economics* 33: 899–904.
Grant, O. (2003) Globalisation versus de-coupling: german emigration and the evolution of the Atlantic labour market 1870–1913. *Explorations in Economic History* 40: 387–418.
Greasley, D. and Oxley, L. (1994a) Rehabilitation sustained: the Industrial Revolution as a macroeconomic epoch. *Economic History Review* 47: 760–768.
Greasley, D. and Oxley, L. (1994b) Structural change and unit root testing: british Industrial Production 1700–1913. *Applied Economics Letters* 1: 29–30.
Greasley, D. and Oxley, L. (1995) A time series perspective on convergence: australia UK and the US since 1870. *Economic Record* 71: 259–270.
Greasley, D. and Oxley, L. (1996a) Discontinuities in competitiveness: the impact of World War One on British industry. *Economic History Review* XLIX: 83–101.
Greasley, D. and Oxley, L. (1996b) Technological epochs and British industrial production, 1700–1992. *Scottish Journal of Political Economy* 43: 258–274.
Greasley, D. and Oxley, L. (1997a) Time-series based tests of the convergence hypothesis: some positive results. *Economic Letters* 56: 143–147.
Greasley, D. and Oxley, L. (1997b) Unit roots and British industrial growth, 1922–1992. *Manchester School* 65: 192–212.
Greasley, D. and Oxley, L. (1997c) Endogenous growth or big bang: two views of the first Industrial Revolution. *Journal of Economic History* 57: 935–949.
Greasley, D. and Oxley, L. (1997d) Shock persistence and structural change. *The Economic Record* 73: 348–362.
Greasley, D. and Oxley, L. (1997e) Causality and the first Industrial Revolution. *Industrial and Corporate Change* 7: 33–47.
Greasley, D. and Oxley, L. (1997f) Endogenous growth, trend output and the Industrial Revolution. *Journal of Economic History* 957–960.
Greasley, D. and Oxley, L. (1997g) Convergence in GDP per capita and real wages: some results for Australia and the UK. *Mathematics and Computers in Simulation* 43: 429–436.
Greasley, D. and Oxley, L. (1998a) Vector autoregression, cointegration and causality: testing for causes of the British Industrial Revolution. *Applied Economics* 30: 1387–1397.
Greasley, D. and Oxley, L. (1998b) Causality and the first Industrial Revolution. *Industrial and Corporate Change* 7: 33–47.

Greasley, D. and Oxley, L. (1998c) A tale of two dominions: australia, Canada and the convergence hypothesis. *Economic History Review* 51: 294–318.

Greasley, D. and Oxley, L. (1999) International comparisons on shock persistence in the presence of structural change and non-linearities. *Applied Economics* 31: 499–507.

Greasley, D. and Oxley, L. (2000) British industrialization, 1815–1860: A disaggregate time-series perspective. *Explorations in Economic History* 37: 98–119.

Greasley, D. and Oxley, L. (2004) Globalization and real wages in New Zealand 1873–1913. *Explorations in Economic History* 41: 26–47.

Greasley, D. and Oxley, L. (2010a) Knowledge, natural resource abundance and economic development: lessons from New Zealand 1861–1939. *Explorations in Economic History* 47: 443–459.

Greasley, D. and Oxley, L. (2010b) Clio and the economist: making historians count. *Journal of Economic Surveys* 24: 755–774.

Greasley, D., Madsen, J. and Oxley, L. (2001) Income uncertainty and consumer spending during the Great Depression. *Explorations in Economic History* 38: 225–251.

Greasley, D., Madsen, J. B. and Wohar, M. (2010). Long-run growth empirics and unified theory. School of History, Classics and Archaeology Research Paper, University of Edinburgh, August 2010, pp. 1–34.

Grossman, R. and Imai, M. (2009) Japan's return to gold: turning points in the value of the yen during the 1920s. *Explorations in Economic History* 46: 314–323.

Grubb, F. (2004) The circulating medium of exchange in colonial Pennsylvania, 1729–1775: New estimates of monetary composition, performance, and economic growth. *Explorations in Economic History* 41: 329–360.

Hadri, K. (2000) Testing for stationarity in heterogeneous panel data. *Econometrics Journal* 3: 148–161.

Hansen, B.E. (1992) Testing for parameter instability in linear models. *Journal of Policy Modeling* 14: 517–533.

Harvey, A. (1989) *Forecasting Structural Time Series Models and the Kalman Filter*. Cambridge: Cambridge University Press.

Harvey, A. and Jaeger, A. (1993) Detrending, stylized facts and the business cycle. *Journal of Applied Econometrics* 8: 231–247.

Harvey, A.C. and Koopman, S.J. (1992) Diagnostic checking of unobserved components time series models. *Journal of Business and Economic Statistics* 10: 377–389.

Harvey, A. and Trimbur, T. (2003) General model-based filters for extracting cycles and trends in economic time series. *The Review of Economics and Statistics* 85: 244–255.

Haslett, J. and Raftery, A.E. (1989) Space-time modelling with long-memory dependence: assessing Ireland's wind power resource (with discussion). *Applied Statistics* 38: 1–50.

Hatton, T.J. and Lyons, J.S. (1983) Eighteenth century British trade: homespun or empire made. *Explorations in Economic History* 20: 163–182.

Herranz-Locan, A. (2007) Infrastructure investment and Spanish economic growth, 1850–1935. *Explorations in Economic History* 44: 452–468.

Hickson, C., Turner, J. and McCann, C. (2005) Much ado about nothing: the limitation of liability and the market for 19th century Irish bank stock. *Explorations in Economic History* 42: 459–476.

Hirschman, A.O. (1958) *The Strategy of Economic Development*. New Haven, CT: Yale University Press.

Hodrick, R. and Prescott, E. (1997) Postwar US business cycles: an empirical investigation. *Journal of Money, Credit and Banking* 29: 1–16.

Hoffmann, W.H. (1955) *British Industry 1700–1950*. Oxford: Blackwell.

Horrell, S., Humphries, J. and Weale, M. (1994) An input-output table for 1841. *Economic History Review* 47: 545–566.

Hosking, J.R.M. (1981) Fractional differencing. *Biometrika* 68: 165–176.
Hsiao, C. (1987) Tests of causality and exogeneity between exports and economic growth: the case of the Asian NIC's. *Journal of Economic Development* 12: 143–159.
Hurst, H.E. (1951) Long-term storage capacity of reservoirs. *Transactions of the American Society of Civil Engineers* 116: 770–808.
Im, K.S., Pesaran, M.H. and Shin, Y. (2003) Testing for unit roots in heterogeneous panels. *Journal of Econometrics* 115: 53–74.
Jacks, D. (2006) What drove 19th century commodity market integration? *Explorations in Economic History* 43: 383–412.
Jacks, D. (2007) Populists versus theorists: futures markets and the volatility of prices. *Explorations in Economic History* 44: 342–362.
Johansen, S. (1988) Statistical analysis of cointegrated vectors. *Journal of Economic Dynamics and Control* 12: 231–254.
Johansen, S. (1995) *Likelihood-Based Inference in Cointegrated Vector Autoregressive Models*. Oxford: Oxford university Press.
Jung, W.S. and Marshall, P.J. (1985) Exports, growth and causality in developing countries. *Journal of Development Economics* 18: 1–12.
Keay, I. (2000) Scapegoats or responsive entrepreneurs: canadian manufacturers, 1907–1990. *Explorations in Economic History* 37: 217–240.
Keay, I. and Redish, A. (2004) The micro-economic effects of financial market structure: evidence from 20th century North American steel firms. *Explorations in Economic History* 41: 377–403.
Kendall, M. (1954) *Exercises in Theoretical Statistics*. London: Griffin.
Kennedy, P. (2002) Sinning in the basement: what are the rules? The ten commandments of applied econometrics. *Journal of Economic Surveys* 16: 569–589.
Kim, C.S. and Phillips, P.C.B. (2000) Modified log periodgram regression. Working Paper, Yale University.
Kling, G. (2006) The long-term impact of mergers and the emergence of a merger wave in pre-World-War I Germany. *Explorations in Economic History* 43: 667–688.
Klovland, J.T. (2009) New evidence on the fluctuations in ocean freight rates in the 1850s. *Explorations in Economic History* 46: 266–284.
Klug, A. and Landon-Lane, J. White, E. (2005) How could everyone have been so wrong? Forecasting the Great Depression with the railroads. *Explorations in Economic History* 42: 27–55.
Komlos, J. (1990) Nutrition population growth and the Industrial Revolution in England. *Social Sciences History* 14: 69–91.
Kwiatkowski, D., Phillips, P.C.B., Schmidt, P. and Shin, Y. (1992) Testing the null hypothesis of stationarity against the alternative of a unit root: how sure are we that economic time series have a unit root? *Journal of Econometrics* 54: 159–178.
Landon-Lane, J. and Rockoff, H. (2007) The origin and diffusion of shocks to regional interest rates in the United States, 1880–2002. *Explorations in Economic History* 44: 487–500.
Lauritzen, S.L. (2000) Causal inference from graphical models. In D.R. Cox and C. Klauppleberg (eds), *Complex Stochastic Systems*. London: Chapman & Hall.
Lauritzen, S.L. and T.S. Richardson (2002) Chain graph models and their causal interpretations. *Journal of the Royal Statistical Society Series B* 64: 321–361.
Lazaretou, S. (2005) The drachma, foreign creditors, and the international monetary system: tales of a currency during the 19th and the early 20th centuries. *Explorations in Economic History* 42: 202–236.
Lee, J. and Strazicich, M. (2001) Break point estimation and spurious rejections with endogenous unit root tests. *Oxford Bulletin of Economics and Statistics* 63: 535–558.
Lee, J. and Strazicich M.C. (2003) Minimum LM unit root tests with two structural breaks. *The Review of Economics and Statistics* 85: 1082–1089.

Leung, S.-K. (1992) Changes in the behaviour of output in the United Kingdom, 1856–1990. *Economics Letters* 40: 435–444.

Levine, A., Lin, C.F. and Chu, C.S. (2002) Unit root tests in panel data: asymptotic and finite-sample properties. *Journal of Econometrics* 108: 1–24.

Lew, B. (2000) The diffusion of tractors on the Canadian prairies: the threshold model and the problem of uncertainty. *Explorations in Economic History* 37: 189–216.

Leybourne, S., Kim, T.-H. and Taylor, A.M.R. (2007) Detecting multiple changes in persistence. *Studies in Nonlinear Dynamics & Econometrics*, 11.

Ljunberg, J. and Nilsson, A. (2009) Human capital and economic growth: sweden 1870–2000. *Cliometrica* 3: 71–95.

Lumsdaine, R.L. and Papell, D. (1997) Multiple trend breaks and the unit root hypothesis. *Review of Economics and Statistics* 79: 212–218.

Lutkepohl, H. and Leimers, H.-E. (1992) Granger-causality in cointegrated VAR processes: the case of the term structure. *Economics Letters* 40: 263–268.

MacKinnon, J. (1991) Critical values for cointegration tests. In R.F. Engle and C.W.J. Granger (eds), *Long-Run Economic Relationships*. Oxford: Clarendon Press.

Maddala, G.S. and Wu, S.W. (1999) A comparative study of unit root tests with panel data and a new simple test. *Oxford Bulletin of Economics and Statistics* 61: 631–652. *Manchester School* 65: 192–212.

Mattesini, F. and Quintieri, B. (2006) Does a reduction in the length of the working week reduce unemployment? Some evidence from the Italian economy during the Great Depression. *Explorations in Economic History* 43: 413–437.

McAleer, M. (1994) Sherlock Holmes and the search for truth: a diagnostic tale. *Journal of Economic Surveys* 8: 317–370.

McAleer, M. (2005) Automated inference and learning in modeling financial volatility. *Econometric Theory* 21: 232–261.

McCloskey, D.N. (1994) 1780–1860. In D.N. McCloskey and R.C. Floud (eds), *The Economic History of Britain Since 1700*, 2nd edn (Vol. 1, pp. 242–270). Cambridge: Cambridge University Press.

Michelacci, C. and Zalaroni, P. (2000) (Fractional) beta, convergence. *Journal of Monetary Economics* 45: 129–153.

Mills, T.C. (1991) Are fluctuations in UK. Output transitory or permanent? *The Manchester School* 59: 1–11.

Mills, T.C. (2008) Exploring historical economic relationships: two and a half centuries of British interest rates and inflation. *Cliometrica* 2: 213–238.

Mills, T.C. (2009) Modelling trends and cycles in economic time series: historical perspective and future developments. *Cliometrica* 3: 221–244.

Mishra, T., Prskawetz, A., Parhi, M. and Diebolt, C. (2009) A note on long memory in population and economic growth. AFC Working Paper 6.

Moser, P. and Nicholas, T. (2004) Was electricity a general purpose technology? Evidence from historical patents citations. *American Economic Review* 94: 388–394.

Muscatelli, V.A. and Hurn, S. (1992) Cointegration and dynamic time series models. *Journal of Economic Surveys* 6(1): 1–43.

Neilson, H.B. (2007) UK money demand 1873–2001: a long-run time series analysis and event study. *Cliometrica* 1: 45–61.

Nelson, C.R. and Plosser, C.I. (1982) Trends and random walks in economic time series. *Journal of Monetary Economics* 10(1): 139–162.

Newey, W. and West, K. (1987) A simple positive semi-definite, heteroskedasticity and autocorrelation consistent covariance matrix. *Econometrica* 69(6): 1519–1554.

Ng, S. and Perron, P. (2001) Lag length selection and the construction of unit root tests with good size and power. *Econometrica* 69: 1519–1554.

O'Brien, P.K. and Engerman, S. (1991) Exports and the growth and the British Economy from the glorious revolution to the peace of Amiens. In B. Solow (ed.), *Slavery and the Rise of the Atlantic System* (pp. 177–209). Cambridge: Cambridge University Press.
Officer, L.H. (2005) The quantity theory in New England, 1703–1749: new data to analyze an old question. *Explorations in Economic History* 42: 101–121.
Ogren, A. (2006) Free or central banking? Liquidity and financial deepening in Sweden, 1834–1913. *Explorations in Economic History* 43: 64–93.
Outhwaite, R.B. (1969) *Inflation in Tudor and Stuart England*. London: Macmillan.
Oxley, L. and Greasley, D. (1997b) Using the Kalman Filter in tests of convergence, paper presented at the Modelling and Simulation Society of Australia. MODSIM, Conference, 1997.
Oxley, L. and McAleer, M. (1993) Econometric issues in macroeconomic models with generated regressors. *Journal of Economic Surveys* 7(1): 1–40.
Oxley, L., Reale, M. and Tunnicliffe-Wilson, G. (2009) Constructing structural VAR models with conditional independence graphs. *Mathematics and Computers in Simulation* 79: 2910–2916.
Pagan, A. (1984) Econometric issues in the analysis of regressions with generated regressors. *International Economic Review* 25: 221–247.
Park, J.Y. (1992) Canonical cointegrating regression. *Econometrica* 60: 119–143.
Pearl, J. (2000) *Causality*. Cambridge, England: Cambridge University Press.
Pedroni, P. (1999) Critical values for cointegration tests in heterogeneous panels with multiple regressors. *Oxford Bulletin of Economics and Statistics* 61: 653–670.
Pedroni, P. (2004) Panel cointegration: asymptotic and finite sample properties of fooled time series tests with an application to the PPP hypothesis. *Econometric Theory* 20: 597–625.
Peng, C.K., Buldyrev, S.V., Simons, M., Stanley, H.E. and Goldberger, A.L. (1994) Mosaic organization of DNA nucleotides. *Physical Review E* 49: 1685–1689.
Perron, P. (1989) The Great Crash, the oil price shock and the unit root hypothesis. *Econometrica* 57(6): 1361–1401.
Persson, K.G. (2010) *An Economic History of Europe*. Cambridge: Cambridge University Press.
Pesaran, H., Shin, Y. and Smith, R. (2001) Bounds testing approaches to the analysis of level relationships. *Journal of Applied Econometrics* 16: 289–226.
Phillips, P.C.B. (1986) Understanding spurious regression in econometrics. *Journal of Econometrics* 33: 311–340.
Phillips, P.C.B. (1998) New tools for understanding spurious regressions. *Econometrica* 66: 1299–1325.
Phillips, P.C.B. (2005) Challenges of trending time series econometrics. *Mathematics and Computers in Simulation* 68: 401–416.
Phillips, P.C.B. and Ouliaris, S. (1990) Asymptotic properties of residual based tests for cointegration. *Econometrica* 58: 165–193.
Phillips, P.C.B. and Perron, P. (1988) Testing for a unit root in time series regression. *Biometrika* 75(2):335–346.
Phillips, P.C.B. and Yu, J. (2009) Dating the timeline of financial bubbles during the subprime crisis. Singapore Management University, Economics and Statistics Working paper series, No. 18-2009.
Prados de la Escosura, L. and Sanz-Villarroya, I. (2009) Contract enforcement, capital accumulation, and Argentina's long-run decline. *Cliometrica* 3: 1–26.
Priestley, M. (1981) *Spectral Analysis and Time Series*. New York: Academic Press.
Rapach, D. and Wohar, M. (2004) Testing the monetary model of exchange rate determination: a closer look at panels. *Journal of International Money and Finance* 23(6): 867–895.

RATS (Regression Analysis of Time Series) 7.3 (2010) http://www.estima.com/. Last accessed 21 September 2010.
Rea, W., Oxley, L. Reale, M. and Mendes, E. (2008a) Long memory or shifting means? A new approach and application to realized volatility. Dept Economics WP 04/2008, http://www.econ.canterbury.ac.nz/RePEc/cbt/econwp/0804.pdf. Last accessed 21 September 2010.
Rea, W., Oxley, L. Reale, M. and Mendes, E. (2008b) The empirical properties of some popular estimators of long memory processes. http://www.econ.canterbury.ac.nz/RePEc/cbt/econwp/0815.pdf.
Rebelo, S. (1991) Long-run policy analysis and long-run growth. *Journal of Political Economy* 99: 500–521.
Ricciuti, R. (2008) The quest for a fiscal rule: Italy, 1861–1998. *Cliometrica* 2: 259–274.
Robinson, P. (1994) Semi-parametric analysis of long memory time series. *Annals of Statistics* 22: 515–539.
Robinson, P. (1995) Log-periodogram of time series with long range dependence. *Annals of Statistics* 23: 1048–1072.
Robinson, P. (2003) *Time Series with Long Memory*. Oxford: Oxford University Press.
Rostow, W.W (1963) *The Economics of Take-Off into Sustained Growth*. London: Macmillan.
Rousseau, P.L. (2009) Share liquidity, participation, and growth of the Boston market for industrial equities, 1854–1897. *Explorations in Economic History* 46: 203–219.
Rousseau, P. and Sylla, R. (2005) Emerging financial markets and early US growth. *Explorations in Economic History* 42: 1–26.
Sabate, M., Gadea, M. and Escario, R. (2006) Does fiscal policy influence monetary policy? The case of Spain, 1874–1935. *Explorations in Economic History* 43: 309–331.
Sanz-Villarroya, I. (2005) The convergence process of Argentina with Australia and Canada: 1875–2000. *Explorations in Economic History* 42: 439–458.
Sarferaz, S. and Uebele, M. (2009) Tracking down the business cycle: a dynamic factor model for Germany 1820–1913. *Explorations in Economic History* 46: 368–387.
Schmidt, P. and Phillips, P.C.B. (1992) LM tests for a unit root in the presence of deterministic trends. *Oxford Bulletin of Economics and Statistics* 54: 257–287.
Schwert, G. (1989) Tests for unit roots: a Monte Carlo investigation. *Journal of Business & Economic Statistics* 7: 147–159.
Shafer, G. (1996) *The Art of Causal Conjecture*. Cambridge, MA: MIT Press.
Siklos, P. (2008) The Fed's reaction to the stock market during the Great Depression: fact or artefact? *Explorations in Economic History* 45: 164–184.
Simon, J. (1994) Demographic causes and consequences of the Industrial Revolution. *Journal of European Economic History* 23: 141–159.
Sims, C.A. (1972) Money, income and causality. *American Economic Review* 62: 540–552.
Sims, C.A. (1980) Macroeconomics and reality. *Econometrica* 48: 1–48.
Sims, C.A., Stock, J. and Watson, M. (1990) Inference in linear time series models with some unit roots. *Econometrica* 58: 161–182.
Solomou, S. and Shimazaki, M. (2007) Japanese episodic long swings in economic growth. *Explorations in Economic History* 44: 224–241.
St. Aubyn, M. (1999) Convergence across industrialized countries (1890–1989). New results using time series methods. *Empirical Economics* 24: 23–44.
STAMP (Structural Time Series Analyser, Modeller and Predictor) 8.3 for OxMetrics (2010) http://stamp-software.com/. Last accessed 21 September 2010.
STATA 9, 10, 11 (2010). STATA Corporation. http://www.stata.com/. Last accessed 21 September 2010.

Streb, J., Wallusch, J. and Yin, S. (2007) Knowledge spill-over from new to old industries: the case of German synthetic dyes and textiles (1878–1913). *Explorations in Economic History* 44: 203–223.

Sullivan, R.J. (1989) England's "Age of Invention": the acceleration of patents and patentable invention during the Industrial Revolution. *Explorations in Economic History* 26: 424–452.

Tattara, G. (2003) Paper money but a gold debt: Italy on the gold standard. *Explorations in Economic History* 40: 122–142.

Temin, P. (2002) Price behavior in ancient Babylon. *Explorations in Economic History* 39: 46–60.

Temin, P. and Voth, H.-J. (2005) Credit rationing and crowding out during the Industrial Revolution: evidence from Hoare's Bank, 1702–1862. *Explorations in Economic History* 42: 325–348.

Terasvirta T. (1998) Modelling economic relationships with smooth transition regressions. In A. Ullah and D. Giles (eds), *Handbook of Applied Statistics*. New York: Dekker.

Toda, H.Y. and Phillips, P.C.B. (1991) Vector autoregression and causality: a theoretical overview and simulation study. Working Paper 977, Cowles Foundation, New Haven, CT.

Toda, H.Y. and Yamamoto, T. (1995) Statistical inference in vector autoregressions with possibly integrated processes. *Journal of Econometrics* 66: 225–250.

Tong, H. (1990) *Non-linear Time Series: a Dynamical System Approach*. Oxford: Oxford University Press.

Toniolo, G., Conte, L. and Vecchi, G. (2003) Monetary Union, institutions and financial market integration: Italy, 1862–1905. *Explorations in Economic History* 40: 443–461.

Tsoulouhas, T.C. (1992) A New Look at demographic and technological change England 1550–1839. *Explorations in Economic History* 29: 169–203.

Vahid, F. and Engle, R.F. (1993) Common trends and common cycles. *Journal of Applied Econometrics* 8: 341–360.

Van Nieuwerburgh, S., Buelens, F. and Cuyvers, L. (2006) Stock market development and economic growth in Belgium. *Explorations in Economic History* 43: 13–38.

Vogelsang, T.J. (1997) Wald-type tests for detecting breaks in the trend function of a dynamic time series. *Econometric Theory* 13: 818–849.

Waldenstrom, D. (2002) Taxing emerging stock markets: a beneficial policy? Evidence from the Stockholm Stock Exchange, 1907–1939. *Explorations in Economic History* 39: 29–45.

Weidenmier, M.D. (2000) The market for confederate cotton bonds. *Explorations in Economic History* 37: 76–97.

Weisdorf, J. and Sharp, P. (2009) From preventive to permissive checks: the changing nature of the Malthusian relationship between nuptiality and the price of provisions in the nineteenth century. *Cliometrica* 3: 55–70.

Whittaker, J.C. (1990) *Graphical Models in Applied Multivariate Statistics*. Chichester: Wiley.

Wrigley, E.A. (1988) *Continuity, Chance and Change: the Character of the Industrial Revolution in England*. Cambridge: Cambridge University Press.

Yousef, T.K. (2000) The political economy of interwar Egyptian cotton policy. *Explorations in Economic History* 37: 301–325.

Yule, G. (1926) Why do we sometimes get nonsense correlations between time series? A study in sampling and the nature of time series. *Journal of the Royal Statistical Society* 89: 1–64.

Zivot, E. and Andrews, D.W.K. (1992) Further evidence on the Great Crash, the oil price shock, and the unit root unit hypothesis. *Journal of Business and Economic Statistics* 10: 251–270.

INDEX

Note: 'n.' after a page number indicates the number of a note on that page.